International Institute of Philosophy
Institut International de Philosophie

La philosophie contemporaine

Chroniques nouvelles

par les soins de
GUTTORM FLØISTAD
Université d'Oslo

Tome 4
Philosophie de l'esprit

Martinus Nijhoff Publishers Dordrecht/Boston/Lancaster 1986

Contemporary philosophy

A new survey

edited by
GUTTORM FLØISTAD
University of Oslo

Volume 4
Philosophy of mind

Martinus Nijhoff Publishers Dordrecht/Boston/Lancaster 1986

Distributors:

for the United States and Canada

Kluwer Boston, Inc.
190 Old Derby Street
Hingham, MA 02043
USA

for all other countries

Kluwer Academic Publishers Group
Distribution Center
P.O. Box 322
3300 AH Dordrecht
The Netherlands

Library of Congress Catalog Card Number: 81-3972

ISBN 90-247-3059-7 (hardback)
ISBN 90-247-3300-6 (paperback)

First edition 1983
Second printing 1986

Published under the auspices of the International Council of Philosophy and Humanistic Studies and of the International Federation of Philosophical Societies, with the support of UNESCO.

Publié sous les auspices du Conseil International de la Philosophie et des Sciences Humaines et de la Fédération Internationale des Sociétés de Philopsophie, avec le concours de l'UNESCO.

PRINTED IN THE NETHERLANDS

Contents/Table des matières

G. Fløistad, Preface — VII

G. Fløistad, Introduction — 1

J. Perry, Personal identity and the concept of a person — 11

D.M. Armstrong, Recent work on the relation of mind and brain — 45

M. Pastin, Philosophy of perception — 81

G.H.R. Parkinson, Spinoza's philosophy of mind — 105

C. Taylor, Hegel's philosophy of mind — 133

A. Hannay, Kierkegaard's philosophy of mind — 157

R.K. Shope, The significance of Freud for modern philosophy of mind — 185

B. Terrell, Brentano's philosophy of mind — 223

D.W. Smith, Husserl's philosophy of mind — 249

T. Sheehan, Heidegger's philosophy of mind — 287

B. Stroud, Wittgenstein's philosophy of mind — 319

VI   *Contents*

H. Hall, Merleau-Ponty's philosophy of mind   343

P. Skagestad, American pragmatism   363

G. Skirbekk, Pragmatism in Apel and Habermas   387

J.F. Rosenberg, Wilfrid Sellars' philosophy of mind   417

Abbreviations used by some contributors   441

Index of names   443

Index of subjects   451

Preface

This publication is a continuation of two earlier series of chronicles, *Philosophy in the Mid-Century* (Firenze 1958/59) and *Contemporary Philosophy* (Firenze 1968), edited by Raymond Klibansky. Like the other series, these chronicles provide a survey of important trends in contemporary philosophical discussion from 1966 to 1980.

The need for such surveys has, I believe, increased rather than decreased over the last years. The philosophical scene appears, for various reasons, more complex than ever before. The continuing process of specialization in most branches, the emergence of new schools of thought, particularly in philosophical logic and the philosophy of language, the convergence of interest (though not necessarily of opinion) of different traditions upon certain problems, and the increasing attention being paid to the history of philosophy in discussions of contemporary problems are the most important contributory factors. Surveys of the present kind are a valuable source of knowledge of this complexity and may as such be an assistance in renewing the understanding of one's own philosophical problems. The surveys, it is to be hoped, may also help to strengthen the Socratic element of modern philosophy, the dialogue or *Kommunikationsgemeinschaft*.

So far, four volumes have been prepared for the new series. The present chronicles in the *Philosophy of Mind* (Vol. 4) follow upon chronicles in the *Philosophy of Language and Philosophical Logic* (Vol. 1) and chronicles in the *Philosophy of Science* (Vol. 2) and chronicles in the *Philosophy of Action* (Vol. 4). Each volume contains, as a rule, fifteen chronicles, each 25 pages long. However, this rule has been broken in all volumes. In some cases, it turned out to be impossible to receive chronicles in time for the date of publication. In others, the authors, if they thought it necessary in view of their topic, were allowed to exceed the allotted number of pages. For these reasons, certain philosophical disciplines, particularly the Philosophical Logic of Volume 1, and the Philosophy of Action in Volume 3, are' covered less satis-factorily than others, apart from the fact that the volumes are of unequal length. The first two chronicles of Volume 3 are also partly overlapping.

Most of the chronicles, as to be expected, are written in English, some in French and one in German. The German contributors, except one, thought it necessary to write in English in order to be read. This is, I think, a most regrettable state of affairs. It indicates that major parts of the philosophical community will no longer have access to important sources of the history of philosophy in their original version.

The topics surveyed in the four volumes belong squarely within the Western philosophical tradition and do little justice to philosophies or ways of thinking in other cultures. This should be kept in mind in the preparation of further volumes. The idea of a trans-cultural philosophy is still very unclear.

Bibliographical references, with a few exceptions, follow the pattern introduced in *Philosophy in the Mid-Century*. The publications discussed in each chronicle are indicated by reference numbers in square brackets, corresponding to the order in which they appear in the text. The bibliographies themselves follow at the end of each chronicle, arranged in alphabetical order.

The bibliographies are selected by the authors themselves and contain, as a rule, only those works they took to be of special interest for the topics under discussion.

I am most grateful to a number of persons who in various ways have assisted in the preparation of the new series. My thanks are first of all due to the former president of the Institut International de Philosophie, Georg H. von Wright, who, in addition to writing the introduction to Part 2, Philosophical Logic, of Volume 1, has given valuable suggestions concerning the topics to be surveyed as well as the contributors to all volumes. The former editor of the Chronicles, Raymond Klibansky, who has devoted much of his eminent scholarship and his time to the editorial work of the earlier Chronicles, provided me with much useful experience. Espen Schaanning, M.A., undertook most conscientiously the unpleasant task of reviewing the methods of reference and the bibliographies to make them comply with the given model. Hannelore Brown-Knauff, M.A., of Martinus Nijhoff Publishers, has contributed most valuable editorial assistance to all volumes.

My thanks are also due to UNESCO for their financial support and to Martinus Nijhoff Publishers, The Hague, for their willingness to publish the Chronicles. The Secretariat of the Institut International de Philosophie deserves special recognition for its most helpful assistance in administrative matters. The Secretariat has also been responsible for the contact with UNESCO and the Publisher.

Lastly, I want to thank all the scholars from various countries, whose contributions have made it possible to complete the new series of Chronicles.

University of Oslo, February 1982   Guttorm Fløistad

Introduction

GUTTORM FLØISTAD

What is the human mind? In view of the variety of answers given in the history of philosophy, no definite answer appears to be possible. This is however in itself a significant answer to the question. If it is true, ontological statements about the mind are always provisional or at most valid only for a certain period of time. Or, in view of the revival now and then of historical theories of the mind, it is even conceivable that such theories, after having been false for a longer or shorter period of time, may become true again.

This "indefinite thesis" of the mind is not without support. For one thing, history has taught us that the mind should not be regarded as en entity existing independently of its surroundings, of history and historical change. This is most obvious in philosophies identifying the mind with its actions and cognitions, for instance that of Spinoza. Changes in actions and cognitions are changes of one's mind. But it also seems to hold true for philosophies regarding the mind as existing "outside" the world, as a "substance" on its own, for instance that of Descartes. His "mechanization" of the world picture certainly forced him to distinguish ontologically between mind and world — and, consequently, between mind and body. The changing views of the mind in philosophies of this type from Descartes onwards suggest however that the alleged ontological distinction between mind and world is after all merely conceptual. Thus Hume's "bundle theory" of the "I" appears to be a straightforward product of his general empiricism — just as the laws governing movements and processes in nature may have contributed to the substance view of thought in Descartes.

Contemporary philosophy. A new survey. Vol. 4, pp. 1–10.
© 1983, Martinus Nijhoff Publishers, The Hague/Boston/London.

I

The present collection of chronicles covers a great variety of topics in the philosophy of mind. Most of them discuss historical conceptions from Spinoza onwards; some deal with important problems in the contemporary philosophy of mind, for instance the problems of personal identity, of the mind—body relation and of perception.

The lack of historical and systematic completeness in this collection of chronicles is to a large extent compensated by the fact that the main types of the philosophy of mind are variously represented. The main types, as indicated already, are in fact only two, and they are constructed according to the two possible ways of looking at the mind's existence: The mind is either regarded as existing by itself, and as having an identity of its own, as in Descartes, or seen as an entity necessarily existing in relation to the world, and whose identity consists in, or is constituted by these relations, as in Spinoza.

The chronicles may be said to clarify and deepen these basic conceptions of the mind in various ways. Thus Brentano and Husserl obviously continue the Cartesian tradition. Although intentionality as the basic feature of consciousness by definition connects the mind with the external world, it obviously still makes sense to search for a pure ego, as the ultimate source of the constitution of objects in consciousness (cf. Terrell, Smith). The chronicles on perception, on personal identity and on the mind—body relation are all entirely based on the Cartesian mind—world and mind—body dichotomy — without his rationalism.

Our perceptions involve in general a contingent relationship between mind and world and consequently create almost insoluble problems concerning, for instance, the justification of our beliefs or concerning general and specific "warrant principles" for the relation of basic and non-basic propositions (cf. Pastin). To conceive of personal identity in terms of memory or in terms of bodily identity through space and time cannot but yield a contingent and highly individualistic conception of personal identity.

The "relational" conception of the mind is most clearly presented and discussed in the chronicles on Spinoza, Kierkegaard, Hegel, Heidegger and Merleau-Ponty. But Freud, the later Wittgenstein and Sellars have also contributed to this conception.

Spinoza, at the outset, identifies the human mind with its knowledge. The human mind, he says, consists of a complex idea. It turns out that an idea is nothing else than an idea of the *interaction* of the body with its natural surroundings. An idea is consequently itself the product of such interactions. This indicates why it is possible to identify knowledge with the human mind. Knowledge is primarily conceived of as active or dynamic. Knowledge is essentially an expression of a cognitive *activity* (cf. Parkinson).

To Kierkegaard, man is in general "a relation" that is conscious of itself. And it is just this relational character of the mind that contains in it the capacity for a religious transcendence towards God (cf. Hannay). And Hegel, like Spinoza, thinks that the mind is to be conceived in terms of its *actions* (cf. Taylor). And actions combined with self-reflection necessarily make the environment part and parcel of the mind's identity, of the self.

Heidegger and Merleau-Ponty are no less explicit on this point. To Heidegger, "world" is simply worked out as a structure of *Dasein* (cf. Sheehan), a view that led Merleau-Ponty to conceive of man as consisting of active skills, which from the outset involve both him in his sourroundings and his surroundings in his personal identity.

Wilfrid Sellars seems to move in the same direction when he, explicitly rejecting Cartesianism, holds that the scientific image of man (which certainly is impersonal and in many respects world-independent), needs to be enriched in order to be able to accommodate man as a person and a living organism (cf. Rosenberg).

A main argument for including Freud in the Spinozistic tradition is due to the concept of knowledge in psychoanalytic theory: Knowledge does not, as is susually the case in analytical theories of knowledge, merely *represent* objects in the external world; knowledge is primarily *experiential*, it has existential impact. Otherwise psychoanalysis would not be possible — irrespective of one's interpretations of the unconscious (cf. Shope).

The experiential character of knowledge applies to the Spinozistic tradition in general. It is precisely this characteristic of knowledge that makes objects in the world enter into the identity of man. The later Wittgenstein had presumably this experiential feature of knowledge in mind when he turned various uses of language into forms of life (cf. Stroud). On this view, the actual uses of language are certainly to be taken into account in a conception of personal identity.

Pragmatism is a complex movement comprising a number of distinct figures. The experiential character of knowledge is certainly present in Peirce's theory of concept-formation and in Goodman's view of the mind's role in shaping our world (cf. Skagestad). And Habermas and Apel attempt to overcome a prevailing restrictive self-interpretation by showing a deeper sense of rationality (cf. Skirbekk). Their extended notion of rationality obviously has Hegelian overtones: it relates primarily not to the individual but to society at large. A community is rational if it allows for "a free dialogue" and if consensus is obtained through argument. Thus, if philosophers of these traditions were two write on personal identity, they would end up by advocating some sort of collective identity preceding the personal one in each individual — as compared with the conception of personal identity in the Cartesian tradition, which appears to be strictly individualistic.

With a view to clarifying these two main approaches in the philosophy of mind, I shall select a few viewpoints from the chronicles for a brief further presentation and discussion. The viewpoints concern mainly the mind—body and the mind—world relation.

II

The relation of mind and body is a major problem in the philosophy of mind in the Cartesian tradition. Given that mind and body are ontologically distinct, a host of problems arise, well-known from contemporary analytical philosophy and philosophy of science. The problem of reducing mental processes to bodily processes or to processes in the brain, or, in general, of reducing psychology and biology to physics, has thus been widely discussed.

Among the leading reductionists or materialists are J.J.C. Smart and D.M. Armstrong. Extensive research programmes have been set forth by others (The Oppenheim-Putnam programme). The working hypothesis of this reductionism is that the concepts and law-statements of a hypothetically completed physics suffice, in principle of least, to give an account of all natural phenomena (cf. Armstrong).

Certain mental phenomena appear, however, to stand in the way of a total fulfilment of this "physicalist dream". Sensation, for instance, appears to have qualities that brain processes seem to lack. And the qualities in question are the secondary qualities. Beliefs and purposes seem like-wise to resist elimination. To say, as do Armstrong and Lewis, that they are occupants of causal roles or that they are the causes of certain responses rather than the effects of certain stimuli, does not seem quite satisfactory.

Reductionists and dualists (non-reductionists) alike encounter other difficulties too, for instance in the explanation of action. Actions are obviously the result of a co-operation of mind and body, of mental causes (reasons) or intentions and bodily movements and brain activity. And how are they correlated? A main problem arises from the fact that one and the same mental cause or intention may give rise to a variety of bodily movements and one and the same bodily movement may embody a variety of mental causes or intentions. The answers given, for instance, by Davidson and von Wright do not seem to settle the difficulties. Davidson thinks that the mental reason or cause of an action may be given a physical interpretation, whereas von Wright holds that intentions that guide actions are not causes at all, but linked with the bodily movements in question from the outset.

In view of the immense amount of intellectual energy and ingenuity that has been put to work on these problems over the years, it is rather baffling to observe that they hardly exist in the "Spinozistic" approach. In Spinoza, mind and body may certainly be conceptually distinguished by the faculty of reason. Ontologically however, mind and body, mental and bodily processes, are united, which unity may be grasped by intuition or "intuitive science". This unity is sometimes expressed by saying that the body is "consciously lived" (Harris).

This view of the unity of mind and body comes close to what Merleau-Ponty has to say: the body is never a mere physical thing. It is always a *lived* body. And, correspondingly, the mind is not a sort of abstract thinking entity, it is always embodied, that is, situated in a body in a certain time and place. The mind makes the body a living body, and the body makes the mind situated (cf. Hall).

Merleau-Ponty is obviously inspired by Heidegger, who wants to avoid the (according to him) misleading terminology of mind and body altogether and instead speaks of man as *Dasein*. Among the connotations of this notion is certainly "situated being". In order to preserve the idea of man as a concrete entity, Heidegger went so far as to begin his philosophical analyses by describing the way of being of practical man, the man of "everyday life" and the implications for a view of man in general. No mention is made of mind and body, nor of consciousness. It is obvious, however, that the unity of mind and body is a unity in *doing* something, be it in the use of utensils or of social and physical objects for scientific purposes or of language. The analysis of practical man aims at clarifying what doing something means.

What then are the main problems of the phenomenological analysis of doing something? Now, doing something has long since been the object of analysis in analytical philosophy. This analysis has, however, been restricted by and large to doing something with words, to using language. The underlying ontology, or concept of the world, does not seem to have evoked the same interest. Pragmatism as a theory of meaning, truth and knowledge has of course gone some way in modifying a one-sided commitment to physical reality. Quine's thesis of ontological relativity, and above all Goodman's more comprehensive ontology of physical objects, of social phenomena and of art, may be interpreted as a tendency more fully developed in the phenomenology of Heidegger and Merleau-Ponty. Goodman's view that there is no such thing as *the* world, there are many actual worlds, and that worlds are made, not found, that what is before me is what I make of it, certainly goes beyond a philosophy of the use of language. It is an analysis of the mind's activity in a broader sense.

In Heidegger and Merleau-Ponty the ontology is brought out in analysis of understanding and of perception of the world, respectively. It turns out that the human activity displayed in understanding and perceptions, and interacting with phenomena in the world (physical, social, historical), yields an ontology that is more fundamental than the various phenomena "taken by themselves alone". This "taken by themselves alone" is rather an abstraction, a second-hand ontology, derived from the interaction of mind and world. And the reason is simply that the various phenomena, in order to be regarded as what they are in themselves, necessarily have to be subjected to the mind's activity in understanding and perception.

This, furthermore, is the reason why ontology, or our concept of the world, is essential for a philosophy of mind. Any view of the world exhibits the mind's constitutive power. There is, in fact, according to this approach, no other way of getting to know the mind. The mind's knowledge of the world, as Heidegger puts it, necessarily involves the mind's self-knowledge, and vice versa.

This is not obvious when, as in the Cartesian tradition, the subject (or mind) is confronted with the world as its object; in other words, when the subject-object distinction is taken as fundamental and our ontology concerns the object-side only. It is as if the ontology can be presented without any trace of the subject's activity in thought and perception. The mind hides itself and disappears behind its results. This process is beautifully stated by Erwin Schrödinger in his book *Mind and Matter*: Speaking about modern natural science he says, the consciousness could only "prescribe for itself the gigantic task of creating an objective external world, by withdrawing itself from its own concept-formations and exclude itself from them".

This is also a true description of the Cartesian tradition in philosophy. Not so the Spinozistic tradition. The subject-object distinction, just as the "purified" object-ontology, is second-hand. In order to be able to draw a distinction between itself and some object, the mind must already by acquainted with the object. The object must be constituted in consciousness, in the mind's perception and understanding. And in the act of object-constitution which simultaneously is the mind's self-constitution, the mind is united with its object.

As is to be expected, there is a parallel between the views on the subject-object and mind-body relation in the two traditions. Those who think that the mind is separated from and confronted with a world, are also likely to regard the mind as distinct from its body. And those who take the mind to be united with the world, also think that mind and body form a unity, or vice versa.

What then does the ontology which unites both world *and* mind look like, for instance, in Heidegger and Merleau-Ponty? If one were to give the barest possible description, or rather indication of a description, as I am, it would go something as follows. Our perception and understanding of things always reflect a certain use of things. When we are using things for some (theoretical or practical) purposes, we are perceiving and understanding them within a specific context, determined by the overall purpose. Our constitution of objects in consciousness is a constitution of these objects within a specific context. This property of the mind's constitutive power means that it is situated in space and time. True, the contextual character of the mind's constitution may differ in clarity and preciseness; it may range from the vaguest feeling of what the situation is about, as is often the case in everyday life, to a fully articulated structure. The point is that the contextual character of the mind's constitutive power in perception and understanding is a genuine property of the mind, irreducible to any perception or understanding of particular things. The contextual (or structural) character of the mind's perception and understanding is rather the condition for things appearing to the mind or consciousness at all, that is, for the mind's intentional constitution of things. The contextual or structural character of our perceptions and understanding is, in other words, a deeper layer in our perceptions and understanding than intentionality. Intentionality is thus never directly directed towards objects or their intentional correlates in consciousness.

Heidegger characterizes the original contextual or structural property of understanding with such difficult terms as *Bewandtnisganzheit* and *Erschlossenheit*. *Bewandtnisganzheit* signifies, roughly, the context or use-structure within which particular things are mutually related to or involved in each other, and, moreover, understood in their relevant aspect or perspective. The fact that it is the understanding that relates the things to each other (in accordance with the relations that are possible between things) and thereby suggests the way the mind is united with the world. The term *Erschlossenheit* carries these ideas a bit further. It signifies the original disclosure of the world; that is, the structure of certain things, which at the same time is a disclosure of the "I" in that specific situation. The "I" is then always living in one possible world, or rather in an ever-changing possible world.

Heidegger obviously tries to capture the active or dynamic character of our understanding or our mind.

Merleau-Ponty expresses similar views in a more familiar language. His starting-point is the active or lived body, which unites mind and body in a continuum of functions. The human subject is then defined as the ensemble of skills which actively involve it, the subject, in the world, and the structure of the world is a function of the subject being situated and at home in it. The structure of the experiences or perceived world is therefore "correlative with the functional organization" of the active or lived body (cf. Hall). This meaningful structure and the objects that are structured and thus appear within it, cannot therefore (and this is also Heidegger's view) be understood as independent of human subjectivity. That, moreover, is the reason why the world we interact with cannot be treated as an array of physical properties, but must be treated as a system of significant contexts or situations, whose meaning depends on the experience or perceptions of the subject. Those who do so, that is, who regard nature as consisting of physical objects and processes, existing independently of the mind to the mind, overlook the constitutive power of human experience, in particular human perceptions.

As is apparent from these introductory remarks, the question as to what the mind is, is still an open question. In the contemporary philosophy of mind the question itself appears in fact to be more indefinite than ever before. Rationalist philosophers of the seventeenth century give the impression of having a fairly clear view of the ontological and cognitive potentialities involved in the human mind. Heidegger, who among modern philosophers most explicitly relates himself to classical metaphysics, cannot be said to have made any progress. On the contrary, he concedes to having failed in his attempt to understand Being, that is, the total context to which the mind may relate itself in its self-knowledge. What he claims to have shown in some detail is the truth of an old axiom, that the mind necessarily depends on the world for its existence and self-knowledge and that the mind's self-knowledge is involved in every knowledge of the world. If there is anything to such a view, it is certainly this, that it effectively explains the increasing indefiniteness, if not to say bewildernment as to what the human mind really is and how it is to be explained. The mind's dependence on the world carries the complexity and value-plurality of the modern world into the human mind itself.

Traditional philosophy often claimed to provide man and the sciences with broader or even ultimate perspectives. The need for such perspectives is as pressing as ever before. Such a need is perhaps the most striking feature of the human mind. The problems involved here are, I take it, a serious challenge to the contemporary philosophy of mind and to philosophy in general.

Personal identity and the concept of a person

JOHN PERRY
Stanford University

Philosophers approach the concept of a person from two directions. In ethics and political philosophy it often is taken as primitive, or at least familiar and not requiring elucidation, but persistent inquiry and difficult problems make a deeper look inevitable. In discussing abortion, for example, one can hardly invoke principles about rights and welfare of persons concerned, without facing the question about which concerned parties are, in fact, persons, and what that means. One moves remorselessly from issues of rights and responsibilities to questions of consciousness, self-awareness, and identity — from the moral to the metaphysical.

From the other direction, no comprehensive epistemology or metaphysic can avoid the question of what persons — our primary examples of knowers and agents — are, and how they fit into the universe, whether as illusion, phenomena, or things in themselves. Answers to this question will have consequences in the ethical sphere.

These approaches meet in the problems of freedom and in the problem the recent history of which I discuss: personal identity. It is the identity of the knower over time that seems to be both the ground and the result of empirical knowledge, and identity of the moral agent that seems presupposed by notions of responsibility, guilt, decision, and freedom.

I shall discuss a number of contributions by philosophers to our understanding of personal identity. I shall follow a specific path through the literature, which means I shall have to ignore a number of contributions that lie to one side or the other. The discussion is mainly metaphysical and epistemological, but questions of ethical significance are posed.

PERSONAL IDENTITY FROM LOCKE TO SHOEMAKER

Our path will begin with Sydney Shoemaker's seminal book, *Self-Knowledge and Self-Identity* [1], published in 1963. But before starting on the path proper, it will be helpful to glance at the historic sources of the problems Shoemaker discusses. Although questions of personal identity are central to Idealism, from Kant to Royce, Shoemaker's book skips over this tradition (except, perhaps, as it enjoys a twilight existence in Wittgenstein's thought) and, like so much of twentieth century analytical philosophy, picks up the problem as it was left by empiricist and common sense philosophers of the seventeenth and eighteenth centuries.

The most important of these was John Locke, who added a chapter on personal identity to his *Essay Concerning Human Understanding* [2] in 1694. Identity of persons consists in continuity of consciousness, and this seems to be provided by links of memory: "as far as this consciousness can be extended backwards to any past action or thought, so far reaches the identity of that person ..." (section 9). Thus Locke appears to analyze self-identity in terms of self-knowledge, and provides the theme of Shoemaker's book and the dominant topic in the discussions to follow.

Locke distinguished identity of person from identity of spiritual substance on the one hand and identity of human body ("identity of man") on the other. The second distinction he argues for with a striking thought experiment: "For should the soul of a prince, carrying with it the consciousness of the prince's past life, enter and inform the body of a cobbler, as soon deserted by his own soul, everyone sees he would be the same person with the prince, accountable only for the prince's actions ..." (section 15). The use of thought experiments which are putative cases of "body-transfer" was to become a focus of discussion two hundred and seventy years later, but at the time Locke wrote his distinction between identity and person and identity of soul or psiritual substance was more controversial. "Let anyone reflect upon himself, and conclude that he has in himself an immaterial spirit, which is that which thinks in him, and, in the constant change of his body keeps him the same: and is that which he calls himself: let him also suppose it to be the same soul that was in Nestor or Theristes, at the siege of Troy ... but he now having no consciousness of any of the actions either of Nestor or Theristes, does he conceive himself the same person with either of them? Can he be concerned in either of their actions? attribute them to himself, or think them his own, more than the actions of any other man that ever existed?" (section 14). Locke also held that it is possible, for all we know, that consciousness can be transferred from one substance to another, so "two thinking substances may make but one person." (section 13). This outraged Joseph Butler: "... in a strict and philosophical manner of speech, no man, no being, no mode of being, nor any thing, can be the same with that, with which it hath indeed nothing the same. Now sameness is used in this latter sense when applied to persons. The identity of these, therefore, cannot consist with diversity of substance" [3; see also 4].

The idea that personal identity could be analyzed in terms of memory was used by twentieth century empiricists who attempted to analyze the self as a logical construction from momentary experiences. This project, more Humean than Lockean, requires a relation between those experiences which will group them into sets of "co-personal" experiences. Though Hume rejected Locke's memory theory [5], and Locke himself did not hold a bundle theory, the two doctrines seem to fit together naturally: we use memory to hold the bundle together through time. The clearest expression of this view comes from H.P. Grice in his fine essay "Personal Identity" [16]. Grice labors to discredit the pure ego theory of the self, a descendant of the view that personal identity consists in sameness of spiritual substance, and to put in its place a "modification of Locke's theory of personal identity." We can understand Grice's subtle and sophisticated theory as the result of successive accommodations to counterexamples, starting with Locke's view. Reconstructing Locke's view within Grice's framework, we begin with experiences. Those that can be known by introspection to be simultaneous belong to the same *total temporary state* or *t.t.s.* (p. 88). Thus we may imagine the realm of experience broken into discrete bundles, each t.t.s. being the experiences belonging to a single person at a given time. Locke's theory then is seen as giving us a principle for stringing these bundles together through time, giving us persons as enduring entities. His view is simply that t.t.s A and t.t.s B belong to the same person if and only if the latter contains an experience that is a memory of some element of the earlier. But this permits Reid's famous brave officer paradox: the boy is the officer (for the officer remembers stealing apples), and the general is the officer (for the general remembers leading the charge), but, since the general doesn't remember anything the boy thought or did, the general is not the boy [4].

Grice's final theory goes roughly as follows. Consider the relation t.t.s A has to t.t.s B if either one could contain a memory of an experience contained in the other. Any set of experiences which is closed under this relation, and contains no subsets closed under it, we may call a Grice set. (A set x is closed under a relation R if anything that has R to any member of x is in x.) T.t.s.'s are members of the same Grice set if and only if they are stages of a single person. The theory gets around the brave officer paradox, and other problems of Grice's own devising, by allowing indirect memory links, such as that between the general and the boy, to confer identity.

Between the publication of Grice's article and the publication of Shoemaker's book, Ludwig Wittgenstein exerted tremendous influence on philosophy, and Shoemaker's perspective and theoretical approach were very Wittgensteinian in some respects. In particular, Shoemaker makes heavy use of the concept of a criterion and of the assymetries between first- and third-person reports. Shoemaker is also sympathetic to Butler and Reid, trying to bring out epistemological insights that motivate their criticisms of Locke, without adopting their metaphysics of immaterial substances. Shoemaker did not conceive of himself as building on Grice's work, and as in fact severely critical of aspects of Grice's view, and of much that Locke had said. Yet, perhaps ironically, a chief effect of Shoemaker's books was to precipitate an increasingly productive re-examination of Locke's ideas.

SELF–KNOWLEDGE AND SELF–IDENTITY

A main theme in Shoemaker's book is that problems about self-knowledge have led philosophers to misconceptions about self-identity, and about the nature of selves in general. Self-knowledge is that which would be characteristically expressed in sentences containing the word "I". The problems have to do with the assymetry between such statement and the third-person statements which are, in some sense, equivalent to them. One who says "I see a tree," for example, will normally find a tree in his visual field, but not a person looking at one, or at least not himself, the person whose seeing he is reporting. And yet someone else who reports the same episode of vision in the third person by saying, for example, "Jones sees a tree," will have to see a person and identify that person as Jones, as well as seeing a tree. Now one who thinks that in the first instance, one *must* have seen, or somehow been aware of, or at least inferred the presence of, the tree-seer as well as the tree seen, and must have identified the person so perceived or inferred as a person appropriately referred to with "I", is likely to be led to the conception of the self as a non-physical thing, simply because no physical thing seems available to fill this role. Shoemaker finds such conceptions in McTaggart, Russell, and others. But these theories, he thinks, all wrongly assume that in order to be entitled to say "I perceive an X" I must perceive more than an X. In fact, says Shoemaker, it is a distinguishing characteristic of first-person experience statements that *their being true* entitles one to assert them. The problem of identifying the perceiver as "me" does not arise, and so the mysterious thing so identifiable need not be found nor postulated. That there should be this entitlement, Shoemaker accounts for in two ways. First, that such first-person statements are generally true when made is not contingent, but necessary. Second, it is simply a fact, indeed, a very general fact of the sort it is easy, as Wittgenstein had emphasized, to overlook, that we can teach individuals to use such sentences as "I see a tree" just when they see a tree, and in doing so we need not be and would not be providing them with criteria which they can use to identify themselves.

Similarly, in the case of a statement like "I remember going to the store," or "I broke the window," there are no first-person criteria which one must apply, to determine *who* is remembering, or went to the store, or broke the window. Now philosophers, like Locke and Grice, who are drawn to the view that personal identity consists of links of memory, may have been led to this view by supposing that we must have criteria of personal identity that we apply in our own cases, and finding nothing but memory that could play this role. Philosophers, like Reid and Butler, who emphasize the special nature of, and indefinability of, personal identity, may have seen that no criterion is applied in our own case, but misinterpreted this to mean that identity is directly observed, and consists in the identity of immaterial substance. In both cases, philosophers have been led away from the view that persons are physical beings by the fact that one need not use a bodily criterion of personal identity in a first-person report of what one did, or remembers doing, in the past.

But if we see that rather than a non-bodily criterion being applied, or a non-bodily fact being observed, it is simply the fact that one is doing the remembering that entitles one to say that it is oneself who went to the store, we shall be free to agree with Shoemaker that identity of body is the fundamental criterion of personal identity.

Although Shoemaker criticizes the memory theorists severely, as being motivated by a mistaken epistemology, and defends bodily identity as the fundamental criterion of personal identity, he does allow that memory is *a* criterion of personal identity, and one that can conflict with the fundamental criterion. Early in the book he introduces the case of Brownson, a twentieth century version of Locke's cobbler and prince — a case that was to perplex and intrigue philosophers for years to come:

> It is now possible to transplant certain organs ... it is at least conceivable ... that a human body could continue to function normally if its brain were replaced by one taken from another human body ... Two men, a Mr. Brown and a Mr. Robinson, had been operated on for brain tumors, and brain extractions had been performed on both of them. At the end of the operations, however, the assistant inadvertently put Brown's brain in Robinson's head, and Robinson's brain in Brown's head. One of these men immediately

> dies, but the other, the one with Robinson's head and
> Brown's brain, eventually regains consciousness. Let us call
> the latter 'Brownson' ... When asked his name he auto-
> matically replies 'Brown.' He recognizes Brown's wife and
> family ..., and is able to describe in detail events in Brown's
> life ... of Robinson's past life he evidences no knowledge at
> all. (pp. 23–24)

Shoemaker does not say that Brownson is Brown. But he does
say that if people did say this, they would not be making a mistake, nor even necessarily deviating from our present criteria, or
debying the primacy of the bodily criterion. They might simply be
allowing it to be over-ridden by other criteria in some circumstances (p. 247).

At this point, some feel a certain frustration with Shoemaker's
conclusions. If Brownson is Brown, or even if that is something we
might decide was true without inconsistency, then personal identity is not bodily identity, and, it seems, persons are not simply
live humans. What then is personal identity? Here the notion of a
criterion of identity, and other notions and modes of argument
reflecting a Wittgensteinian merger of epistemological and metaphysical questions, seem to obscure rather than illuminate issues.
That memory is a criterion of personal identity means that it
could not be discovered not to be good evidence for personal
identity (p. 4). But that does not mean that memory is logically
necessary or logically sufficient for personal identity. The same
goes for bodily identity. So the identity of Brown is not settled:
we have a conflict of criteria that usually don't conflict, and it
appears we must leave it at that.

But it is not clear why Locke's theory, or Grice's modification
of it, could not take hold here. Grice might agree with Shoemaker's main conclusions, but argue that his theory is consistent
with them, and partly explains them. Memory is *a* criterion simply
because personal identity consists in links of memory. Shoemaker
argues that we cannot apply the memory criterion, or even have a
concept of memory, without presuming a stable relation between
bodily identity and links of memory. That is why the bodily identity criterion is fundamental. But Grice, it seems, could accept
that bodily identity was the fundamental criterion of personal

identity, and that the assumption of a close correlation between bodily identity and links of memory is a premise of the whole enterprize of talking about persons, without giving up the claim that personal identity *consists in* links of memory. Just this strategy was adopted by Antony Quinton in "The Soul" [7], in which a version of the memory theory is defended.

A key consideration against the memory theory in Shoemaker's book is that since we employ no criterion of identity in first-person reports of past thought and action, we do not employ the memory criterion. But while being misled about this might have played a role in motivating the memory theory, it does not seem to provide a decisive objections, as Shoemaker was to point out later himself. Grice's view is that if I remember an experience, it it mine. This is not to say that I use the fact that I remember it as a criterion for deciding that it is mine.

In spite of Shoemaker's criticisms of the memory theorists, and his reluctance to unequivocally allow Brownson to be Brown, the overall effect of his book on most philosophers was not to produce the conviction that personal identity is simply bodily identity. In the first place, the example of Brownson takes on a life of its own in the mind of the reader; to many Shoemaker's reluctance to straightforwardly identify Brownson with Brown underestimates the force of his own example. Second, Shoemaker's probing studies of various examples, claims, and positions, while not always proving the conclusions he draws, always impress one with the depth of the problems involved. Third, Shoemaker's point that we typically apply no criterion in first-person judgments about the past has seemed a point in favor of the memory theory, in spite of his own use of it as a contrary argument. Finally, Shoemaker does allow that memory is *a* criterion. Locke had part of the truth. Even though memory may not be enough to make Brownson unequivocally Brown, even Shoemaker admits it is enough to prevent him from clearly being Robinson.

DIVIDING SELVES AND MULTIPLYING MINDS

Before publication of Shoemaker's book, Bernard Williams had put forward a clever argument against the memory theory. In

"Personal Identity and Individuation" Williams constructs the case of Charles, a twentieth century man who shows every sign of remembering the actions and experiences of Guy Fawkes: "Not only do all Charles' memory-claims that can be checked fit the pattern of Fawkes' life as known to historians, but others that cannot be checked are plausible, provide explanations, and so on." [8, 9] The case is designed to give us all the evidence we might want to say we have a case like that of Locke's cobbler. But, Williams points out, we are not forced to say that Charles remembers what Fawkes did, rather than merely that he claims to do so. And he comes up with an impressive argument to clinch the point:

> If it is logically possible that Charles should undergo the changes described, then it is logically possible that some other man should simultaneously undergo the same changes, e.g., that both Charles and his brother Robert should be found in this condition. What should we say in this case? They cannot both be Guy Fawkes, if they were, Guy Fawkes would be in two places at once, which is absurd. Moreover, if they were both identical with Guy Fawkes, they would be identical with each other, which is also absurd... . We might instead say that one of them was identical with Guy Fawkes ... but this would be an utterly vacuous manoeuvre, since there would be *ex hypothesi* no principles determining which description to apply to which. So it would be best, if anything, to say that both had mysteriously become like Guy Fawkes... . If this would be the best description of each of the two, why would it not be the best description of Charles if Charles alone were changed? (p. 9)

In a reply to an article of Robert Coburn's [10], Williams makes the principle behind this argument explicit. "The principle of my argument is ... that identity is a one-one relation, and that no principle can be a criterion of identity for things of type T if it relies only on what is logically a one-many or many-many relation ... 'being disposed to make sincere memory claims which exactly fit the life of ...' is not a one-one, but a many-one relation... ." [10, 9]

Williams' "Reduplication Argument" provided an interesting

challenge to those who wished to defend some version of the memory theory. But it also stirred interest in more general problems of identity and individuation, problems on which attention was also focused as a result of Peter Geach's provocative writings on identity. [11. 12] David Wiggins, in his pioneering study, *Identity and Spatio-Temporal Continuity* [13], adopts a condition very much like Williams' requirement that a criterion of identity be one-one:

> If f is a substance concept for *a* then *coincidence under f* must be a determinate notion, clear and decisive enough to exclude this situation: *a* is traced under f and counts as coinciding with *b* under f, and *a* is traced under f and counts as coinciding with *c* under f while nevertheless *b* does not coincide under f with *c*. (p. 38)

Wiggins distinguishes the concept of a person from that of a human body, and a person from his or her body. And he incorporates into his notion of a person the memory criterion of personal identity. But he claims, in opposition to Shoemaker's analysis of the Brownson case, "... that no correct spatio-temporal criterion of personal identity can conflict with any correct memory-criterion or character-continuity of personal identity." Wiggins then accepts both the importance of memory and Williams' condition on criteria of identity. How can he escape the reduplication argument?

In Williams' notion of the memory "criterion" there is again a merging of epistemological and metaphysical considerations. Surely it is not *claiming* to remember that Locke or Grice thought constituted identity, but some relation of memory for which such claims are evidence. Wiggins is quite clear-headed about this. He generally keeps questions of what constitutes identity and questions of how it is known clearly distinguished. In the present case this is manifested by his adoption of a causal theory of memory, adopted from Martin and Deutscher [14]. Not it is much easier to imagine two persons sincerely claiming to have done what one person did in the past than it is to imagine two persons whose claims are both caused by the previous action in the way appropriate to be memories. The memory criterion, interpreted as a causal criterion, is much more plausibly one-one.

Even if this were enough to avoid the reduplication argument, it would not vindicate Wiggins' claim that the memory criterion, properly conceived, cannot conflict with the spatio-temporal continuity requirement. For in the Brownson case the causal requirement appears to have been satisfied.

Wiggins says that they cannot conflict because the two criteria "inform and regulate on another reciprocally" when the memory criterion is properly founded in the notion of causation: "... indeed they are really aspects of a single criterion. For the requirement of spatio-temporal continuity is quite empty until we say continuity *under what concept* ... and we cannot specify the right concept without mention of the behavior, characteristic functioning, and capacities of a person, including the capacity to remember some sufficient amount of his past." (p. 46) In the final analysis, Wiggins says, we should "analyze *person* in such a way that coincidence under the concept *person* logically requires the continuance in one organized parcel of all that was causally sufficient and causally necessary to the continuance and characteristic functioning, no autonomously sufficient part achieving autonomous and functionally separate existence." (p. 55) Thus, as I understand it, Wiggins allows that Brownson is Brown, the brain being the "organized parcel."

Wiggins points out, however, that building causality into the memory criterion does not totally preclude the reduplication problem:

> Suppose we split Brown's brain and house the two halves in different bodies ... there is memory and character and life in both brain transplants ... . In this case we cannot simply disregard their (claimed) memories. For we understand far too well *why* they have these memories. On the other hand, if we say each is the same person as Brown, we shall have to say Brown I is the same person as Brown II. (p. 53)

Wiggins reasons that we cannot take both Brown I and Brown II to be the same person as Brown, for they are not the same as each other. And he reasons that even if half of the brain is destroyed, and the other half transplanted, we do not have identity: "... one of the constraints which should act on us here is the likeness of what happens to the surviving half in this case to what happens in the unallowable double transplant case ... ." (p. 56)

Wiggins here agrees with the key move in Williams' original argument. If there were two survivors, we could not say they both were the original. But both would have just the relation to the original that a sole survivor would have. So the relation the sole survivor would have cannot be identity, or enough to guarantee identity. Now one might criticize this by pointing out that the relation differs, in the latter case, in that there is no competitor. And Shoemaker, in an article to be discussed below, does take just this attitude towards the reduplication case: causally based memory *without competition* is sufficient for identity. It is natural to reply, on Wiggins' behalf, that this added element of lack of competition does not seem the right sort of difference. Why should who I am be determined by what is going on elsewhere in the world — the presence or absence of a competitor to the identity of the person whose thoughts and actions I remember? This line of thinking will lead us naturally to the insistence not only that the criterion or principle of identity for persons (and perhaps for anything) be logically one-one, but that it be, in some sense intrinsically so rather than as a result of an *ad hoc* stipulation that competitors defeat identity. Here, however, there is a problem. It is not clear that there are any such intrinsically one-one empirical relations. As Richard Gale [15] points out, it is not even clear that Williams' favored criterion of bodily continuity is logically and intrinsically one-one. Can we not imagine a situation in which there are two bodies, either of which by itself would be clearly reckoned as a later stage of a given body?

Another alternative is to allow both of the survivors to be the original. This is assumed to be incoherent, due to the logical properties of identity, by Williams, Wiggins, and Shoemaker. In "Can the Self Divide" [16], however, I argued that if we were careful we could allow this, without incoherence — or that at least we could say everything we wanted to say, giving each of the survivors full credit for the past of the original.

Like Wiggins', my views [17] were set within a general approach to individuation developed as a response to Geach's [11, 12] thesis of relative identity, the thesis that there is no such thing as identity, but only different kinds of "relative identity," and that objects can be identical in one of these ways and not in another. My point of view was derived from Frege [18] and Quine [19], and emphasized the distinction between identity, a relation that is a part of logic and which every object or entity of any kind or type has to itself, and various relations, *unity relations*, which were closely related to identity but which were different for various kinds and types of objects.

The undeniable phenomenon motivating doctrines of relative identity is the *relativity of individuation*. Imagine a checkerboard. We can think of it as eight rows, as eight columns, as 64 squares, or in a variety of other ways. That is, we can individuate it, break it up into individuals for the purpose of description, in different ways. To these different ways of thinking of the same hunk of reality, there seem to be different relations that correspond to identity. Imagine pointing to a checkerboard, saying "this is the same as that." If one is thinking of it as rows, the sentence will only be true if the pointings are side by side, the same distance from the bottom of the board (roughly). If we are thinking in terms of columns, one pointing must be above the other. This suggests that identity is a different relation, depending on whether we are talking about rows or columns. It appears that we need to distinguish between row identity and column identity. This crude example captures one motivation people have had for accepting Geach's doctrine, indeed, the conclusion seems almost forced upon us. If I point at the very same places, side by side, saying first, "This is the same row as that," and next, "This is the same column as that," what I say first will be true and what I say second will be false. So the relations asserted to obtain between the identified individuals must, it seems, be different. (Geach has more sophisticated arguments, of course.)

If we think of rows and columns as sums of squares grouped according to different relations — *being above* and *being beside* — and consistently follow through on this, all of these difficulties, and the motivation for relative identity, will disappear. Being beside and being above are not two kinds of identity, but relations between squares used to construct two different kinds of objects. The problem with "This is the same as that" is not that it hasn't been said what sort of identity is at stake, but that the objects referred to have not been fully identified. And "This is the same row as that " and "This is the same column as that" do not assert different relations of the same objects, but the same relation, identity, of different objects, a row in the first case, and two columns in the second. Thus, like Wiggins, I was unconvinced by Geach's doctrine. In many ways Wiggins' view is that of well-behaved relative identity, however; he does not emphasize, and in some cases (where temporal parts are needed to make the distinction) seems not to allow, the distinction between the unity relations and identity. (See Shoemaker [20].)

This distinction, however, allows us to see a fundamental flaw in Williams' reduplication argument. Williams claims that any criterion of identity must be logically one-one. Now it seems perfectly clear that the evidential relations we have for identity need not be one-one. If X looks exactly like you, that is good evidence that X is you, not because of logic, but because of the rarity of what are called "identical twins." What Williams has in mind are clearly the relations that are constitutive of identity, the relation that parts have if they are parts of the same person (as I would put it). That is, his principle is that unity relations must be one-one, because identity is.

But in fact unity relations need not, and often do not, share the logical properties of identity. It is more convenient to think about this in terms of the traditional conception of identity as an equivalence relation (reflexive, symmetrical, and transitive), for the notion of one-one becomes awkward when comparing relations between parts (the unity relations) to relations between wholes (identity). Now many unity relations are not, even as a matter of fact, much less as a matter of logic, equivalence relations. In general, where K's are a certain kind of entity with spatio-temporal parts, the formal "x and y are parts of a single K" gives us the unanalyzed unity relation for K's. Now consider, for example, highways. The roadbed of the Golden Gate Bridge and the portion of U.S. 101 that goes by Candlestick Park are parts of a single highway, as are the roadbed of the Golden Gate Bridge and that part of California Highway 1 that goes by the Pillar Point Fishing Pier. But the part of 101 that goes by Candlestick and the part of 1 that goes by Pillar Point are not parts of a single highway. (The situation is the familiar one of different highways merging to cross a bridge.) Now it might seem that if the unity relation for highways is not an equivalence relation, then highway identity must not be either — a counterexample to the one should provide a counterexample to the other. But one finds that an attempt to produce a counterexample is blocked by a failure of reference. "The highway that crosses the Golden Gate Bridge," or "This highway" as said on the bridge, fail to refer, for there are two highways that cross the bridge. Thus mechanisms of reference act as fuses, which by failing keep the logical shortcomings of unity relations from being passed on to identity.

In "Can the Self Divide," this idea was worked out in some detail, in a way that allowed us to say, without contradiction, and without abandoning any of the traditional properties of identity, that each of the survivors of a reduplication case did all of the things the original had done, and that he was to do all of the things each of them did. The abstract point that unity relations need not share the logical properties of identity has been more convincing than the particular solution proposed, however. Criticisms by David Lewis [21] and Terence Leichti [22] have weakened my faith that my intuitions about what to say in a reduplication case were as inevitably the product of careful reflection, and that my scheme embodied them in so completely an unobjectionable way, as I had thought. I would now prefer to speak of "individuative crises" occasioned when unity relations that have been reliably equivalence relations (though not logically) cease to have that character, to which we can respond in a number of ways, the present concept underdetermining the matter.

"Can the Self Divide" was one of three papers [16, 23, 24] in which I defended Grice's memory theory. It seemed to me that Grice had been clearer about the structure of identity than his successors, and that since a careful distinction between identity and unity was built into his account, the reduplication argument did not touch it. This still seems to me correct, even if we adopt the view that what to say in a case of reduplication is left indeterminate by our concept of personal identity rather than being as intuitively clear as I had supposed. In the later papers, I argued that Grice's point of view, when stripped of its goal of logical construction, leads to a plausible causal theory of personal identity, and that an account can be given, within this framework, of the importance of personal identity. In my thinking on each of these matters the distinction between the unity relations and identity loomed large; I thought it was a necessary first step to clarity on these issues. In reviewing the literature for this article, I find my earlier attitude rather unfounded, and think it must have led me to be insufficiently appreciative of others, particularly Shoemaker and Wiggins. Perhaps emphasis on the distinction between unity and identity is not so *necessary* a first step as I had thought!

Another approach to the reduplication case is taken by Roderick Chisholm [25]. Chisholm wondered how we might face the propsect of splitting, like an amoeba. He concludes, "There is no possibility whatever that *you* would be *both* the person on the right and the person on the left. Moreover, there *is* a possibility that you would be one or the other of these two persons. And finally *you* could be one of those persons and yet have no memory at all of your present existence." (p. 179)

Chisholm draws on Shoemaker for support. He says he agrees with Shoemaker's contention that first-person psychological statements are not known to be true on the basis of criteria. He thinks a consequence of this is, '... it makes sense to suppose ... that you are in fact the half that goes off to the left and not the one that goes off to the right even though there is no criterion at all by means of which anyone could decide the matter." (p. 182) These reflections on reduplication come at the end of an article whose main object is to defend a version of Bishop Butler's claim that there is a "loose and popular" as well as a "strict and philosophical" sense of identity. Personal identity, unlike the identity of ships and carriages and trains and rivers and trees and in general "compositia" or evolving systems thereof, is identity in the strict and philosophical sense. Identity in the loose and popular sense is typically vague, open ended, defeasible and, ultimately, a matter of convention, of how we choose to talk. In puzzling cases, decision by courts or other agencies is appropriate. But none of this is applicable to personal identity, according to Chisholm. He considers Peirce's ([26], p. 355) example of someone who is to be operated upon, without anaesthetic, with a drug administered beforehand which wipes out memories during the operation, and one administered after that restores these but leaves no memories of the operation. Chisholm has no doubt that it is the person in question who will feel pain during the operation, but he considers someone — perhaps someone tempted by Grice's theory — who is not so sure. He says it ought to be obvious to such a person that the adoption of a convention, a way of talking, or a practice by a judge or a whole community, cannot in the least affect the question he is worrying about.

In his reply to Chisholm's paper at the Oberlin Colloquium [27], Shoemaker begins to develop a line of thinking which goes significantly beyond his book, and introduces ideas and problems that dominated the study of personal identity for the next decade. "What we need to clarify," he says, "is the nature of that interest we have in personal identity, and in particular that special concern that each of us has for his own future welfare." (p. 117) Shoemaker entertains the idea that it might be appropriate for one who knows he is to undergo fission, to anticipate the experience of both offshoots, while not supposing that he would be identical with either. These themes are developed in an important paper Shoemaker was to publish three years later.

PERSONS AND THEIR PASTS

In "Persons and Their Pasts" [28], published in 1970, Shoemaker gives a much more sensitive and sympathetic treatment of the memory theory than he had in *Self-Knowledge and Self-Identity*. He says that he is defending Locke's view that persons have, in memory, a special access to facts about their own past histories and their own identities, and he is also defending the non-trivial nature of Grice's claim (suitably interpreted) that "one can only remember one's own experiences." This would be trivial if there were some general mode of access to past experiences, our own others', and "remembered" were simply a title for the subset of experiences so known that happened to have been ours. It is non-trivial if memory (of some sort) is an independently specifiable mode of knowing of past experiences and what we mean, or part of what we mean, by calling an experience "ours" is that it is remembered. In that case, the limited access we have in memory would be constitutive of the notion of a single person.

Shoemaker considers two criticisms of the memory theory. One is that it is circular, a charge originally made by Butler; Shoemaker had earlier made a version of this criticism himself. The other is the reduplication argument, not in the form in which Williams originally advanced it, but as put forward by Wiggins and Chisholm, with appropriate causal links between the survivors and the original.

Those who charge the memory theory with circularity acknowledge a strong conceptual link between personal identity and memory, but see this as simply the upshot of the fact that personal identity is a logically necessary condition for memory. If it is a part of our concept of memory that one can only remember events one witnessed or participated in, then it is hardly surprising that memory is a sufficient condition for identity with a past witness or participant. But the analysis of personal identity in terms of memory would be circular.

Shoemaker suggests an analysis of memory for the purposes of considering this charge, which goes more or less as follows:

X remembers event e *if and only if*

1) X is in a cognitive state S;
2) Y was aware of when it happened, in virtue of being in cognitive state S';
3) Cognitive state S' corresponds to S;
4) Y's being in S' and X's being in S are elements in an M-type causal chain;

The cognitive state mentioned in 1) is intended to be the sort of state one could be in whether remembering or only seeming to; to distinguish apparent from real memory we need the rest of the analysis. Clause 2) captures part of what is called the "previous awareness condition": if one remembers an event, one must have been aware of it at the time it occurred. By using "Y" instead of "X" in its statement, the part of the analysis that seems to lead to circularity, the condition that the previously aware person be the rememberer, is split off for separate consideration. Clause 3) makes the plausible point that what is remembered must correspond to what one perceives or experiences, though exactly

what this involves is not explained at any length. Clause 4) requires that the present memory activity be caused by the earlier
perceptual activity *in the right way*, that is, in the way that it is
usually caused in memory. Clause 5), finally, is the isolated condition split off from the previous awareness condition, the element in the analysis that makes the use of memory to analyze
identity seem circular.

Shoemaker then introduces two new notions. X *quasi-remem-
bers* e if conditions 1) — 3) are satisfied. X $quasi_c$-remember e if
conditions 1) — 4) are satisfied. Thus the statements that one can
only quasi-remember one's own past experiences, or that one can
only $quasi_c$-remember one's own experiences, would certainly not
be trivial. If we find that either of these notions assigns the same
past event and experiences to a person as does the "unstripped"
notion of memory, then we can say that the additional clauses
are really just redundant. If, for example, we find that one quasi-
remembers just those past events that one would be said to remember, then one can say that clause 5) is really not necessary
for the analysis of memory: memory is just $quasi_c$-memory.
5) would be true, but now we could look on its truth as a consequence of the nature of memory as given by 1) — 4) *and* the
non-circular analysis of personal identity in terms of that notion
of memory.

Shoemaker concludes that quasi-memory is not a very interesting notion. The strong conceptual link between memory and
personal identity is brought out in two principles. The first is
the (unstripped) previous awareness condition. The second is
what Shoemaker calls preservation of immunity to first person
misidentification. This notion is a descendant of the idea in *Self-
Knowledge and Self-Identity* that one needs to criterion for first-
person identification. Used in the book as a basis for criticism of
the memory theory, this immunity is now seen as something the
memory theory goes some way towards explaining. Shoemaker
brings in the helpful notion of memory "from the inside". When
I remember a past thought or action from the inside, then I can
identify myself as the past thinker or doer, without identifying
the thinker or doer as someone who fits a certain description or
satisfies certain criteria. Now, insofar as we can understand quasi-
memory at all, neither the previous awareness condition nor the

principle of preservation of immunity to misidentification seem to hold for it.

For quasi$_c$-memory, however, the picture is quite different. When we add the causal requirement, we get a notion almost indistinguishable from ordinary memory. Virtually any situation I can imagine in which the conditions for quasi$_c$-memory are met is a situation in which the conditions for memory are met. This strongly suggests that personal identity *can* be analyzed in terms of quasi$_c$-memory, that clause 5) can be seen as a consequence of this analysis, and that the memory theory need not be circular.

The need for qualification comes from the second criticism of the memory theory that Shoemaker considers. The way the world is, M-type causal chains neither branch nor merge. Given this orderly behavior, quasi$_c$-memory seems indistinguishable from memory. But it is imaginable that M-type causal chains should not behave in such an orderly way; this is just what we imagine when, with Wiggins, we imagine halves of a brain transplanted to different bodies, or with Chisholm, we imagine splitting like an amoeba. In these cases Shoemaker supposes that we "cannot identify both of the physiological offshoots of a person with the original person, unless we are willing to take the drastic step of giving up Leibniz's Law and the transitivity of identity..." (p. 28) Given such ill-behaved causal chains, I *could* quasi$_c$-remember from the inside an experience or action that wasn't mine. For this reason, the analysis of personal identity in terms of quasi$_c$-memory is not totally straightforward. But we can get a logically sufficient condition for personal identity: quasi$_c$-memory with no branching. Basically, Grice and Locke are vindicated.

Towards the end of the article, Shoemaker picks up the question he raised in the reply to Chisholm. In a case in which there has been branching, Shoemaker thinks that neither of the branch persons is identical with the original. But each would quasi$_c$-remember the experiences and actions of the original person. Now which of these facts is important? That they *do* quasi$_c$-remember, or that they are not identical? As Shoemaker puts it, "If I [quasi$_c$-remember] from the inside a cruel or deceitful action, am I to be relieved of all tendency to feel remorse if I discover that because of fission someone else [quasi$_c$-remembers] it too?" (p. 284). Shoemaker thinks not. It is the quasi$_c$-memory that is important, not the lack of identity. As against this, we might appeal to such facts as that identity is a necessary condition of responsibility for past actions. But then Shoemaker could simply repeat the identity-stripping investigation for the concept of responsibility, and argue that the operative concept is really quasi$_c$-responsibility. No concept has identity more "built into it" than that of survival. Shoemaker thinks that if one is to fission, one will not be identical with either of the survivors. And yet, "The prospect of immanent fission might not be appealing, but it seems highly implausible to suppose that the only rational attitude toward it would be that appropriate to the prospect of immanent death..." (p. 284)

The idea emerging here is that personal identity is important to us *because* it involves certain relationships to past and future persons, rather than these relationships being important because they constitute identity. This idea was to undergo explicit statement and dramatic development in an important article by Derek Parfit published shortly after Shoemaker's. Before looking at that, however, we must look at an article by Bernard Williams [29] published the same year as "Persons and Their Pasts" [28], in which, once again, the argument against according memory too much importance in personal identity is made subtly but forcefully.

THE SELF AND THE FUTURE

In "Persons and Their Pasts," Shoemaker says that Brownson is Brown, and that his former reluctance to conclude this was a result of overlooking the causal component in the notion of memory — an element which, as we have seen, was emphasized by Wiggins, who himself seems to have accepted that Brownson is Brown. Though remaining more certain of the puzzling nature of the questions raised than of his own conclusions, Bernard Williams remained unconvinced, and in "The Self and the Future" [29] he argues against the possibility of body transfer and the considerations about memory and personal identity that seem to allow it.

To persuade us that matters are not so straightforward, Williams produces what we may call a "Nonduplication Argument". He begins by imagining a case in which the memories associated with two bodies are switched. The process is impeccably causal:

> Suppose it were possible to extract information from a man's brain and store it in a device while his brain was repaired, or even renewed, the information then being replaced: it would seem exaggerated to insist that the resultant man could not possibly have the memories he had before the operation... Hence we can imagine the case we are concerned with in terms of information extracted into such devices from A's and B's brains and replaced in the other brains... (p. 47)

Williams calls the resulting persons the "A-body person" and the "B-body person". We may represent the situation with this diagram:

	History of Body-A	*History of Body-B*
Later time	A-body person (memories of B's life)	B-body person (memories of A's life)
Earlier time	A	B

Williams then poses a problem for A and B. Each is asked at the earlier time to choose one of the bodies to be tortured at the later time, the other to receive $100,000. This choice is to be made on selfish grounds. Williams assays the results of various possible combinations of choices, and seems to find in them a strong argument for describing the case as one of body transfer. For example, if A chose that the B-body person be rewarded, and this is done, then the B-body person will be happy about a choice he will seem to remember making. It is natural to report this as "Someone got what he wanted", and it seems this someone must be someone who had body A and then had body B. Indeed, Williams' discussion up to this point puts the case for the possibility of body transfer about as effectively as it has been put.

But then he pulls the rug out from under us. "Let us now consider something apparently different... Someone tells me that I am going to be tortured tomorrow ... when the moment of torture comes I shall not remember any of the things I am now in a position to remember ... but will have a different set of impressions of my past." (pp. 51-52) Now this sounds awful: to be tortured is a frightful prospect, and the additional bits of information about loss of memory and acquisition of false belief just make things worse. But, Williams says, this is really just a variation on the original case. It corresponds to the left side of the diagram above, the history of body A. "What we have just been through is of course merely one side, differently represented, of the transaction which was considered before; and it represented it as something one could rationally, perhaps even cheerfully, choose out of the options there presented." (pp. 52-53)

Williams tells us that these and other considerations leave him "not in the least clear which option it would be wise to take if one were presented with them before the experiment." (p. 62) But his cautious advice is that "if we were the person A then, if we were to decide selfishly, we should pass the pain to the B-body person." (p. 63)

In a review of Williams' *Problem of the Self*, I [30] criticized this argument. It seemed to me that its plausibility as an argument against the possibility of body-transfer, and so as an argument against conceptions of personal identity such as Locke's and Grice's that admit this possibility, rested on leaving certain details of the original case rather hazy. Consider the case we would have if in Shoemaker's example Brown's body with Robinson's brain had survived as well as Robinson's body with Brown's brain. Now if we were to look at half of this situation, it would not seem at all plausible to describe it as Williams has described the "left half" of his case. Imagine that Brown's present body is to be tortured after the brain-exchange takes place. It would seem quite misleading to say to Brown that he was to suffer loss of memory, and then be tortured. It seems that if he knew just that his brain would be removed and replaced by another before the torture, he might well fear death rather than torture. And if he knew further that his brain were to be put in Robinson's body, which would survive, he might well fear neither torture nor death, though presumably he would have enough worries to occupy himself. Thus if Williams' goal is to show that no convincing case of body transfer has been constructed, his argument falls short; the differences between his case and Shoemaker's are crucial to his argument that his case is not a body transfer, so the argument does not transfer to Shoemaker's case.

Does Williams show that no case of body transfer short of brain transfer can be constructed? It does not seem to me that he does. Our reaction to his case depends on what is meant by extracting information from a man's brain, the process less radical than brain transposition by which Williams secures the causal link necessary for memory. If information has been extracted from A's brain, does this leave A's brain unaffected, as when we make a photocopy of an article? Presumably not, since Williams described the A-body person's state, with respect to memories of A's life, as "total amnesia". But "amnesia" itself is a rather ambiguous word; even in fiction it usually refers not to total eradication of memories (a "brain zap"), but to some state in which they are rendered inaccessible, to be regained, with luck, from some future rap on the head. This would not give us a bloodless approximation to Shoemaker's case, for now the links of possible memory would extend from A at the earlier time to both the A-body person and the B-body person at the later time. This would be a delightfully complicated case to think about, both a double fission and a double fusion, but not one very germane to rejecting the possibility of body transfer, a project which requires rebuttal of the most convincing cases. To the extent that an information extraction is a brain-zap, so that the earlier and later stages of body A are not M-connected and we really do have a bloodless equivalent to Shoemaker's case, it seems we do not have a case in which Williams' description of the left side is at all appropriate. If A knew that his brain was to be zapped, he might well cease to fear torture.

While, at least in my opinion, not convincing, Williams' subtle and stubborn argumentation forces to one'a attention what might be called the phenomenological difficulties of accepting one's identity as the sort of thing which could be a matter for decision. Chisholm [25], it will be recalled, found it simply bizarre to imagine that one's identity could be a matter for decision, a matter that would be decided by convention or litigation or even by social practice. Though not drawn, as Chisholm was, by something like a pure ego or immaterial substance theory, and more in a mood to remind us of difficulties than to establish conclusions,

Williams shares Chisholm's attitude towards the suggestion that personal identity could be a matter of convention. "There seems to be an obstinate bafflement to mirroring in my expectations a situation in which it is conceptually undecidable whether I occur ... The bafflement seems, moreover, to turn to plain absurdity of we move from conceptual undecidability to its close friend and neighbor, conventionalist decision ... as a line to deal with a person's fears or expectations about his own future, it seems to have no sense at all." (p. 61)

While Chisholm was drawn to a metaphysical solution to these problems, Williams seems to think that there is refuge in bodily identity. It seems to me, though, that he has put his finger on something that is not just a baffling consequence of one theory of personal identity, that which emphasizes memory, and is avoided by others, but rather on something that is simply baffling. Let *any* empirical relation R be the candidate for the unity relation for persons. Then *some* philosopher is clever enough to construct a case in the area of R-vagueness, that is, a case where our concepts leave it indeterminate whether R obtains or not, even given all the facts. Then we will have an indeterminate case for the theory that maintains that R is the unity relation for persons. It may be easier for *link of memory* than for *identity of body*, perhaps. But it seems that all of our concepts are formed, as Wittgenstein said, within the context of certain very general assumed facts; by imagining those facts to be otherwise, we can create cases the concept was not designed to handle.

We have seen, in the course of discussions, a shift of attention from persons and their pasts to persons and their futures, a shift called for by Shoemaker in his reply to Chisholm [27], and initiated in the thoughts at the end of "Persons and Their Pasts". A key concept in such a enquiry is that which Williams calls "the imaginative projection of myself as participant in [a future situation]." (p. 59; see also [31]) We can perhaps think of this as the future oriented analogue of Shoemaker's "memory from the inside". Shoemaker's question, whether one should look forward to fission as death, given his belief that one will be identical with neither of the products of fission, is then a proposal to consider imaginative projection of ourselves as participants, when we realize that no participant in the situation will be identical with us. Made sensitive by Williams of the baffling aspects of such questions and proposals, let us return to them.

SURVIVAL WITHOUT IDENTITY

If one is asked why one feels bad about an event of the previous evening, and responds, "Because *I* am the one that committed the outrage," the identity asserted between the present speaker and the participant in the earlier event seems to be bearing an important explanatory role. But in "Persons and Their Pasts", Shoemaker is on the verge of displacing identity from this explanatory role, putting in its place the "identity-stripped" concepts of $quasi_c$-memory, $quasi_c$-fear, $quasi_c$-responsibility, and the like. The importance if identity derives from the importance of these relations, which in our well-behaved world, with no M-fission or M-fusion, can be taken as constitutive of identity. The suggestion that identity is after all not so crucial is also considered by Terence Penelhum, in *Survival and Disembodied Existence* [32], with special reference to what we really want when we hope for survival after death. But the step of pushing identity to the background was made most boldly and unequivocally by Derek Parfit, in his profound, imaginative, and influential article, "Personal Identity", [33]:

> Judgments of personal identity have great importance. What gives them their importance is the fact that they imply psychological continuity. ... If psychological continuity took a branching form, no coherent set of judgments of identity could correspond to, and thus be used to imply, the branching form of this relation. But what we ought to do ... is take the importance which would attach to a judgment of identity and attach this importance directly to each limb of the branching relation. ...judgments of personal identity derive their importance from the fact that they imply psychological continuity.

Parfit thinks that there are cases in which there is no correct answer to a question about personal identity. He refers to the examples of Locke (section 18 of [2]), Prior [34], Bennett [35], and Chisholm, but in particular to that of Wiggins. "My brain is divided, and each half housed in a new body. Both resulting people have my character and apparent memories of my life. What happens to me? (p. 5) To say he does not survive seems odd, Parfit argues: "How could a double success be a failure?" For him to be only one or other seems arbitrary. But to say he survives as both is to violate the laws of identity, Parfit assumes. His solution is that we do not need to have identity to have survival, or at least not to have what is important in survival: "We can solve this problem only by taking these important questions and prizing them apart from the question about identity." (p. 9) When we do this the results are dramatic. While identity is an all or nothing affair, the various identity stripped relations that constitute it when well-behaved, and are what really matters in any case, are often quite plausibly regarded as matters of degree. This is a matter of importance, not only in analytical metaphysics, but in the way we think of ourselves in real life: "Identity is all-or-nothing. Most of the relations which matter in survival are, in fact relations of degree. If we ignore this, we shall be led into quite ill-grounded attitudes and beliefs." (p. 11) Among these are the principles of self interest, and regrets about one's eventual death. He argues: "Suppose that a man does not care what happens to him, say, in the more distant future... We must say, 'Even if you don't care, you ought to take what happens to you then equally into account.' But for this, as a special claim, there seem to me no good arguments... The argument for this can only be that all parts of the future are *equally* parts of *his* future. But it is a truth too superficial to bear the weight of the argument." (p. 26)

Parfit notes that in certain extreme puzzle cases — a network of "persons" who periodically fission and fuse, for example — we are naturally led to think not in terms of continuous persons, but in terms of more or less connected selves, reserving the word 'I' for the greatest detree of psychological connectedness. This way of thinking could be applied even in normal cases, and would embody a recognition that it is psychological connectedness that is what matters, and this would help in avoiding the ill-grounded attitudes and beliefs mentioned above. In "Later Selves and Moral Principles" [36], Parfit argues that thinking in this way, or recognizing the possibility of doing so, undercuts certain arguments against utilitarianism.

In Parfit, we might say, Shoemaker's analytical tool of identity stripping has become an approach to life.

The question of the importance of identity seems to me greatly illuminated by general questions about identity and individuation, and in particular by the perspective sketched in the section on dividing selves. Indeed, as soon as one adopts the perspective that identity is a logical relation, one is implicitly committed to the derivative importance of identity, although not necessarily to Parfit's claim that what matters are relations of degree.

After all, there are many conceivable ways of individuating the world — of choosing unity relations with which to unify our objects. That is, many are conceivable from the point of view of constraints imposed by logic, although most fanciful alternatives would not be possible ways for beings like ourselves (however individuated) to experience or deal with the world. Each way of individuating gives rise to a class of objects, members of which are identical to themselves in as literal and unsullied a sense as I am to myself. Thus, for example, we could think in terms of a kind of object which consisted, during any baseball game or inning thereof in which the San Francisco Giants participate, of the Giants' shortstop for that period. This would be a discontinuous object composed of stages of ordinary men, stages of Le Master and Metzger this season. We could give rules for referring to an assigning predicates to these objects, adjusting things to preserve the indiscernability of the identical. Let us call such entities *longstops*. Then the longstop in the game gets an error or strikes out just in case the shortstop does. But the present longstop may have struck out in the last inning, even if the present shortstop didn't — if Metzger replaced a slumping Le Master, for example.

Last inning's longstop is identical with this inning's longstop in as pure a sense of identity as anything is identical with itself. But the identity is unimportant. That the longstop was injured last inning, and that the *very same longstop* is now playing, gives us no reason to expect limping. That the longstop who is playing now made a good play last inning gives us no reason to cheer when he comes to bat.

Clearly, the importance of the identity of objects of a given kind depends on the unity relation. The choice of a unity relation to be a part of our scheme, and so the presence of objects of the corresponding kind in the scheme, reflects its importance. The importance of identity is in this sense derivative; how could it be otherwise?

But we can also ask why a given unity relation is important — worth fashioning identity out of. In particular, if memory, or some more general kind of psychological continuity or connectedness is important, and the source of the importance of personal identity, why is this so? What is so important about it? I think this question is the one which if often on the mind of philosophers who resist the idea that personal identity is analyzable at all. For we can make the point about the derivative importance of identity from an even more general principle. If, as Locke supposed, personal identity may be analyzed, must not the analysans explain the importance of the analysandum? The idea that any such explanation of the special importance identity has for us must be absurd, leads to the claim that identity is unanalyzable and primitive. Butler [3], for example, thinks that if personal identity is analyzable, then it is not strict identity after all but something else, and that if this were so it would be "... a fallacy upon ourselves to charge our present selves with anything we did, or to imagine our present selves interested in anything which befell us yesterday, or that our present self will be interested in what will befall us tomorrow."

While I think that there is no distinction to be drawn between strict and loose identity of the sort that Butler imagines, if we hold that personal identity is analyzable, it seems his challenge must be met. Of Parfit's analysis we might ask: "Why is it important, and why do we care in a special way, about what will happen to someone tomorrow who is psychologically directly connected with me?" Now it is no longer open to us to say the most natural thing, that it is because psychological connectedness is sufficient for identity, and so he will *me* if he is so connected with me. We have concluded that such an appeal to identity is not ultimate, but gives way to the explanation in terms of connectedness.

I tried to deal with this problem in "The Importance of Being Identical" [24], which appeared in Amelie Rorty's anthology *The Identities of Persons* [38]. The attempt led to conclusions which I found peculiar at the time, and still find peculiar, but of which I reconvince myself each time I reflect upon the matter. It seemed clear that a theory of personal identity should be causal; I adopted a descendant of the memory theory that fully relied on the fact that memory is a causal notion. Now in general, attempts to explicate concepts in causal terms make reference to the *normal* mode of causation. It is not enough for me to remember a past event that the event have caused my present memory impression; it must have done so in the right way. If I spill soup on my grandmother as a child, and am told of it so often as an adolescent that as an adult I have e clear memory-like impression, then my spilling has caused the impression. But I do not remember, for it was not caused in the right way.

The account of why identity should be important was built around the fact that we know what to expect from ourselves in the normal case, and can expect continued commitment to the values we have. But it is hard to see why an atypical causal chain that provided the same guarantees should not be just as good, even though, as seemed and seems clear to me, if it is atypical enough it doesn't provide identity. I came to the conclusion that it shouldn't matter:

> Suppose the following. A team of scientists develops a procedure whereby, given about a month's worth of interviews and tests, the use of a huge computer, a few selected particles of tissue, and a little time, they can produce a human as like any given human as desired... I have an incurable disease. It is proposed ... that a duplicate be created ... and simply take over my life... He would not be me. The relation between my terminal and his initial states is too unlike the [normal causal relations which preserve psychological continuity between earlier and later stages of humans] to be counted, even given the vagueness of the concept of a person, as an instance of it. But ... I would have the very same legitimate reasons to act now so as to secure for him future benefits as I would have if he were me. (p. 83)

I meant to include by this the full appropriateness of "imaginatively projecting myself" into the benign imposter's future experiences. Such a position still seems to me a natural and inevitable outcome of Locke's original idea.

SPLIT BRAINS

While the literature on personal identity through time must rely on contrived puzzle cases, contemporary neurosurgery has provided us with real puzzle cases when we wish to consider identity at a time. The behavioral results of brain bisection, an operation that has been performed for the treatment of epilepsy in certain unusual cases, have led some scientists involved to say that two separate "subjects of consciousness" have been created within a single body. This result has seemed to Thomas Nagel [39] to place the very idea of a single person into difficulties, and has moved Roland Puccetti [40] to argue that, since we all differ from split-brain patients at most in the form of communication that takes place between our hemispheres we are really two persons in a sense. Recently, Charles Marks in *Commissorutomy, Consciousness and the Unity of Mind* [41] has surveyed the philosophical, psychological, and medical literature and come to a much more conservative conclusion.

BIBLIOGRAPHY

Bibliographical remarks. Amelie Rorty's anthology, *The Identities of Persons* [38], contains twelve essays on personal identity and related topics, many of which pick up the path of discussion we have followed. There is an extensive bibliography. A number of papers from historical and modern authors are reprinted in my anthology *Personal Identity* [42]. There is also a good bibliography in Godfrey Vesey's helpful book *Personal Identity: A Philosophical Analysis* [42]. An important book by Roderick Chisholm was published in 1976 [44]; perhaps Chisholm's book and the essays in the Rorty volume will prove a good point of departure for some future survey.

Bennett, J. [35] The Simplicity of the Soul. *Journal of Philosophy* LXIV (1967).
Butler, J. [3] *The Analogy of Religion*, first appendix: Of Personal Identity, 1736. Pages references are to [42].

Chisholm, R. [25] The Loose and Popular and Strict and Philosophical Senses of Identity. In Norman S. Care and Robert H. Grimm (Eds.), *Perception and Personal Identity*. Cleveland 1969.
– [44] *Person and Object*. La Salle, Ill. 1976.
Coburn, R.C. [10] Bodily Continuity and Personal Identity. *Analysis* (1960).
Frege, G. [18] *Grundlagen der Arithmetik*. Breslau 1884; trans. by J.L. Austin, *The Foundations of Arithmetic*, 2nd ed. New York 1960.
Gale, R. [15] A Note on Personal Identity and Bodily Continuity. *Analysis* XXIX (1969).
Geach, P. [11] *Reference and Generality*. Ithaca 1962.
– [12] Identity. *Review of Metaphysics* (1969).
Grice, H.P. [6] Personal Identity. *Mind* 50 (1941). Page references are to [42].
Hume, D. [5] *Treatise of Human Nature*, Book I, Part IV, section 6: Of Personal Identity. Page references are to [42].
Leichti, T. [22] *Fission and Identity*. Doctoral dissertation, UCLA, 1975.
Lewis, D. [21] Survival and Identity, in [38].
Locke, J. [2] *Essay Concerning Human Understanding*, Book II, Chapter 27: Of Identity and Diversity. Page references are to [42].
Marks, C.E. [41] *Commissurotomy, Consciousness and Unity of Mind*. Montgomery, Vt. 1980.
Martin, C.B., and Deutscher, M. [14] Remembering. *Philosophical Review* LXXV (1966).
Nagel, T. [39] Brain Bisection and the Unity of Consciousness. *Synthese* 22 (1971). Reprinted in [42].
Parfit, D. [33] Personal Identity. *Philosophical Review* LXXX (1971). Reprinted in [42].
– [36] Later Selves and Moral Principles. In Alan Montefiore (Ed.), *Philosophy and Personal Relations*. London 1973.
Peirce, C.S. [26] *Collected Papers*, Volume V. Cambridge 1935.
Penelhum, T. [32] *Survival and Disembodied Existence*. London 1970.
Perry, J. [16] Can the Self Divide? *Journal of Philosophy* LXIX (1972).
– [17] The Same F. *Philosophical Review* LXXIX (1970).
– [23] Personal Identity, Memory, and the Problem of Circularity, in [42].
– [24] The Importance of Being Identical, in [38].
– [30] Review of [9]. *Journal of Philosophy* LXXIII (1976).
– (Ed.) [42] *Personal Identity*. Berkeley and Los Angeles 1975.
Puccetti, R. [40] Brain Bisection and Personal Identity. *British Journal for the Philosophy of Science* 24 (1973).
Prior, A. [34] *Time, Existence and Identity*. Proceedings of the Aristotelian Society, 1966.
Quine, W.V. [19] Identity Ostension and Hypostasis. In *From a Logical Point of View*. New York 1963.
Quinton, A. [7] The Soul. *Journal of Philosophy* 59 (1962). Page references to [42].

Reid, T. [4] Essays on the Intellectual Powers of Man, Chapters 4 and 6 of the essay *Of Memory*. Page references are to [42].
Shoemaker, S. [1] *Self Knowledge and Self-Identity*. Ithaca 1963.
– [20] Wiggins on Identity. *Philosophical Review* LXXIX (1970).
– [27] Comments. Cf. [25].
– [28] Persons and Their Pasts. *American Philosophical Quarterly* (1970).
Rorty, A. (Ed.) [38] *The Identities of Persons*. Berkeley and Los Angeles 1976.
Vesey, G. [43] *Personal Identity: A Philosophical Analysis*. Ithaca 1974.
Wiggins, D. [13] *Identity and Spatio-Temporal Continuity*. Oxford 1971.
Williams, B. [8] *Personal Identity and Individuation*. Proceedings of the Aristotelian Society, 1956-57. Page references are to [9].
– [9] *Problems of the Self*. Cambridge 1973.
– [10] Bodily Continuity and Personal Identity. *Analysis* (1960). Page references are to [9].
– [29] The Self and the Future. *Philosophical Review* LXXIX (1970). Page references are to [9].
– [31] *Imagination and the Self*. Proceedings of the British Academy, 1966. Page references are to [9].

Recent work on the relation of mind and brain

D.M. ARMSTRONG
University of Sydney

1. INTRODUCTORY

The decade 1966-1976 saw an immense amount of valuable philosophical discussion concerning the relation between mind and brain. As a result, it has seemed best to be selective, both with respect to topics and to authors. Many important books and papers have had to be passed over. This chronicle confines itself almost entirely to cases where new philosophical positions, or striking new lines of argument, have been developed about the relation of mind and brain.

I should like to thank Michael Devitt, Elizabeth Prior, Gregory Currie and Keith Campbell for their advice and assistance. I also sent a draft of this survey to a number of persons whose work is discussed. In many cases they sent me very helpful comments.

2. BACKGROUND

Philosophical discussion of the relation between mind and brain during our decade was greatly influenced by, indeed was in a large measure a reaction to, three papers published in the previous decade. These were U.T. Place's 'Is Consciousness a Brain Process?' ([1], 1956); Herbert Feigl's 'The "Mental" and the "Physical"' ([2], 1958); and J.J.C. Smart's "Sensations and Brain Processes" ([3], 1959). A brief account of these articles is an essential preliminary.

Contemporary philosophy. A new survey. Vol. 4, pp. 45–79.
©*1983, Martinus Nijhoff Publishers, The Hague/Boston/London.*

All three authors were Scientific Realists. They were Realists, because they believed that the physical world exists independently of the minds which are aware of it. They were *Scientific* Realists because they believed that the best account which we have of this world is furnished by contemporary natural science. They held that the theoretical entities in terms of which science gives an account of macroscopic physical objects and processes have a real existence. Indeed, a table or a rock, they held, is a swarm of fundamental particles.

Smart was further inclined to accept, as a high level scientific hypothesis, the thesis of Physicalism. It seemed to him that the concepts and law-statements of physics, or, at any rate, the concepts and law-statements of a hypothetically completed physics, suffice, in principle at least, to give an account of all natural phenomena. Biology, in particular, he thought, does not require the postulation of fundamentally new properties or new laws. The bodies of animals and of ourselves, for instance, are nothing more than extremely complex physical systems operating according to purely physical principles. Contemporary science, he thought, had rather conclusively vindicated the Cartesian dream of a physicalist biology. Place's and Feigl's positions were quite close to those of Smart's, although neither, in different ways, went quite so far with their Physicalism.

Descartes had not been willing to extend his Physicalism about the body to the mind. To these authors, however, such an extension was the obvious next step. Was it likely that a materalist account could be given of the whole of nature with the exception of one tiny corner?

The question therefore arose 'How is it possible to give a physicalist account of the mental?' All these authors felt the attractions of Behaviourism, taken not as a methodology but as a doctrine of the nature of mind. If to have a mind is simply to behave in certain sophisticated ways, if there are no inner mental processes such as thoughts and images, then there is no obstacle to a physicalist account of human beings and the higher animals. As a result, Place and Smart were inclined to give Ryle's *Concept of Mind* ([4], 1949) and Wittgenstein's *Philosophical Investigations* ([5], 1953) a Behaviourist reading, and, given this reading, to accept much of what Ryle and Wittgenstein said.

But it seemed that Behaviourism could not be the whole truth about the mind. As Place said in his article:

> ...there would seem to be an intractable residue of concepts clustering around the notions of consciousness, experience, sensation and mental imagery, where some sort of inner process story is unavoidable.

So what was the physicalist to do about the phenomenal, the sensory, what Feigl called the 'raw feels'?

Place suggested that sensations, etc., simply consisted of processes in the brain. He compared this speculative identification to the once speculative, but now established, identification of lightning with the motion of electrical charges. In neither case can the identification be made simply by semantic, conceptual or logical analysis. Statements about lightning do not *mean* the same as statements about electrical charge. Nevertheless, *as a contingent matter of fact*, lightning is a motion of electric charges. Similarly, statements about sensations do not mean the same as statements about brain processes. Nevertheless, Place argued, it may be a contingent matter of fact that sensations are brain processes. If so, although a Behaviouristic account of sensations is incorrect, a Physicalist account of sensations can still be given.

In Place's view, what had prevented so many other thinkers from identifying sensations with brain processes is what he called the 'phenomenological fallacy'. The fallacy consists in arguing that when I have a green after-image, it is entailed that there is something green in my mind or brain. If we allow this inference, then, says Place:

> We have on our hands an entity for which there is no place in the world of physics.

To have a green after-image, however, is in fact, he argues, only to have the sort of experience which we normally have when we look at a green patch of light. There are no things called 'after images', which are green, there are only experiences-as-of-imaging-something-green. It it these experiences, Place asserts, which are identical with brain processes.

This doctrine was further worked out by Smart. (In the early nineteen fifties both he and Place were at the University of Adelaide.) Smart wrote:

> When a person says, "I see a yellowish-orange after-image", he is saying something like this: *There is something going on which is like what is going on when* I have my eyes open, am awake, and there is an orange illuminated in good light in front of me, that is, when I really see an orange.

Place had talked of 'experiences', but, as Smart points out, his own italicized phrase is completely *topic-neutral*. It just says that there is *something* going on, something described only in terms of the sort of stimulus which characteristically brings it about. As a result, the identification of this something with a brain-process is not at all a difficult notion. (The difficulty with Smart's view lies rather in his analysis of after-image statements.)

It is noteworthy that the third member of our trio of forerunners, Feigl, appears to bestow definite properties upon his 'raw feels'. From Place's point of view, he commits, or comes very close to committing, the 'phenomenological fallacy'. As a result, Feigl finds the identification of sensations with brain processes much more difficult to argue for. He is hard put to it to meet the objection that the raw feels have different properties from their neurological bases, and so are, by Leibniz's Law, different entities.

In general, it may be said that the analytical details of Feigl's essay did not have the same influence as the proposals of Place and Smart. It was rather the huge mass of considerations brought together in Feigl's long paper (together with the wealth of references in his bibliography) which helped during subsequent years to create philosophical interest in a 'central state' physicalist view of the mind.

It should be observed, finally, that an important difficulty concerning the *secondary qualities* remained in the positions of Place and Smart. Their analyses of sensation involved the notion of such things as *green* and *orange* physical objects (or surfaces) acting as stimulus-objects. But the Physicalist Dream (to adopt Michael Devitt's phrase) seems to have no more place for colours in the physical world than it does for after-images in the mind.

Smart was very much aware of the problem. He tried to solve it by producing a subjectivist analysis of secondary qualities in terms of the sensory discriminations made by 'normal' observers, where 'normal' was given the special definition that a normal percipient is one who can make more discriminations than any other perceiver. He then gave as a (rough) definition of 'This is red' the statement 'A normal percipient would not easily pick this out of a clump of geranium petals though he would pick it out of a clump of lettuce leaves'. (Besides [1], see his [6], (1963, Ch. 4.)

3. THE CAUSAL ANALYSIS

So much as background to our decade. A fairly direct development of the Place-Smart view is to be found in the work of D.K. Lewis [7, 8] and D.M. Armstrong [9].

First, Lewis and Armstrong generalize the identification of sensations and brain processes to apply to *all* mental processes, states, events, etc. (For simplicity, I shall simply talk about states in future. It is to be noted that the generalization to all mental states becomes explicit in Lewis only in his [8].) Not only perceptual states such as after-imagings, but, for instance, beliefs and purposes are now conceived of as inner states, states which are then identified with states of the brain.

Ryle had compared such states as beliefs to *dispositions*, such as the brittleness of glass. (His mental dispositions are dispositions for outward behaviour.) But Ryle does not conceive of brittleness and other dispositions as actual states of the disposed thing, states whose concrete nature might be identified by later scientific research. Armstrong in particular, however, argued for such a 'Realistic' view of dispositions. As a result, he was able to admit the generally dispositional nature of mental attributions; yet also to distinguish mental states from outward behaviour; and then to defend the hypothesis that mental states are in fact states of the brain.

Second, and bound up with this generalization of Place's and Smart's view, Lewis and Armstrong put forward a general account of the concept of a mental state. Place and Smart had given a (rather rudimentary) analysis of sensation-statements as asserting the occurrence of inner processes of a sort typically produced by certain physical stimuli. But in the case of beliefs and purposes, now also to be treated as central states, there seemed no possibility of explicating our concepts of such things in terms of typical stimuli. Beliefs and purposes are, rather, states which are thought of as typically bringing about certain behaviour. They are the causes of certain responses, rather than the effects of certain stimuli.

Lewis produced an elegant formula. He proposed that mental states are given to us in consciousness as nothing more than the *occupants of causal roles*. Sensations play the causal role of being typically brought about by certain stimuli acting upon the body. Beliefs, purposes, etc., and *also* sensations, occupy the causal role of bringing about, or enabling the bringing about, of certain sorts of behaviour. The particular causal role differs for different sorts of mental state. Among their causal roles, mental states participate in certain causal transactions with other mental states. For instance, if a person has the belief-state with the content 'if p, then q' but lacks both the belief that p and the belief that q, then *acquiring* the belief that p will (typically) give rise to acquiring the belief that q. Consciousness of a mental state is itself a mental state. Our concept of such consciousness, therefore, is also to be explicated purely in terms of its particular causal role.

In [8] Lewis even suggests that *all* theoretical identification is of this nature. Something (whether particular, property, or whatever) which is originally known or hypothesized merely as that which uniquely fills a certain causal role is subsequently more concretely identified. In the particular case of the mental states, the causal roles are to be defined, according to Lewis, by that collection of psychological platitudes, which is 'common knowledge' among us all (we know the platitudes, know that others know them, and so on). Armstrong's specifications of the causal roles placed less weight on psychological platitudes. His analyses, in their general form, much more resembled the logical analyses to be found in Ryle's *Concept of Mind* [4] while differing greatly in content from Ryle).

As is the case with Smart's more rudimentary account, if the general truth of either of these accounts of mental states be granted, then the identification of mental states with states of the brain, whether or not it is actually correct, becomes an identification of an unpuzzling *sort*. There remains the weighty task of trying to establish the truth of these sorts of account. Lewis does not undertake it. Armstrong, however, devotes a large portion of his book trying to show that, under analysis, the mental concepts exhibit just that topic-neutrality which clears the way for the scientific identification of mental states with states of the central nervous system.

What of the problem of the secondary qualities? Smart's Subjectivist account in terms of the powers of objects to produce in us suitable selective or discriminatory capacities, had been subjected to damaging criticism by Michael Bradley ([10], 1963). Would it not be possible, Bradley asked, for ordinary objects to produce in a subject exactly the right selective or discriminatory capacities, and yet for that subject to see a world of uniform grey? It seemed that Smart's analysis had failed to capture colour-*quality*.

Armstrong therefore proposed a completely Objectivist account of the secondary qualities ([9], Ch. 12). Colours, sounds, tastes, smells and so forth were taken to qualify physical objects, surfaces, etc. and were then straightforwardly identified with whatever properties of a physically respectable sort scientific investigation discovered to be well-correlated with the secondary qualities. For instance, heat, perceived or felt heat of objects, was identified with the motion of the molecules of the hot object. The model proposed for such an identification was that where a complex property of objects is grasped by a perceiver as a simple, unanalysable, 'gestalt'. Theoretical reasons may be given for thinking that the epistemologically simple property is, in fact, ontologically complex. This Objectivist account solves many problems for the Physicalist. But it remains very implausible phenomenologically.

When Lewis in his [8] argued that *all* theoretical identification was a matter of identifying the occupants of causal roles, he was committed, consistent with Physicalism, to giving a causal role account of the secondary qualities. In f. 15 he argued that colour-sensations can be defined in terms of the effect of coloured objects on the perceiver, and colours in terms of the colour-sensations which they produce in perceivers. But he maintained that this circularity was not vivious.

In general, it may be said that those philosophers who seek to identify mental and physical states are always left with a problem about the location and status of the secondary qualities. They have perhaps not given the problem the attention which it deserves.

4. THE DISAPPEARANCE VIEW

We have seen that those who identify sensations with brain processes face the difficulty that sensations appear to have properties which brain processes lack, and *vice-versa*. If this appearance corresponds to reality, then, by Leibniz's law, sensations and brain processes cannot be identical. Feigl recognized that this was a major difficulty for his position.

On the view put forward by Place and Smart, and further developed by Lewis and Armstrong, sensations are replaced by the having-of-sensations, and then a purely topic-neutral account of what it is to have a sensation is given. However, many philosophers have doubted whether this programme of producing a topic-neutral account can succeed.

Suppose, then, as is quite possible, that one remains in sympathy with the doctrine of Physicalism, yet one accepts neither the straightforward identification of sensations with brain processes nor the topic-neutral account. There is at least one further strategy available. One can deny that there are such things as sensations. More broadly, one can deny the existence of mind. It is not the case that the mind is the brain. There are no minds. There are only brains.

Such a view was advocated by Paul Feyerabend [11, 12] in the decade before that one which we are concerned with. In our decade it was defended, in a somewhat more cautious form, by Richard Rorty [13, 14].

Consider caloric fluid. We now believe that there is no such thing. Nevertheless, there does exist a real phenomenon to which the name 'caloric fluid' was applied. This phenomenon is the motion of molecules. Hence we can say that, although the motion of molecules is not caloric fluid, it *is* the thing which was (wrongly) called 'caloric fluid'. Again, we now believe that there are no witches. Nevertheless, in the past there did exist certain unhappy or disturbed old women to whom the word 'witch' was applied. Hence we can say that, although the women were not witches, they were persons who were (wrongly) called 'witches'.

Using these analogies, Rorty argues that it is an intelligible suggestion that there are no sensations or other mental activities. There are things to which terms such as 'sensation' are applied. But these things are in fact brain entities and so cannot be sensations. It follows that although certain brain processes are not sensations (because nothing is), these processes are the things which are (wrongly) called 'sensations'.

A spectacular theoretical advantage over the theories which identify sensations with brain processes immediately accrues. If the identification is correct, then by Leibniz's Law sensations and brain processes have exactly the same properties. But if certain brain processes are merely things to which the word 'sensation' is wrongly applied, then there is no necessity for the brain processes to have the properties which we attribute to sensations. At the same time, we can explain what it is that people talk about when they talk about sensations.

However Rorty does not actually deny that there are sensations. His position is rather that it is a plausible view that there are no sensations. If neurophysiological theory develops in the way he expects it to develop, then this plausible view will be upheld.

The dialectical situation concerning this 'Disappearance' or 'Eliminative' view may be illuminated by considering the parallel situation in the debate about Free Will and Determinism. Many philosophers hold that Free Will and Determinism can be true together. We are free when we choose what to do, or, perhaps, we are free when we choose, and furthermore the situation in which we choose is one where certain further empirically ascertainable conditions (such as absence of coercion) obtain. It is irrelevant that the choice may be fully determined by antecedent factors. This is the Reconciliationist position. The parallel to this position in the mind-brain debate is the view that mental states either are, or can intelligibly be said to be, physical states of the brain.

In the Free Will debate, however, there are philosophers who believe that Free Will and Determinism are incompatible. Among these anti-Reconciliationists there are those who are disposed to assert Free Will and so to deny the truth of Determinism. This is the Libertarian view. But others accept Determinism and therefore deny that there is any free will (Hard Determinism). Anti-Reconciliationists about the mind/body problem are those who take the existence of mental states to be incompatible with Physicalism. This also gives rise to two possible positions. There are those who respond to the (believed) incompatibility by rejecting Physicalism. They are like the Libertarians. But Feyerabend and Rorty respond by denying that there are mental states. Their position resembles the Hard Determinists.

The parallel with the Free Will debate shows that, while the Disappearance view avoids the difficulties involved in maintaining a strict identity between the mental and the physical, it is peculiarly vulnerable to attack from the anti-Materialist. For the latter can argue that the proposition that there are sensations, etc., is much more intuitively acceptable than is the Physicalist hypothesis.

The anti-Materialist case will be especially strong if it can be successfully argued that there is a fairly firm distinction to be drawn between the language of observation and the language of theory. If such a distinction can be drawn, and if theory must take epistemological second place to observation, then the Disappearance view is clearly in trouble. For if anything is 'given', surely mental states are given (in one's own case). Richard Bernstein [15] argues against Rorty in this way.

In his reply to Bernstein, Rorty [16] therefore argues, as many contemporary philosophers are inclined to argue on independent grounds, that the distinction between observation and theory is not an absolute one. All observation is theory-laden, including the deliverances of introspection. To claim to be directly aware of sensations is to make a theoretical claim which we may come to have scientific reasons to think false.

In his 1970 paper [14] Rorty tries to develop his argument further by giving 'marks of the mental' which are incompatible with Physicalism. He appeals to *incorrigibility*: the special epistemological authority which each of us appears to have about our own current mental states.

Rorty does not hold that it is logically impossible for us to be mistaken about our current mental states. Nevertheless, he argues, we are the ultimate authorities, the final court of epistemological appeal, concerning our current sensations and thoughts. He restricts this incorrigibility to sensations and thoughts. About other mental states, such as our beliefs and purposes, we have only near-incorrigibility. They are accounted mental only by a certain courtesy, because our epistemological authority about them approaches, but does not attain to, our authority concerning sensations and thoughts.

Materialists have objected to doctrines of incorrigibility that our special authority about the occurrence and nature of our own mental states might in the future be overthrown, for instance by evidence obtained by electroencephalograms. Such data, in conjunction with a powerful enough brain theory, might persuade us that even sincere reports of current mental states should be rejected. (See, for instance, Gregory Sheridan [17].)

Rorty accepts that our special authority about our own mental states might be overthrown in this way. Indeed, he expects such an overthrow to occur in the future. However, he urges, in Disappearance spirit, that this overthrow will show that so-called mental states are not mental states at all, but are *mere* brain states.

5. FUNCTIONALISM

We have seen that Lewis and Armstrong give their *preliminary* account of mental states purely in terms of the causal relations holding between those states, on the one hand, and sensory stimulation, behavioural output, and further mental states in the same mind, on the other. A very similar doctrine has been expounded by a number of philosophers, in particular Hilary Putnam and Jerry Fodor, under the label 'Functionalism'. An influential earlier paper of Putnam's is his [18] (1960), but within out decade the view is more fully developed in his [19].

Lewis and Armstrong take their Causal analysis to be *preliminary* to physicalist identifications. Putnam, however, takes his Functionalism to be an *alternative* to the view that mental states are physico-chemical states of the brain. Indeed, he says in [19] that one of the advantages of the view which he takes is that, unlike the Materialist view, it is compatible with Dualism about the mind. Putnam's remark here seems to be based upon misunderstanding, in particular a misunderstanding of Smart. The predecessor of Functionalism was Smart's topic-neutral account of sensations, not his identification of sensations with brain processes. Furthermore, Smart saw as one of the advantages of his topic-neutral formula that it was at least logically compatible with Dualism! Lewis' and Armstrong's later causal theories made a similar bow to anti-Materialism.

However, there is a feature of Putnam's Functionalism which does seem genuinely to differentiate his position from Smart, Lewis and Armstrong (and which unites him with Fodor [20, 21]). It is that he takes Functionalism to be a psychological rather than a conceptual theory.

But even here it may be that the apparent opposition can be largely reconciled. We may take Smart, Lewis and Armstrong to be offering accounts of our first, our preliminary, 'fix' upon mental states. Whether or not we admit the notion of conceptual analysis, it seems that, if we are to understand talk about mental states, there must be such a first fix. This preliminary understanding, they argue, is functional (causal). Now it is easily imaginable that this original functional characterization should be greatly developed, sophisticated, (perhaps even amended) by progress in psychological theory, *although this theory still stayed at the functional level.*

A parallel with genetic theory may be helpful. Pre-Mendelian commonsense had a vague genetic theory. It recognized that organisms could inherit particular characteristics. ('He has his mother's eyes.') But, except for even more imprecise talk about 'blood', the mechanism of inheritance was specified functionally only. This vague theory constituted genetics' 'first fix'. It corresponds to the Smart-Lewis-Armstrong theory of what constitutes our first fix upon the mental. After Mendel, a sophisticated theory of the inheritance of characteristics was developed, but for a long time the theory remained a purely functional one. In the same way, it may be suggested, Putnam and Fodor are pointing to the way that a preliminary functional view of the mental may be developed and sophisticated by psychology, while still remaining purely functional.

Putnam and Fodor were also critical of other aspects of the programme of identifying mental states with states of the brain. Place had drawn an analogy between the identification of sensations and brain processes and the identification of lightning with electric discharges. Fodor argues that the latter identification was a case of micro-analysis or reductive analysis, but that functional or causal role identifications are not of this nature. Instead, he offered as a model for the identification of mental states with brain states the identification of *valve lifters* (objects characterized in engineering functional terms) with *camshafts* (objects characterized by reference to their physical structure).

It may be remarked in passing that, even if Fodor's point be conceded, the model of micro-analysis may still have great importance for physicalists in the case of the secondary qualities. A purely functional characterization of the secondary qualities may not prove possible.

The identification of lightning with an electric discharge may be called a *type-type* identification. The property of being lightning, or the event-kind lightning, is identified with the property of being an electric discharge, or the event-kind electric discharge. By contrast, it is not the case that being a valve lifter is being a camshaft, or that the kind valve lifter is the kind camshaft. The reason for this is that although in many engines the function of valve lifting is performed by camshafts, it is perfectly possible to have quite other sorts of valve lifter. (Nor is every camshaft a valve lifter.) As a result, although we can say that *this* valve lifter is a camshaft, or even that valve lifters are generally camshafts, we cannot say that valve lifters are camshafts. We can only make *token-token* identifications.

Under the influence of such models as the identification of lightning with an electric discharge, physicalists about mental states had tended to think in terms of type-type identifications. As a result, they had often thought of the *evidence* for a physicalist account of mental states as a matter of establishing one-one correlations between mental states of a certain type, and physical states of a certain type, and then hypothesizing that this one-one correlation was in fact identity. (Opponents were regularly found who conceded the correlation, but denied the identity.)

But the Functionalists pointed out that, given a functionalist account of mental states, there need be no such one-one correlations. It is completely possible that very different sorts of things should all perform the same function. Putnam stressed the analogy with computers. Mental states may be compared with *computational* states of a computer, states characterized in 'software' terms. The same computational state type, and its complex computational relations to other state types, may be physically realized by all sorts of different mechanisms. Why should biological mechanisms be any different from computing mechanisms in this respect? As a result, the correlations which we may expect to exist between a certain type of mental state and a certain type of physical state are not necessarily one-one. They may be one-many. Furthermore, the many may be indefinitely many.

Fodor particularly stressed the point that, once one-one correlation was abandoned, there could be no reduction of psychological types and psychological laws to physiological types and physiological laws.

A very influential paper published in the previous decade by Oppenheim and Putnam [22] had put forward the thesis of the Unity of Science, conceived of as involving the reduction of psychology to biology, and biology in turn to chemistry and physics. This programme looked forward to the reduction of psychological types and psychological laws to physiological types and physiological laws. Fodor pointed out that, once one-one correlation between the psychological and the physiological was abandoned, such reduction was impossible.

This important point, whose force was widely appreciated, nevertheless led to a good deal of confusion. Some philosophers took it that the Oppenheim-Putnam programme of scientific reduction was an essential part of the doctrine of Physicalism or Materialism. So it seemed to them that to accept what Fodor had to say was to reject Physicalism and/or Materialism.

At the same time, however, Fodor's argument seemed to leave a central core of Physicalism (Materialism) unaffected. While the argument seemed to show that a mental type cannot be identified with a physical type, it had no tendency to cast doubt upon the view that each mental *token* — each individual sensation, thought, etc. – was a purely physical brain token. Individual pains might still be physical states of the brain. After all, different sorts of computer hardware are simply different *hardware*. Valve lifters which opperate according to a different pattern from camshafts are simply different *bits of machinery*. The relative autonomy of psychology, as it is envisaged by Fodor, stands in no necessary conflict with the Physicalist Dream.

The situation here may perhaps be illuminated by recalling an older uncertainty about the interpretation of the doctrine of Phenomenalism. According to what may be called 'translation Phenomenalism', statements about physical objects could actually be translated (in principle!) into statements about actual and possible sense-data or sense-impressions. This view corresponds to the view that psychological types can be identified with physiological, and ultimately with physical, types. (In the latter case, of course, the identity is not conceived of as *semantically* guaraneed.) The philosophical failure of translation Phenomenalism led some philosophers to say that Phenomenalism had been refuted.

But it is possible to abandon translation Phenomenalism and yet hold fast to a form of Phenomenalism. For it can still be maintained that, although physical-object statements cannot be translated into sense-datum statements, the truth-makers for each true physical-object statement are nothing but certain actual and possible sense-data. We might call this doctrine 'ontological Phenomenalism'. It is compatible with the falsity of translation Phenomenalism. Ontological Phenomenalism corresponds to the view that each mental token is identical with some purely physical token. Just as each physical object statement is made true by some purely sense-datum state of affairs, so each mental token statement is made true by some purely physical state of affairs.

It appears, then, that it is perfectly reasonable to deny that psychology is reducible to physiology, and yet to hold fast to the rest of the Physicalist programme. What can this doctrine be called except a form of Physicalism?

Before leaving the topic, it may be worthwhile to notice that the point that the correlations between mental and physical types may be one-many rather than one-one was not as original as the Functionalists seemed to believe. One-many correlations had already been explicitly envisaged by Feigl in [2].

However, Functionalism has also thrown up one further problem. There remains the difficult metaphysical question 'What is a functional property?' (The corresponding question for Lewis and Armstrong is 'What is a causal role?') Putnam spoke of functional properties as *second-order* properties [23]. This may suggest that he thought of them as properties of properties. Particulars, such as brains or portions of brains, have properties. Second-order properties would then be properties of these properties. Putnam, however, following Russell, calls such one-level-up properties 'properties of higher *type*'. By contrast, properties of higher *order* are properties of ordinary particulars, such as brains. A second-order property of a brain would be the property of possessing some (first-order) property, such that the latter property played some functional role. For instance, an object may have the (first-order) property of being a camshaft. As a result, the object may also have the (second-order) property of possessing some property playing the functional role of valve lifter.

The question then arises whether these second-order properties are really properties over and above first-order properties. If that is what they are, then they seem to be an extra, and mysterious, element in the ontological situation. But perhaps it can be argued that they are simply the original (first-order) properties, although picked out in a rather special way. We are led here into ontological and semantic questions to which those engaged in discussing the relation of mind and brain have given only peripheral attention.

6. DAVIDSON'S ANOMALOUS MONISM

The position developed by Donald Davidson in [24] and [25] has a number of points of resemblance to the Functionalist position, although he is not especially concerned to stress the functional character of mental states.

Davidson holds that each individual mental token is a physical token. Every sensation is a brain process. At the same time he denies that there are any strict laws linking the mental with the physical. He agrees that there are reasonably reliable psycho-physical generalizations. But he maintains that these generalization are not capable of being refined into strict laws. As a result, he agrees with the Functionalists that there are no type-type identities between the mental and the physical. He is particularly concerned to deny that there are any strict *causal* laws linking the mental and the physical, for instance, between mental events and behavioural effects. (Equally, he denies that there are any strict laws linking the mental with the mental.) He calls his token-token physicalism 'Anomalous Monism'.

The principle of Mental Anomaly leads Davidson to a certain paradox. He wishes to hold that mental events and physical events interact causally. Human bodily actions, for instance, are *actions* because they have a certain sort of mental cause. (See his famous paper 'Actions, Reasons and Causes' [26].) He calls this the Principle of Causal Interaction. Davidson also holds that any events related as cause and effect fall under strict laws. He calls this the Principle of the Nomological Character of Causality. (He defends the Principle in [27]. Quantum interactions may not be deterministic, but, Davidson points out, physicists treat them as governed by strict laws nevertheless. For the probabilities involved are sharply fixed.)

These two Principles seem to conflict with the Principle of the Anomalism of the Mental. How can mind act upon matter, or matter upon mind, and yet there be no strict laws governing the interaction?

Davidson points out that the paradox is rather easily resolved when we realize that a particular cause and its effect are governed by a strict law only relative to certain descriptions of these events. The collision of the *Titanic* with an iceberg caused the *Titanic* to sink. But not every collision of a liner with an iceberg causes that liner to sink. What we believe, however, is that there exists some true general description of the *Titanic*'s collision and the subsequent disaster (involving the ship, the ice and the further circumstances) such that, under that description, the events involved exemplify strict law. As is normal in such cases, we do not know what that description is. But we do not doubt that it exists. Similarly with simpler, more homely, cases such as that of the stone breaking the window.

Once this point is grasped, Davidson points out, the Anomalism of the Mental ceases to be paradoxical. When a certain desire plus certain beliefs and perceptions is followed by motion of the limbs, this sequence may well be causal, and so governed by a strict law, but it is not a strict law under these or any other purely *mental* descriptions. It may well be possible to explain why the action was done in mental terms, by specifying the purposes and beliefs involved. But such explanations will not involve anything more than rough-and-ready generalizations. ('Those who want W and believe B will generally do D.') It will not be possible, even in principle, to refine these generalizations into a strict law except at the cost of completely deserting the mental vocabulary. What vocabulary will serve for strict laws, then? As a Physicalist (in the ontological sense), Davidson thinks that it will be necessary to pass over into the vocabulary of theoretical physics. But there are no strict correlations between that vocabulary and our mental vocabulary.

For Davidson, then, the Anomalism of the Mental is completely compatible with the purely physical nature of the mental. This is not a particularly spectacular result, of course, nor does Davidson regard it as such. But now follows something more interesting. It is argued that the three premisses: the Principle of Causal Interaction, the Principle of the Nomological Character of Causality, and, finally, the non-existence of precise psycho-physical laws, can be put together to give good reasons for thinking that the mental is purely physical. The premisses can be used to *support* ontological Physicalism.

As Davidson says in [24], the argument is quite simple:

> Suppose m, a mental event, caused p, a physical event, then under some description m and p instantiate a strict law. This law can only be physical, ... But if m falls under a physical law, it has a physical description, which is to say it is a physical event. An analogous argument works when a physical event causes a mental event.

Could someone who accepted the premisses of this argument react by accepting the identity of mental and physical events, but at the same time postulate extra properties of the physical events in question, properties which are constitutive of mentality and are of a non-physical nature? Davidson, I think, would reject the implied ontology of objective properties, but in any case the suggestion seems not to meet his argument. For suppose, first, that these properties bestow no power, active or passive, upon the tokens which they are properties of. In effect this condemns what is peculiarly mental to causal impotence, contrary to the Principle of Causal Interaction. Suppose, alternatively, that the properties do bestow causal power. By an obvious extension of the Principle of the Nomological Character of Causality the properties must bestow a *law-governed* power. But then it follows that there must be precise psycho-physical laws, in contradiction to a premiss already granted.

The really critical premiss in Davidson's argument seems to be his contention that there are no precise psycho-physical laws. Furthermore, if the argument for the identity of the mental with the physical is to have any bite, the premiss will have to be supported by considerations which do not already, independently, presuppose the truth of a physicalist theory of the mind. This means that Davidson cannot, for instance, appeal in support of this premiss to the considerations advanced by Putnam and Fodor against type-type materialism. For they appeal to the fact that functionally similar mental states can be realized by very different material systems. But in so doing they argue from the physicalist framework which Davidson is trying to supply an argument for adopting.

Perhaps this accounts for the fact that Davidson's argument against strict psycho-physical laws is not easy to assess.

The argument begins, though it does not end, in the *holistic* character of mental causality. This is a point well appreciated in contemporary discussions of the philosophy of mind. For instance, if we consider the way in which beliefs and desires issue in behaviour, then it can be rather easily seen that belief X and desire Y will issue in behaviour Z only against some mental 'background'. I can want a drink, perceive the public-house before me, and believe that I have only to step inside for my desire to be satisfied. But do I take the step? What if I believe that my enemy is within, and want not to meet him more than I want the refreshment? I may then refrain from taking the step. But what if the belief that my enemy is within has temporarily slipped my mind (under influence of thirst, perhaps)? The original behaviour may then be reinstated. And there may be further mental factors, which, if present, would change the situation again, and so on indefinitely. The finding of precise laws linking the mental and the physical begins to look difficult.

However, as Davidson remarks, this sort of holism is to be found in the sphere of the purely physical as much as in the sphere of the mental. Given a certain set-up in a machine, a certain pattern of operation may result. But there may well be no law that this sort of set-up must produce this sort of pattern of operation. The existence of this set-up may be physically compatible with an indefinite range of further factors which, if they are present, will in some way disrupt the pattern. Yet we think that this is compatible with the existence of strict physical laws governing all these situations.

However, according to Davidson, there is something which sets apart the holistic realm of the mental from the holistic realm of the physical. Davidson shares with Causal theorists and the Functionalists the view that the mental is essentially something posited to explain behaviour. Once again, he points out, this does not set the mental apart from the theoretical postulations of physical science. But now follows the decisive difference. In postulating mental states, according to Davidson, we must inevitably attribute a certain amount of coherence, rationality and consistency to the person who has the states. We must use what has been called (though not by Davidson) the Principle of Charity in interpreting behaviour. (For the Principle, see N.L. Wilson [28].)

This principle has no parallel in physical theory. And because the Principle is in some degree vague, and because of the possibility of more than one equally charitable interpretation, the behavioural facts allow there to be a certain 'slack' in the interpretation of these facts. Nor is this slack epistemological only. It is a slack in the facts of the case. (Davidson points here to the influence on his thought of W.V. Quine's doctrine of the indeterminacy of translation [29].)

This is the reason why Davidson thinks that psycho-physical generalizations could never be precise laws, however far psychology might develop. He is then able to use this premiss, in conjunction with the less controversial premisses, in the rather surprising argument for ontological Physicalism already given.

7. KRIPKE'S ARGUMENTS AGAINST MATERIALISM

Place, Feigl and Smart were moved by their sympathy with the Physicalist Dream. The authors whom we have discussed so far are similarly sympathetic. They do not want to make any *ontological* distinction between the mental and the physical. But although such views dominated our decade, anti-Physicalist positions did receive some support. In two widely discussed papers [30, 31], Saul Kripke proposed a number of novel and exciting theses in semantics. These theses, he held in turn, could be used to cast doubt upon the identification of mental states with states of the brain.

Kripke distinguishes between *rigid* and *non-rigid* designators. A rigid designator is a referring expression which designates the same object in every possible world. Proper names and general names, are, for the most part, rigid designators. For instance, 'Hesperus' (the Greek name for the Evening star) and 'heat' are rigid designators. Kripke does not accept a full-blooded metaphysics of possible worlds, although he does think that it is an objective fact that the world might have been different in various ways. For him, to say that 'Hesperus' and 'heat' designate the same thing in all possible worlds means that, in whatever way the actual world might have been different from the way it actually is, nevertheless 'Hesperus' and 'heat' still designate the same object and quality respectively. (That is, if they designate at all. It is allowed that what they designate may not exist.) The contrast here is with a descriptive phrase such as 'the inventor of bifocals'. As a matter of fact, this phrase designates Benjamin Franklin. But we can easily conceive of the world being different so that, although 'the inventor of bifocals' would still designate somebody, that somebody would not be Franklin. This phrase is therefore a non-rigid designator.

It should be noted that a non-rigid designator can be used to fix the reference of a rigid designator. For instance, we could introduce a name 'F', and use it to designate *rigidly* whatever person is actually designated by the non-rigid designator 'the inventor of bifocals'.

Acceptance of this plausible seeming distinction between rigid and non-rigid designators immediately leads, according to Kripke, to some philosophically surprising consequences. If 'Hesperus' is a rigid designator, then so presumably is 'Phosphorus' (the Greek name for the Morning star). If 'heat' is a rigid designator, then so presumably is 'motion of molecules'. Since it is true that Hesperus is Phosphorus and also true (we may assume) that heat is motion of molecules, it follows that these truths are *necessary* truths. 'Hesperus' designates the same object in every possible world, 'Phosphorus' designates the same object in every possible world, Hesperus is Phosphorus, so it is necessary that Hesperus is Phosphorus. Similarly for heat and the motion of molecules.

But how is it possible that these truths should be necessary? Are they not paradigms of empirical truths, in one case an early, in the other case a comparatively late, discovery of natural science? In reply to this objection Kripke draws a sharp distinction, a distinction which he thinks the philosophical tradition has slurred, between the *epistemological* notion of an *a priori* truth, and the *ontological* notion of a necessary truth. That Hesperus is Phosphorus, and that heat is motion of molecules, are truths known *a posteriori*. But, Kripke argues, this is compatible with their being necessary truths.

With this (all too brief) preliminary, let us now consider the situation of a type-type materialist who holds, say, that pain is identical with the firing of C-fibres. (Kripke thinks that the argument will hold against other forms of Materialism, but it is convenient to restrict ourselves to this case, implausible though it is both in its general form and in its details.) Such Materialists characteristically say that the identity is contingent. But if Kripke's semantic argument is correct, it seems that the identity cannot be contingent. For if 'heat' and 'motion of molecules' are rigid designators, so surely are 'pain' and 'firing of C-fibres'. Hence it seems that the Materialist ought really be arguing that the proposition that pain is the firing of C-fibres is a *necessary* truth, though a necessary truth known *a posteriori*, as a result of scientific investigation.

As Kripke recognizes, just by itself this result need not disturb the Materialist unduly. The Materialist would have been wrong in his characterization of the logical status of the Materialist propositions, but the propositions themselves are not impugned. But now Kripke attempts to tighten the screw. Kripke concedes, indeed wishes to assert, that the truths that Hesperus is Phosphorus, and that heat is motion of molecules, inspire in us a very strong *illusion of contingency*. Though they are necessary, yet they appear to us to be contingent, and allowing that they are known *a posteriori* is insufficient to explain why they appear contingent. According to Kripke, this illusion of contingency can only be explained by specifying a *contingent associated discovery* (to use the phrase adopted in Michael Levin's [34]) involving non-rigid designators.

It is a necessary truth that Hesperus is Phosphorus. Nevertheless, it is perfectly conceivable that there should have been two distinct heavenly bodies, observed at the same times and places as Hesperus and Phosphorus and presenting the same appearance to us as Hesperus and Phosphorus do. Our situation in that case would have been *epistemologically indistinguishable* from our actual situation *before* the establishing of the identity of Hesperus and Phosphorus. Now, in the imagined situation, and so equally in our actual situation before the astronomical discovery, we were able to designate Hesperus and Phosphorus (this heavenly body, presenting such and such an appearance, at this time, from this place; that heavenly body...). These preliminary designators were used to fix the reference of the rigid designators 'Hesperus' and 'Phosphorus'. But the preliminary designators themselves are non-rigid designators. Hence it is a contingent truth that the bodies *so designated* are identical. This truth, then, is the contingent associated discovery which explains what has to be explained: the illusion that it is a contingent truth that Hesperus is Phosphorus.

Similarly, it is a necessary truth that heat is motion of molecules. The presence of heat is recognized, in the first place at least, by sensations of heat. Now although heat (characteristically) produces sensations of heat in us, it is conceivable that it should not have done so. It is conceivable that what *we* call sensations of heat might have been produced in us by some other property of physical objects. Our situation then would have been epistemologically indistinguishable from our actual situation before the establishing of the identity of heat with motion of molecules. Now, in the imagined situation, and so equally in our actual situation before the nature of heat was established, we were able to designate heat. We did so as 'that property of physical objects which characteristically produces *these* sorts of sensations in us'. This preliminary designator was used to fix the reference of the rigid designator 'heat'. But the preliminary designator itself is non-rigid. Hence it is a contingent truth that heat *so designated* is the same thing as molecular motion. This truth, then, is the contingent associated discovery which explains what has to be explained: the illusion that it is a contingent truth that heat is the motion of molecules.

Turning now to the contention that pain is the firing of C-fibres, it is clear that it, too, produces a stubborn appearance of contingency. Yet, if Kripke's argument has been correct, the proposition, if true at all, is true necessarily. The Materialist is therefore under an obligation to find a contingent associated discovery which will explain the illusion of contingency. He must describe a possible situation, epistemically indistinguishable from our actual situation *before* the identification of pain with the firing of C-fibres, where something epistemically indistinguishable from pain is picked out by a non-rigid designator, and then this something turns out not to be the firing of C-fibres. If he can do this, he has specified a suitable non-rigid designator for pain. It will be a contingent fact that pain *so designated* is identified with the firing of C-fibres. In this way, the illusion of the contingency of the identification of *pain* with the firing of C-fibres will be satisfactorily explained.

But, Kripke claims, the Materialist is unable to meet this challenge. The only possible situation which is epistemically indistinguishable from our situation before the identification of pain with the firing of C-fibres is the situation where we are actually in pain. So it seems that the Materialist must fail to explain why his contention appears to be a contingent one. Hence his identification lies under the greatest suspicion.

Despite the ingenuity of Kripke's argument, it has not found much favour in the subsequent literature. Criticism by Feldman [32], Lycan [33] and Levin [34] has not sought to attack Kripke's semantics. Instead, it has been argued that, even granting Kripke his general position on identity, he has failed to show that, for example, pain cannot be a firing of C-fibres.

It is a premiss of Kripke's argument that 'pain' is a rigid designator. It has been pointed out that this contention can be, and has been, questioned. According to Causal theorists, and to Functionalists, pain is *whatever* plays a certain causal or functional role in our life. Since quite different sorts of things could possibly play such a role (including both material and immaterial processes), 'pain' is not on these views a rigid designator. It is an analytic consequence of the view that 'pain' is not a rigid designator that what is in fact pain might possibly not have been pain. Pain might in fact be firing of C-fibres, but, in a different possible world, the firing of C-fibres might occur, but not be pain. Kripke himself regards this consequence as a *reductio* of the view that 'pain' is a non-rigid designator. His opponents, however, do not concede this. It seems that the matter requires to be argued much more fully than Kripke argues it.

Suppose, however, that Kripke is right in taking 'pain' to be a rigid designator. Let it be granted that 'firing of C-fibres' is also a rigid designator. Does Kripke's argument then succeed (granted also his general position)? Michael Levin argued that the topic-neutral analyses of sensation-statements favoured by Smart, Lewis and Armstrong fail as *analyses*. But he thinks that these 'Australian descriptions', as he calls them, are the only *facts* which we know about pains. As a result, when we wish to use 'pain' in a rigid way (which, he agrees with Kripke, is the way that we use it), the only way we have of fixing the reference of 'pain' is by using Australian descriptions. 'Pain' designates rigidly that phenomenon which the appropriate Australian descriptions designate non-rigidly.

Given this view, Levin is able to provide a 'contingent associated discovery' to parallel the necessary truth that pains are certain sorts of brain processes. It is the discovery that the phenomena which answer to certain Australian descriptions are in fact certain sorts of brain processes.

Suppose, now, that Levin's argument is rejected for some reason. Is there any other way that Kripke's argument might be rejected, while still conceding to Kripke all that has so far been conceded? Kripke emphasizes that to be in pain is to feel pain, or to have a sensation of pain. This seems relatively uncontroversial just by itself. But as Lycan points out, Kripke in speaking of 'feeling pain' or 'having the sensation of pain' may be assuming the doctrine that pain is identical with the impression or awareness of being in pain. There are, however, quite weighty arguments for saying that the cognitive state which is the impression or awareness of being in pain is distinct from the pain itself. Given this, it is plausible to hold that the cognitive state can exist in the absence of pain, that is, that it is possible to think one is in pain but be mistaken. (See Armstrong [9], Ch. 6, Sec. 10.)

The truth of such a view might then affect Kripke's argument. For consider a false impression of being in pain. A person under such an impression will be in a state epistemically indistinguishable from one who is actually in pain. This appears to give to the Materialists who maintains that pain is (necessarily) a firing of C-fibres his 'associated contingent discovery'. It is the discovery that what ordinarily bring about impressions of being in pain are firings of C-fibres.

8. CAMPBELL'S NEW EPIPHENOMENALISM

Kripke has no positive suggestion to make about the relation of mind and brain. He confines himself to his critique of Materialism. Keith Campbell's short book *Body and Mind* [35] may be the best elementary introduction to the mind-body problem as it was seen in our chosen decade. In his last chapter Campbell sketches a position which he calls a 'New Epiphenomenalism'. It is an attempt to come to a compromise with Materialism.

Classical epiphenomenalism is a form of Dualism, but a Dualism which wishes to make its peace with Materialism, in particular with neurophysiology. Epiphenomenalists hold that the mental exists, but that it is distinct from the material brain. Suitable conditions in the brain bring the mental into existence, and determine its nature, but the mental is unable to affect the brain in any way. Everything we say or do, for instance, is brought about by the physical brain working according to purely physical principles.

This method of trying to keep the peace by almost completely separating the combatants leads to many counterintuitive consequences, as Campbell briefly points out. Consider, for instance, the problem of how our knowledge or belief that there are other minds besides our own can be rationally justified. If Epiphenomenalism is true, then everything that other human bodies do, in-

cluding their mouths making sounds, would be the same, even if
these bodies were brain-automata who lacked any minds. It seems
that the consistent Epiphenomenalist can have no reason to believe in the existence of other minds.

Nevertheless, Campbell thinks, a *limited* Epiphenomenalism
may still have value. He wishes to limit his Epiphenomenalism,
because he is inclined to go a long way with the Causal analysis
of the mental. The mental is primarily that which plays a certain
causal role. Furthermore, Campbell identifies that which as a
matter of fact plays this causal role with physical processes in
the brain working according to physical laws.

However, like many who have been attracted to the Causal
analysis (or else to Functionalism), Campbell thinks that these
theories leave something out. What is left out is the experience
of phenomenal qualities. Campbell, indeed, is prepared to accept
the idea that the experien*ced* quality of pain or itch, or of perceiv*ed* colour, may turn out to be purely physical properties of
the brain, and of visual surfaces, respectively. They are physical
properties of brain and surface clumsily and/or indeterminately
apprehended. But, Campbell maintains, the experien*cing* of pain,
or the perceiv*ing* of colour, involve qualities which escape the
Materialist net.

When, for instance, we experience a burning pain, over and
above the recognition that it is characteristically the effect of a
certain sort of stimulus, and over and above the recognition that
it characteristically has effects upon our behaviour and upon our
other current mental states, there is a special phenomenal quality
associated with the experiencing. A Causal or a Functional analysis
fails to capture this phenomenal quality. In general, these analyses
leave our mental life qualityless. Clearly, what we have here once
more is a version of that King Charles' head, the problem of the
secondary qualities. Campbell thinks that the problem defeats a
complete Materialism.

If extra qualities must be postulated, what do they qualify?
Campbell does not want to go so far with Dualism as to postulate
an extra substance or substances. So, instead, he takes the phenomenal qualities to be properties of the brain-items which, in his
view, play the causal role of being an experience of pain, or a perceiving of a colour. A physical thing, a brain-item, has extra prop-

erties which ordinary, non-mental, physical things lack. (These properties can, of course, be observed, by introspection, only by the person who is having the experience.) Although this view is not a Dualism of substances, it may fairly be called a Dual-*Attribute* view. It should be noticed that the view involves taking *properties* with ontological seriousness. If instead, for instance, attributions of properties are analysed in terms of the mere application of predicates (that is, linguistic expressions) to the objects involved, then talk of extra attributes seems to lose its force. Where there are no attributes, there cannot be extra attributes.

We come finally to Campbell's New Epiphenomenalism. The old Epiphenomenalism made its mental objects causally impotent. Campbell, in parallel fashion, makes his phenomenal qualities causally impotent. They bestow no power upon the brain-objects which they are properties of. It is allowed that Materialism gives us the whole *causal* truth about the world. The *operations* of the brain are purely physical.

Campbell's compromise has obvious phenomenological appeal. Moreover, it answers some of the objections which can be brought against orthodox Dualism and Epiphenomenalism. But other objections remain.

First, as Campbell recognizes, his view faces the same problems concerning evolution and embryonic development which face all anti-Materialist views except those of a very extreme sort. At what point in the evolution of ever more physiologically complex forms of life, and at what point in the development of the embryo, do these properties emerge? Given our present biological knowledge, any answer to this question seems to be utterly unmotivated and *ad hoc*. At a certain arbitrary moment in the history of evolution, and the history of the individual, objects which previously had nothing but ordinary physical properties acquire these new phenomenal properties. Suddenly there are experiences of colour, smell, pain. The past history of science does not encourage us to rest with such brute, inexplicable, facts.

The problem of emergence would be solved if the phenomenal properties were properties of *all* matter: a form of the panpsychist hypothesis. But this alternative hypothesis seems utterly untestable.

As might be expected, the specifically Epiphenomenalist side of

Campbell's view also leads to problems. Frank Jackson [36] pointed out that Campbell is stuck with a mini-version of the old Epiphenomenalists' problem of what warrant they have for postulating other minds. Have we any good reason for thinking that others besides ourselves have experiences of phenomenal qualities (not to speak of experiences of the *same* phenomenal qualities as ourselves)? Since anything that the others *say* about the nature of their experience is purely physiologically determined, what reason have we to think that they are like us? Campbell admits that this is a problem.

Jackson tries to sharpen the dilemma by pointing out that it holds even for Campbell himself. Campbell believes that he has experienced phenomenal qualities in the past. But he only believes this because he remembers or thinks he remembers it. By hypothesis, his memories are purely physiologically determined and would be exactly the same as they are even if the qualities had been absent in his past mental life.

A final turn of the screw is possible. Has Campbell any reason to think that he is *currently* experiencing any phenomenal properties? He feels quite sure that he does experience them, of course. But feeling quite sure is a belief-state, and a belief-state, for Campbell, is a *purely* physiological entity. What reason has he, then, when he turns reflective philosopher, to think that his conviction that he is experiencing phenomenal qualities is rational?

9. NAGEL'S DOUBTS ABOUT MATERIALISM

Two papers by Thomas Nagel [37, 38] articulate doubts about Materialism.

The first of these papers is based upon the now famous split-brain observations made by R.W. Sperry and others. It is known that the two hemispheres of the brain serve somewhat different functions. They monitor somewhat different sensory areas, and they have different motor capacities. In most persons only the left, or 'dominant', hemisphere is capable of giving rise to speech. The major link between the two hemispheres is the bridge-like *corpus callosum*. If the latter is severed (an indicated treatment for some forms of severe epilepsy), then detailed testing shows, what ordinary observation reveals neither to the clinical observer nor to the patient, that the two hemispheres are associated with something remarkably like separate seats of consciousness.

The question arises whether we should say that these people have one mind or two. Nagel considers five interpretations of the situation. The *first* is that the patients have a mind associated with the left hemisphere, but that the right hemisphere is a mere automaton. The *second* differs from this only in allowing that there may be some isolated conscious mental phenomena associated with the operations of the right hemisphere. Nagel rejects these hypotheses, saying that the only reason to accept them is that the patient cannot give any *testimony* about the mental activities associated with the right hemisphere. This, however, is question-begging, because that hemisphere lacks the power of speech, and there can be consciousness without speech.

Although denied speech, the right hemisphere is capable of reasonably extensive and sophisticated mental integration. There is no reason to think that a person who had been deprived of the left hemisphere would not still be a person, albeit a diminished person.

Should we then take the *third* view, and say that the patients have two minds, one being associated with each hemisphere? This is rejected by Nagel on the grounds of the highly integrated character of the patient's relation to the world in ordinary circumstances, that is, when not subjected to special tests. Those who observe them, and, more importantly, they themselves, find it completely natural to think of them as single persons with a single mind.

But to take the *fourth* view and allow that the integration is the integration of a single mind, also leads to difficulties. Suppose that there are two experiences going on in a consciousness simultaneously. It seems to be part of what we mean by the notion of a *single* consciousness that we can be conscious of some of the simpler relations between the two experiences. For instance, if the experiences are both colour-experiences, then we can be directly aware that the colour qualities associated with the experiences are the same or are different. But for many of the simultaneous experiences of split-brain patients, this sort of co-consciousness is lacking. They appear to have something approaching two streams of experiences, each internally well-organized, but each quite substantially disassociated from each other.

A *fifth* hypothesis, that the patients normally have one mind, but that two minds are temporarily brought into existence during the time that they are exposed to the sophisticated tests devised by Sperry and others, is judged by Nagel to be arbitrary and *ad hoc*.

The fact is, Nagel concludes, that they can neither be described as persons who have just one mind, nor as persons who have two or more minds:

> These cases fall midway between ordinary persons with intact brains (between whose cerebral hemispheres there is also cooperation, though it works largely via the corpus callosum), and pairs of individuals engaged in a performance requiring exact behavioural coordination, like using a two-handed saw, or playing a duet. In the latter type of case we have two minds which communicate by subtle peripheral cues; in the former we have a single mind.

It is clear that the further metaphysical inferences to be drawn from this conclusion are ambiguous. The results might be thought to play into the hands of a Disappearance view like that of Rorty. If we cannot say concerning certain individuals whose mental functioning in normal conditions appears to themselves and others to be normal whether they have one mind or two, is this not some reason for discarding the concept of *mind*? Nagel is aware that this sceptical conclusion can be drawn.

However, we have also seen the two-edged nature of arguments designed to support a Disappearance view. If it begins to appear that the notion of *a* mind lacks a proper physiological basis, those who trust in physiology may be inclined to doubt whether there are such things as minds. But others will simply conclude that there are minds even if minds lack a physiological basis, and so be led away from Materialism. Nagel can see that the argument cuts both ways, but seems drawn in the second direction.

Nagel's dissatisfaction with Materialism is much more clearly and definitely articulated in his [38]. Like Campbell and others, he thinks that Functionalism, the Causal theory, etc., leave something essential out. For Campbell what is left out is the experience of qualities. For Nagel it is the *subjective point of view*.

In order to bring this out, he considers bats. A bat has a sufficiently complex nervous system to make it likely that it has a mental life, even if of a primitive sort. Their way of life, and their sonar-like method of navigation in caves, ensure that this mental life is utterly different from ours. But although we cannot grasp it save in the dimmest possible way, or perhaps not at all, there must be some way of experiencing that bats enjoy. There must be a way of experiencing which is what it is like to be a bat. Being a bat involves having a subjective point of view.

Materialists identify experiences, whether of bats or ourselves, with purely physical brain processes. Nagel asserts that this identification is unintelligible. It is of the essence of a physical process that it can be apprehended in different ways, from different points of view. But a point of view itself is not something which can be truly apprehended from different points of view. You have, as it were, to be inside the point of view, or else you have not apprehended it. You have to *be* a bat, or the human being, each with their different sorts of experiential point of view. Hence experiences cannot be a physical process. Subjective experience cannot be objective brain process.

It is clear that, if the relation between experience and brain process cannot be that of identity, then Nagel needs to go on, in a complete theory, to give some positive account of what the relation really is. This, however, he says that he is unable to do.

10.   INTERACTIONIST DUALISM

The position which is completely opposed to Materialism is Interactionist Dualism. In opposition to materialist reduction, it takes the mind to be an immaterial substance (or, in 'Bundle' versions, a collection of immaterial junior substances). Nor is this mind thought to be impotent with respect to the material world, as it is thought to be in Epiphenomenalist theories. The mind interacts with the body, in particular with the brain. But although such full-blooded Dualism is still favoured by some philosophers, our decade saw little theoretical development of the position.

John Beloff's interesting book *The Existence of Mind* [39], written in 1962, argued for Dualism. In that work, among other considerations, he pointed to the importance for the philosophy of mind of the results, or lack of results, in parapsychology (psychical research). In his [40], which does fall in our decade, he devotes a chapter to parapsychology. He argues very plausibly that the present state of these investigations is so confusing that we can hardly come to any conclusion, one way or the other.

But he does go on to contend that it is in this field, and this field alone, that we can hope to find decisive considerations against the identification of the mind with the physical brain. His position is thus quite close to those physicalists who maintain that the truth or falsity of the identification must be decided on the basis of scientific, rather than purely philosophical, considerations.

Mention may also be made of the position of Karl Popper ([41] Ch. 3 and 4, and, in 1977, with the neurophysiologist John Eccles, [42]). Popper distinguishes between World 1, the material world; World 2, the world of mental processes; and World 3. World 3 is a realm which bears a resemblance to Plato's realm of Forms, and to Frege's realm of objective thought-contents. But, by contrast with Plato's and Frege's eternal realms, World 3 is man-made. In particular, it is a product of World 2, although, once brought into existence, it exists independently of, and reacts back upon, World 2. It is a world of conjectures, theories and intellectual systems.

Popper favours an immaterialist, or Dualist, account of World 2. World 2 interacts both with World 1 and World 3, and so serves to link them. Two features of his position, however, have the result that his position remains very unworked out. First, there is his resolutely epistemological, anti-ontological, attitude. As a consequence, he rejects such questions as 'What is mind?', which he thinks can only lead to trivial debates about the use of words. Second, he is much more interested in World 3 than World 2. Indeed, he thinks that that World 2 processes, that is, mental processes, can hardly be interestingly studied except in terms of the World 3 intellectual contents which they are graspings of.

In Eccles' contribution, although there is an attempt to work out a theory of mind-brain interaction, it is the brain and its workings, not the postulated immaterial mind, which remains the focus of interest. He attempts to identify the points and processes in the brain which might plausibly be regarded as the locus, on the material side, of mind-brain interaction.

BIBLIOGRAPHY

Armstrong, D.M. [9] *A Materialist Theory of the Mind.* Routledge and Kegan Paul, 1968.
Beloff, J. [39] *The Existence of Mind.* Macgibbon and Kee, 1962.
— [40] *Psychological Sciences.* Crosby Lockwood Staples, 1973.
Bernstein, R.J. [15] The Challenge of Scientific Materialism. *International Philosophical Quarterly* 8 (1968): 252-257.
Bradley, M. [10] Sensations, Brain-Processes and Colours. *Australasian Journal of Philosophy* 41 (1963): 385–393.
Campbell, K. [35] *Body and Mind.* Doubleday Anchor, 1970.
Davidson, D. [24] Mental Events. In L. Foster and J.L. Swanson (Eds.), *Experience and Theory*, pp. 79-101. University of Massachusetts Press, 1970.
— [25] Psychology as Philosophy. In S.C. Brown (Ed.), *Philosophy of Psychology*, pp. 41-52. Macmillan, 1974.
— [26] Actions, Reasons and Causes. *Journal of Philosophy* 60 (1963): 685-700.
— [27] Causal Relations. *Journal of Philosophy* 64 (1967): 691-703.
Feigl, H. [2] The 'Mental' and the 'Physical'. *Minnesota Studies in the Philosophy of Science* 2, pp. 370–497. University of Minnesota Press 1958. Reprinted separately with a Postscript, University of Minnesota Press, 1967.
Feldman, F. [32] Kripke on the Identity Theory. *Journal of Philosophy* 71 (1974): 665-676.
Feyerabend, P.K. [11] Mental Events and the Brain. *Journal of Philosophy* 60 (1963): 295-296.
— [12] Materialism and the Mind-Body Problem. *Review of Metaphysics* 17 (1963): 49-66.
Fodor, J.A. [20] *Psychological Explanation.* Random House, 1968.
— [21] *The Language of Thought.* Thomas Crowell, 1975.
Jackson, F. [36] Review of Keith Campbell's Body and Mind. *Australasian Journal of Philosophy* 50 (1972): 77-80.
Kripke, S. [30] Identity and Necessity. In M. Munitz (Ed.), *Identity and Individuation*, pp. 135-164. New York University Press, 1971.
— [31] Naming and Necessity. In G. Harman and D. Davidson (Eds.), *Semantics of Natural Language*, pp. 253-355. Reidel, 1972.
Levin, M. [34] Kripke's Argument against the Identity Thesis. *Journal of Philosophy* 72 (1975): 149-167.

Lewis, D.K. [7] An Argument for the Identity Theory. *Journal of Philosophy* 43 (1966): 17-25.

— [8] Psychophysical and Theoretical Identifications. *Australasian Journal of Philosophy* 50 (1972): 249-258.

Lycan, W. [33] Kripke and the Materialists. *Journal of Philosophy* 71 (1974): 677-689.

Nagel, T. [37] Brain Bisection and the Unity of Consciousness. *Synthese* 20 (1971): 396-413.

— [38] What is it like to be a bat? *Philosophical Review* 83 (1974): 435-450.

Oppenheim, P., and Putnam, H. [22] Unity of Science as a Working Hypothesis. In H. Feigl, M. Scriven and G. Maxwell (Eds.), *Minnesota Studies in the Philosophy of Science*, Vol. II, pp. 3-36. University of Minnesota Press, 1958.

Place, U.T. [1] Is Consciousness a Brain Process? *British Journal of Psychology* 47 (1956): 44-50.

Popper, K.R. [41] *Objective Knowledge*. Oxford 1972.

Popper, K.R., and Eccles, J.C. [42] *The Self and its Brain*. Springer International, 1977.

Putnam, H. [18] Minds and Machines. In S. Hook (Ed.), *Dimensions of Mind*, pp. 130-164. Collier-Macmillan, 1960.

— [19] Psychological Predicates. In W.H. Capitan and D.D. Merril (Eds.), *Art, Mind, and Religion*, pp. 37-48. University of Pittsburgh Press, 1967.

— [23] On Properties. In N. Rescher (Ed.), *Essays in Honour of Carl G. Hempel*, pp. 235-254. Reidel, 1969.

Quine, W.V.O. [29] *Word and Object*. M.I.T. Press, 1960.

Rorty, R. [13] Mind-Body Identity, Privacy, and Categories. *Review of Metaphysics* 19 (1965): 24-54.

— [14] Incorrigibility as the Mark of the Mental. *Journal of Philosophy* 67 (1970): 399-424.

— [16] In Defense of Eliminative Materialism. *Review of Metaphysics* 19 (1970): 24-54.

Ryle, G. [4] *The Concept of Mind*. Hutchinson, 1949.

Sheridan, G. [17] The Electroencephalogram Argument against Incorrigibility. *American Philosophical Quarterly* 6 (1969): 62-70.

Smart, J.J.C. [3] Sensations and Brain Processes. *Philosophical Review* 58 (1959): 141-156.

— [6] *Philosophy and Scientific Realism*. Routledge and Kegan Paul, 1963.

Wilson, N.L. [28] Substances without Substrata. *Review of Metaphysics* 12 (1959): 521-539.

Wittgenstein, L. [5] *Philosophical Investigations*. Blackwell, 1953.

Philosophy of perception

MARK PASTIN
Arizona State University

1. OVERVIEW

Current philosophy of perception has its roots in the assumptions of what is sometimes called "the Cartesian epistemological tradition". These assumptions are: (1) That to understand what knowledge is one must understand what justified belief is; (2) That the justification of a person S's belief in a contingent proposition is always at least partly constituted by S's perceptual judgments ('I see that this is red', 'I hear that a dog is barking', 'I smell (that) the house (is) burning', etc.); (3) That whenever S judges perceptually S has a sensory experience; (4) That S's perceptual judgment derives its warrant at least partly from propositions about the accompanying sensory experience; (5) That these sensory propositions are self-warranted — They do not derive *all* of their warrant from other propositions. (This interpretation is defended in Firth [1] and critiqued in Pastin [2].) Current philosophy of perception has its roots in these assumptions in that it has developed from a series of attempts to defend, elaborate, or criticize some of these assumptions, particularly, assumptions (3) to (5). In the period following World War II much attention was given, notably by Austin [3] and Wittgenstein [4], to attacking assumptions (3) and (4), that perceptions have a sensory component essential to their warrant. On the other hand, Ayer [5] and C.I. Lewis [6] tried to explain how assumptions (3) to (5) work, how empirical knowledge can be based on self-warranted propositions about sensory experience, by defending versions of linguistic

Contemporary philosophy. A new survey. Vol. 4, pp. 81--104.
© 1983, Martinus Nijhoff Publishers, The Hague/Boston/London.

phenomenalism. The attacks on sensory experience as a constituent of perceptual judgments having a key epistemological role seem to have had their hearing and are no longer at center stage. Recognition of a sensory component in perceptual judgment seems to have deflated these attacks. Current trends in the psychology of perception also seem to place more emphasis on the sensory component of perception. (See Carterette [7] and Pastin [2].) There is renewed interest in the proper characterization of sensory experience (objectual vs. adverbial) and in analysis of the role of sensory experience in perceptual judgment by Castañeda [8], Clark [9], Grossmann [10], Hintikka [11], Jackson [12], and Sellars [13, 14]. Interest in linguistic phenomenalism has receded for two reasons. Roderick Chisholm's attack on phenomenalism in [15] seems decisive (but see Firth [16]), and there is general doubt concerning the notion of meaning equivalence presupposed by linguistic phenomenalism. This dissatisfaction with phenomenalist approaches has pushed other approaches, discussed below, to the fore.

2. SKEPTICISM, CERTAINTY, AND COHERENCE

With a weakening of the influence of ordinary-language philosophy on epitemologists has come renewed interest in skepticism. While the issues of whether foundational propositions, presumably, either perceptual or sensory propositions, may be certain or incorrigible have not been settled, the issues of certainty or incorrigibility of foundations have not figured as centrally in discussions of skepticism as in the past. Acceptance of the principle that *if there are no certain* (foundational) *propositions then no propositions can be warranted* as a *sine qua non* of foundationalism is less prevalent. Thus I formulate the assumptions of the Cartesian tradition above in terms of self-warranted, not certain or incorrigible, sensory propositions. For discussions of foundationalist views which do not require certain foundations, see Alston [17, 18], Cornman [19], Firth [20, 21], Pastin [22, 23], and Sellars [24].

One recent approach to skepticism has been to maintain that skepticism, while at least *prima facie* capable of meaningful formulation, is to be presumed false at the outset of epistemological investigation. This approach is in the tradition of the common sense philosophies of Thomas Reid and G.E. Moore. H.H. Price [25] and Roderick Chisholm [26] adopt this approach when they defend a principle of perceptual acceptance ('If S believes that he sees something red, he is warranted in believing that there is something red') as the only or best alternative to skepticism. More recently, John Pollock takes this approach as the basis for his theory of evidence in *Knowledge and Justification* [27]. Gilbert Harman [28, 29] has ably defended this approach. He says, "Much of epistemology ... is best seen as a response to the thesis that no one ever has the slightest reason to believe anything... the problem is not to find an argument against skepticism, it is to find out what is wrong with an argument for skepticism" ([29], p. 41). The philosophy of perception will then seek to undermine arguments for skepticism concerning the senses. Harman posits not only inferential principles of warrant, but actual unconscious inferences in perception to undermine such skepticism. The key point about this approach is that it treats the epistemic enterprise in a way radically different from other branches of philosophy. The epistemological enterprise, as traditionally conceived, seeks an analysis of the concepts of knowledge, warrant, perception, and sense experience. Skepticism *may* appear as a view that has to be considered, given the nature of epistemic concepts as revealed by the proceeding analysis of epistemological concepts. It is worth noting that even Descartes' method of doubt is a method, and that Hume's skepticism is a *result* of what he found *upon inspection of* certain concepts. Skepticism is a possible but not desired *outcome* of an analysis of epistemic concepts. To assume the falsity (or truth) of skepticism *prior to analysis* surely is dogmatism of an anti-philosophical kind. Can one *assume*, prior to analysis of concepts of human action, that free will must be upheld, or, prior to analysis of theological concepts, that God exists? Surely, the critical stance of philosophy precludes these approaches to non-epistemological matters, suggesting that analogous approaches are unacceptable in epistemology. The issue of epistemological dogmatism is yet to be fully examined in the literature.

Another recent approach to skepticism has been to take it seriously as an epistemological position. Unger argues that skepticism is the correct view ([30, 31]), and Lehrer argues for a more tolerant attitude towards skepticism, as preferable to dogmatism, and for recognition that the most stringent standards of knowledge can not be satisfied ([32], 33]). Still, skepticism is not widely embraced.

A final approach to skepticism has been to argue that the assumptions of the Cartesian epistemological tradition, or anything that resembles these assumptions sufficiently to yield a foundational epistemological view, lead inevitably to skepticism, that all foundational views are therefore false, and, finally, that the only viable alternative is to embrace a coherentist epistemology (Rescher [34, 35], Rorty [36], Williams [37] and Harman [29]). This approach is a development of the approach to skepticism considered above of presuming skepticism false as a basis for epistemological theory. But this approach is broader, arguing not just for specific principles needed to avoid skepticism with respect to particular kinds of claims, but that a general coherentism is needed to avoid skepticism. Coherentism maintains that beliefs are warranted on the basis of their "coherence" in a comprehensive system of propositions. Since coherence, whether purely deductive or more broadly construed, is not by itself sufficient to distinguish warranted from non-warranted beliefs, further factors are needed. A usual move is to impose the further restriction that a coherent system must include as much as consistently possible of what a person believes, perhaps weighted in accordance with the person's assignnments of probabilities or strength of belief. Coherentism is not a theory of perception, but it does have consequences for the epistemology and metaphysics of perception. Principles relating to the warrant of sensory and perceptual propositions, and to the warranting of non-perceptual propositions by perceptual proposition, are to be validated in terms of their place in a coherent system of propositions. Perhaps the most difficult question for coherentism is whether it can explain the apparently central role of perception in the warrant of empirical knowledge, for example, whether it can explain why it is not reasonable, as a policy, to ignore perceptions that conflict with one's belief system. It is arguable that the coherentist can not answer these questions (Pastin [38]) or, that, if he does, his coherentism becomes indistinguishable from foundational views with respect to its stance towards toward the assumptions of the Cartesian epistemological tradition, or other similar foundationalist assumptions (Firth [20], Sellars [24]).

Both non-skeptical approaches to the skeptical challenge bring us to the issue of principles of perception, principles concerning the warrant of sensory and perceptual propositions and their warranting of other propositions. These principles are at the center of current epistemological controversy.

3. PRINCIPLES OF PERCEPTION

Current controversy over the status of principles of perception presupposes very little specific epistemic theory, certainly nothing so specific as the basic assumptions of the Cartesian tradition. Some epistemology is presupposed. It is assumed that a satisfactory epistemology acknowledges that a class of perceptual propositions is central to the warrant of other propositions. Most epistemologists allow that there is a point at which the physical world impinges on our consciousness, that here there is a transition from something non-cognitive and sensory to conceptual cognition, and that the cognitions formed at this point are essential to warranted belief about the world. These "border" cognitions are taken to be distinguished by content or subject matter as perceptual. The analysis of perceptual cognition is not at issue here. It is assumed that the (propositional) objects of perceptual cognitions have some degree of self-warrant for the cognizer, some warrant not attributable to inferential relations to other propositions warranted for the cognizer. It is these self-warranted perceptual cognitions that are essential to the warrant of propositions about the physical world. Discounting the self-warrant of perceptual cognitions requires abandonment of warrant attributions to other apparently warranted propositions. While this presupposed epistemology is, broadly speaking, empiricist, it is not Cartesian and encompasses most traditional views of perception and perceptual knowledge.

This epistemology poses our central question: What relations are there between self-warranted objects of perceptual cognitions (henceforth, basic propositions) and other warranted contingent propositions about the physical world (henceforth, non-basic propositions) in virtue of which the former contribute to the warrant of the latter? Extreme views offer simple answers to this question. If one accepts virtually any proposition as basic — this is one variant of coherentism, then there is no *special* problem about warranting relations between basic and non-basic propositions. That is, there is no problem about warranting relations between basic and non-basic propositions (as distinguished within foundational views — the coherentist does not recognize this distinction) that does not arise concerning warranting relations among non-basic propositions. This approach vitiates the presupposed subject-matter distinction constitutive of the basic/non-basic distinction, and may be unable, via the reasoning of Section 2, to explain the central role of perception in the warrant of our beliefs about the physical world. Coherentist views also have inherent difficulties not related to their treatment of perception (Lehrer [33], Pastin [38]). Reductionists, including linguistic phenomenalists, also have a simple answer. They acknowledge a *prima facie* difference in subject matter between basic and non-basic propositions, but argue that on deeper analysis non-basic propositions share their subject matter with basic propositions. If a reductionist holds that the form of a basic proposition is 'I sense ϕ-ly', propositions about physical objects will be taken to be about actual and possible sensings. Granting, what is not obvious, that reports of individual sensings (to stick with a particular reductionist view) can warrant counterfactuals about what would be sensed, basic propositions support non-basic propositions via statistical induction — inferring from a sample of actual and possible sensings to a population of sensings. (Sellars argues against this in [39].) We reviewed some criticisms of reductionist approaches in Section 2.

If we accept neither coherentist nor reductionist views, it becomes more difficult to answer our question about the warranting relations between basic and non-basic propositions. There is much to recommend the view that warranting relations are supervenient on non-epistemic relations. That is, if (proposition) p warrants (proposition) q for (person) S at (time) t, then there is a non-epistemic relation between p and q which, together with other facts (p is warranted for S at t), suffices for p to warrant q for S at t. A non-epistemic relation is a relation that can be explicated without appeal to the concepts of warrant or warranting. One thing recommending this view is that in some cases, e.g., where q can be deductively or inductively inferred from p, a non-epistemic relation is an essential element of conditions sufficient for p to warrant q. Consistency suggests that there is an underlying non-epistemic relation in all cases of warranting. Further, pointing to an underlying inferential relation seems to be *part of* an appropriate philosophical defense of a claimed warranting relation. However, short of accepting a reductionist view, holding that warranting relations from basic to non-basic propositions are supervenient is problematic.

Even reductionists do not hold that non-basic propositions warranted by basic propositions are, generally, deducible from basic propositions. Whether basic/non-basic warranting relations supervene on inductive relations is a complex question given the variety of relations that may be counted as inductive. It is useful to distinguish "categorematic" and "transcategorematic" inductive relations. Categorematic relations, paradigmatically "enumerative" induction, relate propositions affirming that entities of one category belong to another category (ϕ_1 is a ψ, ϕ_2 is a ψ, ϕ_n is a ψ) to other propositions affirming that other entities of the first category also belong to the second (ϕ_{n+1} is a ψ, All ϕs are ψs). *Trans*categorematic relations relate propositions affirming that entities of one category belong to another category to propositions affirming that these or other entities belong to yet other categories — examples given below. On non-reductionist views, warranting relations between basic and non-basic propositions can not be based on categorematic inductive relations. The point is Berkleyan. The "ground" proposition of a categorematic inductive relation employs the same categories as the "amplifying" proposition. If the subject-matter difference constitutive of the basic/non-basic distinction is bridged by categorematic relations, it is bridged in the "ground" proposition. This does not answer questions about the warranting of non-basic propositions by basic propositions; the questions are reclassified as questions about the warrant of "ground" propositions of categorematic inductions.

Surely, it may be contended, the problem is that categorematic relations are too narrow a class of inductive relations. The transcategorematic inductive relations cited to explain basic/non-basic warranting relations are a mixed lot. I consider three types. The first stype are relations formulated in "special principles" such as Price's Principle of Confirmability [25], Chisholm's Principle of Perceptual Taking [26], and similar principles recently propounded by Pollock [27] and others. (Sellars may accept such principles as "derivative" principles [24].) The gist of these principles is that if S takes himself to perceive that x is ϕ, then that x is ϕ^* (ϕ^* is ϕ or a related property) is warranted for S. Such principles are special in several respects. The principles are content-specific, ordinarily applying to attributions of proper and common sensibles, when contrasted with deductive and categorematic inductive principles (principles formulating categorematic inductive relations). The principles are local; they apply only to relations between basic and non-basic propositions, and do not apply within the class of non-basic propositions. Finally, as noted in the discussion of the first approach to skepticism (Section 2), the principles often are recommended only on the ground that they circumvent skepticism.

There are objections specific to each special principle. The most serious objections depend on the fact that the principles are formulated in terms of what a subject believes about his perceptions rather than the sensory experiences which, arguably, ground these beliefs (Firth [40], Heidelberger [41]). Even if the objections are overcome, the principles (or the relations they formulate) do not provide a basis for warranting relations. The content-specificity and local applicability of the principles contribute to the impression that they are *ad hoc* skepticism defeaters. Allowing that skepticism is false, the fact that a principle circumvents skepticism does not adequately justify the principle. At any rate, the principles are inappropriate as a *non-epistemic* basis on which warranting relations supervene since the principles themselves are stated in epistemic terms. No one has suggested a non-epistemic formulation of a relation underlying these principles. (But see the comments below on causal transcategorematic relations.)

The second type of transcategorematic inductive relations are neither content-specific nor local. They are abductive inferential relations (Peirce), including the relations of inference to the best explanation now widely appealed to in epistemic contexts (Harman [22], Williams [37], Sellars [24], and others). I think that these relations can not be given adequate formulation without employing epistemic concepts. For instance, inference to the best explanation surely consists partly of inference to that explanation which is most highly warranted, given the warrant of background propositions and propositions to be explained. The form of the conclusion of a Peircean abductive inference is that *there is reason to suppose* that such and such is the case. So, even if principles of best explanation are given the explicit formulation which they notably lack so far, it is unlikely that they provide a non-epistemic basis for warranting relations. There are other objections to the abductive approach — e.g., Lehrer [33] has argued that if the best explanation is not good, inference to the best explanation can not yield warranted belief.

The third category of transcategorematic relations are causal relations. They include relations formulated in traditional Lockean principle of inference from effect to cause (Mackie [42]) and relations formulated in principles of warrant via reliability (Armstrong [43]) or discrimination among relevant alternatives (Goldman [44], Dretske [45], Stine [46]). Principles of inference from effect to cause, such as those of Descartes and Locke, may well be neither local nor content-specific. The current view (Mackie [42]) is that such principles are acceptable only if they can be subsumed under best-explanation or categorematic inductive principles. If this is true, and I think it is, these principles are open to our earlier objections to best-explanation and categorematic principles, and thus do not provide a non-epistemic basis for warranting relations.

Reliability and discrimination approaches have wider current acceptance. The reliability approach states that a belief is warranted if it is formed in a reliable way. For instance, a perceptual belief is warranted if it arises out of a perceptual process that, in *a specified range of circumstances*, is likely to yield true beliefs. The discrimination approach states that a belief is warranted if the believer usually can distinguish cases in which the belief is true from *relevant cases* in which it is false. Thus, a perceptual belief is warranted if the believer is able to distinguish cases in which the belief is false. These approaches are neither local (they are part of general analyses of warranted belief in terms of reliability or discrimination), content-specific (the warrant of all beliefs is determined in terms of reliability or discrimination – although the relevant comparison classes vary with belief content), nor dogmatically anti-skeptical. Further, it seems possible to state what it is for a perceptual belief to be reliable or for a believer to be able to perceptually discriminate without employing epistemic concepts, so that these approaches promise to provide a non-epistemic basis for warranting relations.

Despite these positive indications, there are serious problems with these approaches. First, both approaches presuppose a structure which may only be explicable in epistemic terms, and which may presuppose a solution to the problem of how perceptual cognitions contribute to the warrant of non-perceptual propositions. If reliability accounts are not to be overly stringent, in requiring that a belief arise from a process that would be reliable in *any* circumstances, relevant circumstances in which the belief-forming process is reliable must be stated. And the relevant conditions seem to be specifiable only as those in which the believer would be warranted in his belief. Again, the discrimination approach requires that a believer be able to distinguish not among *all* alternatives, but among all relevant alternatives. But, in the case of a perceptual belief, the relevant alternatives, those that are sufficiently perceptually similar to actual case, seem to be specifiable only as those in which one would, on the available sensory evidence, be warranted in one's perceptual belief. Second, these approaches seem to address a different question from that traditionally addressed by epistemologies of perception. The key epistemological question addressed by traditional theories is what is warranted for a person *from that person's perspective*, where a person's perspective is constituted by the perceptual and memory input available to the person – however these are characterized in a particular epistemological theory – and the reasoning of the person from this input. It is logically possible that a certain perceptual belief be warranted for a person, from his perspective, even though the person's belief is not reliable (perhaps no reliable belief-forming process is available in the circumstances) and the person can not discriminate among relevant perceptually similar alternatives (the situation is simply radically deceptive). And the converse situation (reliability or ability to discriminate without perspectival warrant) is also possible. This reflects the difference between the type of warrant at issue in reliability and discrimination approaches and that at issue in our original question about warranting in perception, so that these approaches can not answer the original question.

We began this survey of answers to the question of what relations there are between basic propositions and non-basic propositions in virtue of which the former contribute to the warrant of the latter by hypothesizing that basic/non-basic warranting relations supervene on non-epistemic relations. The survey suggests that, no matter what the independent merits of various principles of perception proposed to answer this question, none yields a relation statable in non-epistemic terms on which basic/non-basic warranting relations supervene. Thus we must abandon the hypothesis of supervenience, or at least suspend judgment concerning it until new perceptual principles are postulated. We must take basic/non-basic warranting relations to be *essentially* epistemic, requiring epistemic notions for their perspicuous formulation, or else conclude that there are no such relations. The latter conclusion is even stronger than typical varieties of skepticism, which allow the relevant warranting relations but deny that they are satisfied or that their satisfaction yields knowledge. This conclusion could be accepted only on the basis of a convincing argument that non-supervenient basic/non-basic warranting relations are impossible. The possibility of non-supervening *sui generis* warranting relations receives support from another direction. The problem of projectability (Goodman [47]) is that there is no feature of the truth conditions or non-epistemically characterized inferential relations of statements involving "projectable" predicates, such as 'green', versus those involving "non-projectable" predicates, such as 'grue', which explains why inductive inferences from the former statements, but not the latter, transmit warrant. There is nothing in the truth conditions or non-epistemically characterized inferential relations of 'green' and 'grue' statements allowing derivation of 'a_{n+1} *is green* is warranted for S' as opposed to 'a_{n+1} *is grue* is warranted for S' from 'a_1 *to* a_n *are green/grue* is warranted for S' given the non-epistemic facts of S's situation. If there is a difference in point of warranting between projectible and non-projectible predicates, as there certainly seems to be, this difference must be captured in principles formulated in epistemic terms. These considerations support recognition of *sui generis* epistemic principles. There is recognition of this point in the literature (Pollock supports this point [48, 49], [27]), with concern increasing over the nature of *sui generis* epistemic principles.

4. MEANING AND METAPHYSICS

One theme emerging in current epistemological literature is that philosophers ought to focus attention on warrant conditions and warranting relations in attempting to understand basic issues in semantics and metaphysics (Dummett [50, 51] and Putnam [52, 53]). There is a return of interest in the epistemological profiles of physical and theoretical sentences, but not in verificationist attempts to "reduce" physical and theoretical sentences to sentences expressing their verification conditions. This new interest in epistemological profiles is not motivated by concern over the meaningfulness of certain categories of statements. Rather, it is motivated by concern over (1) those features of a statement relevant to understanding the statement — i.e., can more be required than that one grasp the warrant conditions and warranting relations of the statement, and (2) the extent to which a realistic interpretation of physical and theoretical sentences has an empirical basis. In order to address these concerns, one needs an understanding of the nature and extent of *sui generis* epistemic principles including those required to bridge the gap between perceptual cognitions and physical and theoretical sentences. We shall consider the second concern in more detail, since thorough consideration of the first concern would carry us far into the philosophy of language.

A distinction between *general* and *specific* warrant principles will help. General warrant principles are principles that belong to a theory for the expressions 'P is warranted for S at t' and 'P warrants Q for S at t' and related terms of epistemic appraisal, whereas specific warrant principles concern the warrant conditions and relations *specific to certain non-epistemic expressions*. The issue of supervenience can be viewed in terms of whether all warrant principles are general, are principles for epistemic expressions that make no reference to a specific non-epistemic content, in which case it is justifiable to claim supervenience of all epistemic relations on non-epistemic relations. We clarify matters by distinguishing warrant principles not as general or specific *per se* but as general or specific *with respect to specified statements*, or, more accurately, the sentences with which the statements are made. Warrant principles are general with respect to sentences $P_1,...,P_n$ if the principles can be formulated without employing non-logical constituents of $P_1,...,P_n$. Taking names as uniquely satisfiable predicate functions, warrant principles general with respect to $P_1,...,P_n$ can be formulated without restriction to a class of predicate functions including those that occur in $P_1,...,P_n$. The principle '*if P_1&P_2&...&P_n is warranted for S, then P_1 is warranted for S, P_2 is warranted for S,...,P_n is warranted for S*' is general for $P_1,...,P_n$. But the principle *if S takes himself to see that x has (proper or common sensible) ϕ, then that x has ϕ is warranted for S* is not general for P_1 where P_1 is *This is red*. Warrant principles not general with respect to $P_1,...,P_n$ are specific to these sentences.

The category of general warrant principles of interest is that of principles general for all sentences (of a given, expressively rich language) not having an epistemological subject matter, i.e., sentences not containing epistemic predicate functions. These *fully general* warrant principles, or an axiomatization from which these principles follow, can be regarded as constituting a meaning theory, logic, or, if one rejects these as conceptually unsound categories, as a theory of warrant and warranting. One's attitude towards these principles should parallel one's attitude towards principles of a theory of preference or of different types of modalities. The status of fully general warrant principles is a topic of central concern to a comprehensive theory of evidence, but it is not of special concern for our narrower interest in perceptual warranting. Specific warrant principles belong to theories for the sentences, or the non-logical components of those sentences, to which they are specific. These principles include principles of self-warrant for basic propositions, principles of basic/non-basic warranting, and principles of predicate-specific inductive warranting (principles of projectability). The status of these principles has been debated in the literature, and the status of principles of the first two kinds, particularly, principles of basic/non-basic warranting, is central to philosophy of perception.

One possibility if to take such principles, or axioms from which the principles follow, to be principles of meaning for the predicate function constituents of the relevant sentences. (Pollock [54] [49] [27] and Pastin [55] argue for this line. Field [56] can also be viewed as taking this approach.) Whether or not all such principles are meaning principles on such a view is not clear. One might take specific warrant principles as meaning constitutive if grasping those principles partly constitutes understanding the sentence or expression in question (Pollock [27]). Something like this may be implicit in Wittgensteinian talk of criteria as meaning constitutive. (Sklar [57] discusses this.) But it is unclear whether there is a determinate set of principles, grasp of which is essential to understanding a sentence or expression, or whether the fact that one must grasp a principle to understand an expression shows that the principle is a principle of meaning rather than, say, a truth about the expression so fundamental that one could not understand the expression without grasping this truth. An important virtue of this approach is that it breaks the idea the meaning principles or semantical principles are strictly deductive. There is no reason to exclude inductive, epistemic, or other types of principles from theories of meaning. However, there is apprehension about appropriate criteria for sorting principles into principles of meaning as opposed to fundamental, non-meaning constitutive truths on a topic, and little point to arguing for a particular sorting. The issue is what reason there is to regard the principles as true, what sort of support they can be given. Declaring the principles to be meaning or semantical principles does not resolve this issue. (See Harman [29].)

A second possibility is to take basic/non-basic warranting principles to be validated in terms of their coherence in our belief systems (Harman [28, 29], Sellars [24], Williams [37]). This approach may take the form of a first-order foundationalism, allowing a sorting of warranted propositions as basic and non-basic, with a second-order coherentism justifying epistemic principles in terms of their fit in a person's overall belief system. Sellars [24] thus speaks of a Firth-Bosanquet. This approach may also take the form of pure coherentism, not allowing a distinction between basic and non-basic propositions, in which epistemic principles, like all other propositions, are justified in terms of their fit in a person's belief-system. Such an approach is open to general problems with coherentist epistemic views, some of which were examined earlier (Section 2). A further problem arises which is specific to the attempt to justify epistemic principles. Many subjects believe nothing so esoteric as these principles, so that the principles apparently do not figure centrally in their belief-systems. Thus epistemic principles might turn out to be only very weakly justified on pure coherentist approaches.

A final approach takes basic/non-basic warranting principles as contingent, non-basic propositions (Alston [17], Pastin [58]). This approach requires jettisoning of the usual assumption that attributions of warrant and of self-warrant are iterative. If the claims 'P is warranted for S' or 'P is self-warranted for S' are non-basic, then it is possible for these claims to be true but neither warranted nor self-warranted for S, or for anyone else. While it is widely assumed in the literature that warrant and self-warrant attributions are iterative, there is no convincing argument that this is the case. Consideration of the epistemological status of basic/non-basic warranting principles, and of the iteration of warrant and self-warrant attributions, underscores the need for accounts of the meaning of the epistemic expressions involved in attributions of warrant, self-warrant, and warranting − of what exactly is being claimed in making such attributions. It can not be plausibly argued that the claim that P is self-warranted for S is non-basic, or that it is basic, unless we know what is being said of P and S in claiming that P is self-warranted for S. If 'P is warranted for S' means that P is something that S would believe if S's beliefs were ideally formed in respects that are specified (in terms of S's sensory and memory input, reasoning abilities, motivation, etc.), then 'P is warranted for S' is contingent, and evidence for this claim will consist of evidence concerning what beliefs S and other subjects have in circumstances approaching the relevant sort of ideality (Pastin [58]). Other analyses of warrant attributions may not support their classification as non-basic. The point is that resolution of controversies concerning the epistemological status of basic/non-basic warranting principles requires that epistemologists deal with meta-epistemic questions of a sort they recently seem reluctant to face. (The last detailed response to such questions in Chisholm [26].) At least some accounts of the meaning of warrant attributions, e.g., the ideal belief account, support classification of warrant principles as non-basic.

The three approaches to the status of specific warranting principles, including the basic/non-basic warranting principles at issue in philosophy of perception, are not exclusive. The final approach of taking such principles to be non-basic, contingent truths comports naturally with a foundationalist epistemology which treats these principles as it treats other empirical generalizations. But a coherentist could take specific warrant principles to be contingent propositions justified by their role in a belief system. The first and third approaches can be combined if one adopts the view that some meaning principles are contingent, and the first and second views are compatible if one justifies meaning principles in terms of fit in a belief system.

Whatever status is accorded to specific warrant principles, allowing that there are warrant principles for non-epistemic sentences which are not eliminable in favor of non-epistemic principles raises two important questions: (1) How much should theories (be they theories of meaning or simply theories capturing important truths) for non-epistemic sentences, sentences composed of non-epistemic predicate functions, say about the warrant conditions and relations of the sentences? A narrower version of this question applies to sentences expressing the propositions involved in perceptual warranting, in basic/non-basic warranting relations. (2) What consequences does inclusion of specific warrant principles in theories for non-epistemic, including physical and theoretical, sentences have for understanding non-epistemic features of these sentences, particularly, the internal structure and ontological import of the sentences? I conclude this essay by briefly examining these questions.

I think the correct answer to the first question is that theories for non-epistemic sentences, whatever else we regard as proper goals for such theories, should "fully determine" the warrant conditions and relations of the sentences. This answer sets an upward bound, to be called "epistemic completeness", on what epistemic content can be expected from theories for non-epistemic sentences. As a first approximation, we can say that an epistemically complete theory for non-epistemic sentences $P_1,...,P_n$, when combined with a general theory of warrant and relevant non-epistemic background information, allows derivation of the warrant conditions and relations of $P_1,...P_n$. Since each of $P_1,...,P_n$ has warranting relations to many other sentences, we must clarify which of these sentences are encompassed by epistemic completeness. I restrict attention to warrant relations among the sentences $P_1,...,P_n$, with the caveat that ideally $P_1,...,P_n$ is a broad enough set of sentences to be closed under relevant warranting relations. Our first approximation suggests three factors determining the warrant conditions and relations of non-epistemic sentences. These are: (a) basic facts, which include the epistemic information expressed in the specific warranting principles, constituting a theory for the non-epistemic sentences; (b) facts formulated in non-epistemic terms concerning the conditions of use of the sentences; and (c) warrant principles that are fully general, as characterized above, with respect to the non-epistemic sentences being considered. A more precise statement of the goal of epistemic completeness can be given: A theory for non-epistemic sentences $P_1,...,P_n$ is epistemically complete for these sentences just in case the theory provides sufficient information of type (a) to allow derivation, when combined with information of types (b) and (c), of the warrant conditions of $P_1,...P_n$ and of the warrant relations among $P_1,...,P_n$.

It is obvious that much has to be said to make the goal of epistemic completeness acceptably precise (Pastin [55]). For instance, allowable non-epistemic information used in deriving warrant conditions and relations, as well as restrictions on principles of derivation, must be specified. And the reasonableness of this goald needs considerable defense. I limit defense to consideration of two salient objections to setting the goal of epistemic completeness.

First, if epistemic information is to be part of a theory for non-epistemic sentences, then surely "having this information" is part of understanding the sentences. But we apparently can fully understand a sentence without knowing all of its warrant conditions and relations. Second, we often find new ways to determine whether a sentence, *which we fully understand*, is warranted. These considerations are not incompatible with the goal of epistemic completeness. Apparent incompatibility rests on the idea that epistemic completeness requires that *all* warranting conditions and relations of a sentence be *stated* in a theory for the sentence. What is actually required is that the theory, given what it says about a certain sentence *and* related sentences, when combined with factual information and general warrant principles, determine the warrant conditions and relations of the sentence. The goal of epistemic completeness is also compatible with discovery of warrant conditions and relations of understood sentences. On the reading of warrant attributions (in terms of ideal belief) outlined earlier (this section) statements of warrant conditions and relations are contingent. Truths about warrant conditions and relations are subject to discovery as other contingent truths are. One who regards warrant attributions as conceptual, necessary, or analytic truths can also correctly point out that there are truths in these categories, often involving familiar sentences, which can be discovered.

Despite apparent stringency of the goal of epistemic completeness, problems arise more from ease of satisfying the goal than from difficulty in satisfying it. Information expressible in sentences of the forms 'P is warranted for a person at a time in conditions $C_1,...,C_n$' and 'P is warranted *by* Q for a person at a time in conditions $C_1,...,C_n$' *result from* an espitemically complete theory for P and Q. Epistemic information could not be incorporated in the theory in postulates of these forms, at least if the theory is to encompass a significant chunk of a natural language. Incorporating the information whole sentence by whole sentence would be an interminable task. The theory presumably consists of postulates for predicate functions (of the forms 'VSVtVx(⌜Fx⌝ is warranted for S at t iff___)' and 'VSVtVxVy(⌜Fx⌝ warrants ⌜Gy⌝ for S at t iff___)' where 'Fx' and 'Gy' are non-epistemic predicate functions and the blanks are filled with non-epistemic information about 'Fx' and 'Gy'), and postulates for generating warrant conditions and relations of sentences composed of the predicate functional components out of the conditions and relations of the components. While the predicate functional/componential approach is ultimately to be pursued, we view the *results* of epistemically complete theories in terms of information about whole sentences.

I argue in Pastin [55] that if *only* epistemic information expressed in sentences of the above forms, stating warrant conditions and relations for whole sentences, result from a theory for non-epistemic sentences, the theory can satisfy the conditions of epistemic completeness. I employ general epistemic assumptions acceptable within even a strict empiricist framework. It is not appropriate to repeat the argument here. The strategy is to allow the theory to specify warrant conditions and relations of (sentences expressing) basic propositions and warrant relations between basic and (sentences expressing) non-basic propositions. The substantive problem in arguing epistemic completeness for a theory, given this background, is to show that warranting relations among sentences expressing non-basic propositions are derivable from the theory. Sentences expressing basic propositions, for which warrant conditions and relations result from the theory, are taken as a medium of exchange for warranting relations among sentences expressing non-basic propositions. Not only can it be argued in this way that a theory for non-epistemic sentences is complete, but the argument does not require specification of the *internal* structure of non-epistemic sentences. In fact, an argument of this form can be carried through for compound sentences, expressing a theory, part of a theory, a belief system, or some other unit of discourse. This undermines the sometimes supposed inconsistency between holistic views of meaning and empiricist epistemologies.

The possibility of arguing the epistemic completeness of a theory for ron-epistemic sentences, while offering simplification and reconciling empiricist epistemologies with current semantical holism, is problematic with respect to the second question posed by incorporation of specific warrant principles in theories for non-epistemic, notably, physical and theoretical, sentences: What consequences does including specific warrant principles in theories for physical/theoretical sentences have concerning the internal structure and ontological import of the sentences? Let us call those results of a theory for non-epistemic sentences which state epistemic information about the sentences the *empirical component* of the theory. The *empirical component* is further restricted to results stating warrant conditions for sentences expressing basic propositions and results stating warranting relations between sentences expressing non-basic propositions and sentences expressing basic propositions. The argument in Pastin [55] supports the conclusion that a theory for non-epistemic, physical/theoretical sentences can be epistemically complete *strictly on the basis of empirical component* results for warrant conditions and relations of *whole* sentences. What the theory says about the internal structure of the sentences (what names, quantifiers, modifiers, predicate functions, etc. are constituents of the sentences) is not part of the empirical component, and is not necessary for establishing epistemic completeness. The empirical component of an epistemically complete theory is indifferent to, and does not determine, the internal structure of non-epistemic sentences. Since it is widely recognized as a *necessary* condition for determining the ontological import of sentences (what entities exist if the expressed propositions are true) that the referential and predicational elements of the sentences be distinguished, these considerations suggest that the empirical component of an epistemically complete theory, the totality of empirically relevant information in the theory, does not determine the ontological import of physical/theoretical sentences.

Consideration of some examples confirms this suggestion. We can imagine a people who have conceptual schemes which allow that reality is occasionally undetectably "gappy". In this scheme the world is usually as it seems to be, full of middle-sized physical objects, or, when it is not, it is possible in principle to find out that it is not. But in rare cases it seems that there is such and such an object when there is not, and there is, in principle, no way to find out that there is not. These people have words ('chairhole', 'bookhole') applicable in rare cases — although they do not *know* when 'book' as opposed to 'bookhole' applies. Epistemically complete theories for 'This is a book' and 'This is a bookhole' have the same empirical components, despite the fact that these sentences are contraries and have constituents with different referents. The philosophical literature provides two further types of illustration. Reductionist programs to translate physical and theoretical sentences into an evidentially more basic jargon would, if successful, yield translations of physical/theoretical sentences having the same warrant conditions and relations in terms of basic sentences as the original sentences, but differing from the original sentences in referential import. Thus, on one reading, C.I. Lewis wished to translate (preserving identity of proposition expressed) physical sentences into conjunctions of subjunctive conditional sensory sentences. Given a successful program of this sort, epistemically complete theories for a sentence and its translation would have the same empirical components — since the point of these programs is to translate physical/theoretical sentences into the empirical evidence relevant to them. But the sentence and its translation obviously differ in referential import. Finally, Quine's famous examples [59], used first to illustrate indeterminacy of translation and later to support the theses of inscrutability and relativity of reference, offer cases of sentences identically related to basic sentences (so that theories for the sentences will have the same empirical components) but having both different constituents (terms, predicate functions) and constituents with different referents. Epistemically complete theories for 'This is a rabbit', 'This is a temporal rabbit stage', 'This is an undetached rabbitpart', and 'Rabbithood there' have the same empirical components, even though these sentences differ in internal structure and ontological import.

The idea that the empirical component of a theory for non-epistemic sentences does not determine the internal structure or ontological import of these sentences, or at least the general idea that empirical evidence can not settle questions of internal structure, reference, or ontological import, is gaining acceptance in the recent epistemological literature (Dummett [49, 50], Putnam [52], Rorty [36], Williams [37]). There is some propensity to draw anti-realistic conclusions, to the effect that various ontological claims are meaningless, that there is no way the world is, that non-epistemic sentences do not have uniquely correct models, from this epistemic underdetermination. These conclusions may be correct. But the fact that the empirical component of epistemically complete theories does not settle questions of internal structure or ontological import does not itself yield these conclusions. In addition, accounts are needed of how the empirical component of a theory relates to non-empirical epistemic information in the theory, of how epistemic information in the theory relates to non-epistemic information in the theory, and of what *non*-epistemic considerations bear on questions of internal structure and ontological import. Principles *bridging* epistemic and non-epistemic information are as much needed to support anti-realistic inferences as they are to support realistic inferences. Indeed, the problem of justifying principles of perceptual acceptance is a micro-case of the general problem of providing acceptable bridge principles. Philosophies of perception are likely to address questions concerning the relations between epistemological and ontological assessment in the future, questions that originally motivated phenomenalism, idealism, direct realism, representative realism, and causal realism. Hopefully, these philosophies will offer answers that serve as models for the pressing, more general questions concerning the relations between empirical evidence and the world such as it is.

BIBLIOGRAPHY

Alston, W.P. [17] Self-Warrant: A Neglected Form of Privileged Access. *American Philosophical Quarterly* 13 (1976): 257-272.
- [18] Two Types of Foundationalism. *The Journal of Philosophy* 73 (1976): 165-185.
Armstrong, D.M. [43] *Belief, Truth and Knowledge.* Cambridge 1973.
Austin, J.L. [3] *Sense and Sensibilia.* Oxford 1962.
Ayer, A.J. [5] *The Foundations of Empirical Knowledge.* London 1940.
Butchvarov, P. *The Concept of Knowledge.* Evanston 1970.
Carterette, E.C. and Friedman, M.P. (Eds.), [7] *Handbook of Perception,* Volume I. New York 1974.
Castañeda, H. Consciousness and Behavior. In H. Castañeda (Ed.), *Intentionality, Minds, and Perception,* pp. 121-158. Detroit 1967.
- [8] Perception, Belief, and the Structure of Physical Objects and Consciousness. *Synthese* 35 (1977): 285-351.
Chisholm, R.M. [15] The Problem of Empiricism. *Journal of Philosophy* 45 (1948): 512-517.
- [26] *Perceiving: A Philosophical Study.* Ithaca 1957.
- *Theory of Knowledge,* 2nd ed. Englewood Cliffs, N.J. 1977.
Chisholm, R.M. and Swartz, R.J. (Eds.), *Empirical Knowledge.* Englewood Cliffs, N.J. 1973.
Clark, R. Old Foundations for A Logic of Perception. *Synthese* 33 (1976): 75-99.
- [9] Sensuous Judgments. *Nous* 7 (1973): 45-55.
Cornman, J. [19] On Acceptability without Certainty. *The Journal of Philosophy* 74 (1977): 29-47.
Dretske, F.I. [45] *Conclusive Reasons.* In G.S. Pappas and M. Swain (Eds.), pp. 41-60.
Dummett, M. [50] What is a Theory of Meaning? (I). In S. Guttenplan (Ed.), *Mind and Language,* pp. 97-138. London 1975.

Dummett, M. [51] What is a Theory of Meaning? (II). In G. Evans and J. Mc
    Dowell (Eds.), *Truth and Meaning: Essays in Semantics*, pp. 67-137.
    London 1976.
Field, H. [56] Logic, Meaning and Conceptual Role. *Journal of Philosophy*
    74 (1977): 379-409.
Firth, R. [1] Sense Experience. In E.C. Carterette and M.P. Friedman (Eds.)
    [7], pp. 3-18.
— [16] Radical Empiricism and Perceptual Relativity. *The Philosophical
    Review* 59 (1950): 164-183, 319-331.
— [20] Coherence, Certainty, and Epistemic Priority. In R.M. Chisholm and
    R.J. Swartz (Eds.), pp. 459-470.
— [21] The Anatomy of Certainty. *The Philosophical Review* 76 (1967):
    3-27.
— [40] Chisholm and the Ethics of Belief. *The Philosophical Review* 70
    (1959): 493-506.
Goldman, A.I. [44] Discrimination and Perceptual Knowledge. In G.S.
    Pappas and M. Swain (Eds.), pp. 120-145.
Goodman, N. [47] *Fact, Fiction, and Forecast*, 3rd ed. Indianapolis 1973.
Grosmann, R. [10] *The Structure of Mind*. Madison, Wis. 1965.
Harman, G. [28] *Thought*. Princeton 1973.
— [29] Epistemology. In E.C. Carterette and M.P. Friedmann (Eds.) [7],
    pp. 41-55.
Heidelberger, H. [41] Chisholm's Epistemic Principles. *Nous* 3 (1969): 73-
    82.
Hintikka, J. [11] The Logic of Perception. In N. Care and R. Grimm (Eds.),
    Perception and Personal Identity, pp. 140-173. Cleveland 1969.
Jackson, F. [12] On the Adverbial Analysis of Visual Experience. *Meta-
    philosophy* 6 (1975): 127-135.
Lehrer, K. [32] Skepticism and Conceptual Change. In R.M. Chisholm and
    R.J. Swartz (Eds.), pp. 47-58.
— [33] *Knowledge*. New York 1974.
Lewis, C.I. [6] *An Analysis of Knowledge and Valuation*. La Salle, Ill. 1946.
Mackie, J.L. [42] *Problems From Locke*. Oxford 1976.
Pappas, G.S. and Swain, M. (Eds.), *Essays on Knowledge and Justification*.
    London 1978.
Pastin, M. [2] Review of Handbook of Perception, Volume I. *Erkenntnis* 12
    (1978): 293-303.
— [22] Modest Foundationalism and Self-Warrant. In G.S. Pappas and M.
    Swain (Eds.), pp. 279-288.
— [23] C.I. Lewis's Radical Foundationalism. *Nous* 9 (1975): 407-420.
— [38] Foundationalism Redux. *The Journal of Philosophy* 71 (1974):
    709-710.
— [55] Meaning and Perception. *The Journal of Philosophy* 73 (1976):
    571-585.
— [58] A Decision Procedure for Epistemology? *Philosophical Studies*
    35 (1979): 257–268.

Pollock, J.L. [27] *Knowledge and Justification*. Princeton 1974.
— [48] Criteria and Our Knowledge of the Material World. *Philosophical Review* 76 (1967): 28-60.
— [49] Perceptual Knowledge. *Philosophical Review* 80 (1972): 287-319.
— [54] The Structure of Epistemic Justification. *American Philosophical Quarterly Monograph Series*, No. 4 (1970): 62-78.
Price, H.H. [25] *Perception*. London 1932.
Putnam, H. [52] Realism and Reason. In H. Putnam [53], pp. 123-140.
— [53] *Meaning and the Moral Sciences*. London 1978.
Quine, W.V. [59] *Word and Object*. Cambridge, MA 1960.
Rescher, N. [34] *The Coherence Theory of Truth*. Oxford 1973.
— [35] Foundationalism, Coherentism, and the Idea of Cognitive Systematization. *The Journal of Philosophy* 71 (1974): 695-708.
Rorty, R. [36] The World Well Lost. *The Journal of Philosophy* 69 (1972): 649-665.
Sellars, W. [13] Empiricism and the Philosophy of Mind. In R.M. Chisholm and R.S. Swartz (Eds.), pp. 471–541.
— [14] The Adverbial Theory of the Objects of Sensation. *Metaphilosophy* 6 (1975): 144-160.
— [24] Givenness and Explanatory Coherence. *The Journal of Philosophy* 70 (1973): 612-624.
— [39] Phenomenalism. In W. Sellars, *Science, Perception, and Reality*, pp. 60-105.
— *Science and Metaphysics*. London 1967.
Sklar, L. [57] *Semantic Analogy*. Manuscript.
Sosa, E. On Our Knowledge of Matters of Fact. *Mind* 83 (1974): 388-405.
Stine, G. [46] Skepticism, Relevant Alternatives and Deductive Closure. *Philosophical Studies* 29 (1976): 249-261.
Unger, P. [30] Two Types of Skepticism. *Philosophical Studies* 25 (1974): 77-96.
Williams, M. [37] *Groundless Belief*. Oxford 1977.
Wittgenstein, L. [4] *Philosophical Investigations*. Oxford 1953.

Spinoza's philosophy of mind

G.H.R. PARKINSON
University of Reading

1. Although the term 'philosophy of mind' has no rigid definition, one may take it to include philosophical discussions of the problem of mind-matter relations, and of the nature of thinking, perception, emotion and will. It also includes investigations into the nature of the self, and in particular the unity of the self; again, its concern with the nature of the will covers the question of whether human beings may be said to have free will. The philosophy of Spinoza contains some distinctive answers to such questions, but because of the compression and obscurity of his writings, there has been considerable disagreement as to the exact nature of these answers. In consequence, most Spinoza scholarship has been expository in character. This remains true of the period 1968–78, which has seen much activity in the field of Spinoza studies, partly connected with the commemoration in 1977 of the tercentenary of Spinoza's death. Nevertheless, by no means all of the scholars who have written on Spinoza during this period have seen their task as merely one of historical scholarship; on the contrary, many of them see Spinoza's philosophy as containing insights that are relevant to the present day.

Studies of Spinoza's philosophy of mind have, in the past, concentrated almost exclusively on the *Ethics*, in which his mature views on the subject are stated. His early views, which are contained in the *Short Treatise on God, Man and his Well-Being*, have been discussed only in so far as they are thought to throw light on the *Ethics*. This is partly because of the obvious immaturity of the *Short Treatise*, and partly because of uncertainty as

Contemporary Philosophy. A new survey. Vol. 4, pp. 105–131.
©*1983, Martinus Nijhoff Publishers, The Hague/Boston/London.*

to how much of it is Spinoza's own work and how much is that of his pupils. This comparative neglect of the *Short Treatise* has continued. In a paper published just before the period covered by this chapter, R. Boehm [1] has argued that the Dutch text of the *Short Treatise* that has come down to us is Spinoza's own version, and not (as had previously been supposed) a Dutch translation of a lost Latin original. But even if Boehm is correct (and his arguments are very strong), this does not affect the view that the ideas presented in the work are manifestly immature and poorly presented.

It might be thought that a discussion of the philosophy of mind that is expounded in Spinoza's *Ethics* would omit the metaphysical doctrines that are contained in Part I and would concentrate on Parts II and III, which contain Spinoza's views about the mind in general and the emotions in particular. In fact, however, Part I is very relevant to Spinoza's philosophy of mind, for it is here that he lays the foundations of his theory of substance and its attributes, which is central to his account of the relations between mind and body. Our survey will begin by considering some recent discussions of Spinoza's theory of attributes.

2. One of the most important events in Spinoza scholarship during the period 1968-78 was the publication of two volumes in which Martial Gueroult ([2, 3]) commented on the first two parts of Spinoza's *Ethics*. (The author's death prevented him from carrying out his plan of writing a commentary on the whole work.) Gueroult's commentary is very much that of a historian of thought. He is not concerned to present a Spinoza for our times, but concentrates on the task of presenting the thought of Spinoza as it really was. At the same time, his commentary is by no means a conservative work; on the contrary, some of its theses are quite radical. Of these, perhaps none is more challenging or important than Gueroult's interpretation of Spinoza's theory of substance and its attributes.

Answers to the question, 'What is the relation between Spinoza's substance and its attributes?' fall into one or other of two groups, of which one may be called the 'subjective' interpretation of the substance-attribute relation and the other the 'objective' interpretation. According to the subjective interpretation, the attributes of extension and thought do not really belong to substance. Substance is indeed thought of *as* extended and thinking, but really it is neither. The objective interpretation denies this, and says that (according to Spinoza) when substance is thought of as extended and thinking, it is thought of as it really is. In a long appendix to [2] (Appendice III: 'La controverse sur l'attribut') Gueroult examines, and rejects, the subjective interpretation, paying particular attention to the arguments of one of its most influential defenders, H.A. Wolfson [4]. This leaves him with the problem of explaining the nature of the objective relation that, according to him, exists between substance and its attributes. Some supporters of the objective interpretation argue that the attributes belong to substance in the sense that they are its predicates, but Gueroult's position is quite different. He offers a new defence of a view propounded by another commentator on Spinoza's *Ethics*, Lewis Robinson, in 1928 [5]. For Robinson, Spinoza's substance is not something that is outside its attributes, it is no 'ens absolute indeterminatum', no Aristotelian 'prime matter'. The unity of substance is to be found, not *behind* the attributes, but *in* the attributes; it is a unity, not of sameness, but of difference. The fact that the various attributes of substance do not form separate worlds is shown by the prevalence in them of one and the same world-law.

Gueroult's defence of this thesis rests on a special reading of the first eleven propositions of Part I of the *Ethics*. In these propositions, Spinoza makes various assertions about the nature of substance, before proving in Proposition 11 that substance — or more exactly, substance consisting of infinite attributes — necessarily exists. Gueroult calls attention to the fact that, in the course of these propositions, Spinoza says certain things about substance which seem to contradict what he says later. He speaks of *two* substances (Eth. I Prop. 2), of 'substances and their affections' (Eth. I Prop. 6 Cor.) and of 'the modifications of substances' and 'the truth of substances' (Eth. I Prop. 8 Schol. 2), despite the fact that he says later (Eth. I Prop. 14 Cor. 1) that there is only one substance. An obvious way out of the difficulty (and it is, incidentally, the one followed by Robinson in [5]) is to say that Spinoza's language in the early propositions is only provisional. That is, we are to supplement these propositions with the hypothetical proposition 'If there exist one or more substances'; this is then replaced by categorical propositions, as Eth. I Prop. 11 establishes that *at least* one substance (God) exists, and Eth. I Prop. 14 Cor. 1 establishes that *at most* one substance exists. However, Gueroult does not follow this path. He draws a distinction between different types of substances, and says that Props. 1-8 deal with substances of one attribute (e.g. thought, extension), and that Props. 9-10 concern a substance that is constituted by an infinity of attributes, whose existence is established in Prop. 11. More than this, Gueroult argues that Props. 1-8 are not to be viewed as entirely hypothetical; on the contrary, Eth. I Prop. 7 (which states that it pertains to the nature of substance to exist) contains an ontological argument for the existence of at least one substance of one attribute. All this has an important bearing on the problem of the relation of the attributes to the one infinite substance. The attributes, Gueroult argues, are not qualities or predicates of the one infinite substance, *they are substances*, each of which is constituted by a single attribute. What makes them belong to the one infinite substance is not the fact that they are predicates of one subject, but the fact that their causal activity (by which they produce themselves and their modes) is one and the same. The act by which thought is the efficient cause of itself and of its modes is identical with the act by which extension is the efficient cause of itself and of its modes. Spinoza's theory of the relation between substance and its attributes is often called an 'identity theory'; Gueroult might not object to this description, provided that the identity is seen as one of act, not of subject.

Gueroult's interpretation has been powerfully criticised by André Doz [6], who argues that the function of the first ten propositions of the *Ethics* is to establish the elements of Spinoza's theory of substance by means of partial truths, which involve hypotheses which are progressively eliminated. As to Gueroult's reading of Eth. I Prop. 7, Doz replies that the purpose of this proposition is not to establish that a substance necessarily exists, but is simply to prove that there is a necessary connexion between the nature of a substance and existence. Gueroult's account of the relation between the one infinite substance and its attributes has also been criticised by Alan Donagan [7]. Donagan attacks Gueroult's view that the attributes are things that are absolutely different as to their essence, but absolutely identical as to the causal act by which each produces itself and its modes. This, says Donagan, separates the causal activity of a substance from its essence in a way that is quite un-Spinozist. If there is only one causal act by which all the attributes of God exist, then there must, for Spinoza, be only one essence which involves their existence, and it is this essence which each attribute expresses — as, indeed, Spinoza himself says in Eth. I Props. 19 and 20.

3. Whereas Gueroult finds the unity of Spinoza's infinite substance to lie in the unity of a causal act, E.M. Curley, in a book on Spinoza's metaphysics [8], finds it to lie in a unity of a very different kind. Curley's approach to Spinoza is distinctive in that he makes a conscious use of some of the concepts and results of twentieth-century analytical philosophy; his aim, he says, is to see Spinoza through lenses ground by Russell, Moore and Wittgenstein. He has in mind here certain views about propositions and facts which, he claims, are characteristic of the British empiricist philosophy of the early years of this century. These views (which correspond fairly closely to Russell's logical atomism) are first sketched by Curley, and then applied to Spinoza's metaphysics. Curley begins by distinguishing between three types of propositions, which he calls 'singular propositions', 'accidental generalisations' and 'nomological generalisations'. Singular propositions ascribe a property to one object, or state that a relation holds between two or more objects. Accidental generalisations may be either universal ('All F is G') or particular ('Some F is G'). When universal — e.g. 'All the books in this room are about philosophy' — they do not have what Kant called true or strict universality. However, a nomological generalisation is always strictly universal, and when true is necessarily true. Such generalisations are commonly called 'laws of nature'. Propositions of these three types are not logically independent of each other. A singular proposition follows logically from a law or set of laws, together with a set of antecedent conditions; nomological propositions themselves are capable of being organised into a deductive system, in which some figure as axioms and others as theorems derived from them. Now, according to the philosophy that Curley sketches here, the world mirrors our description of it. For each distinct type of proposition there is a corresponding type of fact; there are singular facts, accidentally general facts and nomological facts, and it is by virtue of the existence of facts that propositions are true. Just as propositions are not independent of each other, neither are facts; wherever there is a relation of logical dependence among propositions, there is a relation of causal dependence among the corresponding facts. So, singular facts depend on other singular facts and on nomological facts, and derivative nomological facts depend on basic nomological facts.

Curley claims that this system can be applied to Spinoza's metaphysics with illuminating results. Consider, for example, the relations between the attribute of extension and its infinite and finite modes. According to Curley, the attribute of extension consists of the basic nomological facts; its infinite modes are the derived nomological facts and the finite modes are the singular facts. Similar relations hold in the attribute of thought, except that here the relations are between propositions and not between facts. We come now to the question that chiefly concerns us here: namely, what is the relation between the attributes of thought and extension? In what sense are they attributes of one substance? Curley answers that the relation between thought and extension is one of identity — identity between true proposition and fact. The set of true propositions, says Curley, is the world conceived under the attribute of thought, and the set of facts is the world conceived under the attribute of extension. But these are not two worlds, they are one. Here, it is important to realise that when Curley says that true popositions and facts are identical, he is not making the point that (e.g.) 'It is true that p' has the same meaning as 'It is a fact that p'. His use of the term 'proposition' is idiosyncratic. Unlike most philosophers, he does not understand a proposition to be that which is true or false, that which is affirmed, denied, entertained, doubted etc. As he uses the term, a proposition is related to a fact somewhat as, in Aristotle, form is related to matter. Curley says that any concrete situation is analysable into two elements: an abstract pattern which can characterise many situations, and a particularising element which makes it *this* situation. Curley proposes to call the abstract pattern the 'proposition' and the particularising element the 'fact'. This, then, is how we are to read Curley's interpretation of Spinoza's claim that a mode of extension and its corresponding mode of thought are one and the same thing: namely, as equivalent to the claim that facts and true popositions are identical. As he himself notes, this interpretation is close to one already defended by Wolfson [4] − namely, that Spinoza's view of the mind-body relation is in essence the same as the Aristotelian view that the soul is the form of the body.

Of Curley's interpretation, one may ask (i) whether his elucidatory model is coherent and (ii) whether it fits Spinoza's text. (i) It is by no means certain that the model is coherent. When Curley speaks of the various types of propositions (singular, nomological etc.) he is using the term 'proposition' in its standard sense and not in the special sense that he later gives to it. Indeed, one may doubt whether one can speak of *true* propositions in Curley's special sense. Abstract patterns are not true; what is true is what is asserted, believed, etc. (iii) But even if we grant that the model is coherent, its applicability to Spinoza is very questionable. In an article on Spinoza's identity theory, T.L.S. Sprigge [9] has argued that to regard the distinction between attributes as one between facts and true propositions makes it resemble the distinction between essence and existence. But, argues Sprigge, the distinction between essence and existence holds within each attribute; the relation between attributes is between different sorts of essences together with their actualisations. Sprigge also criticises Curley's suggestion that particular modes of thought are abstract patterns, and says that on the contrary they are existences or occurrences, which are quite as concrete as the modes of extension.

4. Sprigge [9] offers his own interpretation of the substance-attribute relation and argues that, as so interpreted, Spinoza's views are very much a 'living option'. Sprigge rejects the subjective interpretation, though he says that it contains an element of truth. In talking about the attributes, Spinoza is indeed talking about different ways of grasping reality. The distinction between the attributes, then, is a conceptual one, as the subjective interpretation claims; but it is a distinction between different *valid* concepts. But if extension and thought are radically distinct properties, how can the same reality possess both? Sprigge first discusses each attribute in isolation, beginning with the attribute of thought. He argues that we have to take seriously Spinoza's 'panpsychism'; the attribute of thought has to be seen, not as a system of true propositions, but as ideas actually entertained within a cosmic mind. We have to look at Spinoza, then, not from the standpoint of logical atomisim (as Curley does) but from the standpoint of nineteenth-century philosophical idealism. When discussing the attribute of extension, Sprigge concentrates on Spinoza's views about the human body. He suggests that Spinoza saw the human body, not as the aggregate of its physical parts, but rather as a certain formula instantiated in the parts. The formula, as a feature really present in the physical world, *is* the body whose existence is reported in the human being's consciousness.

How, then, does Spinoza see the relation between mind and body? Sprigge suggests that we take seriously Spinoza's remark (Eth. II Prop. 13 Cor.) that the human body exists as we sense it ('prout ipsum sentimus'). Sprigge's interpretation of this has, as he notes, affinities with one suggested by C.D. Broad in 1930 [10]. According to Broad, Spinoza saw each idea as (at least in part) an act of direct acquaintance with a 'sensum', by which Broad means the objective constituent of a sensation. Spinoza, says Broad, saw this sensum as a physical state, and argued that the act of sensing and the sensum are not distinct events, but are distinct aspects of a single event. Sprigge, for his part, says that Spinoza's views about the identity of mind and body can be interpreted as follows. The ideas of the modifications of a person's body are just the same thing as those physical manifestations themselves. The modifications count as physical by virtue of their structural properties (we are presumably to bear in mind the view that the body *is* a certain formula); they count as mental by virtue of the feeling aspect which gives them their concrete individuality.

Sprigge summarises his interpretation of Spinoza as follows. (i) Our mind consists wholly in presentations of states of our body, and especially of our brain. (ii) These presentations actually are these bodily states, as felt from the inside. (iii) They belong to a cosmic whole of presentation; the bodily states involved are *all* bodily states, and it is this totality which is felt from the inside.

This interpretation, Sprigge argues, fits best with Spinoza's system as a whole; moreover, the view presented may actually be true. (i) and (ii) are close to the currently popular mind-brain identity theory; but Spinoza's view has its own distinctive advantages. It forbids us to regard mind as just a special sort of physical object, and it gives a rational place to the religious aspirations of mankind by seeing the universe as a unity which is both material and spiritual.

There are several difficulties in this interpretation of Spinoza, some of which Sprigge sees and tries to answer. His suggestion that, according to Spinoza, the sensory qualities and the feelings that we experience are literally in the physical processes that accompany consciousness is hard to reconcile with Spinoza's broadly Cartesian approach to physics — that is, his insistence that mind and matter are utterly distinct. However, Sprigge thinks that there is no clash with any specific affirmation made by Spinoza. Another difficulty discussed by Sprigge is this. If the idea of a bodily state really is that bodily state, considered from the inside, should not a person's consciousness contain parts which correspond to each of its physical parts? Yet it seems that it does not. Sprigge's answer seems to be that the consciousness of an organism as a whole could be an idea which is at a higher level than the ideas of its parts, and as such need not be aware of each part separately. A further objection, which Sprigge does not discuss, is to his view that it is the feeling aspect of bodies that gives them their individuality. There seems to be no evidence for this, and there is ample evidence for the contrary view that there are individuals both in the attribute of thought and in the attribute of extension.

5. It was mentioned in the last section that Sprigge believes Spinoza's philosophy to have something in common with absolute idealism. He was not the first to take this view, which may be found (for example) in the books on Spinoza written by H.H. Joachim [11, 12], himself an idealist philosopher. Nor is he the only present-day interpreter of Spinoza to see his philosophy through Hegelian lenses. In his recent book *Salvation from Despair* E.E. Harris [13] expresses admiration for Joachim's work, and interprets Spinoza in a way which owes much to the con-

cepts of philosophical idealism. Harris has since elaborated his views in a number of articles, three of which [14-16] have particular relevance to Spinoza's philosophy of mind.

As its title suggests, Harris' book is primarily concerned with Spinoza's moral philosophy — a philosophy which, Harris argues, provides an antidote to the mood of despair that is very prevalent today. But Spinoza's moral philosophy cannot be divorced from his metaphysics, and it is in the course of his discussion of Spinoza's metaphysics that Harris offers a challenging interpretation of the theory of attributes. In effect, Harris sees Spinoza's philosophy as displaying a tendency — unrecognised by its author — towards idealism. Harris sees in Spinoza, besides his express view that there is a plurality of attributes, an implicit view that there is only one attribute, which is substance's infinite self-completeness [13, 14]. Substance, Harris argues, is not only a whole, it is a *dialectical* whole. It is a concrete universal, a self-differentiating system whose principle of organisation determines the nature of its parts. (On these grounds, incidentally, Harris [16] criticises Curley's views [8] about the attributes. Curley, says Harris, is not wrong in drawing attention to the importance of nomological facts and nomological propositions, but he fails to recognise that Spinoza's nomological facts are concrete universals.) The attributes expressly recognised by Spinoza must, Harris argues, be seen in the context of the single dialectical whole. This whole has various manifestations, which constitute a scale of forms of reality; the more self-contained, the more comprehensive a manifestation is, the more real it is. The attributes of thought and extension are to be located on this scale. Spinoza implicitly takes the view (to be stated expressly by Hegel) that matter is less coherent, less real than mind. So the attribute of extension occupies the lower part of the scale and the attribute of thought occupies the upper part, the highest stage of all being God's self-awareness [14]. But it is the *same* whole which is manifested, more or less adequately, at each stage, and it is in this way that (as Spinoza asserts) the order and connexion of ideas is the same as the order and connexion of things.

It is hard to resists the conclusion that Harris is confusing what he thinks Spinoza *ought* to have believed with what he *did* believe. It is by no means certain that Spinoza's substance is a dialectical whole of a Hegelian type; it is surely quite certain that Spinoza did not think that the attribute of extension is in any way inferior to that of mind. But let us leave this aside, and consider the way in which Harris explains Spinoza's views about mind-body relations. In Spinoza's opinion, says Harris, mind is the body as felt or sensed; it is, as contemporary phenomenologists would say, the body as consciously 'lived' [15]. The relation between mind and body is that of form to matter, and it is in this sense that there is only one series of events, each of which is both idea and bodily process [13]. At first sight, this Aristotelian interpretation of the relations between mind and matter might not seem to be consistent with the dialectical interpretation of the attributes described above; but doubtless the view is that the units of a lower phase of the dialectical whole are the matter of which the corresponding units of the higher phase are the form. This preserves the consistency of Harris' interpretation; but whether his dialectical approach to Spinoza is the right one remains a matter for doubt.

6. We turn now from recent interpretations of Spinoza's views about mind-matter relations to discussions of his theories about the individual human mind. There is general agreement among scholars that what Spinoza says about the nature of the human mind has to be seen in the context of the theory of the nature of the human body that is sketched in the axioms, lemmata and postulates that follow Eth. II Prop. 13. Spinoza begins with an outline of his physics, describing the way in which certain 'most simple bodies' (*corpora simplicissima*) combine to form what he calls 'individuals' — classes of such 'most simple bodies' which are able to retain their identity, despite changes in their component parts. All this has concerned bodies in general; Spinoza then lays down a number of postulates concerning the human body in particular before going on to explain the nature of 'the formal being of the human mind' in Eth. II Prop. 15. Our concern here is not with Spinoza's physics in general, but with the relation between what he says about 'individuals' and his views about the unity of the human mind. Eth. II Prop. 15 poses a problem. Spinoza has stated in Eth. II Prop. 11 that the first thing that constitutes the actual being (*actuale esse*) of the human mind is

the idea of some thing that actually exists, and he adds in Eth. II Prop. 13 that this thing is a body — more specifically the human body, *our* body (Eth. II Prop. 13, Cor. and Schol.). In Eth. II Prop. 15 Spinoza states that this idea is not simple, but is composed of many ideas. The problem is, how we are to take this assertion; and here there is disagreement among scholars. Spinoza might be thought to mean that the human mind is simply a class of ideas, i.e. simply a collection of mental states, such as thinking, willing or feeling. Such ideas would not of course be independently existing particulars; this would make of an idea a kind of substance, whereas Spinoza regards it as a mode of thought. Still, the overall view would be that the unity of the human mind is the unity of a class, where the members of the class are modes of the attribute of thought. Douglas Odegard [17] argues that this was not Spinoza's view. Spinoza, says Odegard, does not maintain that the proposition 'That mind is thinking' simply means 'That collection of mental states includes thinking'; neither, on the other hand, does he maintain that the mind is a substance or substratum underlying mental states. The mind is not a substance, but is a complex idea, but it is also *an idea*, and not just a class of ideas.

What, then, is that body of which (according to Spinoza) the human mind is the idea? In other words, what is that body which is in a sense identical with the human mind, in that both are expressions in different attributes of one and the same state of substance? This is the main problem to which Odegard addresses himself. The short answer is that the body in question is the human body: the whole human body, and not just a part of it. This, says Odegard, is implied by two propositions in the *Ethics* which may be regarded as providing criteria for the concept of body in the equation 'mind = body'. The first of these is Eth. II Prop. 12, which states that everything that happens in the object of the idea that constitutes the human mind must be perceived by the human mind. Taken in conjunction with Eth. II Prop. 13, this means that nothing can occur in the human body without being perceived by the human mind. This implies, says Odegard, that the body that is identical with the human mind — the body of which the human mind is the idea — is a body such that the human mind perceives everything that occurs in it. It must therefore be the whole human body and not just a part of it, such as the brain.

Eth. II Prop. 12 is indeed a strong argument in favour of Odegard's thesis. However, what Spinoza says in this proposition involves an obvious difficulty, which leads us further into his philosophy of mind. The difficulty is simply that there seem to be very many things that occur in the human body and yet are *not* perceived by the human mind. Discussing this problem (which is touched on by Sprigge [9], see Section *4* above), Odegard refers to some suggestions made by G.H.R. Parkinson in 1954 [18]. Parkinson suggested that two answers are open to Spinoza. (i) He could agree that a man does not (e.g.) perceive everything that happens in his body at cellular level. There are indeed ideas of what happens at cellular level, but such ideas do not constitute the *human* mind. Rather, they constitute the minds of the cells, which, like all other individuals, are 'animated' (cf. Eth. II Prop. 13 Schol.). (ii) The alternative is to say that the human mind does indeed perceive all that happens in the human body, but that it is not *conscious* of all of it. Some of its perceptions are unconscious perceptions, corresponding to what Leibniz called 'little perceptions'. So one does perceive, e.g., the cellular activity of the human body, though one is not conscious of this activity — somewhat as, according to Leibniz, one has unconscious perceptions of each moving particle of water when one hears the roar of the sea. Odegard finds neither explanation satisfactory and offers his own, which involves the notion of 'nontactual feeling'. Nontactual feelings are those that do not involve touch: e.g. feeling a chill in one's foot, or the feeling of an energy change in one's body as it moves from one point to another. These are perceptions which other human beings do not share, and indeed could not share, unless they somehow came to share the body itself. Now, such feelings typically encompass the *whole* body; further, an embodied mind cannot normally be conscious without nontactually feeling its own body. In Eth. II Prop. 12, then, Spinoza is saying that a human mind must perceive whatever occurs in the body that can be perceived by nontactual feeling. Odegard adds that many of the things that we nontactually feel are not noticed by us, and to that extent Parkinson's comparison with Leibniz is accurate.

Eth. II Prop. 12 provides Odegard with one of the criteria of the body that is the object of the human mind; the second criterion is provided by Eth. II Prop. 26. This concerns, not our non-tactual feelings of our own bodies, but our perceptions of external bodies; it states that when the human mind perceives any external body as actually existing, it does so solely through the ideas of the modifications of its own body. This suggests that the body that is identical with the human mind is the body such that, through the ideas of its modifications, the mind perceives external bodies. But, as Odegard notes, whereas the first criterion allowed us to say that the body that is identical with the human mind is the *whole* human body, it is not certain that the second criterion will allow us to go so far. Could not Spinoza simply be referring to the central nervous system? Odegard doubts this. He says that it is indeed true that in passages such as Eth. II Prop. 17 Cor. Spinoza seems to focus attention on the central nervous system; but he does not seem to think that the perception of an external body depends on this system alone.

7. A radically different interpretation of Spinoza's view about personal identity is offered by Ruth Saw [19]. Saw brings two main objections to what Spinoza says about personal identity. (i) It is seriously incomplete. (ii) It commits Spinoza to the view that self-identity is an illusion. (i) She sees a logical gap between Spinoza's axiom 'Man thinks' (Eth. II Ax. 2) and the account of 'individuals' given in the sketch of physics that follows Eth. II Prop. 13. Her point is that if we are to accept as axiomatic the proposition 'Man thinks', we should be given grounds for his unity as a thinking being. But all that Spinoza does in his sketch of physics is to explain the unity of man as a *physical* being. It may be replied that what is lacking here can be supplied from Spinoza's metaphysics. He has explained the sense in which the human body is one; but (by his theory of the attributes) mind and body are expressions in different attributes of one and the same state of substance, so a similar account can be given of the unity of the human mind. Saw answers that this is not enough. We need an independent account of the unity of the human mind, not one that borrows from physics. Further, we are not given terms for the simplest elements of thinking, that would cor-

respond to 'most simple bodies' in the attribute of extension. (ii) More serious, perhaps, is a problem posed by the identity of the human mind through duration. Spinoza asserts that we may call a human body 'the same' body as long as it preserves the same proportion of motion and rest. If the proportion changes, the identity is destroyed; so we do not say, for example, that the embryo is the same body as the one that is born, or that the living body is the same body as the corpse (*Short Treatise*, Part II, Preface). Saw argues that this has damaging consequences. If, say, the living body is not identical with the dead body, must not Spinoza also say that the man of now is not identical with the man of a moment ago, or of the moment to come? But if a human mind is a series of momentary states, how can it follow through an argument? How, indeed (since to state a proposition takes time) can it even grasp a single proposition?

Odegard does not discuss Saw's criticisms, but he would doubtless argue that what he has said about the mind as the idea of the human body is a sufficient answer. An explicit reply to Saw is given by Lee C. Rice [20] in a paper on Spinoza's views about individuation. Rice draws attention to the respect in which Spinoza's account of personal identity agrees with that of Hume. When Hume begins his inquiry into the nature of personal identity in his *Treatise of Human Nature*, he does so by way of an examination of what it means to talk about the same material object — e.g. the same ship, the same living organism. Spinoza, too, thinks that the identity of a human person does not differ in principle from the identity of a ship. Rice would doubtless agree that there are important differences between the two philosophers' theories of personal identity. Spinoza, for example, does not say that the idea of personal identity is the work of the imagination, nor would he say (with Hume) that 'the identity, which we ascribe to the mind of man, is only a fictitious one'. What Rice emphasises is that, for Spinoza as for Hume, personal identity is not a special case. As to Saw's point that, if Spinoza sees the change from life to death as so decisive, then he must also admit that earlier changes in the living being involve loss of identity, Rice replies that this does not follow. For Spinoza, to talk of the preservation of identity is to talk of a relation or balance which is *more or less* constant. Rice adds that this does not make of personal identity a purely conventional matter. The criteria of identity are indeed established by convention; but whether or not these criteria are satisfied is not a matter of convention. Here one may wonder whether Rice has not pushed Spinoza too close to Hume. Spinoza says that the preservation of the identity of an individual lies in the preservation of *the same* ratio of motion and rest among the parts (Lemma 5 after Eth. II Prop. 13), not in the preservation of *more or less* the same ratio. His point would be that the component parts of an individual may change, whilst the same ratio is preserved; it is unlikely that he would say that the criteria of identity are in any way conventional.

8. We come now to that part of Spinoza's philosophy that concerns the causation of human actions. According to Spinoza, what a human being does is partly determined by external factors, since every finite mode is determined from outside (Eth. II Prop. 9). But it is also determined by the human being's *conatus*, that endeavour to persevere in one's own being that is displayed, not only by human beings, but by absolutely all things. Our main concern here is with the *conatus* of human beings and with the way in which this determines human actions; but before this is considered, there is something to be said about Spinoza's deterministic theory in general, within the context of which his account of the actions of human beings is to be placed.

According to Spinoza, each existing thing necessarily has a cause, by reason of which it exists (Eth. I Prop. 8 Schol. 2, III). In nature, there is nothing that is contingent (Eth. I Prop. 29): things could not be produced by God in any other way or any other order from that in which they were produced (Eth. I Prop. 33). It is such remarks that have led to Spinoza's philosophy being called a form of 'determinism'; the question is, how precisely this term is to be understood in his case. In a book on Spinoza first published in 1951, Stuart Hampshire [21] expressed the view that Spinoza's determinism is of a Laplacean type; that is, that Spinoza believed that it is in principle possible to give a complete explanation of every state of the universe. Such an interpretation is widely held, but it has recently been challenged by Arne Naess [22] in the course of a discussion of the question whether freedom is consistent with Spinoza's determinism. Laplacean determinism, Naess argues, is a determinism of *events*; it asserts that the state of the universe at any given moment determines in all details the state of the universe at the next moment. In other words, it is concerned with determination in time, or what Naess calls 'antedetermination'. Naess points out that this is not the only sort of determination; there is also determination into which time does not enter, as when (say) two angles in a triangle determine the third. Naess argues that there is in Spinoza no direct reference to determination in time. The determination that Spinoza asserts is one between *classes* of things; he says nothing about particular individuals at a particular date. What concern him especially are the consequences that follow necessarily from the nature of things, and in particular from the nature of human beings. In sum, Naess' view is that Spinoza is concerned with essential relations between classes of particulars; he is not concerned with unique particulars and the way in which they operate in time.

What Naess says is at least partly true; Spinoza does speak of the timeless relations between classes, particularly in the *Ethics*. But it is possible that what Naess says about Spinoza's determinism is not the whole truth. In a discussion of Spinoza's views about miracles and natural law, G.H.R. Parkinson [23] defends the Laplacean interpretation of Spinoza by appealing to evidence from the *Tractatus Theologico-Politicus*. He points out that in this work, Spinoza says (e.g.) that everything is determined by universal laws of nature to exist and act in a certain way (Gebhardt [24] iii, p. 58), and that in nature nothing happens that does not follow from its laws (Gebhardt [24] iii, p. 83. Cf. pp. 91, 229, 264). One may add that the overall pattern of argument in Chapter 6 of the *Tractatus Theologico-Politicus*, in which Spinoza attacks the concept of miracle, tells against the view that his determinism is purely one of essential relations between classes. A miracle (if it occurred) would be an *event*; an event which, according to Spinoza, either (a) contradicts the order of nature, or which at any rate (b) cannot be explained in terms of any laws of nature. In arguing against miracles in sense (b), Spinoza says that no event is inexplicable; every event follows necessarily from the laws of nature.

A defender of Naess' thesis might perhaps reply that the *Tractatus Theologico-Politicus* contains only a popularised and imprecise account of Spinoza's views. It is not clear what is imprecise about the attack on miracles in Chapter 6 of that work; but in any case one can bring arguments against Naess from the *Ethics* itself, and in particular from what it says about the remedies for the passions (summarised in Eth. V Prop. 20 Schol.). Of most relevance here is the remedy that lies in the very knowledge of the passions (Eth. V Prop. 4 Schol.). Spinoza asserts that if we get to know a passion clearly and distinctly — if we see how it follows from necessary laws — then we can master it. Here he is surely talking about the various particular passions to which we are subject; *this* feeling of anger, say, rather than anger in general.

Naess has also expounded Spinoza's views about freedom in a short book [25] on Spinoza's concepts of freedom, emotion and self-subsistence. This is a valuable attempt to make clear the structure of some of Spinoza's central arguments, using the techniques of modern deductive logic. However, the book has relatively little to say about problems of interpretation, and in particular about the problems that concern Spinoza's philosophy of mind.

9. After this survey of problems in Spinoza's determinism in general we come now to a concept that plays an important part in that determinism. This is the concept of *conatus*; of the endeavour that each thing has, in so far as it is 'in itself', to persevere in its own being. The concept of *conatus* is closely related to Spinoza's concept of power, in that he speaks of this endeavour as a 'power' (Eth. III Prop. 7). Our account of recent discussions of *conatus* must, therefore, also cover discussions of Spinoza's concept of power.

There is general agreement among commentators on Spinoza that his philosophy has to be seen in dynamic terms; that is, that the concept of power is a fundamental one for him. The problem is to determine exactly what Spinoza understood by the term 'power' and by the *conatus*, the 'endeavour' that is closely related to it. In a discussion of Spinoza's views about the power and freedom of man, G.H.R. Parkinson ([26]; cf. also Fløistad [26a] and [26b]) considers this problem. He notes that for Spinoza, there is an intimate connexion between power or endeavour on the one hand, and essence on the other; indeed, Spinoza seems sometimes to identify them, as in Eth. III Prop. 7 and Eth. IV Prop. 53. The implied view seems to be that to say that P is in the power of X is to say that P follows from the essence of X. Parkinson observes that such a view is at variance with ordinary usage. For example, Spinoza would doubtless say that certain consequences follow from the essence of a circle; but we do not normally speak of the *power* of a circle. In his paper, Parkinson suggests that Spinoza might reply that a circle is a mere 'entity of reason', and that the identity between power and essence holds only in the case of real entities. However, there is another, and perhaps better solution, which allows Spinoza to say that it is proper to speak of the power of a circle, whatever the ordinary usage of terms may be. Here it is necessary to refer to Spinoza's views about definition, and more specifically about genetic definition. (The importance of genetic definition for Spinoza, incidentally, is repeatedly stressed by Gueroult [2]; see also a valuable article by Herman de Dijn [27] about the historical context of Spinoza's theory of definition.) For Spinoza, the connexion between essence and definition is that a definition must express the essence of a thing (*Tractatus de Intellectus Emendatione*, Gebhardt [24] ii, p. 34); now, it is Spinoza's view that a definition must express an efficient cause, i.e. must be a genetic definition (Ep. 60; cf. Gebhardt [24], p. 35). So, for example, Spinoza's definition of a circle is that it is that space which is described by a line of which one end is fixed and the other mobile. If one views definitions in this way, then to talk about the power of a geometrical figure becomes less puzzling.

However, Spinoza's use of the term 'power', whereby to say that X has a certain power is to say that certain things follow from its essence, may seem to contradict ordinary usage in another respect. We would ordinarily say that a thing may have the *power* to do P even if it never actually *does* P; not all power need be exercised. Parkinson suggests that Spinoza would say that this is true, but only to a certain extent: namely, of things other than God. Spinoza would point out that his account of power or *conatus* concerns what each thing does in so far as it is in itself (*in se*), i.e. in so far as it is independent. But only God is *in se*; only in the case of God does everything that is in his power actually exist, and this is why God cannot be conceived except as acting (Eth. II Prop. 3 Schol.). In the case of finite modes, such as human beings, the situation is different. To say that each man, in so far as he is 'in himself', endeavours to preserve his own being is to say that it follows from his essence (regarded as something which is independent) that he *will do* those things which preserve his own being. But in fact a man is not independent, and his acts do not follow from his essence alone. In other words, to speak of the power of a finite mode X is to speak of what X will do *if not interfered with*, and what it will do in such circumstances is preserve its own being.

Parkinson asks next how Spinoza claims to prove the truth of his doctrine of *conatus*. Eth. III Prop. 6 contains a deductive proof of the doctrine that is both obscure and unconvincing; however, Spinoza also offers an empirical argument in favour of his views. This is supplied by his assertion that the mind, in so far as it is in itself, endeavours to persevere in its being, *and is conscious of this endeavour* (Eth. III Prop. 9). Parkinson points out that there is an obvious difficulty here. As finite modes, we are affected by an infinity of other things (Eth. I Prop. 28): how, then, can we be aware of the endeavour of either our body or our mind as it is in itself? Perhaps Spinoza might try to justify his theory of *conatus* in another way: namely, by regarding it as a scientific hypothesis. Such a hypothesis would be justified to the extent that it enables Spinoza to explain human behaviour. But if one takes the theory of *conatus* in this way, one has difficulty in reconciling it with Karl Popper's thesis that for a theory to be scientific, it must in principle be falsifiable. One might at first think that Spinoza's theory of *conatus* is not only falsifiable, but actually false — refuted by the existence of such people as suicides and martyrs. Spinoza would reply that the suicide, for example, is not 'in himself', but is mastered by external causes (Eth. IV Prop. 20 Schol.; cf. Eth. IV Prop. 18 Schol., 'Tertio'). Similar objections would be dealt with in the same way; so it seems that nothing can refute the theory of *conatus*, and it cannot therefore be claimed to be scientific.

Parkinson suggests that there are two ways in which the theory of *conatus* could be seen as significant. (i) It could simply point out that human beings are not merely static, but endeavour to act in various ways. Such an assertion would be empirical, but tame. (ii) However, the doctrine can also be interpreted in a way which is neither empirical nor tame. The unfalsifiability of the doctrine may reflect the fact that it is a moral theory, not a scientific theory. It becomes clear from Spinoza's moral philosophy that the 'being' that each man, in so far as he is in himself, endeavours to preserve is his rationality, and that in so far as a man is rational he is truly himself. This is clearly not a scientific proposition; rather, Spinoza is setting up a moral standard of human behaviour.

The last aspect of the theory of *conatus* discussed by Parkinson is the sense in which *conatus* can be called a cause. The scholastics would have explained a thing's endeavour in terms of final causation, i.e. in terms of the end towards which the agent strives. Spinoza expressly rejects this view, and says that *conatus* has to be seen as an efficient cause. Particularly illuminating is a passage in Eth. IV Pref., in which Spinoza illustrates his view by the example of someone building a house. The scholastics would have said that this activity has to be explained through its final cause, namely having somewhere to live. Spinoza, on the other hand, says that it has to be explained by an efficient cause, namely somebody's 'appetite' for building the house. ('Appetite' in Spinoza refers to *conatus* as manifested both in extension and thought: Eth. III Prop. 9 Schol.). The question is, how appetite functions as an efficient cause. It might be thought that Spinoza views appetite or *conatus* as a kind of inner thrust, which drives body and mind somewhat as the uncoiling of a spring drives the wheels of a clock. Parkinson suggests that this is not Spinoza's view. Rather, Spinoza is saying that the building of the house has to be seen *in the light of* (or, as Spinoza would say, as following from) the agent's endeavour to preserve his own being.

10. Spinoza's rejection of explanation in terms of final causes could be called his rejection of the idea of teleological explanation. It must be stressed, however, that when the word 'teleological' is used in the context of discussions of Spinoza's theory of *conatus*, it can have a different sense. This sense is to be found, for example, in an article in which Wolfgang Bartuschat [28] discusses the implications of Spinoza's view that individuality (*Selbst-*

sein) is not thinkable apart from its relation to a transcendent absolute. According to Bartuschat, this does not mean that an individual fulfils itself in a striving beyond itself; rather, the individual's striving is self-related. *Conatus* is an endeavour to preserve *one's own* being; it is not an endeavour to transcend oneself, and in particular it is not an attempt to approach a transcendent God who is the *telos* of the creature's self-fulfilment. Bartuschat puts this by saying that Spinoza's *conatus* is nonteleological.

Bartuschat's view of *conatus* is sharply opposed to that defended by Errol Harris in his book on Spinoza [13]. Harris admits that there are passages in Spinoza that can be construed as an attack on teleology, such as the famous attack (Eth. I, Appendix) on the view that all things are brought about by God for his own inscrutable purposes. But this, says Harris, is an attack on false teleology; there is another concept of teleology — true teleology — which is implicit in Spinoza's own thought. A teleological process of this kind is a mutual determination of past, present and future events. In such a process the end, as potential, is already present at the beginning; equally, each phase of its realisation is determined by what has gone before. Further, the process in question is one that tends towards greater perfection, towards the realisation of the infinity that is implicit in each finite thing. The principle that motivates this process is the *conatus* of each particular thing to persist in its own being; *conatus*, in other words, is a striving towards greater completeness or perfection. It is in this sense, says Harris, that Spinoza's system is teleological.

This conflict of opinion between Bartuschat and Harris seems irreconcilable. It has already been suggested (cf. Section 5 above) that Harris is inclined to substitute for Spinoza's actual views the views that he believes Spinoza ought to have held. Here, too, the Spinoza presented by Bartuschat seems closer to the actual philosopher than the one presented by Harris.

11. This survey of recent work on Spinoza's philosophy of mind concludes with his theory of the emotions, which is to be found in what he says about the *affectus*. Some English translators, indeed, render *affectus* as 'emotion', but this is not altogether satisfactory. Spinoza recognises desire (*cupiditas*) as one of the three primary *affectus* (Eth. III Prop. 11 Schol.), and most philosophers would distinguish desire from the emotions. Lee C. Rice [29] has recently brought further objections to the translation of *affectus* by 'emotion', arguing (a) that it suggests that the *affectus* resemble the emotions in that they result from body-mind interaction, and (b) that it suggests passivity, whereas some *affectus* are active. But though the term *affectus* may not be equivalent to emotion, there is no doubt that many of the *affectus* discussed by Spinoza – e.g., love, hope and fear – are emotions.

One of the most interesting of recent studies of Spinoza's theory of the emotions is contained in Jerome Neu's book [30] *Emotion, Thought and Therapy*. As its title suggests, this is not wholly, or even primarily, a work of Spinoza scholarship. Neu discusses Hume as well as Spinoza, and he discusses them, not just in their own right, but as representatives of two different philosophical analyses of the emotions. These analyses differ in the role that they ascribe to feeling and thought in the emotions. In ordinary usage, the term 'feeling' is sometimes equivalent to 'emotion', but Neu uses the former term in a narrower sense to refer to what he calls 'felt sensations'. His view seems to be that whereas love, for example, is an emotion, the glows and pangs that love involves are to be called 'feelings'. According to Neu, Hume treats emotions as being in essence feelings, to which thoughts are attached only incidentally. Spinoza, on the other hand, treats emotions as essentially thoughts, to which feelings are incidentally attached. Neu argues that not only is Spinoza nearer the truth here, but that his account of the way that thoughts are built into emotions gives us an understanding of Freudian theory and therapy.

The book, though not always quite accurate in matters of scholarship, is rich in ideas. Neu begins his detailed discussion of Spinoza with a short account of *conatus*, and then discusses pleasure (*laetitia*) and pain (*tristitia*) which, together with desire (*cupiditas*: roughly speaking, *conatus* that is self-aware) form the three primary *affectus*. Neu, incidentally, seems to have no objection to calling desire an emotion; however, it is not desire which concerns us here, but what are undeniably emotions, such as pleasure and pain. Neu's interpretation of Spinoza's account of pleasure and pain is somewhat confused. He notes, quite correctly, that Spinoza views pleasure as a passage from a less to a greater perfection, and pain as a passage from a greater to a less perfection; that is, pleasure and pain are respectively an increase or decrease of power. However, Neu seems in error when he suggests that Spinoza regards pleasure and pain as states of the whole individual, and as such to be distinguished from the more localised sensations or moods. Among such sensations or moods Neu lists what Spinoza calls *titillatio* (pleasurable exitement), *hilaritas* (cheerfulness) *dolor* (painful suffering) and *melancholia* (melancholy). But in fact Spinoza says expressly that cheerfulness and melancholy relate to the body as a whole, and pleasurable excitement and painful suffering to a part of the body (Eth. III Prop. 11 Schol.). There is no suggestion that pleasure and pain always relate to the body as a whole; rather, they relate either to the body as a whole or to a part of it.

After discussing pleasure and pain, Neu considers Spinoza's account of one of the derivative emotions, namely love. The primary emotion of pleasure is an element in the emotion of love; what makes the emotion *love* is the type of thought involved. (Love is 'Pleasure accompanied with the idea of an external cause', Eth. III Prop. 13 Schol., and, as Neu rightly remarks, an 'idea' in Spinoza is not an image or feeling, but can express a whole thought or proposition). Neu adds that in Spinoza's account, the thought of the loved object does not simply accompany some essential core of feeling; rather, the object of love appears in the idea of the cause, and so is in a sense internal to the emotion. In sum, the lover's emotion depends on his belief; more specifically, his belief that X is the external cause of the pleasure that he feels. There is much truth in Neu's account, but his remarks could mislead. In saying that pleasure is an element in the emotion of love, and that what makes the emotion one of love towards X is the lover's belief that X is the external cause of his pleasure, Neu may seem to suggest that pleasure is a mere feeling, and that the entire thought-element in the emotion of love is the belief that X is the cause of the pleasure felt. But this cannot be so; Spinoza's view is that *any affectus* (including the primary ones) involves an idea (cf. Eth. II Ax. 3). It seems, rather, that two ideas are involved in the love for X: the idea of X as simply existing (involved in the emotion of pleasure) and the idea of X as the external cause of the pleasure.

Neu now proceeds to a distinction which is vital to Spinoza's moral philosophy: namely, that between active and passive emotions. For Spinoza, an active emotion is one which can be explained solely by reference to the individual's nature as a person (i.e. as an individual mind-body); a passive emotion is one which has to be explained by reference to external causes. Neu considers the objection that one cannot have an active emotion towards anything that is outside oneself, for any such thing must by definition be external to one's nature. His reply is, in effect, that one cannot indeed have an active emotion towards any *particular* external thing. The actions of the mind involve 'adequate ideas', i.e. involve understanding; and what we understand is not, say, one external thing in isolation, but the whole system of things, i.e. Nature as a whole. Neu suggests, then, that there can logically be only one object of active emotion, namely the whole of Nature; further, since the contemplation of the whole of Nature can be accompanied only by pleasure (for it is then that our power of thought is at its greatest) it seems to follow that the only active emotion can be love. Neu notes that Spinoza does not in fact say that active emotion has only one object; one may add that he certainly thinks that there are active emotions other than love — e.g. self-satisfaction (*acquiescentia in seipso*) (Eth. IV Prop. 52) and glory (*gloria*) (Eth. IV Prop. 58). Neu does not try to explain away this apparent inconsistency, but perhaps a way out is provided by Spinoza's third kind of knowledge, 'intuitive knowledge'. This, Spinoza explains, is knowledge of particular things (Eth. V Prop. 36 Schol.); so the person who has such knowledge of things could, and indeed would, love them.

Neu concludes his book by considering the relations between Spinoza's philosophy and Freudian psycho-analysis. Freudian therapy stresses the importance of self-knowledge; Spinoza's theory of the emotions shows *how* self-knowledge can function as a means of liberation. If, as Spinoza stresses, beliefs are built into emotions, this explains how (for example) the uncovering of the elements of childish fantasay embodied in the emotions can help to transform those emotions. Neu remarks that one may also draw specific comparisons between Spinoza and Freud, though he adds that some qualifications have to be made. For example, Spinoza's *conatus* has often been compared with Freud's *libido* (e.g. Hampshire [21]). The comparison, says Neu, has a point, but must be made with caution. The two concepts can be compared only if one takes *libido* to include, not just the sexual impulses, but all other impulses. Again, Freud came to oppose to the *libido* the death-instinct, a concept for which there is no place in Spinoza. Any drive to self-destruction, Spinoza would say, must be external to that endeavour to persevere in our own being which is essential to us.

BIBLIOGRAPHY

Bartuschat, W. [28] Selbstsein und Absolutes. In R. Bubner, K. Cramer and R. Wiehl (Eds.), *Spinoza, 1677-1977. Neue Hefte für Philosophie* 12, pp. 21-63. Göttingen, 1977.

Boehm, R. [1] *'Dieses war die Ethic und zwar Niederländisch, wie sie Spinosa anfangs verferttiget'. Spinozas 'Korte Verhandeling' — eine Übersetzung aus einem lateinischen Urtext? Studia Philosophica Gandensia* 5 (1967): 175-206.

Broad, C.D. [10] Spinoza. In *Five Types of Ethical Theory*, pp. 15-52. London 1930.

Curley, E.M. [8] *Spinoza's Metaphysics: An Essay in Interpretation.* Harvard 1969.

De Dijn, H. [27] Historical Remarks on Spinoza's Theory of Definition. In J.G. van der Bend (Ed.), *Spinoza on Knowing, Being and Freedom*, pp. 41-50. Assen 1974.

Donagan, A. [7] Essence and the Distinction of Attributes in Spinoza's Metaphysics. In M. Grene (Ed.) *Spinoza*, pp. 164-181. New York 1973.

Doz, A. [6] Remarques sur les onzes premières propositions de l'Ethique de Spinoza. *Revue de Métaphysique et de Morale* 81 (1976): 221-261.

Fløistad, G. [26a] Spinoza's Theory of Knowledge. *Inquiry* 12 (1969): 41-65.

— [26b] Mind and Body in Spinoza's Ethics. *Synthese* 37 (1978): 1-13.

Gebhardt, C. (Ed.) [24] *Spinoza Opera.* Heidelberg 1924-1926. 4 vols.

Gueroult, M. [2] *Spinoza, I. Dieu (Éthique, 1).* Paris 1968.

— [3] *Spinoza, II. L'âme (Éthique, 2).* Paris 1974.

Hampshire, S. [21] *Spinoza.* Harmondsworth 1951; 2nd ed., London 1956.

Harris, E.E. [13] *Salvation from Despair: A Reappraisal of Spinoza's Philosophy.* The Hague 1973.

Harris, E.E. [14] The Order and Connexion of Ideas. In J.G. van der Bend (Ed.), *Spinoza on Knowing, Beind and Freedom*, pp. 103-113. Assen 1974.

Harris, E.E. [15] Body-Mind Relation in Spinoza's Philosophy. In J.B. Wilbur (Ed.), *Spinoza's Metaphysics: Essays in Critical Appreciation*, pp. 13-24. Assen 1976.
— [16] Finite and Infinite In Spinoza's System. In S. Hessing (Ed.), *Speculum Spinozanum, 1677-1977*, pp. 197-211. London 1977.
Joachim, H.H. [11] *A Study of the 'Ethics' of Spinoza*. Oxford 1901.
— [12] *Spinoza's 'Tractatus de Intellectus Emendatione'*. Oxford 1940.
Naess, A. [22] Is Freedom consistent with Spinoza's Determinism?. In J.G. van der Bend (Ed.), *Spinoza on Knowing, Being and Freedom*, pp. 6-23. Assen 1974.
— [25] *Freedom, Emotion and Self-Subsistence: The Structure of a Central Part of Spinoza's Ethics*. Oslo 1975.
Neu, J. [30] *Emotion, Thought and Therapy: A Study of Hume and Spinoza and the Relationship of Philosophical Theories of the Emotions to Psychological Theories of Therapy*. London 1978.
Odegard, D. [17] The Body identical with the Human Mind: A Problem in Spinoza's Philosophy. In E. Freeman and M. Mandelbaum (Eds.), *Spinoza: Essays in Interpretation*, pp. 61-84. La Salle 1975.
Parkinson, G.H.R. [18] *Spinoza's Theory of Knowledge*. Oxford 1954.
— [26] Spinoza on the Power and Freedom of Man. In E. Freeman and M. Mandelbaum (Eds.), *Spinoza: Essays in Interpretation*, pp. 7-33. La Salle 1975.
— [23] Spinoza on Miracles and Natural Law. *Revue Internationale de Philosophie* 31 (1977): 145-157.
Rice, L.C. [20] Spinoza on Individuation. In E. Freeman and M. Mandelbaum (Eds.), *Spinoza: Essays in Interpretation*, pp. 195-214. La Salle 1975.
— [29] Emotion, Appetition and Conatus in Spinoza. *Revue Internationale de Philosophie* 31 (1977): 101-116.
Robinson, L. [5] *Kommentar zu Spinozas Ethik. Erster Band: Einleitung: Kommentar zum ersten und zum zweiten Teil der Ethik*. Leipzig 1928.
Saw, R.L. [19] Personal Identity in Spinoza. *Inquiry* 12 (1969): 1-14. Also in S.P. Kashap (Ed.), *Studies in Spinoza*, pp. 86-100. Berkeley 1972.
Sprigge, T.L.S. [9] Spinoza's Identity Theory. *Inquiry* 20 (1977): 419-445.
Wolfson, H.A. [4] *The Philosophy of Spinoza*. Harvard 1934; 2nd ed. New York 1958. 2 vols.

Hegel's philosophy of mind

CHARLES TAYLOR
McGill University

As with any highly systematic body of thought, Hegel's philosophy of mind can be reconstructed from many perspectives. Each one gives us something, though some are more illuminating than others. But I believe that it is particularly illuminating to see Hegel's Philosophy of mind though the perspective of his philosophy of action. This is, of course, hardly a surprising doctrine. Mind (Geist) for Hegel is thoroughgoing activity (Tätigkeit). But I think the insights from this perspective can be enlivened and made more penetrating if we relate Hegel's thought to a set of perennial issues that have been central to the philosophy of action in modern times. This is what I want to attempt in this paper.

At the same time, a study of this kind can also be interesting in another way. Understanding Hegel's contribution to the developing modern debate on the nature of action helps us to understand the historical development of this debate. And this, I would like to argue, is important for understanding the debate itself.

I

We can perhaps identify one fundamental issue which has been open in the philosophy of action in modern times. To do so, of

* An earlier version of this paper was read at the conference on Hegel and the Philosophy of Action, sponsored by the Hegel Society of Great Britain, Merton College, Oxford, September 1981.

course, requires some interpretation of the history of modern philosophy, and this as always can be subject to controversy. The precise question which defines this issue was not asked in the seventeenth and eighteenth century, and is rather one which is central to our twentieth century debate. But I want to claim nevertheless that different answers to this question were espoused earlier, as one can see from a number of related philosophical doctrines which *were* expressly propounded, and which depend on these answers. I hope the plausibility of this reading will emerge in the course of the whole argument.

This being said, I will baldly identify my central issue in un-ashamedly contemporary terms: what is the nature of action? or otherwise put, what distinguishes (human) action from other kinds of events? What are the peculiar features of action?

One family of views distinguishes actions by the kind of cause which brings them about. Actions are events which are peculiar in that they are brought about by desires, or intentions, or com-binations of desires and beliefs. As events, actions may be de-scribed among other ways as physical movements. (Although one would have to be generous with the term 'physical move-ments', so as to include cases of non-movement, as, e.g., with the action we would describe as 'He stood still'.) In this, they resemble a host of other events which are not actions. What distinguishes them is a peculiar type of psychological cause, that they are brought on by desires or intentions. Of course, to hold this is not necessarily to hold that psychological explanations are ultimate. One can also look forward to their reduction to some neuro-physiological or physical theory. But in that case, the burden of distinguishing action from non-action would be taken over by antecedents differently described: perhaps some peculiar kind of firing in the cortex, which was found to be the basis for what we identify psychologically as desire.

A view of this kind seems to have been implicit in much of Donald Davidson's work [1] and [2]. But the basic conception goes back, I believe, at least to the seventeenth century. A con-ception of this kind was in a sense even more clearly at home in the basically dualist outlook common both to Cartesian and em-piricist philosophies. Qua bodily movements actions resembled all other events. What distinguished them was their inner, "mental" background. Within the bounds of this outlook, there was a clear ontological separation between outer event and inner background.

Against this, there is another family of views which sees action as qualitatively different from non-action, in that actions are what we might call intrinsically directed. Actions are in a sense inhabited by the purposes which direct them, so that action and purpose are ontologically inseparable. The basic intuition here is not hard to grasp, but it is difficult to articulate it very clearly. What is in any case clear is that this view involves a clear negation of the first: we cannot understand action in terms of the notions of undiscriminated event and a particular kind of cause; this is to explain it in terms of other primitive concepts. But for the second view, action is itself a primitive: there is a basic qualitative distinction between action and non-action. To the extent that action can be further explicated in terms of a concept like 'purpose', this turns out not to be independently understandable. For the purpose is not ontologically separable from the action and this means something like: it can only exist in animating this action; or its only articulation as a purpose is in animating the action; or perhaps a fundamental articulation of this purpose, on which all others depend, lies in the action.

This second view thus resists the basic approach of the first. We can't understand action by first identifying it as undifferentiated event (because it is qualitatively distinct), and then distinguishing it by some separably identifiable cause (because the only thing which could fill this function, the purpose, is not separably identifiable). One of the roots of this doctrine plainly is Aristotle's thesis of the inseparability of form and matter, and we can see that in contrast to Cartesianism and empiricism, it is plainly anti-dualist. This is not to say that proponents of the first view are necessarily dualist – at least not simply so; just that their conception permits of dualism, whereas the qualitative distinction thesis does not.

One of the issues which is thus bound up with that about the nature of action is the question of dualism. Another which I want briefly to mention here is the place of the subject. It is clear that the distinction between action and non-action is one that occurs to us as agents. Indeed, one can argue plausibly (Taylor [3]) that a basic, not further reducible distinction between action and what just happens is indispensable and ineradicable from our self-understanding as agents. That is, it is impossible to function as an agent at all unless one marks a distinction of this kind.

In this context, we can understand part of the motivation for the first, or causal theory of action, as lying in the aspiration to go beyond the subjective standpoint of the agent, and come to an understanding of things which is objective. An objective understanding in this sense would be one which was no longer tied to a particular viewpoint, imprisoned in the categories which a certain viewpoint imposes. If agency seems to impose the qualitative conception of action, then the causal one can appear as a superior analysis, an objective portrayal of the way things really stand, of the real components of action *an sich*. This drive for objectivity, or what Bernard Williams [4] has called "absolute" descriptions, was one of the animating motives of both Cartesianism and empiricism.

Now Hegel is clearly a proponent of the second, qualitative conception of action. And indeed, he emerges out of a climate in which this conception was staging a comeback after the ascendancy of Cartesian and empiricist views. In one sense, the comeback can be seen to start with Leibniz, but the tenor of much late eighteenth century thought in Germany was of this stamp. The reaction against dualism, the recovery of the subject, the rehabilitation of Aristotle-type inseparability doctrines — notably in the conception of the aesthetic object in Kant's third critique — all pushed towards and indeed, articulated themselves through this understanding of action. I now want to develop its ramifications to show how central it is to Hegel's thought, and in particular his theory of mind.

II

The first important ramification of the qualitative theory is that it allows what I shall call agent's knowledge. The notion is that we are capable of grasping our own action in a way that we cannot come to know external objects and events. In other words, there is a knowledge we are capable of concerning our own action which we can attain as the doers of this action; and this is different from the knowledge we may gain of objects we observe or scrutinize.

This qualitative distinction in kinds of knowledge is grounded on the qualitative view of action. Action is distinct in that it is directed, aimed to encompass ends or purposes. And this notion of directedness is part of our conception of agency: the agent is the being responsible for the direction of action, the being for whom and through whom action is directed as it is. The notion of action is normally correlative to that of an agent.

Now if we think of this agent as identical with the subject of knowledge, then we can see how there can be different kinds of knowledge. One kind is gained by making articulate what we are doing, the direction we are already imprinting on events in our action. As agents, we will already have some sense, however dim, inarticulate or subliminal, of what we are doing; otherwise, we could not speak of directing at all. So agent's knowledge is a matter of bringing this sense to formulation, articulation or full consciousness. It is a matter of making articulate something we already have an inarticulate sense of.

This evidently contrasts with knowledge of other objects, the things we observe and deal with in the world. Here we are learning about things external to our action, which we may indeed act with or on, but which stand over against action.

Now the first, or causal view, cannot draw this contrast. To begin with, we can see why it wasn't concerned to: because the contrast is one which is evident from the agent's standpoint; agent's knowledge is available to the knower only qua agent, and thus from his standpoint. It cannot be recognized as knowledge from the absolute standpoint. Thus, for the causal view, my action is an external event like any other, only distinct in having a certain kind of cause. I cannot claim to know it in some special way.

Of course, what I can claim "privileged access" to is my desire, or intention — the cause of my action. And here we come to the closest thing to an analogous distinction within the causal view to that between agent's and observer's knowledge. In the original formulations of Cartesianism and empiricism, I am transparently or immediately aware of the contents of my mind. It may be accorded that I am immediately, even incorrigibly aware that I want to eat an apple, or that I intend to eat this apple. But of the consequences of this desire or intention, viz., my consuming the apple, I have knowledge like that of any other external event: I observe it.

We might then contrast the two views by noting that the causal view too recognizes two kinds of knowledge, but it draws the boundaries quite differently, between "inner" and "outer" reality. But we would have to add that this difference of location of the boundary goes along with a quite different view of what the knowledge consists in. The notion of immediate or incorrigible knowledge makes sense in the context of dualism, of a separate domain of inner, mental space, of which we can say at least that its *esse* entails its *percipi*. The contrast will be something like that between immediate and inferential knowledge, or the incorrigible and the revisable.

Once we draw the boundary the way the qualitative theory does, there is no question of incorrigibility. We may never be without some sense of what we are doing, but coming to have knowledge is coming to formulate that correctly, and we may only do this in a partial or distorted fashion. Nor is this knowledge ever immediate; it is, on the contrary, mediated by our efforts at formulation. We have, indeed, a different mode of access to what we are doing, but it is questionable whether we should dub this access 'privileged'. Neither immediacy nor incorrigibility are marks of agent's knowledge.

Now in a sense this idea of agent's knowledge originates in modern thought with Vico. But since his work didn't have the influence it deserved in the eighteenth century, we should perhaps see Kant as the important seminal figure. Not that Kant allowed a full-blooded notion of agent's knowledge. Indeed, he shied away from using the word 'knowledge' in this context. But he made the crucial distinction between our empirical knowledge of objects on the one hand, and the synthetic a priori truths which we can establish on the other, about the mathematical and physical structure of things. In Kant's mind it is clear that we can only establish the latter with certainty because they are in an important sense our own doing.

Perceiving the world involves not just the reception of information, but crucially also our own conceptual activity, and we can know for certain the framework of empirical reality, because we ourselves provide it.

Moreover, in Kant's procedure of proof of these synthetic a priori truths, he shows them to be essential conditions of undeniable features of experience, such as, e.g., that we mark a distinction between the objective and the subjective in experience, or that the 'I think' must be able to accompany all our representations. Later he will show the postulates of freedom, God and immortality as essential conditions of the practice of determining our action by moral precepts. If we ask what makes these starting points allegedly undeniable, I think the answer can only be that we can be sure of them because they are what we are *doing*, when we perceive the world, or determine our action on moral grounds (I have argued this further in Taylor [5]).

Kant thus brings back into the centre of modern epistemological debate the notion of activity and hence of agent's knowledge. Cartesian incorrigibility, the immediate knowledge I have of myself as a thinking substance, is set aside. In its place come the certainties which we don't have immediately, but can gain, concerning not some substance, or any object of knowledge whatever, but the structures of our own activity. What we learn by this route is only accessible by this route. It is something quite different from the knowledge of objects.

This has been an immensely influential idea in modern philosophy. One line of development from Kant lies through Schopenhauer, who distinguished our grasp of ourselves as representation and as will, and from this through Wittgenstein into modern British analytical philosophy, e.g., in Miss Anscombe's notion of 'non-observational knowledge' ([6], pp. 13-15).

But the line which interests us here passes through Fichte. Fichte's attempt to define subject-object identity is grounded on the view that agent's knowledge is the only genuine form of knowledge. Both Fichte and Schelling take up Kant's notion of an 'intellectual intuition', which for Kant was the kind of agent's knowledge which could only be attributed to God, one through which the existence of the object itself was given (B72), or one in which the manifold is given by the activity of the self (*selbstthätig*, B68). But they make this the basis of genuine self-knowledge by the ego; and then of all genuine knowledge in so far as object and subject are shown to be identical.

The category of agent's knowledge has obviously taken on a

central role, has exploded beyond the limits that Kant set for it; and is, indeed, the principal instrument by which these limits are breached and the realm of inaccessible noumena denied. But the extension of agent's knowledge obviously goes along with a re-definition of the subject. He is no longer simply the finite subject in general that figures in the Critiques, but is related in some way to a single infinite or cosmic subject.

Hegel is obviously the heir to this development. He takes up the task of demonstrating subject-object identity, and believes himself to be alone capable of demonstrating this properly. What is first seen as other is shown to be identical with the self. It is crucial to this demonstration that the self cease to understand itself as merely finite, but see itself as part of spirit.

But the recognition of identity takes the form of grasping that everything emanates from spirit's activity. To understand reality aright is to understand it as 'actuality' (translating *Wirklichkeit*), i.e., as what has been actualized. This is the crucial prerequisite of the final stage, which comes when we see that the agent of this activity is not foreign to us, but that we are identical to (in our non-identity with) spirit. The highest categories of the Logic, those which provide the entry into the absolute Idea, are thus those linked with agency and activity. We move from teleology into the categories of life, and then from knowledge to the good.

The recognition thus requires that we understand reality as activity, but it requires as well that we come to understand in a fuller way what we are doing up to the point of seeing what spirit is doing through us. Coming to this point, we see the identity of the world-activity with ours.

Thought thus culminates in a form of agent's knowledge. Only this is not just a department of what we know alongside obser-ver's knowledge, as it is for our ordinary understanding. Rather, observer's knowledge is ultimately superceded. But the distinc-tion is nonetheless essential to the system, since its crucial claim is that we only rise to the higher kind of knowledge through a supercession of the lower kind.

And this higher knowledge is far from immediate. On the con-trary, it is only possible as mediated through forms of expres-sion, among which the only adequate medium is conceptual thought. And this brings us to another ramification of the qualitative view, which is also of central importance for Hegel.

III

On the qualitative view, action may be totally unreflecting, it may be something we carry out without awareness. We may then become aware of what we are doing, formulate our ends. So following on a conscious desire or intention is not an inescapable feature of action. On the contrary, this degree of awareness in our action is something we come to achieve.

In achieving this, we also transform our activity. The quality of consciously directed activity is different from that of our unreflected, semi-conscious performance. This flows naturally from the second view on action: if action is qualitatively different from non-action, and this difference consists in the fact that action is directed, then action is also different when this direction takes on a crucially different character. And this it does when we move from unreflecting response, where we act in much the same manner as animals do, to conscious formulation of our purposes. Our action becomes directed in a different and stronger sense. To become conscious is to be able to act in a new way.

Now the causal theory doesn't allow for this kind of qualitative shift. Indeed in its original, dualist variant, it couldn't even allow for unreflecting action. Action is essentially caused by desire or intention, and on the original Cartesian-empiricist model, our desires were essentially features of inner experience. To have a desire was to feel a desire. Hence on this view, action was essentially preceded by a cause of which the agent was aware. This amounted in fact to making conscious action, where we are aware of our ends, the only kind of action. It left no place at all for totally unmonitored, unconscious activity, the kind of action animals engage in all the time, and we do much of the time.

And even when the causal theory is disengaged from its dualist or mentalist formulation, where the causes of action are seen as material, and hence quite conceivably largely unconscious, the theory still has no place for the notion that action is qualitatively transformed in becoming conscious. Awareness may allow us to intervene more effectively to controll what comes about, but action remains essentially an undifferentiated external event with a certain kind of cause.

Now this offshoot of the qualitative view: that action is not essentially or originally conscious, that to make it so is an achievement, and that this achievement transforms it; this also is crucial to the central doctrines of Hegel. I want to look at two of them here.

1. The first is what I have called elsewhere (Taylor [7]) the 'principle of embodiment'. This is the principle that the subject and all his functions, however 'spiritual' they may appear, are inescapably embodied. The embodiment is in two related dimensions: first, as a 'rational animal', i.e., as a living being who thinks; and secondly, as an expressive being, that is, a being whose thinking is always and necessarily in a medium.

The basic notion here is that what passes in modern philosophy for the 'mental' is the inward reflection of what was originally external activity. Self-conscious understanding is the fruit of an interiorization of what was originally external. The seeming self-coincidence of thought where I am apparently immediately aware of my desires, aims and ideas, which is foundational to Cartesianism, is understood rather as an achievement, the overcoming of the externality of an unconscious, merely instinctive life. It is the fruit of a negation of what negates thought, not itself a positive datum. This understanding of conscious self-possession as the negation of the negation if grounded on the conception of action I have just been outlining. In effect, it involves seeing our mental life fundamentally in the category of action. If we think of the constituents of mental life, our desires, feelings, ideas, as merely given, as the objects which surround us in the world are given, then it is plausible to think of our knowledge of them as privileged. They appear to be objects which we cannot but be aware of, if we are aware at all. Our awareness of them is something basic, assured from the start, since it is essentially involved in our being aware at all.

In order to understand mental life as something we have to achieve understanding of, so that self-transparency is a goal we must work towards, we have to abandon the view of it as constituted of data. We have to understand it as action, on at least one of two levels, if not both.

On one level, we have to see self-perception as something we do, something we can bring off, or fail to bring off, rather than a feature of our basic predicament. This means that we see it as the fruit of an activity of formulating how things are with us, what we desire, feel, think, etc. In this way, grasping what we desire or feel is something we can altogether fail to do, or do in a distorting or partial, or censored fashion. If we think through the consequences of this, I believe we see that it requires that we conceive selfunderstanding as something that is brought off in a medium, through symbols or concepts, and formulating things in this medium as one of our fundamental activities.

We can see this if we leap out of the Hegelian context and look at the quite different case of Freud. Here we have the most notorious doctrine of the non-self-transparency of the human psyche. But this is mediated through a doctrine of self-understanding through symbols, and of our (more or less distorted and screened) formulation of our desires, fears, etc. as something we do. For although these formulations occur without our wilful and conscious intent, they are nevertheless motivated. Displacements, condensations, etc. occur where we are strongly motivated to bring them off.

But, on a second level, we may also see the features of ourselves that self-perception grasps not as simply givens but as themselves bound up with activity. Thus desires, feelings may not be understood as just mental givens, but as the inner reflection of the life-process that we are. Our ideas may not be conceived as simple mental contents, but as the precipitates of thinking. And so on.

Hegel understands mental life as activity on both these levels. In a sense, the first can be thought to represent the influence of Kant. It was Kant who defended the principle that there is no perception of any kind which is not constituted by our conceptual activity. Thus there is no self-awareness, as there is no awareness of anything else, without the active contribution of the 'I think'. It was the contribution of the new, richer theory of meaning that arose in the wake of Romanticism to see that this constitutive thought required an expressive medium. Freud is, of course, via Schopenhauer, the inheritor both of this Kantian doctrine and of the expressivist climate of thought, and hence, also through Schopenhauer, of the idea that our self-understanding can be very different in different media, as well as distorted in the interests of deeper impusles that we barely comprehend.

The making activity central on the second level is also the fruit of what I want to call the expressivist climate of thought, which refused the distinctions between mind and body, reason and instinct, intellect and feeling, which earlier Enlightenment thought had made central. Thought and reason were to be understood as having their seat in the single life-process from which feeling also arose. Hence the new vogue for Aristotelian inseparability doctrines, of form and matter, of thought and expression, of soul and body.

Hegel's theory of mind is built on both these streams. Our self-understanding is conceived as the inner self-reflection of a life-process, which at the outset fails to grasp what it is about. We learn through a painful and slow process to formulate ourselves less and less inadequately. At the beginning, desire is unreflected, and, in that condition, aims simply for the incorporation of the desired object. But this is inherently unsatisfactory, because the aims of spirit are to recognize the self in the other, and not simply to abolish otherness. And so we proceed to a higher form of desire, the desire for desire, the demand for recognition. This too starts off in a barely self-conscious form, which needs to be further transformed. And so on.

In this theory, activity is made central on both levels: a) on the second, more fundamental level, what is to be understood here, the desire, is not seen as a mere psychic given, a datum of mental life. On the contrary, it is a reflection (and at first an inadequate one) of the goals of a life-process which is now embodied and in train in the world. Properly understood, this is the life-process of spirit, but we are at the outset far from seeing that. So the active life-process is primary, even in defining the object of knowledge.

Then b) on the first level, the achievement of more and more adequate understandings is something that comes about through our activity Sof formulating. This takes place for Hegel, as we shall see later, not only in concepts and symbols, but also in common institutions and practices. E.g., the institution of the master-slave relationship is one "formulation" (and still an inadequate one) of the search for recognition. Grasping things through symbols, establishing and maintaining practices, are things we do, are to be understood as activities, on Hegel's theory.

And so we have two related activities. There is a fundamental activity of Spirit, which it tries to grasp through the various levels of self-formulation. These two mutually conditioning activities are at first out of phase, but they are destined in the end to coincide perfectly. That is because it will come clear that the end of the whole life-process was that spirit come to understand itself, and at the same time the life-process itself will be entirely transparent as an embodiment of this purpose.

But this perfect coincidence comes only at the end. And it only comes through the overcoming of non-coincidence, where what the pattern of activity is, differs from what this pattern says. And so the distinction between these two dimensions is essential for the Hegelian philosophy: we could call them the effective and the expressive. Each life form in history is both — the effective realization of a certain pattern and, at the same time, the expression of a certain self-understanding of man and hence also of spirit. The gap between these two is the historical contradiction which moves us on.

And so for Hegel, the principle of embodiment is central. What we focus on as the mental can only be understood in the first place as the inner reflection of an embodied life-process; and this inner reflection is itself mediated by our formulation in an expressive medium. So that all spiritual life is embodied in the two dimensions just described: it is the life of a living being who thinks, and his thinking is essentially expression. This double shift from Cartesianism, from a psychology of immediate self-transparency, to one of achieved interiority, of the negation of the negation, is obviously grounded in the qualitative understanding of action, and the central role it plays here. The mental life has a depth which defies all immediate self-transparency, just because it is not merely self-contained, but is the reflection of a larger life-process; while plumbing this depth is in turn seen as something we do, as the fruit of the activity of self-formulation.

Once again, we see that the Hegelian understanding of things involves our seeing activity as all-pervasive. But the activity concerned is as it is conceived on the qualitative view.

2. We can thus see that this offshoot of the qualitative view, which sees action as first unreflecting, and reflective understanding as an achievement, underpins what I call the principle of embodiment in Hegel's thought. But we saw above that for this conception reflective consciousness transforms action. And this aspect too is crucial to Hegel's theory.

His conception is of an activity which is at first uncertain or self-defeating because its purposes are barely understood. The search for recognition is, properly understood, a demand for reciprocal recognition, within the life of a community. This is what our activity is in fact groping towards, but at first we do not understand it in this way. In a still confused and inarticulated fashion, we identify the goal as attaining one-sided recognition for ourselves from others. It follows that our practice will be confused in its purpose and self-defeating. For the essential nature of the activity is not altered by our inadequate understanding of it; the true goal of the search for recognition remains community. Our inadequacy of understanding only means that our action itself is confused, and that means that its quality as directed activity is impaired.

We can see this kind of confusion, for instance, at the stage where we seek to answer our need for recognition through an institution like that of slavery. We are already involved here with what will turn out to be the only possible solution to this quest, viz., community; because even the institution of the master-slave relation will typically be defined and mediated by law, a law which bind all parties, and which implicitly recognizes them as subjects of right. Within this framework, the relations of domination, of ownership of man by man, contradict the basic nature of law. If we think of our building and maintaining these institutions as an activity we are engaged in together, which is how Hegel sees it, then we can see that our activity itself is confused and contradictory. This is, indeed, why it will be self-defeating, and why this institutional complex will eventually undermine and destroy itself.

A new form of society then will arise out of the ruins of this one. But the practices of this new society will only be higher than previous ones, to the extent that we have learnt from the previous error, and now have a more satisfactory understanding of what we are engaged in. And indeed, it is only possible to accede eventually to a practice which has fully overcome confusion and is no longer self-defeating if we finally come to an understanding which is fully adequate.

But throughout this whole development we can see the close relation which exists between the level of our understanding and the quality of our practice. On this view, our action itself can be more or less firmly guided, more or less coherent and self-consistent. And its being one or the other is related to the level of our self-understanding.

We are reminded here of a common conception of the Romantics, well expressed in a story of Kleist, that fully coherent action must either be totally unreflecting, or the fruit of full understanding. The birth of self-conciousness on this view disrupts our activity, and we can only compensate for this disruption by a self-awareness which is total. Hegel takes up this conception with an important difference. The crucial activity is that of Spirit, and it aims for self-recognition. As a consequence, there is no such thing as the perfection of totally unreflecting activity. The earliest phases of human life are even then phases of spirit, and the contradiction is present between their unconsciousness and what they implicitly seek.

In sum, we can see that this ramification of the qualitative theory of action involves a basic reversal in the order of explanation from the philosophy that Cartesianism and empiricism bequeathed to us. It amounts to another one of those shifts in what is taken as primitive in explanation, similar and related to the one we mentioned at the outset.

There I pointed out that for the Cartesian-empiricist view, action was something to be further explained, compounded out of undifferentiated event and a certain kind of cause. The cause here was a desire, or intention, a "mental" event; and these mental occurrences are taken as primitives by this kind of theory, and part of the explanatory background of action.

But the qualitative view turns out to reverse this order. The "mental" is not a primitive datum, but is rather something achieved. But more, we explain its genesis from action, as the reflective understanding we eventually attain of what we are doing. So the status of primitive and derived in explanation is reversed. One theory explains action in terms of the supposedly more basic datum of the mental; the other accounts for the mental as a development out of our primitive capacity for action.

IV

The qualitative view also brings about another reversal, this time in the theory of meaning, which it is worth examining for its own sake, as well as for its importance to Hegel.

I said above that for this view, becoming aware of ourselves, coming to self-consciousness, is something we do. We come to be able to formulate properly what we are about. But this notion of formulation refers us to that of an expressive medium.

One way to trace the connection is this: if we think of self-consciousness as the fruit of action, and we think of action as first of all unreflecting bodily practice, which only later comes to be self-understood; then the activity of formulating must itself conform to this model. That is, our formulating ourselves would be at first a relatively unreflective bodily practice, and would attain only later to the self-clarity required for full self-consciousness.

But this is just what we see in the new expressive theories of meaning which arose in the later eighteenth century, and which Hegel took over. First, the very notion of expression is that of self-revelation as a special kind of bodily practice. The Enlightenment theory of signs, born of the epistemological theories of the seventeenth century, made no fundamental distinction between expressive and any other form of self-revelation. You can see that I am afraid of a recession by the fact that I'm selling short; you can see that I'm afraid of you by the expression on my face; you can see that it's going to rain because the barometer is falling. Each of these was seen as a 'sign' which points beyond to something it designates or reveals. Enlightenment theorists marked distinctions between signs: some were by nature, some by convention. For Condillac, there were three kinds, accidental, and natural signs, and signs by institution.

But the distinction they quite overlooked was the crucial one

for an expressivist, that between 'signs' which allow you to infer
to their 'designatum', like the barometer does to rain, and true
signs which express something. When we make something plain
in expression, we reveal it in public space in a way which has no
parallel in cases of inference. The barometer 'reveals' rain indirect-
ly. This contrasts with our perceiving rain directly. But when I
make plain my anger or my joy, in facial or verbal expression,
there is no such contrast. This is not a second-best, the dropping
of clues which enable you to infer. This is what manifesting
anger or joy *is*. They are made evident not by or through the
expression but in it.

The new theories of meaning, which start perhaps with Herder's critique of Condillac, involved a fundamental shift. They
recognize the special nature of those human activities which reveal things in this special way. Let us call them expressive activities. These are bodily activities. They involve using signs, gestures,
spoken or written words. And, moreover, their first uses are relatively unreflecting. They aim to make plain in public space how
we feel, or how we stand with each other, or where things stand
for us. It is a long slow process which makes us able to get things
in clearer focus, describe them more exactly, and above all, become more knowledgeable about ourselves.

To do this requires that we develop finer and more discrimi-
nating media. We can speak of an embodiment which reveals in
this expressive way as a 'medium'. Then the struggle for deeper
and more accurate reflective self-understanding can be understood
as the attempt to discover or coin more adequate media. Facial
expressions do much to make us present to each other in our
feelings and desires, but for self-understanding, we need a refined
and subtle vocabulary.

This amounts to another major reversal in theory. The Enlightenment account explained meaning in terms of the link of des-
ignation or 'signifying' between word and object. This was a link
set up in thought. In Locke's theory, it was even seen as a link set
up through thought, since the word, strictly speaking, signified
the idea of the object. Meaning is explained here by thought,
which once again is seen in the role of explanatory primitive. In
this conception, expression is just one case of the signifying relation, which is seen as constituted in thought.

But for the expressive theory, it is expression which is the primitive. Thought, that is, the clear, explicit kind of thought we need to establish new coinages, new relations of 'signifying', is itself explained from expression. Both ontogenetically and in the history of culture, our first expressions are in public space, and are the vehicles of a quite unreflective awareness. Later we both develop more refined media, in concepts and images, and become more and more capable of carrying out some part of our expressive activity monologically; that is, we become capable of formulating some things just for ourselves, and hence of thinking privately. We then develop the capacity to frame some things clearly to ourselves, and thus even to coin new expressions for our own use. But this capacity, which the Enlightenment theory takes as a primitive, is seen here as a late achievement, a change we ultimately come to be able to ring on our expressive capacity. This latter is what is now seen as basic in the order of explanation.

In our day, a similar radical reversal was carried out in the theory of meaning by Ludwig Wittgenstein, who took as his target the view which emerges out of modern epistemological theory, to which he himself had partly subscribed earlier. What I have called the Herderian theory is very reminiscent therefore of Wittgenstein's.

But Hegel wrote in the wake of the earlier expressive revolution. And one can see its importance for his thought by the crucial place in it of what I have called the notion of medium. The goal of spirit is clear, self-conscious understanding. But the struggle to attain this is just the struggle to formulate it in an adequate medium.

Thus Hegel distinguishes art, religion and philosophy as media, in ascending order of adequacy. The perception of the absolute is embodied in the work of art, it is presented there (*dargestellt*). But this is in a form which is still relatively inarticulate and unreflecting. Religious doctrine and cult bring us closer to adequacy, but are still clouded by images and 'representations' (*Vorstellungen*). The only fully adequate form is conceptual thought, which allows both transparency and full reflective awareness. But attaining our formulation in this medium is the result of a long struggle. It is an achievement; and one which builds on and required the formulations in the other, less adequate media. Philosophy doesn't only build on its own past. For in earlier ages, the truth is more adequately presented in religion (e.g., the early ages of Christianity), or art-religion (at the height of the Greek polis). In coming to its adequate form, philosophy as it were catches up. True speculative philosophy has to say clearly what has been there already in the images of Christian theology.

Thus for Hegel too thought is the achievement whereby our expression is made more inward and clear. The attainment of self-understanding is the fruit of an activity which itself conforms to the basic model of action, that it is at first unreflecting bodily practice and only later attains self-clarity. This is the activity of expressing.

V

I have been looking at how the qualitative theory of action and its ramifications underlie Hegel's philosophy of mind, for which in the end everything is to be understood in terms of the all-pervasive activity of Spirit. I have been arguing that we can only understand the kind of activity here involved if we have in mind the qualitative view.

But there are also some important features of human historical action on Hegel's view which only make sense against this conception. I want to mention two here.

1. The first is this: all action is not in the last analysis of individuals; there are irreducibly collective actions. The causal view was inherently atomist. An action was such because it was caused by desire, intention, some 'mental' state. But these mental states could only be understood as states of individuals. The mental is what is 'inner', which means within each one of us. And so action is ultimately individual. That is to say, collective actions ultimately amount to the convergent action of many individuals and nothing more. To say 'the X church did so-and-so', or 'the Y party did such and such' must amount to attributing converging action to clumps of individuals in each case. For what makes these events actions in each case is their having inner mental causes, and these

have to occur or not occur discretely within individuals.

By contrast, the qualitative view does not tie action only to the individual agent. The nature of the agency comes clear to us only when we have a clear understanding of the nature of the action. This can be individual; but it can also be the action of a community, and in a fashion which is irreducible to individual action. It can even conceivably be the action of an agent who is not simply identical with human agency.

Hegel, of course, avails himself of both of these latter possibilities. In his conception of public life, as it exists in a properly established system of objective ethics (*Sittlichkeit*), the common practices or institutions which embody this life are seen as our doing. But they constitute an activity which is genuinely common to us, it is ours in a sense which cannot be analyzed into a convergence of 'mine's.

But for Hegel, there is a crucial level of activity which is not only more than individual, but even more than merely human. Some of what we do we can understand also and more deeply as the action of Spirit through us. In order to arrive at a proper understanding, we thus have to transcend our ordinary self-understanding; and to the extent that our common sense is atomist, we have to make two big transpositions; in the first, we come to see that some of our actions are those of communities; in the second, we see that some are the work of Spirit. It is in the *Phenomenology of Spirit* that we see these transitions being made. The first corresponds to the step from Chapter V to Chapter VI (here Hegel speaks of the community action by using the term 'Spirit'). The second is made as we move through the discussion in the third part of Chapter VI into the chapter on Religion.

2. Following what I have said in earlier sections, human action is to be understood in two dimensions, the effective and the expressive. This latter dimension makes it even clearer how action is not necessarily that of the individual. An expression in public space may turn out to be the expression essentially of a common sentiment or purpose. That is, it may be essential to this sentiment or purpose that it be shared, and the expression may be the vehicle of this sharing.

These two features together — that action can be that of a community, and that it also exists in the expressive dimension — form the crucial background to Hegel's philosophy of society and history. The *Sittlichkeit* of a given society not only is to be seen as the action of a community, or of individuals only so far as they identify themselves as members of a community (an 'I' that is 'We', and a 'We' that is 'I', *PhG* 140); it also embodies and gives expression to a certain understanding of the agent, his community and their relation to the divine. It is this latter which gives us the key to the fate of the society. For it is here that the basic incoherence underlying social practice will appear as contradiction, as we saw with the case of the slave-owning society above. Hegel's notion of historical development can only be properly stated if we understand social institutions in this way, as trans-individual action which also has an expressive dimension. By contrast, the causal view and its accompanying atomist outlook induces us to explain institutions in purely instrumental terms. And in these terms, Hegel's theory becomes completely unformulable. We cannot even begin to state what it is all about (I have developed this further in Taylor [8]).

VI

I have been arguing that we can understand Hegel against the background of a long standing and very basic issue in modern philosophy about the nature of action. Hegel's philosophy of mind can be understood as firmly grounded on an option in favour of what I have been calling the qualitative view of action and against the causal view.

I have tried to follow the different ramifications of this qualitative view, to show their importance to Hegel's thought. I looked first at the notion of agent's knowledge, and we saw that the system of philosophy itself can be seen as the integration of everything into a form of all-embracing agent's knowledge. I then followed another development of the qualitative view, which shows us action as primordially unreflecting bodily practice, which later can be transformed by the agent's achievement of reflective awareness. We saw that Hegel's conceptions of subjectivity and its development are rooted in this understanding. I then argued that the expressive revolution in the theory of meaning could be seen as an offshoot of this same view of action; and that Hegel is clearly operating within the expressive conception. Finally we can see that his theory of history supposes not just the expressive dimension but also the idea of irreducibly common actions, which only the qualitative view can allow.

One part of my case is thus that Hegel's philosophy of mind can be illuminated by making this issue explicit in all its ramifications. This is just in the way that we make any philosophy clearer by spelling out more fully some of its deepest assumptions. The illumination will be the greater the more fundamental and pervasive the assumptions in question are for the theory under study. Now my claim is that for Hegel the qualitative theory of action is very basic and all-pervasive, and the above pages have attempted to show this. Perhaps out of deference to Hegel's shade, in this anniversary year, I shouldn't use the word 'assumption', since for Hegel everything is ultimately demonstrated. But my claim stands that the thesis about action I have been describing here is quite central to his philosophy.

But this is only one side of the gain that one can hope for in a study of this kind. The other, as I said at the outset, is that we should attain some greater understanding of the historical debate itself by situating Hegel in it. I think this is so as well, but I haven't got space to argue it here.

What does emerge from the above is that Hegel is one of the important and seminal figures in the long and hard-fought emergence of a counter-theory to the long dominant epistemologically-based view which the seventeenth century bequeathed us. This can help explain why he has been an influential figure in the whole counter-movement where this has been the case. But what remains to be understood is why he has also often been ignored or rejected by major figures who have shared somewhat the same notions of action, starting with Schopenhauer but by no means ending there.

Perhaps what separates Hegel most obviously and most profoundly from those today who take the same side on the issue about action is their profoundly different reading of the same genetic view. For Heidegger, for example, the notion that action is first of all unreflected practice seems to rule out altogether as chimerical the goal of a fully explicit and self-authenticating understanding of what we are about. Disclosure is invariably accompanied by hiddenness; the explicit depends on the horizon of the implicit. The difference here is fundamental, but I believe that it too can be illuminated if we relate it to radically different readings of the qualitative view of action, which both espoused in opposition to the epistemological rationalism of the seventeenth century.

BIBLIOGRAPHY

Anscombe, G.E.M. [6] Intention. Oxford 1957.
Davidson, D. [1] Actions, Reasons and Causes. *The Journal of Philosophy* 60 (1973), No. 23.
— [2] Freedom to Act. in T. Honderich (Ed.), *Essays on Freedom of Action*. London 1973.
Fackenheim, E. *The Religious Dimension in Hegel's Thought*. Boston 1967.
Harris, H.S. *Hegel's Development: Toward the Sunlight*. Oxford 1971.
Henrich, D. *Hegel in Kontext*. Frankfurt 1967.
Labarrière, P.J. *Structures et mouvement dialectique dans la Phénoménologie de l'Esprit de Hegel*. Paris: Auber-Montaigne, 1968.
Kelly, G.A. *Hegel's Retreat from Eleusis*. Princeton 1978.
Plant, R. *Hegel*. Bloomington, Ind. 1973.
Taylor, C. [3] Action as Expression. In C. Diamond and J. Teichman (Eds.), *Intention and Intentionality*. London 1979.
— [5] The Validity of Transcendental Arguments. *Proceedings of the Aristotelian Society*, pp. 151-165. 1978-79.
— [7] *Hegel and Modern Society*. Cambridge 1979.
— [8] Hegel's "Sittlichkeit" and the crisis of representative institutions. In Yirmiahu Yovel (Ed.). *Philosophy of History and Action*. London and Jerusalem 1978.
— *Hegel*. Cambridge 1975.
Williams, B. [4] *Descartes*. London 1978.

Kierkegaard's philosophy of mind

ALASTAIR HANNAY
University of Trondheim

1. The influence of Søren Kierkegaard's writings on the course
of philosophical debate in the last two decades has been predict-
ably less than the burgeoning literature on this profound and complex thinker would ordinarily suggest. Those acquainted with
Kierkegaard's writings appreciate the reasons — not least the
complexity of the thought, the difficulty of 'reducing' it to a
systematic, or at any rate consistent, locutionary series, or even
to a string of clearly defined and independently contestable
claims. There is also the apparently insoluble problem of the
'illocutionary' force to be attributed to the various works themselves, individually or in their appointed categories ('aesthetic',
'dialectical', 'religious') — the difficulty among others, that the
works in the two former categories may not be intended to express Kierkegaard's own claims, or even to claim assent at all but,
as Louis Mackey proposes [1], to address the reader's intelligence
in some less direct way. There is also (to what is for the most
part a studiously agnostic professional public) the apparent
parochiality of what Kierkegaard says is the principal theme of
his work, 'how to become a Christian' — or in fact even more
narrowly, 'how to become a Christian in Christendom'. Not necessarily finally, but surely most effectively, there is the absence of
any clear connexion between the highly interesting claims Kierkegaard or his pseudonyms seem to make and the problems which
have occupied the centre of the wider philosophical stage in the
1960s and 1970s.

In view of the difficulties of interpretation (the first and second

Contemporary philosophy. A new survey. Vol. 4, pp. 157–183.
©*Martinus Nijhoff Publishers, The Hague/Boston/London.*

reasons), it is not surprising that a large proportion of the work on Kierkegaard, indeed a significant part of almost every work on Kierkegaard, is concerned with offering one theory of how to read him and with rebutting rival theories. There is obviously a genuine need to solve such difficulties, and the depth and detail of some recent publications, whether they aim to provide a systematic interpretation of the entire corpus (as in the very different cases of Louis Mackey's *Kierkegaard: A Kind of Poet* [1] and Gregor Malantschuk's *Dialektik og Eksistens hos Søren Kierkegaard*, translated as *Kierkegaard's Thought* [2]) or a part (as, for instance, in John W. Elrod's *Being and Existence in Kierkegaard's Pseudonymous Works* [3] and Mark C. Taylor's *Kierkegaard's Pseudonymous Authorship: A Study of Time and the Self* [4]), have helped in large measure towards doing so. But readers can hardly be expected to judge the merits of the new proposals without a comprehensive acquaintance with the original texts; and even where, as in the latter two works, the discussion is of quite specific and central Kierkegaardian concepts and theses which could well prove interesting and constructive in a larger forum, the exegetical burden tends to inhibit the further analyses and comparisons needed to make them available there. The general effect, it might be said, is to preserve whatever is excellent in the renaissance of Kierkegaard scholarship (and there is very much) for an already established, even if expanding, circle of Kierkegaard scholars.

Some Kierkegaardians may not be troubled by this. They may say that the so-called centre of the philosophical stage is only that part of it which happens, for essentially trivial reasons and only for the time being, to be best lit. Time will show that the framework and manner in which Kierkegaard presents his thought is the enduring one, and that, as Mackey claims, 'in parting company with [the then] modern philosophy' Kierkegaard, although 'perhaps the most extreme antiphilosopher of modern times', was actually 'rejoin[ing] the *philosophia perennis*' ([I], p. 268). It would, however, be presumptuous as well as complacent to assume that the issues which occupy present modern philosophy, as well as the methods with which it deals with them, were entirely foreign to the *philosophia perennis*, and if participation in the *philosophia perennis* really matters it would be safer to assume that the more lasting results would be obtained by a joint exertion that allows concessions from both sides. In the remainder of this chronicle I shall drawn attention to a few topics where I suggest it might be profitable to search for links between the interesting things Kierkegaard seems to be saying, though not always with the greatest precision and clarity, and certain familiar problems and points of view in current philosophy of mind, broadly conceived. The point of the exercise is to chart the extent to which Kierke-gaardian issues have their counterparts in (let us tendentiously call them) less sectarian discussions, to gain some idea of the degree of mutual interest and relevance.

2. Kierkegaard describes the person or self in terms which to the casual eye suggest the now widely discredited Cartesian pola-rity of *res cogitans* and *res extensa*. Since most contemporary dis-cussion in current philosophy of mind is concerned with the ela-boration of acceptable alternatives to Cartesian dualism, this could be one place where the connexion can be made quite straightforwardly. But that is not so. Or at least it is not a con-nexion that can be made straightforwardly with the contemporary critique and attempted replacement of Cartesian dualism. The terms which Kierkegaard uses to describe the person or self as a synthesis of two elements (infinitude/finitude, possibility/ necessity, eternity/temporality) are drawn not from Descartes but from Hegel (and Aristotle). There are two very important differences between the Hegelian and the Cartesian polarity. In the first place, in the tradition stemming from Descartes philo-sophy of mind focuses attention on the relation between mind, or consciousness, and its physical vehicle, the body; the debate is one in fundamental ontology as to whether the human mind is *sui generis* or can be explained in principle as a complex natural (i.e. physical) phenomenon. But the relation upon which the Hegelian tradition focuses is that between mind, or conscious-ness, and its *object*, the world. Secondly, for contemporary phi-losophy of mind, as for Descartes himself, the notion of the mind's object is that of an 'outside' (i.e. extra-mental) reality which true judgments 'represent' in consciousness. In the Hegelian tradition it would be more apt to say that the mind's object is contained *in* rather than that it was represented *by* our true

thoughts; or, as one commentator puts it, that '[t]hought and the determinations through which it operates (the *Denkbestimmungen*, or categories) are not the apanage of a subject over against the world, but lie at the very root of things' ([5], p. 225). The Hegelian idea of an objective world is linked to that of shareable meaning rather than to that of common reference. Roughly, the commonness of the common world lies in the Fregean idea that a thought must be something people can share rather than in the Strawsonian idea of a unique system of publicly observable and enduring spatiotemporal entities ([6], Part One).

These aspects of the Hegelian polarities determine the nature of the philosophical problems posed by the oppositions in question. The overriding problem is that of reconciling them. Why is *that* a problem? Because the latter element in each opposition represents a limitation of the subject's fundamental nature. Traditionally finitude or finiteness is the limitation of distinctness, and is a logical consequence of being something of a certain sort; necessity is the logical property of something's being as it has to be by power of reason; while temporality implies successiveness and so exposure to change. As Mark Taylor points out in his useful discussion of the oppositions, Kierkegaard not only departs from the traditional use of these terms but also tends to regard them as interrelated aspects of the same limitation ([4], pp. 91 ff.). Broadly, and in the corresponding order, the aspects are being merely particular, being constrained by accidents of environment and endowment, and lacking a stable centre, or essence. The most crucial departure from the tradition is the use of the term 'necessity' in connexion with situational rather than rational or logical constraint; Kierkegaard denies ([7], pp. 67-78) that anything actually occurs with necessity and, in the absence of its previous function of determining choices, applies the term by association to factors limiting them. Again broadly — and the parallel here was as far as I know first pointed out by Jean Wahl ([8], see, e.g., p. 166) — the problem facing the subject is the one described by Hegel in his account of the Unhappy Consciousness as the subject's separation from the source of its own nature. What the 'particular individual' needs is (in Hegel's terms) its 'oneness ... with the Unchangeable', or 'the reconciliation ... of [its] individuality with the universal' ([9], § § 213 and 210).

One difference between today's philosophy and the philosophy Kierkegaard so violently opposed is that for the former this is not a genuine problem at all. The Aristotelian framework of essences and unchangeable truths in which Hegel's philosophy is embedded has gone the way of all metaphysics. But then Kierkegaard's reason for opposing his philosophical contemporaries was that neither did he believe it was a philosophical problem. So how do Kierkegaard and our (post-positivist, linguistically turned) contemporaries differ? And if Kierkegaard's point is that the problem is genuine but not philosophical, how can this be reconciled with the claim that in opposing his own philosophical contemporaries he was rejoining the *philosophia perennis*?

First, Kierkegaard's opposition to speculative idealism is that it claims the problem can be solved conceptually. The oneness and reconciliation are to be unifications in *thought*, brought about by advancing to a higher point of view. According to Hegel, consciousness 'becomes Spirit by *finding* itself therein', in an '*aware [ness]* of the reconciliation of its individuality with the universal'. Its 'joy' is then found in the 'peace' of 'self-assurance', and its 'blissful enjoyment' is that of perfect 'vision' ([9], § § 210 [emphases added] and 232, and [10], p. 318). In these quotations we see the tendency in Hegelian philosophy to personify abstract ideas and Kierkegaard's argument is in effect that, if the problem is, as it should be, really posed by actual persons of themselves, it becomes clear (for reasons given in [7] and [11]) *both* that the conceptual solution is abstract, irrelevant, and self-defeating, *and* that it involves misconceptions simultaneously of the nature of personal existence and of the role of philosophy in helping to solve the problem as it does indeed arise there. If it is true that post-positivist philosophy would in general reject whatever metaphysical assumptions must be made for the problem to be able to arise there, this would not put it in a position significantly different from that of speculative idealism in Kierkegaard's eyes. Speculative idealism *thinks* it is addressing the issue but isn't. Post-positivist philosophy isn't addressing it either; the difference is simply that it doesn't aim to do so. Kierkegaard's criticism of the philosophical style of his contemporaries is one he would no doubt find good reason to repeat today:

> If thought in our time had not become something queer, something one learns parrot-fashion [*noget Tillært*], thinkers would make a quite different impression upon people, as was the case in Greece, where a thinker was also someone whose thinking inspired him to a passionate interest in his own existence; and as was also once the case in Christendom, where a thinker was someone whose faith inspired him to try to understand himself in the existence of faith ([11], 1, p. 15, quoted in Lowrie's translation in [1], pp. 324-325).

The answer to the second question, then, as the reference indicates, is that Kierkegaard saw himself as returning to the Greek tradition. More specifically, he saw himself as returning to and continuing from where Socrates had left off. Kierkegaard describes himself (in the shape of his philosophical or 'dialectical' *persona*, Johannes Climacus) as 'going further than Socrates' ([7], p. 99). The respect in which Socrates was going in the right direction was that he was an *existential* thinker; while the respect in which he did not go far enough in that direction was that (in Plato's version; see the important footnote on [11], 1, p. 172) he continued to assume that essential truth lay within the scope of human cognitive capacity. Kierkegaard's 'advance' on Socrates is his rejection of this assumption; while it was the philosophical tradition's acceptance of it which made the culmination of that tradition in Hegel's 'System' a colossal diversion. Ideally, Kierkegaard's own philosophical project should have been that of showing the path *out of* Greek philosophy (paganism), *via* Socrates (existential thought and irony), *to* the antiphilosophical, non-humanist position where the only saving truths have to be conceived as based on paradox (religiousness B). But there were obstacles: the philosophical tradition itself and its off-shoot, organized religion. Kierkegaard had to contend with an ideology which offered easy ways out of the hard epistemological truths of his advanced position, which encouraged people to believe that they could be saved by being incorporated *into* the essential truth simply as effective members of existing Danish society, or even that they were already saved because they had been baptized into the Danish State Church. In respect of the ideology Kierkegaard saw himself as a Socrates (see [4] and especially [12]) demolishing the protective fabric of illusions that prevented people from posing the problem of reconciliation as a personal one, as a problem their reflection on which could inspire them to a passionate interest in their own existence.

If we now return to the schema of oppositions which we said formed the basis of Kierkegaard's account of the person or self, we find two things which distinguish Kierkegaard's account from the kinds with which we are most familiar in contemporary philosophy. In the first place, the oppositions apply differently according to the subject's understanding of its own relation to essential truth. Thus in paganism, or in what Kierkegaard calls 'immanent' positions generally, the subject as it were straddles the opposition; it is assumed that it can establish its relationship to the essential truth (to the eternal) by some form of action or style of life within the subject's own power of performance — in the ethical but not yet religious sphere by asserting a social self, and in the as yet only paganly religious sphere by a form of self-annihilation involving withdrawal from existence. In either case existence, the *individual's* existence, whether in self-assertion or in self-annihilation, is thought to be in some way encompassed by the eternal; while in Kierkegaard's advanced position, instead of the opposition occurring within existence, it is placed 'absolutely between existence and eternity' ([11], 2, p. 238).

The second distinctive feature is Kierkegaard's use of the term 'self'. It is introduced into the schema as a 'third term' which 'mediates' the opposites, establishing them as elements in a 'synthesis'. Against the Hegelian background one might expect the synthesis to be the solution of the problem, the reconciling of the opposites in a higher unity; but it appears rather to be the first grasp of the problem itself. In a discussion of sin and sensuality we are told that 'the synthesis is first posited in the sexual as a contradiction ... and, like every contradiction, as a task the history of which begins at that very moment' ([13], p. 142; cf. p. 160 where the German 'Widerspruch' is added in parentheses). In an often-quoted passage, sometimes regarded as a deliberate parody of the Hegelian style but in effect a neat though spare definition of the self's place in the synthesis, we read:

> The human being is a synthesis of infinity and finitude, of temporality and eternity, of freedom and necessity, in short a synthesis. A synthesis is a relation between two [factors]. Considered in this way the human being is not yet a self. ... In the relation between two [factors] the relation [itself] is the third [factor] as a negative entity [*Enhed*], and the [other] two relate themselves to the relation, and in the relation to the relation; this is the way in which the relation between soul and body is a relation when soul is the determining category [*under Bestemmelsen Sjel*]. If, on the other hand, the relation relates itself to itself, then this relation is the positive third [factor], and this is the self ([14], p. 73).

In plainer language, the self is not to be identified simply with a relation which allows us to classify human beings as a species of psychophysical entity; for then the self would be a merely dependent factor, mirroring the interactions of the other two. Kierkegaard's self is a controlling rather than a controlled factor, this being the respect in which it is said to belong properly to the category of 'spirit'. In Hegelian terms 'spirit' is synonymous with 'freedom' and the freedom of spirit is that spirit exists 'in and with itself' ([15], p. 17). Kierkegaard need not deny that psychophysical organisms *lacking* a self are nevertheless controlled, in the sense that they have an organized repertoire of advantageous responses to their immediate environments. But beings whose mental life is correctly located in the category of spirit are not confined in this way to the instinctual closure of immediacy. Kierkegaard refers (in *The Concept of Anxiety*) to spirit as a kind of function or force 'present' in man ([13], p. 137; cf. p. 185), and which 'constitutes' ([13], pp. 162 and 170) the psychophysical synthesis, whose components, soul and body, are variously said to be 'united' ([13], p. 137), 'bound' ([13], p. 142), 'sustained' ([13], pp. 170 and 176) by, or to 'rest' ([13], p. 142) in it. Spirit also 'posits' ([13], p. 142) the synthesis, though only when it, that is to say spirit, ceases to be merely 'dreaming' in man, or present only 'as immediate' ([13], p. 136). The presence of spirit implies not merely an ability to envisage *other* environments than the immediate one; it implies a kind of distancing of the mind from the finite world of particular environments altogether. If we allow that animals are exclusively finite beings in the terms of this discussion, their minds (souls) do not have this distance, they live 'immediate' lives, and the synthesis in their case contains no 'opposition', 'contradiction', or 'task'. While even if a human being who lives the life of immediacy (as in the 'aesthetic sphere') finds no contradiction in his existence, it is still here 'outside' ([11], 2, p. 239). The contradiction is not between *soul* and *body*, but between spirit and the soul in its instinctual role. What Kierkegaard means by saying that man is 'determined as spirit' ([13], p. 138) is that man is always, even if at first only implicitly, conscious of being *essentially* underdetermined as a merely finite being. An interesting parallel can be drawn between Kierkegaard's 'spirit' and Hegel's 'consciousness'. In Hegel this term, distinguished in a corresponding way from 'soul' (*Seele*), refers specifically to the kind of awareness, allegedly specific to man, in which he is set apart from the immediate, instinctual side of his existence, an idea with which Hegel, also with Kierkegaard, associates the notion of spiritual freedom and self-contained existence ([16], § 413).

Hegel talks of the 'path of natural consciousness ... the way of the soul which journeys through the series of its own configurations as though they were the stations appointed for it by its own nature, so that it may purify itself for the life of the Spirit'. The path laid out for the soul 'presses forward to true knowledge' or 'Science', and the point of the journey is to provide the soul with a 'completed experience of itself' in which it finally achieves 'awareness of what it really is in itself' ([9], § 77). Kierkegaard's existing individual is denied any such awareness, and it is, instead, the full awareness of *this* fact that forms the goal of its journey along the path of consciousness. On the other hand, Kierkegaard's spirit, like Hegel's, is the realization of a potentiality specific to the *human* soul. And also like Hegel's the special characteristic of this soul is its sense of a disproportion between natural and merely finite existence on the one hand and the requirements of its autonomy and fulfilment on the other (cf. [13], p. 138). But in the case of Kierkegaard's 'soul', the ideals of fulfilment and freedom are always a 'task', for instance the task of 'winning the sexual into the [eternal] category of spirit' (*at vinde det ind i*

Aandens [evige] Bestemmelse) ([13], p. 162). The instinctual life does not conform *itself* to 'the category of spirit', it has to be brought actively *into* conformity with it; the instinctual life poses a practical problem requiring the individual's active intervention.

How then are this practical task and its solution related to the overriding problem of reconciling the opposites, and to *its* solution? Indeed what kind of reconciliation is at all possible in the absence of a perfect vision of the kind providing it in Hegel? And even if there is one, what advantages, corresponding to the 'joy', 'blissful enjoyment', and 'self-assurance' afforded by the Hegelian vision, can the individual expect from such a reconciliation? Unless there is some sense of its being not only the right but also a satisfying thing to do, unless, at the very least, there is the prospect of some compensation for the losses involved in elevating the instinctual life to the level of spirit, the project will be as 'abstract' as Hegel's own and a matter of indifference to the concretely situated individual to whom Kierkegaard appeals. The answers, given here very briefly, provide introductions to our remaining topics.

First, that Kierkegaard does contemplate some form of reconciliation, and that what he calls 'transfiguring sensuousness into spirit' ([13], p. 169) is a necessary part of it, can be understood, once again, in terms of the Hegelian programme which Kierkegaard's is intended (it is not always sufficiently stressed) to replace as well as to subvert. Hegel's is a monist system in which matter tends towards ideality, and spirit in the end encompasses everything. The material world exists merely in order to give spirit embodiment, spirit has to 'externalize' itself as nature before 'returning to' itself as concrete spirit. For Kierkegaard, however, this monistic scheme leaves out the problematic and compound category of existence. In describing the human being as a compound (of infinitude and finitude, possibility and necessity, and eternity and temporality) Kierkegaard is, as we have seen, referring to the situation of the merely particular, concretely situated, and unstabilized individual concerned with the possibility of reconciling these limitations with their opposites. Since conceptual mediation is an illusion from the point of view of existence (see [11], 2, pp. 60 ff. and 92), the tendency in *thought* should rather be to stress the absolute distinction between these elements. Any tendency to conflate the two, to see the finite as a manifestation of the infinite, as if the terms of this contradiction were still *within* existence, and the reconciliation within the individual's power through ethical self-assertion or religious self-annihilation, must be regarded as a human weakness. The same applies if the tendency is to *say* that the infinite is totally different from the finite and yet to treat or conceive it *as if* it belonged to the familiar realm of the finite all the same ([11], 2, p. 86). The two must be held absolutely apart. But there is still the possibility of a situation corresponding to that of the 'embodiment' of spirit in nature. It is for the *acting* individual to subordinate finite ends to an absolute end, at least to try to reach that 'maximum' which is to 'maintain simultaneously a relationship to the absolute *telos* and to relative ends, not by mediating them, but by making the relationship to the absolute *telos* absolute, and the relationship to the relative ends relative' ([11], 2, p. 99). 'If for any individual', says Kierkegaard, 'an eternal happiness is his highest good, this will mean that all finite considerations [*Momenter*] are once and for all *actively [handlende]* reduced to what has to be given up in relation to the eternal happiness' ([11], 2, pp. 85-86, my emphasis). By 'giving up' the finite (Kierkegaard also talks of 'resignation' [see (11), 2, p. 93] and of 'renouncing everything' [(11), 2, p. 97], the latter as 'the first true expression of one's relationship to the absolute *telos* [there are later expressions, first suffering, the 'essential' expression, then guilt, the 'decisive' expression]), Kierkegaard does not mean turning one's back on it. 'The individual does not cease to be a human being, nor does he divest himself of the manifold composite garment of the finite in order to clothe himself in the abstract attire of the cloister ...' ([11], 2, p. 101). The point is rather that the individual consciously subjects the finite goals that confront him to an overordinate, non-finite end, *genuinely conceived as non-finite*. The result, in form, corresponds to the Hegelian subordination of matter to spirit — putting matter to spiritual use. The difference is that here the transformation of the material occurs not in the material world as such, in things and processes, but in the *manner* in, or nature of the intention by, which changes are brought about in that world by individuals, in their projects, aims, and choices. The unification, which in Hegel's account of spirit is the result of matter striving (self-destructively, as Hegel says) after the realization of its idea, is for Kierkegaard introduced into the world by human agency. But it is not introduced in the sense that a change in the world due to human action of the kind in question is an objectively identifiable manifestation of the infinite. In this respect action is *not* a substitute for mediation. The unification has a purely 'subjective' location, in the individual will.

Secondly, why, when living in the category of spirit (see [14], p. 113) requires the individual to be a 'stranger in the world of the finite' ([11], 2, p. 102), should the individual nevertheless choose that life? Now although the reference to eternal happiness indicates that there is meant to be some form of ultimate satisfaction in it for the individual, it appears that the threshold of satisfaction to which Kierkegaard appeals is considerably lower than in Hegel. It is true that he speaks of a kind of certainty (*Vished*) paralleling Hegel's 'self-assurance', but otherwise, rather than 'joy' or 'blissful enjoyment', all that Kierkegaard can offer his individual is the absence of despair. And even the certainty turns out to be the product of a consciously irrational decision, an 'act of daring' (*Vovestykke*) in which the individual 'risks everything', including his 'thought', which means that the capacity to determine logical possibility has to be renounced if an eternal happiness is to be even so much as an option ([11], 2, pp. 113 and 118). Whatever gravitational pull the prospect of an eternal happiness originally has is replaced, as the consequences of Kierkegaard's advanced position emerge, by the intellectually blind choice, in what he calls the 'passion of the infinite ' (*den uendelige Lidenskab* [11], 2, p. 115), of a goal about which all that can be said is that it is 'the manner of its acquisition' ([11], 2, p. 116). However, we are not to take this to imply a corresponding decrease of interest in the goal of reconciliation itself. On the contrary, it is when, in the *deepest* despair, one faces the full impact of the absolute transcendence of the eternal that being rid of despair becomes the greatest thing one could wish (as water to someone parched with thirst) and differentially on a par with Hegel's joy and blissful enjoyment. The reason why, as Kierkegaard concedes, so few even attempt the life of spirit is not that it has no inherent attraction, it is, he says, because 'most people have still not come particularly deep in their despair' ([14], pp. 112-113).

Despair is described as an incongruity (*Misforhold*) 'in the relation comprising the synthesis' ([14], p. 74). The incongruity, it should be noted, is not the fact that the terms in the synthesis stand opposed to one another: that they do so is a given fact of human existence (see [11], 2, p. 85); and in any case 'it is not up to the existing [individual] to make existence out of finitude and infinity [by putting them together], but being himself composed of [these] to *become qua* existing one of them [namely infinite] ...' ([11], 2, p. 110, original emphasis; cf. [14], p. 88). Furthermore, '[if] the synthesis [itself] were the incongruity, there would be no such thing as despair, for despair would then be something inherent in human nature as such ... something that befell man, something he suffered, like a sickness ... or death' ([14], p. 75). It is essential to Kierkegaard's view that there is an alternative to despair, that despair is an option that the individual chooses, or at least remains in by default. So the incongruity is a feature not of the synthesis, but of the *self*. More accurately, it is that whereby this 'third' factor fails to establish itself, or be 'posited' as a self, fails to 'relate itself to itself' and thus to become the 'positive' third factor in the synthesis.

But this is not the whole story. Despair is said to have two main forms. One is the individual's reluctance to *be* a self, and the other is the 'posited' self's reluctance to accept that it is 'constituted by another' ([14], p. 73). In Hegel's language this latter reluctance would be the posited self's insistence that it has its 'essence' in itself. Hegel's ideal of spiritual freedom as the spirit's existing 'in and with itself' would therefore appear from Kierkegaard's position as a form of despair. The 'formula' for reconciliation, or the 'condition of the self when despair is completely eradicated, [is]: by relating itself to its own self and by willing to be itself, the self is grounded transparently in the Power which posited it' ([14], p. 74). 'The self is freedom', or the achievement by the synthesis (or by the relationship which comprises it) of relating itself to itself (see [14], p. 87). But if the self now freely *refuses* to consider itself a 'derived' (*deriveret*) relationship and presumes to exist (as Hegel would put it) 'in and with itself', it has still failed to be rid of its despair. The self is 'in sound health' and 'free from despair' only when, 'having been in despair', it is 'grounded transparently in God' ([14], p. 88).

Both these answers imply the centrality of will. The first says that reconciliation is a kind of exercise of will, the second that it is an achievement of will. The latter is obviously logically prior: the existence of the achievement is presupposed by the claim that it takes the specified form. The combined view is that reconciliation is the result of the individual's own effort, something which, first of all, points to the truth in the Kierkegaardian share in the frequent claim that the problems Hegel treated as capable of conceptual solution Marx and Kierkegaard interpreted in their different ways as practical; and thereby, secondly, allows us to place Kierkegaard's views on the relation of body, soul, and spirit in their proper philosophical context, which is that of Hegel's *Phenomenology of Spirit*, not philosophy of mind in the modern, more specialized sense.

The pseudonymous author of *The Concept of Anxiety* says it is not necessary for his purpose to enter into any 'pompous philosophical discussion about the relation between soul and body' (though he adds enough to indicate that he could if he wanted); it suffices to say that 'the body is the organ of the soul and thus, in turn, of the spirit' ([13], p. 218). Transforming the soul/body synthesis into the organ of the spirit is the task that first appears, or the 'history' of which begins, with the 'positing' of the synthesis and culminates in the constituting of a 'self' properly so called: a free individual in the sense of one who, to adapt Marx, has brought the psychological conditions of life under conscious control — conditions which, in Marx's terms, if abandoned to chance acquire an independent existence over *against* the individual. The 'synthesis' is the framework in terms of which Kierkegaard describes fulfilment: the individual's decision to 'risk everything' is one by which he does, in a way, 'become infinite' ([11], 2, p. 113); it is a choice in which he accepts an identity apart from and overordinate to the finite, even though, in order to avoid the second main form of despair, this requires accepting that possession of the infinite must take the form of dependence upon God.

But it is also the framework within which the *problems* and *failures* of fulfilment are to be described. The synthesis provides, in its pairs of opposite terms, the basis of a typology of failures, i.e. of forms of despair (in [14]), as well as a kind of hierarchy of growth-levels — first the psychophysical compound in which the body is the organ of soul, and in respect of which spirit is only an open 'possibility', and then this compound as the organ of spirit in the state Kierkegaard calls freedom — which allows Kierkegaard to describe (in [13]) the states of anxiety attending the idea of a transition from a finitely based identity to an infinitely based one. To understand the role of the component terms in the synthesis it would be misleading to think of them, as in contemporary discussion of psychophysical connections, as logically independent coevals in some kind of hierarchically ordered relation to one another. The soul, for instance, is not to be regarded, along with its characteristic bodily expression, as an independent though junior and more earthbound partner of an ascetic spirit. It is rather the state or stage to which the self may regress when under pressure, a state in which the body becomes the organ of the soul rather than of the spirit, though Kierkegaard claims that in thus shunning its spiritual possibility or freedom the self entering this state is divided and the state therefore a morbid one. This attempted regression in fact comprises one important category in Kierkegaard's typology of anxiety, what he calls 'freedom lost psychosomatically' (*Friheden tabt somatisk-psychisk*). It is an anxiety which shuns the good, and among the 'countless multiplicity of [whose] nuances' will be found 'an exaggerated sensibility, nervous affections, hysteria, hypochondria, etc.' ([13], p. 218). The circumstances of which these can be symptoms might be called conditions of life which have acquired an independent existence over against the individual.

3. One way of reading the two main works Kierkegaard devotes to psychological themes is as providing the conceptual tools necessary for the individual's conscious control of such conditions. What these works describe are the psychological attitudes of the individual in its relation to the presupposed and personally demanding ideal of freedom. In [13] we have an account of the individual's growing anxiety in the face of the ideal, both before it takes clear shape in consciousness and after. In [14] we are given classified descriptions of the morbid and psychologically unstable conditions of those who shun the ideal and try, against their better judgment, but also — it is suggested — against the inherent tendency of human consciousness, to make do with something less demanding. Both accounts could be said to provide the conceptual background the individual needs to know his place within the psychological economy, thus enabling him to direct his own psychological affairs instead of being directed by them.

This interpretation strikes me as largely correct but in need of careful qualification. In two respects. First, there is the emphasis Kierkegaard places on the will. It isn't *just* understanding that the individual lacks, as if he already had the correct desire (selfhood, freedom) and needed only the knowledge of what actions will satisfy it; indeed Kierkegaard's assumption seems to be that the gist of the account is something with which the individual is already acquainted, and the details of which will be readily recognized as true. What someone who is a victim of his own psychological economy lacks is, partly, the will to put the knowledge into practice. But only partly, since a significant factor in the weakening of the will is the individual's own description of the attitude he adopts in failing to act so as to satisfy his desire for selfhood and freedom; thus he might say that the conditions really do have an independent existence and that he really is a victim and so not free to do otherwise, or that the attitude is freely adopted because it affords an alternative satisfaction that is the really preferred one. What Kierkegaard gives is an alternative description, a description of the attitude as an inferior option which the individual has chosen deliberately or by default, that is to say as an accountable failure to act on an actually preferred judgment. Here, then, we should be able to find a link with contemporary discussions of *akrasia*, or weakness of will, and self-deception (e.g. [17] and [18]). But there are obvious differences. These discussions are often formal, with examples, usually fairly trivial and nearly always artificial, concocted to make particular logical points. Kierkegaard focuses on one example and seems to claim it is universal. His discussion really belongs to moral psychology, not conceptual analysis. In addition to which it takes for granted an ethico-religious framework that even moral psychologists would consider old-fashioned — a framework which to many will seem simply to have been imposed upon the psychological phenomena from above, though this would be to go too far; Kierkegaard's moral psychology is in the first instance phenomenological; its descriptions of psychological states appeal, if not to *common* experience, at least to what Kierkegaard might plausibly claim are generally available insights. It might be more fruitful to regard the ethical framework not as being arbitrarily superimposed but as an attempted reconstruction of more or less familiar phenomena in terms of a particular theory of human development, a theory which gives a central place to individual responsibility and choice. A better indication of the kind of relation Kierkegaard's moral framework has to his psychological descriptions is to be found in the objection that the framework is arbitrary in another sense: namely that it is simply an ideological solution to admittedly real but not universal psychological problems, problems revealed to Kierkegaard in his own neurosis and by his exceptional powers of self-observation. In other words, that the framework of sin, faith, and redemption is a piece of wishful thinking. For even if the criticism is misguided (and perhaps it is not altogether), its functional interpretation of the relationship between the ethical superstructure and psychological base does at least express recognition of a way in which it would be correct to say that the two are not logically independent of one another.

The second qualification to the claim that the psychological works provide the knowledge the individual needs to be able to control his own psychological economy concerns the role often assigned to knowledge in such a case. Scientific descriptions are parts of scientific explanations, and we usually think of these as causal. Discounting mere curiosity or wonder, the rationale for such descriptions is that, if true, they contribute to our ability to predict and in principle, by manipulation of the causal antecedents, to prevent, compensate for, or contrive the occurrence of the phenomenon in question. Although it is perhaps physical phenomena we think of first here, there seems no reason in principle why at least some psychological phenomena should not be open to similar manipulation. Nevertheless Kierkegaard's descriptions of psychological phenomena are not intended to enable us to *avoid* problems. His account of the conditions of the 'real' possibility of sin ([13], Ch. I), for example, is not intended to enable us to avoid the problem of sin by control of these conditions. Certainly there is a sense in which he intends it to enable us to *solve* the problem of sin, but the solution requires us not to avoid the problem, but to face it. (This point is made in Kresten Nordentoft's *Kierkegaards psykologi* [19], the only major work in the period under review devoted to these aspects of Kierkegaard's thought and their relation to post-Freudian psychology.) The descriptions are in fact best understood as reconstructions of certain psychological phenomena in a non-scientific terminology which interprets them from the point of view of that problem. The aim is to make us aware both of the *kind* of practical solution needed and of the destructive consequences of not giving it that kind of solution. The descriptions *are* thus in a sense diagnostic and cautionary. But unlike scientific psychologists, whose cautions consist in *predictions* of undesirable consequences (pain, death, insanity) of present psychological conditions, predictions which only then disclose to those affected that they are confronted with a (prudential or ethical) choice, Kierkegaard interprets the conditions as themselves *outcomes* of choice in conscious defiance of what the choosers already know to be right.

Establishing causal connexions between (it is usually insisted) logically independent events is only one way of enlarging the scope of our understanding. The connexions can also be, and perhaps must always necessarily be in part, conceptual. According to Hegel's conception of science (philosophical science) they are exclusively conceptual. Phenomena which appear to be only contingently related, or which our currently best descriptions even force us to regard as conceptually irreconcilable, are grasped — that is to say, a conceptual solution of the theoretical problem they confront us with is provided — only if they can be logically united or reconciled under the cover of a new, embracing concept. The ability to come by such concepts, Hegel's speculative reason, has in principle no limits. Hegelian science is therefore all-embracing. Hegel classified psychology, along with (in his senses of these terms) phenomenology and anthropology, as a science of 'subjective spirit' (cf. [13], p. 12), a topic comprising, roughly, the attitudes and dynamics of spiritual emergence from the point of view of consciousness — in contrast to 'objective spirit', by which Hegel meant the public manifestations and historical forms of this emergence, including legal institutions and social morality

(*Sittlichkeit*), but also the socially significant aspects of individual conscience (*Moralität*). In intending his science of spirit to be all-embracing, Hegel meant that no aspect of human life, not even the concepts and principles of individual and social morality, lay beyond its grasp. It is this view which Kierkegaard attacks; the belief that ethical concepts, principles, and problems can be understood by incorporating them within a systematic understanding of the world in general. This, on Kierkegaard's view, is precisely to misunderstand the nature of ethical problems. It is to interpret them not as practical dilemmas facing individual persons and their lives, practical problems, that is, which require specifically ethical, not technical solutions, but as in the end theoretical problems to be solved by advances in comprehension. As if the solutions were to be *found* rather than *made*.

4. Making a solution, in Kierkegaard, means creating the unity of the infinite. Feuerbach said that speculative philosophy's mistake was to conceive the path of philosophy as 'from the abstract to the concrete, from the ideal to the real'. This was to put things upside-down; the starting-point should be the finite, without which 'the infinite cannot be conceived'. Feuerbach observes that '[t]he transition from the ideal to the real takes place only in *practical* philosophy' ([20], pp. 230 and 232). Whatever he meant by that, it is clear that Kierkegaard, too, holds that the proper direction is the reverse of Hegel's and that the problem is a practical one. However, in regard to this practical problem Kierkegaard prescribes a path that not only reverses Hegel's by having the finite (individual) as its beginning and the unity of the infinite as its goal, but is its reverse in another respect too. Hegel's 'path of natural consciousness' goes from private to public, from inner to outer, from individuality to a consummation of the individual in a publicity offering fulfilment in ready-made social roles. The progress is outward from 'immediacy' to the public domain in which spirit finds its own home, and in relation to which any pockets of privacy in the public fabric are wrinkles to be flattened out in further extensions of the common vision of objective truth. Kierkegaard's journey is inwards, as greater insight reveals the inability of the public world to provide for the individual's consummation, and as the role of will (or 'heart') and personal choice are revealed as the resources with which the finite agent must secure any consummation that may be in store for it. In this respect the force of Kierkegaard's injunction to 'become subjective', and of his claim that this is the 'highest task' confronting every individual ([11], 2, p. 131), is that, apart from having to be stood on his head, Hegel also has to be turned outside-in.

5. We said earlier that the Hegelian idea of an objective world was linked to that of shareable meaning rather than common frame of reference. By, at this level of analysis, an admittedly crude and facile inference one might suppose that from the Hegelian point of view the degree to which a person succeeds in becoming *subjective* correlates inversely with the amount of meaning that person has to share, and perhaps that at the extreme of subjectivity a person has no meaning at all to share. Now, as it notoriously happens, this thesis, or rather a thesis answering to this general formulation, is the one presented in *Fear and Trembling* and exemplified in the extreme moral individualism of the knight of faith. The knight of faith, portrayed in a version of the Genesis story of Abraham's willingness, on God's command, to sacrifice his son, Isaac, as proof of his faith, is one who acts in 'concealment' and 'absolute isolation' ([21], pp. 102 and 73). His isolation is that of one who cannot make himself understood, who, whatever he might say in explanation of his action, will not be able to convey its moral point to others. He is a radically recalcitrant wrinkle in the public fabric. The question is whether his 'privacy' has any actual connexion with the notion that objectivity is essentially linked to that of shared meaning — or of common conceptual vision — and if so with what implications for the wider philosophical debate; or whether the 'teleological suspension of the ethical', as Kierkegaard calls the situation exemplified by Abraham, is a breach not of some alleged principle of meaning, but, less radically, of a preferred theory of morality.

The latter interpretation is suggested by Kierkegaard's explanation of Abraham's 'concealment' as being due to his 'doing nothing for the universal' ([21], p. 102). That is to say, there is no overriding communal goal that his action serves and which in the eyes of common morality would justify what to those eyes must otherwise appear to be an incomprehensible repudiation of parental love and responsibility. One might think that Abraham's own reason for his action (that it is a test of his faith — not, of course, in God's existence, since even disobeying God's command demonstrates that, but in God's justice) is one that he, Abraham, understands. So that if there were enough knights of faith to form a community, it might be said of them that *they* shared a common vision of morality, one for which doing something for the universal was *not* an absolute norm. If the knight of faith's isolation is 'absolute', however, we would expect knights of faith to be just as isolated, in the relevant respect, from one another as from those with whom they do not share this vision. It seems that the clue to what this respect is and to what makes the isolation absolute is to be found in Kierkegaard's (or his pseudonym's) saying that the basis of the knight of faith's actions is a principle which defies thought and 'remains in all eternity a paradox'. The principle is that 'the individual as such is higher than the universal' ([21], pp. 52-53).

Hegel says in the *Phenomenology* that there is something which, if you try to convey it in language, you will always misrepresent: namely the particular 'sensuous' content of your experience. Language can only express generality. So what you might mean to say in this case will be 'refuted' by what you actually succeed in saying. Hegel's view is that it is what you *say* that is 'the more truthful' ([9], § 96), as we would expect if objective truth is the content of a perfect vision whose content is conceptual, i.e. a system of relationships, and not some particular or particulars to which you stand in a definite relation. Kierkegaard apparently accepts this view of what language can and cannot express ('As soon as I speak I express the universal' [(21), p. 56] and 'the relief of speech is that it translates [one] into the universal' [(21), p. 102]). But his view as to where there is more truth is the opposite of Hegel's — at least with regard to 'eternal' truth, an essential component in which is the definite relation of the individual *to* the content (the 'how' of the utterer's relationship to the objective 'what' of his utterance, as the distinction is made in [11], 1, p. 169), and therefore also, in the present case, with regard to the transcendent source of eternal value. What is primary in this respect is the 'absolute relationship' in which the individual stands to this

'Absolute'. The relationship itself is absolute because it is unconditional upon any finite consideration on the part of the individual. Apart from this, however, and the fact that the absolute, being transcendent, could not be identified by any general description applicable within the space-time order in any case, the relationship to this transcendent source is parallel to that to the immediate content of experience, or perhaps to any particular thing we try to consider in itself, without the 'mediation' of the universal. What is paradoxical is the idea that the individual, in regard to what he *essentially* is and ought to do, should be prior to the universal, i.e. to what can be thought and said *about* the individual. It is paradoxical in so far as in order to 'understand' the utterances and actions of the individual who adopts this idea, we would have to describe them in terms that constitute a breach of a principle of describability. That the idea defies *thought* would then simply be a consequence of the (not at all self-evident) principle that whatever can be thought can be said.

Most discussion of *Fear and Trembling* in the period covered by these chronicles has focused on the figure of Abraham and the question of the morality and/or general defensibility of his intended action ([22]). Although little of this debate comes more than marginally within the philosophy of mind, it is perhaps worth remarking that a fuller appreciation of the general Hegelian background — of the logical background as well as the practical background presented by Bernstein ([23]) — would have obviated the need for a good deal of it and perhaps directed attention more fruitfully upon the general issues. It is clear, for example, that Kierkegaard *does* envisage a teleological suspension of the ethical, at least in the sense of a Hegelian *Sittlichkeit* ethics, but that he does not mean this to imply a relativization of morality as such to a supramoral authority (see [21], p. 51); and also that we are to take Abraham as an illustration not of the total irrelevance to morality of our moral intuitions but of the unintelligibility of faith (see Dietrichson [22]). So there should be advantages both in the present context *and* in general in a fuller and closer investigation of the principles of meaning and reference underlying Kierkegaard's potentially important accounts not only of the unintelligibility and enforced silence of the knight of faith, but of course also of subjectivity and 'inwardness' (*In-*

derlighed) in connexion with the concepts of truth and communication.

A more useful point of departure for such an investigation would be what Kierkegaard says about the distinction between inner and outer (see Taylor [4], especially the two last chapters). The potential relevance of this distinction for contemporary philosophy of mind should be clear. Kierkegaard's insistence on the distinction itself and more particularly on the centrality of the inner goes against the grain of most recent philosophy of mind, as also (even more so) his claim that faith, the category in which the inner has to be understood if it is to have that centrality Kierkegaard claimed for it, is an aspect of the inner life which has no specific outward manifestation (see [4], pp. 337 ff. and the qualifying footnote on p. 337). In view of Kierkegaard's conception of his own role as that of Socratic gadfly, encouraging people, as it might be said, to prise the mystical shell of absolute idealism away from whatever existential kernel is to be found in Hegel's dialectic, it would be an interesting test of the durability of his thought to place it in contexts where, if true, it should prove fruitfully corrosive. One such context might be the general area of post-Rylean and post-Wittgensteinian philosophy of mind with its questions of 'other minds', the logic of mental concepts, the question of outward criteria for their application, and of the relationship of the inner life to the outer as well as of the implications of this for the learning of the vocabulary of the inner life (see Hampshire [24], especially pp. 81 ff.). Another might be that of the analysis of 'intentionality' or propositional attitudes. Kierkegaard's distinction between the thought's 'how' and its 'what' comes close enough to a current distinction between the 'psychological mode' of a person's concern about some objectively identifiable segment of (past, present, or future) reality and the 'representative content' ([25]) of the corresponding thought to prompt the possibility of extending the modest range of rather simple modes usually mentioned in such analyses to include Kierkegaard's more sophisticated modes (irony, humour, faith, anxiety, despair), as well perhaps — more interestingly philosophically — as the 'life-views' corresponding to the well-known stages or spheres of existence, since these after all are said to be *ways* of experiencing reality.

6. Finally, there is an underlying issue affecting the question of the contemporary philosophical relevance of Kierkegaard's thought quite generally, namely the status of the ethico-religious framework in which it is embedded. For many the 'superimposition' of this framework will weaken the ties of relevance and interest, while for others its being 'presupposed' will strengthen them. Superficially this difference looks non-philosophical, at least in the sense that philosophical differences are held to be ones which can be — and perhaps also actually *tend* to be — discussed philosophically. However, as was suggested earlier, the connexion between the ethical superstructure and psychological base is closer than the notions of superimposition and presupposition imply. A better idea of the connexion is conveyed by Wittgenstein's remark that, as he sees it, 'the Christian faith ... is a man's refuge in [an] *ultimate* torment' ([26], p. 46e, original emphasis). Wittgenstein's comments on religion are clearly coloured by his reading of Kierkegaard. Nevertheless 'refuge' (*Zuflucht*) with its connotation of 'shelter' suggests *flight from* reality, and one may wonder how that notion can be part of the framework within which reality itself is what one is attempting to describe. The answer must of course be that it is a description of *human* reality that the framework is designed to provide. But then a similar question arises in that context too: Why should a framework which selects *this* refuge be the one that accounts most satisfactorily for human reality? If, as Wittgenstein also says, '[t]he Christian religion is *only* for the man who needs infinite help, solely, that is, for the man who experiences infinite torment' (ibid., emphasis added), why should the special needs of *this* man be thought to have universal significance? Now although at first glance it would seem self-defeating to answer this latter question by saying, 'Well at least it can seem so to one who has these needs', there is an important point here nonetheless. It comes to light if we read the claim that the Christian religion is only for the man who needs infinite help as saying not that it has nothing to say to others, but that if you are to understand what it does say you must have or acquire the kind of inner life in which the Christian concepts of sin, faith, and redemption apply. Hampshire has argued that '[e]ntry into a certain "form of life" is a necessary background to using and attaching sense

to [the] concepts ... [which correspond] to the more refined distinctions within the vocabulary of sentiment and emotion' ([24], p. 81). The form of life Hampshire refers to is the 'adult human form of life' with its habits of controlled expression in word and deed. But if, following Cavell's lead ([27]), we regard Kierkegaard's religious stage as a Wittgensteinian form of life, Hampshire's arguments — to the effect that the 'concept of feeling and sentiment' is *derived* from that of inhibited behaviour, in such a way that 'the order in which a person learns the use of two classes of expression' is also that in which he 'acquires the faculties of mind to which the expressions refer' ([24], p. 82) — might be extended or adapted to the feelings and sentiments (needs and hopes) of the person about whose form of expression Wittgenstein says, 'No cry of torment can be greater than the cry of *one* man' ('Ein Notschrei kann nicht grösser sein, als der *eines* Menschen') ([26], p. 45, the first emphasis added to the English translation). In order to account for the 'faculty of mind' Kierkegaard calls 'spirit', as a sense of distance from the finite world, we must allow for both a widening and a transforming of the contexts in which it makes sense to talk of privation (the root sense of the German *Not* here translated 'torment') and correspondingly of refuge or restitution. Thus, beyond the inhibiting of behaviour, we have to focus on the *expansion* in or of a person's consciousness which occurs 'in conjunction with his power to dissociate his inclinations from their immediate natural expression' ([24], p. 82). The solitary individual's cry of torment to which Wittgenstein refers is of course *not* a natural expression, but a manifestation of sensibility possible only for an expanded consciousness involved in a complex and many-levelled relationship with its environment.

These remarks indicate a way of linking Kierkegaard's thought to a discussion in philosophy of mind that has flagged somewhat in recent years. Attention to Kierkegaard might help to revive it. They also define an area where the question of the status of the ethico-religious framework might be fruitfully discussed without prejudice or prior commitment. Hitherto work within or on the expanded consciousness of the 'spiritual' faculty has tended to place itself, and be placed, outside the thronging publicity of the philosophical mainstream. Some of the best of it has appeared in journals of religion and theology (see, e.g., Roberts [28]). It will be interesting to see what developments, or what expansions of the general philosophical consciousness, the chronicler of the next decade's work will have to report.

BIBLIOGRAPHY

Bernstein, R.J. [23] Marx and the Hegelian Background *and* Consciousness, Existence, and Action: Kierkegaard and Sartre. In Bernstein, *Praxis and Action: Contemporary Philosophies of Human Activity*, 1971.

Bogen, J. [22] Kierkegaard and the Teleological Suspension of the Ethical. *Inquiry*, 1962.

Cavell, S. [27] Kierkegaard's *On Authority and Revelation*. In Cavell, *Must We Mean What We Say?*, 1976.

Davidson, D. [17] How is Weakness of the Will Possible? In Davidson, *Actions and Events*, 1980.

Dietrichson, P. [22] An Introduction to a Reappraisal of Fear and Trembling. *Inquiry*, 1969.

Donnelly, J. [22] Kierkegaard's "Teleological Suspension of the Ethical". In Donnelly (Ed.), *Logical Analysis and Contemporary Theism*, 1972.

Elrod, J.W. [3] *Being and Existence in Kierkegaard's Pseudonymous Works*, 1975.

Feuerbach, L.A. [20] *Werke* II, 1903-1910.

Hampshire, S. [24] Feeling and Expression. In J. Glover (Ed.), *The Philosophy of Mind*, 1976.

Hegel, G.W.F. [9] *Phenomenology of Spirit*, trans. A.V. Miller, 1977.

— [10] *Faith and Knowledge*, trans. W. Cerf and H.S. Harris, 1977.

— [15] *The Philosophy of History*, trans. J. Sibree, 1900.

— [16] *Enzyklopädie der philosophischen Wissenschaften im Grundrisse (System der Philosophie, Sämtliche Werke*, Vols. VIII, IX, and X, 1927-1930).

Kierkegaard, S.A. [7] *Philosophical Fragments or a Fragment of Philosophy*, 1962, present author's trans. and references to *Samlede Værker*, Vol. 6, 1963.

— [11] *Concluding Unscientific Postscript to the Philosophical Fragments*, 1941, present author's trans. and references to *Samlede Værker*, Vol. 9 (1) and Vol. 10 (2), 1963.

— [13] *The Concept of Anxiety*, 1981, present author's trans. and references to *Samlede Værker*, Vol. 6, 1963.

— [14] *The Sickness unto Death*, 1954, present author's trans. and references to *Samlede Værker*, Vol. 15, 1963.

— [21] *Fear and Trembling*, 1954, present author's trans. and references to *Samlede Værker*, Vol. 5, 1963.

Mackey, L. [1] *Kierkegaard: A Kind of Poet*, 1971.

Malantschuk, G. [2] *Kierkegaard's Thought*, trans. H.V. and E.H. Hong, 1971.

Nordentoft, K. [19] *Kierkegaards psykologi*, 1972.

Roberts, R.C. [28] Kierkegaard on Becoming an "Individual". *Scottish Journal of Theology* 31. *And* Thinking Subjectively. *International Journal for Philosophy of Religion* 11 (1980): 71-92.

Rorty, Amelie Oksenberg [18] *Akrasia* and Conflict. *Inquiry*, 1980. *And* Belief and Self-deception. *Inquiry*, 1972. See these works for further references.

Russell, B. [22] What is the Ethical in Fear and Trembling? *Inquiry*, 1975.

Santurri, E. [22] Fear and Trembling in Logical Perspective. *Journal for Religion and Ethics*, 1977.

Searle, J.R. [25] What is an Intentional State? *Mind*, 1979. *And* The Intentionality of Intention and Action. *Inquiry*, 1979.

Shmuëli, A. [12] *Kierkegaard and Consciousness*, 1971.

Strawson, P.F. [6] *Individuals*, 1959.

Taylor, C. [5] *Hegel*, 1975.

Taylor, M.C. [4] *Kierkegaard's Pseudonymous Authorship: A Study of Time and the Self*, 1975.

Wahl, Jean [8] *Études Kierkegaardiennes*, 1938.

Wittgenstein, L. [26] *Culture and Value*, trans. P. Winch, 1980.

Further references may be found in the 'Bibliographical Supplement' to J. Thompson (Ed.), *Kierkegaard: A Collection of Critical Essays*, 1972 (which itself contains essays on a variety of topics some of which touch on the themes mentioned in this chronicle), and in A. Hannay, 'A Kind of Philosopher: Comments in Connection with Some Recent Books on Kierkegaard', *Inquiry*, 1975.

The significance of Freud for modern philosophy of mind

ROBERT K. SHOPE
University of Massachusetts, Boston

The aspects of Freud's thought that have generated the greatest amount of recent philosophical discussion, and have provoked significant critical commentary from various psychoanalysts, are those concerning the nature of the unconscious and its connection with conscious thought and conduct. The most important viewpoints may be conveniently grouped according to the details that they would stress in Freud's famous description of the id:

> We approach the id with analogies: we call it a chaos, a cauldron full of seething excitations... It is filled with energy reaching it from the instincts but it has no organization, produces no collective will, but only a striving to bring about the satisfaction of the instinctual needs subject to the observance of the pleasure principle. The logical laws of thought do not apply in the id, and this is true above all of the law of contradiction. Contrary impulses exist side by side, without cancelling each other out or diminishing each other: at most they may converge to form compromises under the dominating economic pressure towards the discharge of energy. There is nothing in the id that could be compared with negation; and we perceive with surprise an exception to the philosophical theorem that space and time are necessary forms of our mental acts. ([1] *22*, 73-74)

I shall consider four types of reactions to the themes involved in this paragraph, which we may call the materialist/energic/systematic emphasis, the hermeneutical/activity-oriented emphasis, the noumenal emphasis, and the causal/intentionalistic emphasis.

1. THE MATERIALIST/ENERGIC/SYSTEMATIC EMPHASIS

Whether or not Freud's metapsychology lacks utility for clinical work (cf. Gill [2], Klein [3], and Schafer [4, 5]), it is of interest to philosophers as speculative metaphysics. Moreover, the latter is often an early stage of scientific theory development (Bloor [6], Galatzer-Levy [7]).

Nagel [8] points out the double-aspect view contained in Freud's thesis that unconscious mental processes and mental processes of which one is conscious are in themselves physical. Nagel remarks that although definition of a double-aspect view stops short of requiring that the process of being conscious of a mental process itself be physical, Freud did adopt the latter materialist view in his early *Project* ([1], *1*, 311). Nagel observes that contemporary philosophy of mind has neglected this particular version of materialism.

Nagel goes too far when he says that Freud's materialism assumes that a single physical or at least objective character is common to all states having a similar appearance to consciousness, e.g., all desires to kill one's father.[1] Freud may only be maintaining of a *given* person's unconscious desire to kill his father that, were it to become conscious, *that* desire would be identical with the physical state with which the unconscious desire is presently identical (or would be identical with a whole of which the latter forms a part). This makes Freud's views compatible with the type of materialism explored by Davidson [9].

Basch [13] mistakenly regards Freud as a dualist. He stresses Freud's praise for Fechner's view that the "scene of action" of dreams is different from that of waking life ([1] *4/5*, 48, 536). Basch maintains that Freud does not construe this as a remark about physical space because Freud goes on to say that Fechner did not mean a change of location in the brain. Basch is correct only to the extent that Freud would not want to speak of a change of location because he believes that dreams *originate* from latent thoughts of the same type that are already found in waking ideational life. However, Basch illegitimately extends this thesis by claiming that "the thinking behind dreams is not peculiar to dream life." (68) This overlooks the fact that the processes of the dream work which form a transition from the latent dream to the manifest dream are said by Freud to be quite different from the rational thought processes of waking life (e.g. [1] *4/5*, 509). Inspired by Fechner's terminology, Freud assigns the stages of this process to a different "psychical locality" which nonetheless is identical with a literally spatial locality. This reading of Freud is borne out by his use of the phrase "scene of action" in the *Outline* ([1] *23*, 144) and in a surprising speculation that was one of the last passages he ever wrote: "Space may be the projection of the extension of the psychical apparatus. No other derivation is probable. Instead of Kant's *a priori* determinants of our psychical apparatus. Psyche is extended; knows nothing about it." ([1] *23*, 300)

Basch claims that a cultural predilection for Cartesian dualism reasserts itself in Freud's resolution to "remain on psychological ground" and to avoid "the temptation to determine psychical locality in any anatomical fashion." ([1], *4/5*, 536) Basch says that this is an inconsistent decision to "*look* upon the brain *not as* a physical entity, but as a 'mental apparatus,' which seems to mean a brain without anatomical properties, i.e., a *non*anatomical entity carrying out mental functions." (70) (emphasis added) But Basch has failed to bear in mind the difference between two concepts of reference, an error repeated by Thickstun and Rosenblatt ([14], 25-26, [15], 269). As Rorty [16] has emphasized, what a remark is referring to in one sense is merely whatever the speaker is talking about but in another sense is, roughly, the actual items to which the speaker is responding when referring in the first sense. If Freud avoids talking about anatomical properties and structures, that does not prevent him from taking himself to be referring in the second sense to items in different spatial localities.[2]

Basch discusses a passage in which Freud suggests that "we should picture the instrument which carries out our mental functions as resembling a compound microscope." ([1] *4/5*, 536) It is noteworthy that an analogy is involved at the end of this suggestion, not the beginning. Freud says that the systems of the mental apparatus are to be distinguished from our "ideas, thoughts, and psychical structures in general" and that the systems "are not in any way psychical entities themselves and can never be accessible to our psychical perception." ([1] *4/5*, 611) They are "like the lenses of the telescope [or microscope], which cast the image," whereas any psychical entity that "can be an object of our internal perception is *virtual*, like the image produced in a telescope by the passage of light rays." ([1] *4,5*, 611) Basch chides Freud for overlooking the fact that an image is not an entity in the telescope but is instead a phase of the viewer's sensory cortex. (71) However, the point of the analogy is that early stages of light transmission in the telescope have the potential, if continued in a normal fashion, to result in things appearing to a viewer which are never located in pieces of the instrument; similarly, early stages of certain mental processes have the potential to result in consciousness of a psychic entity which also is never in pieces of the nervous system affecting the process.

Freud says that "strictly speaking there is no need for the hypothesis that the psychical systems are *actually* arranged in a spatial order," in the way that the system of lenses in a telescope are arranged "behind one another." ([1] *4/5*, 537) But he explains that this means that different psychical processes might move through the psychical systems in different temporal sequences, in contrast to the fixed sequence in which light passes through the lenses of the telescope to the eye. Moreover, just as it is light but not a virtual image which moves through the telescope, Freud says that what is "mobile" in dream formation is "excitation" rather than a psychical structure or entity. Thus, each stage of a given sequence is one in which the exitation "has come under the sway" of a particular system..." ([1] *4/5*, 610). (For further citations see Solomon [17].)

In the *Interpretation of Dreams*, Freud attempts to justify the metaphysical assumptions underlying these analogies by claiming that they explain more than they originally described. For the regressive movement of excitation during dreams from the motor end to the perceptual end of the apparatus would require passage through various "mnemic systems" to those closest to the perceptual end. It would explain the relative loss of logical relations in the representation of the dream-thoughts by the manifest dream, since memory traces of logical relations are laid down in mnemic systems further from the perceptual end. ([1] *4/5*, 543) Whether or not this argument for his theory is methodologically suspect, it does reveal that memory traces are treated as aspects of the systems rather than as ideas, thought, or psychic entities succeptible to introspection. As I have explained elsewhere (Shope [18]), the very concept of a memory trace, e.g., a memory trace of a past occurrence, requires that in recollecting we become conscious not of the memory trace itself but of the past. Any imagery in which the past is consciously represented during our recollection must be regarded as at most partly caused by the trace, rather than identical with it. (Freud was not always careful to respect this requirement; e.g. [1] *23*, 199, 266.)

Our discussion of the telescopic analogy alerts us to the fact that Freud's reference to a seething cauldron carries with it not just the image of the contents of the vessel, e.g., currents of liquid and bits of material against and around which the currents swirl, but also the image of the cauldron's walls, comparable to the sides of the telescope and perhaps its outermost lens. But the latter analogy was intended in discussing the passage from one system to another, so when dealing only with the metaphysics of the id, a different analogy may be useful.

Freud used many analogies in his writings (Thalberg [19]), often biological ones. Indeed, Gill agrees with Schafer [5] that talk of psychic energy and systems is "a derivative of infantile psychosexual fantasies in which the mind is equated with an organ that can ingest, retain, and excrete substances." (Gill [20], 588) As Swanson [21] points out, such an origin does not by it-self prove that metapsychology is unjustifiable as a theory. In any event, the metaphysics of the id does seem to be illuminated by an analogy to a digestive organ, such as the stomach. The analogy will also help to clarify a point that certain psychoana-lysts regard as an inconsistency, namely, that there are some respects in which Freud's description of the id treats it as un-structured and other respects in which structure is ascribed to it.

Just as the gastric juices swirl about food in the stomach, leading to the collision of one piece of food with another, so the mobile cathexes of psychic energy in the id are supposed to help account for mental sequences in the id, where, thanks to the presence of the energic "currents," the activity of one wish, idea, or fantasy brings about the activity of another or its formation from elements of the others. The activity of the successor, in turn, continues the sequence, depending always upon what additional currents may impinge. However, relative to the arrangement created by the chef who prepared the meal, the bits of food now display interrelations that are chaotic, just as, relative to rational thought processes aimed at problem-solving, the sequences in the id are chaotic, reflecting no uniform will. The id is "as we might say, 'all to pieces'." ([1] *23*, 196)

Successful prediction of the collisions of food in the stomach would depend upon knowing the order involved in the muscular motions of the stomach walls and the secretions of new quantities of gastric fluids through those walls. This is akin to detailed information that the psychoanalyst lacks concerning processes in the 'walls' of the 'cauldron' and the influence of the instincts on the id. Given this metaphysics, Freud's commitment to classical determinism was preserved (cf. [1] *23*, 148), even though a requirement for the correctness of Freud's metapsychology is that Freud's "science" be incapable of predicting the phenomena which it explains unless supplemented by some other science.

In one of his earliest critiques of metapsychology, Schafer [22] maintained that there are two concepts of psychic energy in Freud's writings: psychic energy as a scalar quantity, and as a substance. But Schafer relied on a single passage from Freud in attributing the former concept to him, a passage which explicitly speaks only of instincts. So we need to consider the connection in Freud's metaphysics between energy and instincts.

The most consistent reading of Freud's view on the instincts (exclusive of Eros and Thanatos themselves) seems to me to be the following. An instinct is a phylogenetic modification in the living substance ([1] *14*, 120) that is a stimulus or force making a (supposedly constant) impact on the mind (*14*, 118) It has a separate organic basis (*14*, 118) or somatic source of stimulation concerned with one's major somatic needs, of which it is the mental representative or mental expression (*14*, 122; *20*, 200; *12*, 74; *7*, 168) Its representatives, in turn, within the psychic apparatus are wishes, that is, ideas of actions or of states of affairs cathected with psychic energy (part of which may become detatched and is called a quota of affect). (*14*, 152) It is by bringing about such representatives in the id that an instinct may be said to "operate in" the id. (*23*, 197; cf. 145 and *22*,

197) Although Freud sometimes speaks of instincts as "in" the id (e.g., *20*, 200; *23*, 145), he warns that this is a misleading expression since "in the unconscious ... an instinct cannot be represented otherwise than by an idea." (*14*, 121-22)

Thus, what Freud means by speaking of the concept of an instinct as a "concept on the frontier between the mental and the somatic" (*14*, 121-22) is that an instinct causally mediates between processes out in the body, which relate to biological requirements, and events within the portion of the nervous system that is the psychic apparatus, or more particularly, the id. That is, an instinct is a representative *of* somatic processes *to* the mind – a frontier concept in that the analysis of the concept mentions both the mental and the somatic. Since it does mention mental effects of the instinct, it is less misleading to call the instinct mental than to call it somatic, even though it is not an introspectible psychic entity within the apparatus.

A crucial question is whether it is conceptually required that we invoke a concept of psychic energy in order to speak of a given instinct as a "measure" of the demand made on the mind for "work" because it is connected with somatic phenomena. (*14*, 122) Freud did take this step, but not, as Schafer implies, by treating an instinct simply as a scalar quantity. For that would have destroyed any causal role for an instinct. Instead, Freud says that "we picture it as a certain quota of energy *which presses in a certain direction*." (*22*, 96) In the very essay that Schafer mentions, Freud maintains that this "motor factor" is the very "essence" of an instinct. (*14*, 122) It accounts for why an instinct (and not merely a wish) is sometimes called an instinctual impulse even though only its representatives fall within the id. (*14*, 177)

Thus, throughout his career, Freud thought of excitation in terms of the second concept of psychic energy mentioned by Schafer, always comparing it to, although not identifying it with, "an electric charge" spread over a surface, or to "a fluid electric current." (*3*, 60) Actual electric charges and currents are constituted not by pure physical energy but by particles possessing the energy, which makes those particles able to do work and accounts for their exerting physical forces. In the case of static charge, these are forces that come from the location of the larger body over whose surface the charge is spread, and this allows us to speak of the body itself as exerting force. In addition, it is not unusual to speak somewhat loosely of something that exerts a force as itself being a force. So Freud's analogy leads to a metaphysics in which one speaks of an idea within the psychic apparatus as being a causal force, thanks to the psychic energy with which that idea is cathected. One also speaks of instincts outside the psychic apparatus as forces that causally influence it, even though they are 'portions' of psychic energy without ideational content. Some of the 'pooled' energy moves into the id and adheres to ideas (cf. *14*, 152; *20*, 200) analogously to the injection of gastric fluid through the walls of a digestive organ.

Solomon [17] maintains that Pribram [23] has persuasively compared cathexis to the graded nonimpulsive activities of neural tissue, but Swanson [21] has shown that there are important disanalogies.

Some charge that psychic energy theory is *inconsistent*. For example, Schur [24] wonders how Freud could have spoken of a permanent reservoir of libido. But a cauldron may, *à la* Heraclitus, be always filled without always containing the same fluid. Yet to treat the psychic apparatus as an open system has been said by Thickstun and Rosenblatt [14] to contradict conservation laws for psychic energy. Applegarth [25] and Galatzer-Levy [7] offer replies to this type of objection. Horowitz [26] suggests that the apparent contradiction between Freud's different conservation principles may be resolved if they apply to different stages of one's development.

Galatzer-Levy argues that a number of *obscurities* concerning psychic energy may be due to a relatively early stage of theory development. But Thickstun and Rosenblatt [27] emphasize the obscurity of the fate of the energy after discharge, and Applegarth [25] admits that revising the concept of discharge so that it means what Klein [28] calls turning off a drive at its source will require further metapsychological revisions.

Holt [29] argues that Freud's concept of psychic energy is *methodologically* self-defeating because the view that there are different qualities and aims of psychic energy prevents Freud from conforming to his antivitalist metaphysical goals. I have attempted (Shope [30]) to improve Rubinstein's tentative reply [31] that the energy may be "quasi-directional" in the sense that a given type of energy has a "specific affinity for" one type of mental structure, e.g., one type of wish. The affinity might be a basic objective propensity lacking further explanation, or, as the above discussion allows, might be explained by non-introspectible aspects of the id or by the history of the portion of energy, e.g., the sources from which it springs or the path it takes to the instincts. (See Thickstun and Rosenblatt [14], 18 regarding the relevance of historical variables in explanations.)

However, I have argued (Shope [30]) that there are enough *disanalogies* between the concept of energy in physics and the concept of psychic energy to show that the latter is not a concept of energy at all. Thus, the appeal of Freud's metaphysics ought not to trade upon the successful use of the concept of energy in the natural sciences. For example, the concept of energy in psychoanalysis does not relate to the concepts of work and force in the way it does in physics, where the technique called "dimensional analysis" requires that *all* forms of energy have the *dimensions* of work, where work can be *measured* in terms of a force exerted through a distance. (Solomon [17] has misunderstood this point and has charged that I was concerned only with mechanical energy.) Schafer [22] notes that physics does not treat a given variety of energy as varying in degrees of its qualities independently of its quantity.

Because of all these disanalogies, we cannot agree with Solomon that psychic energy terminology provides a neutral, monistic vocabulary which refers "without distinguishing — in sense or reference — neurological from psychological predicates." ([17], 51)

Thickstun and Rosenblatt [14, 15], Swanson [21], and Wallerstein [32] have protested the *ad hoc* nature of explanations mentioning psychic energy, the inability of such explanations to cover all relevant data (such as the existence of pleasurable tension in sexual foreplay), and the fact that the explanations have little clinical use since they can at most allows the prediction that paths of discharge are likely to be the same paths taken in the past.

Galatzer-Levy [7] has responded that psychic energy theory need not be clinically illuminating in order to be true. But an additional objection may be made to the theory even when it is viewed as speculative metaphysics. An interesting metaphysics at least contains arguments justifying one application of its concepts to a higher degree than competing applications of the very same concepts. But Freud is content, for example, after adumbrating the view in the *Interpretation of Dreams* that dreams are wish-fulfillments because they discharge psychic energy, to shift almost off-handedly to the claim that they either discharge *or bind* the energy of the unconscious wish when they prevent it from disturbing sleep. ([1] *4/5*, 578) Commentators have shown that within psychoanalytic theory the mere fact that a force is blocked does not reveal whether it has been reduced in strength. (Shope [33], 436, Thickstun and Rosenblatt [15], 275; [27], 539-41) I have argued (Shope [33, 34]) that psychoanalysts have not provided ways of supporting claims about the energy processes involved in wish-fulfillment to a higher degree than contrary or contradictory claims involving the same energic terminology.

2. THE HERMENEUTICAL/ACTIVITY–ORIENTED EMPHASIS

Some philosophers and psychoanalysts seek to characterize the clinically significant sense of "unconscious" without resort to energic and systematic terminology, or at least without regarding such terminology as more than metaphorical.

One approach, taken by Solomon [35] and Smythe [36], is to explain the concept of unconsciousness by appealing to a dispositional type of analysis, for example, the treatment of wants and desires taken by Brandt and Kim [37]. (Also see Shope [38].) Solomon says that if we avoid a Cartesian emphasis on immediacy as well as the spatial metaphor of a motive's "entering" consciousness, we can treat having a motive as having a complex disposition toward various activities of thought, feeling, and behavior. He adopts an epistemological definition of "unconscious" motives: they are motives whose ascription best explains their possessor's behavior, feelings, or thoughts but are not among the possessor's self-ascribed motives. However, Solomon's definition runs afoul of Smythe's point that we may accept the compulsive hand-washer's report that he *does want* to wash his hands. Moreover, as Radden [39] emphasizes, there are cases where a person does something out of an unconscious motive, or is affected by it, where the person is at the time aware of having the motive, thanks to having reached "a state of familiarity with his or her unconscious mind which would obviate the necessity of his or her carrying out any reasoning or inference in order to assert the presence" of the motive. (27) (This point also tells against Cheney [40], 529, Collins [41], and against one of Audi's characterizations of unconscious wants and beliefs [42], 446n.) Because the person's familiarity with unconscious motives originates in therapy, we might be tempted to avoid Radden's objection by requiring that the possessor of an unconscious motive not *originally* know of its presence on the basis of evidence. But Radden points out that the unconscious motive might originally have been a conscious one and known to be present not on the basis of evidence, yet thereafter have become unconscious. (27-28)

The main difficulty with the above interpretations is that they at best capture the pre-Freudian notion of a preconscious mental state. (also see Cheney [40]) Smythe makes a gesture at overcoming this limitation by adding that repressed unconscious wishes and desires "require more trouble and effort to come to know." ([36], 418) Alternative suggestions are that they cannot be brought into consciousness by any "normal" means (MacIntyre [43]), or that becoming aware of unconscious mental states requires "unusual" effort (Mullane [44]), or requires the assistance of "special techniques" (Alexander [45]). But none of these suggestions fit Freud's famous parapraxis of forgetting the name "Signorelli," which Freud described as an example in which memory of the name was repressed because of its associations with other repressed materials and was involved in the production of some conscious associations during his efforts to remember, yet returned to consciousness when a friend told him the name. ([1] *3*, 290 ff.) (One can even imagine that the name was provided to Freud without his requesting it.) Here, the means of return to awareness hardly seem abnormal or effortful.

This particular example could be dealt with by incorporating in the definition of an unconscious mental state the requirement that one cannot come to know oneself to be in that mental state without either the help of another person or at least some special self-scrutiny. (Audi [42], 447) But it is not clear that even this captures Freud's intent, since Freud could just as well have recalled Signorelli's name thanks to being prompted by a mere record of it. In addition, the term "special" is extremely vague, and could only deal with Radden's cases, mentioned above, if it were construed as allowing for earlier therapeutic priming.

Cases like the Signorelli example also put a severe strain on the attempt by some philosophers to interpret unconscious mental states as ones involving self-deception. Freud says that in such examples one does know that one has the memory of the name even while the actual name is not recalled. ([1] *15/16*, 110) In addition, these are examples where one does not believe the opposite of the repressed information. Those who speak of self-deception regarding what is unconscious says that what is involved in becoming conscious of such items is abandoning the guise of not disclosing certain things to oneself; yet they also speak of the person as one who for a while "cannot" abandon this guise. (Dilman [46]; Fox [47]) One might attempt to deal with this modal element by attributing some motive for forgetting to the person, e.g., the motive of avoiding topics which have painful personal associations. (However, see Cioffi [48].) But the irresistibility of the motive would need to be clarified. In addition, as Radden notes, the motives for some self-deceptions might not be so strong. She also points out that this analysis, rather than characterizing the *status* of, e.g., the memory of the forgotten name, instead speaks of the activity of the person. Indeed, Freud postulates repression in order to explain the unconscious status of a mental phenomenon, rather than including it (as Brenner [49] and Carrella [50] do) in the very definition of "unconscious." Mullane [44] disputes the possibility of regarding repression as an activity of the person. It is also unclear how the concept of self-deception allows us to deal with Radden's cases of realizing that the unconscious state is present thanks to familiarity with one's own neurosis.

Radden doubts that there is any phenomenologically distinct state, such as a special feeling, that always accompanies a conscious mental state and whose absence would help us to define an unconscious mental state. But she suggests that if we follow Freud in appealing to an ordinary sense of the phrase, "conscious of," and do not confuse it with the sense of "conscious that," we may say that one infallibly knows that a mental state of which one is conscious *is* a state of which one is conscious. She calls this a "quality" of our awareness of the state, and defines unconscious mental states as ones that we cannot become conscious of "at the time at which the behaviour and states which they are introduced to explain are occurring, except in a way which is always qualitatively distinguishable from the way in which we are aware of our ordinary conscious mental states." (Radden [39], 34) Regrettably, this definition has the flaw of applying to a mental state only at the time it gives rise to the behavior or other activity it explains. Dropping the temporal qualification from the definition would, of course, incorrectly entail that unconscious mental states never return to consciousness because of external prompting, as in the Signorelli example.

Alexander [45], Collins [41], and Mullane [44] have stipulated that unconscious beliefs and desires would be rejected by the person if they were to become conscious. However, we must avoid any such requirement in our definition because of the Signorelli example. In addition, Radden has pointed out that, according to Freud, one possible fate of a previously unconscious desire is that "the patient's personality may be convinced that it has been wrong and may be led into accepting it wholly or in part." (Freud [1] *11*, 28; also see 54)

However, it is useful to seek a conditional definition as an exegesis of Freud's concept, rather than to employ the unnecessarily strong modal language of Radden's definition. To be sure, Freud himself occasionally uses such language, as when he defines a dynamically unconscious mental state as one which (a) is "not in itself and without more ado capable of becoming conscious." ([1] *19*, 15) But at other places Freud characterizes "unconscious" as indicating those mental states (b) "keeping apart from consciousness in spite of their intensity and activity" (*12*, 262), or as states (c) that "do not penetrate into consciousness, however strong they may have become" (*12*, 262).

We may discover a way to coalesce and to clarify these three characterizations by considering why Freud thought that his early hypnotic experiments in France were sufficient to ground a concept of dynamically unconscious mental states independently of special psychoanalytic data. One implication of these experiments, according to Freud, is that "there is knowledge of which the person concerned nevertheless knows nothing," and it is therefore possible that one may know the meaning of one's dream, symptom, or parapraxis but not know that one knows. ([1] *15/16*, 101-102) Cioffi [48] labels this the "self-intimation thesis." He incorrectly regards it as implying that the person stands in a privileged relation to the "explanations" of his condition. But Freud only invokes hypnotic data in order to show that the person knows *de re* the meaning of his condition, but not to show that the person knows it *de dicto*; that is, the person knows certain mental phenomena, *which* happen to be the meaning of his or her condition, but does not know *that* they are the meaning.

Freud argues for this view in two stages. First, mental experiences during a hypnotic trance were something the subject later sincerely denied knowledge of when politely asked to remember, but could report after "urgent pressure" from the hypnotist. ([1] *15/16*, 103) Secondly, we can therefore expect that in the experiments involving post-hypnotic suggestion the subject had a latent memory of his auditory experiences of the hypnotist's order, e.g., "You will open an umbrella when I return to the room." When the hypnotist returned, "the idea of the action," i.e., the idea of opening-the-umbrella, "grew *active*: it was translated into action as soon as consciousness became aware of its presence." (*12*, 261) But its source, which contains the explanation of its timing, remains unconscious, i.e., the idea of opening-the-umbrella-when-the-hypnotist-returns-to-the-room. The latter idea is thus a mental act in that it arose from the mental phenomenon of experiencing the order (cf. *15/16*, 60-61). Yet it is also active and unconscious.

The ideas that Freud describes as unconscious in these examples are said to be "inaccessible" to the subject, but this means that one's trying to become conscious of them by turning one's attention toward them under some description (e.g., 'what I experienced during the trance' or 'what is leading me to do this') is not sufficient for one to become conscious of them. We may contrast this with a case of getting oneself to become conscious of a forgotten name by utilizing free association, where I must "direct my attention to the substitute names, and allow further ideas in response to them to occur to me..." (*15/16*, 110)

One more point extracted from the example of post-hypnotic suggestion will lead us to a clarification of definition (a) above. If we construe the concept of the strength of a conative mental state not in terms of psychic energy but in terms of the extent to which one's behavior involves one in the state of affairs that the mental state is directed toward, then we may say that the idea of opening-the-umbrella-when-the-hypnotist-returns-to-the-room could not be any *stronger* since the person if fully involved in the state of affairs toward which the idea is directed.

Thus, we may offer the following definition of what is dynamically unconscious, yet avoid the use of energic and systematic terminology: *that which is active but would not become conscious merely because of an increase in its strength and/or one's turning attention toward it.*

There has been considerable disagreement concerning the categories of activity to which Freud assimilates symptoms, parapraxes, and dreams. Alston [51] says that Freud's accounts of these phenomena may involve an "in order to" type of explanation. But we shall see that a number of Freud's explanations do not accomodate easily to this model.

Mullane [52] claims that little Hans "exchanges" fear of his father for fear of horses as a means of reducing anxiety (since horses can be more easily avoided) and he thereby also avoids misconduct that would emanate from the former fear. Cioffi [53] calls attention to Freud's remark: "in order to be free from anxiety and danger, 'Little Hans', therefore, imposed a restriction on his ego." ([1] *20*, 126) However, Freud says that symptoms are created in order to avoid the danger situation of which anxiety sounds the alarm, and adds that in infantile zoöphobias "this danger was castration *or something traceable back to* castration." (*20*, 129) (emphasis added) In Hans' case, the phobia was a fear concerning horses which *consciously* helped to avoid the anxiety that Hans would have felt in the *derivative* danger situations of being near a horse. This concerns the "phobia proper," which Freud calls the "second phase" of the neurosis, occurring later than the original outbreaks of anxiety about horses. (*14*, 155) Freud regards the danger of castration itself as avoided because Hans' erotic and aggressive impulses are repressed.

Cioffi [53] cites a later work in which Freud speaks of an

agorophobic as displacing fear of unconscious feelings of temptation that arise on the street. Freud says that the patient gains
something because "he thinks he will be able to protect himself
better in that way." ([1] *22*, 84) But Freud only says this after
noting that the phobia is ensuent upon situations in which the
patient has "invariably" proved afraid while on the street. Thus,
Freud may be concerned with a "misconstruction by the preconscious" involved in the patient's attempt to discern the source of
the anxiety common to those frequent attacks. (Freud [54], 184;
see [1] *3*, 54, 81, and Cheney [40], 521)

One way of attempting to locate an instrumental aspect in
Hans' phobia would be to regard it in the fashion that Mischel
[55] regards obsessional actions. Mischel says that when a neurotic performs the obsessive act of lunging at a lamp-post with an
umbrella, the neurotic unconsciously identifies the act with
killing his father: "killing him ... is what the neurotic takes himself to be doing *in* lunging at lamp-posts." (75) I have previously
criticized Mischel's approach to obsessive action. (Shope [33])
Applied to Hans' phobic action, Mischel's view might have various
interpretations: (a) Hans unconsciously forms the irrational belief
that horses are his father and that being bitten (or: being bitten by
a horse) is being castrated; Hans unconsciously infers that avoiding
horses will be more likely to fulfill his desire to avoid castration;
(b) Hans forms the unconscious irrational belief that the following
conditional is true: 'If Hans were to be bitten by a horse then that
would be being castrated by Hans' father'; Hans unconsciously
infers that avoiding horses will make it more likely that the antecedent of the conditional not be fulfilled, and thereby accord
with his desire to avoid castration; or (c) Hans has the disposition
to react to perceiving the approach of a horse by forming the unconscious belief that it is his father coming to castrate him; Hans
avoids the former situation in order to fulfil his desire to avoid
castration. (In Mischel [56], interpretation (a) or (b) seems to
be proposed, cf. 221.)

But it is doubtful that anyone can intelligibly be said to hold
the beliefs described in (a), which entail believing that a plurality
(horses) is a single item (Father). All three interpretations have
the type of defect that I have pointed out (Shope [33]), namely,
they attribute beliefs to Hans which Freud never describes as

reaching consciousness in the course of analysis. Moreover, Freud says that the idea of the father's aggression against Hans is subjected to the "mechanism" of displacement, thanks to fortuitous associations that occurred in Hans' experience and the fact that his father and horses belong to the more general class of animals which are both envied and feared. Hans' conflict due to ambivalence is "circumscribed, as it were," when one of the conflicting impulses is "directed to" the substitute object. ([1] *20*, 103) Here, Freud is saying that Hans' impulse to undergo aggression from his father is replaced in consciousness by Hans' phobic impulse (and may also be speaking of energy transfer from the one to the other) rather than considering the unconscious inferences or beliefs indicated in (a), (b), or (c). (Also see [1] *1*, 255-256; [54], 211.)

Another Freudian explanation that is difficult to fit into the mold of unconscious means-end thinking is the Rat-man's obsessive slimming, and its immediate precursor, his obsessive conscious idea that he was too fat (in his native German, *"dick"*) and must make himself thinner. This thought occurred while his lady was in the company of his cousin, Richard, known in his circle as "Dick," of whom the patient was very jealous. An instrumentalist reading might prompt us to suppose that Freud attributes to the Rat-man unconscious beliefs, such as the belief that getting rid of fat is a means to getting rid of his cousin, or that replacing feelings of jealous rage with pains of physical exertion will make life more bearable.

Wollheim [57] objects to the first possibility by claiming that when the Rat-man engages in his regime he is "thereby attacking Richard" in an infantile frame of mind where he is simply unable to distinguish between "acting upon" or "expressing" a desire and, instead, gaining the desired state of affairs. (89, 91) But, as Cioffi [53] has objected, Freud says that the Rat-man's obsessive thought springs from an unconscious desire to kill himself, and that the latter is a defensive impulse against the extreme unconscious hostility which he bears toward his cousin. Thus, Wollheim's criticism of the means-end interpretation is inappropriate.

The slimming obsession is actually one of those obsessive symptoms that are, according to Freud, not substitute satisfactions but a reaction against a repressed impulse. (Freud [1] *20*, 112) Indeed, Freud says that when one is subject to a given type of obsessional symptom, for some time there is an "absence of discharge." (*14*, 185) The Rat-man's suicidal impulse is disguised in the slimming obsession. However, Freud does not impky that the Rat-man believed that losing fat is itself a means toward suicide. Freud explains the detail of the disguise as due to the fact that a word, in this case, "*dick*," is "recklessly employed ... for the purpose of establishing a connection between unconscious thoughts ... and symptoms." (*10*, 189n)

Cioffi [53] says that the slimming compulsion "directly" expresses the self-murderous impulse. (185) However, the obsessive *thought* that set off the strenous self-harmful efforts did not contain the idea of self-harm. Accordingly, commentators who wish to avoid treating the association between "*dick*" and "Dick" as merely leading to a detour where one idea occurs in consciousness instead of another would place weight on Wollheim's suggestion that getting rid of fat "signified" something for the Rat-man. ([57], 89) Thus, we need to consider the possibilities, mentioned by Cioffi [48], that the symptom is an attempt to satisfy a *higher-order* desire, perhaps, (i) a desire to represent or to portray another desire, or (ii) a desire to represent or to portray a desired state of affairs, or, as Radden [39] suggests, (iii) a desire to express — in some ordinary sense of that term — some other desire, even if not to represent or to portray it.

These possibilities must be distinguished from those against which I have previously argued (Shope [33]), namely, that symptoms involving marked displacement or "forced" associations are attempts to satisfy or to fulfill, in some ordinary non-technical sense, the *first-order* desires mentioned above. However, in arguing against the latter thesis, I pointed out that only the incorporation of additional background information, usually including additional beliefs on the part of the patient, would bring the examples close to what in an ordinary sense we can call fulfilling, partly fulfilling, or disguisedly fulfilling the desire. A similar point might be made concerning several of the possibilities mentioned above, which require the *ad hoc* attribution of beliefs to patients that cannot be made conscious by means of therapy.

Ricoeur presents an important and complex referential account of all neurotic behavior, parapraxes, and dreams, which contains a "hermeneutical" emphasis (in one of several sense that he gives the term): these phenomena are purportedly a kind of indirect language whose hidden reference is is the task of interpretation to articulate. Ricoeur [58], 317) Ricoeur agrees ([59], 307) with Lacan's remark ([60], 147) that a symptom is structured like a language whose speech must be realized. Both living metaphors in everyday speech and neurotic symptoms are instances of "the fantastic," for they issue from the work of the productive imagination in Kant's sense) in finding a figure for a second sense of an utterance or an action having an initial, literal sense. ([58], 212-15; [59], 316-19) The fact that there is no analogue in a symptom to the role played by the copula in a metaphorical statement, and thus no parallel to the predicative function that Ricoeur assigns the latter ([58], 245 ff.) may be why Ricoeur relates the reference connected with symptoms to the wider class of signs that he calls (in a non-Freudian sense) "symbols," where an overt sense designates or refers to a second *sense*. ([61], 12, 15, 16) The second sense concerns predicates relevant to a second domain of life even though the symptom may not be *applying* the predicates to anything in that domain.[3]

Ricoeur compares a symptom's representing unconscious contents to the Leibnizian monad's expressing the universe. ([61], 455) He regards Freud's theory of wish-fulfillment as important because "seeking to attain a goal or to satisfy a desire is what we fully understand as the veritable axiom that governs our whole comprehension of human action." (Ricoeur [59], 301)[4] The distortion in dreams and symptom formation is something to which the person "submits ... in order to accomplish by deception the aims of wish-fulfilment." ([62], 184-85) But Ricoeur defends the latter point by regarding the axiom in question in a quite special way. He construes wish-fulfillment not in the sense of the attainment of a desired state of affairs but instead in Husserl's sense of the fulfillment of a "signifying intention." ([61], 30) Partial wish-fulfillment is thus compared to a monad's attaining part of the "perception" toward which it tends. ([61], 455-56)

Ricoeur defends his reading of Freud by numerous citations, some of which I have previously disputed (Shope [63]). Among those which deserve further discussion are the following:

(1) Freud and Breuer assert ([1] 2, 5) that "symbolization"

occurs in both hysterical symptoms and healthy dreams. Ricoeur says that this view is extended to the whole field of repression when hysterical symptoms are treated as "mnemic symbols" of traumatic memories. ([61], 97; [59], 298-99)

But Freud says that symbolization is not present in all hysterical symptoms and requires a different degree of hysterical modification. (2, 176, 178) When present it is a relation in which a bridge is made between the trauma and the symptom by means of words consciously thought during the trauma. In an example of genuine symbolization, as in the case of Frau Cäcelie (2, 179 ff.), "it is as though there were an intention to express the mental state by means of a physical one, and linguistic usage affords a bridge by which this can be effected." (3, 34) However, one must not overlook Freud's intentional inclusion of the phrase, "as though." Breuer described these cases as involving "some ridiculous play upon words or associations by sound" occurring when one's "critical powers are low," which indicates that he was not inclined to regard the similarity in sound as serving an intention to express something. (2, 209, 216)

(2) Freud and Beuer call an hysterical symptom a "mnemic symbol" involved in rememoration, which leads Ricoeur to maintain that the symbol's "significative value" is that it "counts as" the traumatic scene. (Ricoeur [59], 299)

One aspect of a symptom's being a mnemic symbol is its being an undistorted "portion" of a traumatic memory, and its containing "traces of the process to which it owed its origin." (Freud [1] 2, 96, 92; cf. 11, 29) This reveals Freud's reason for not speaking of mnemic symbols in connection with other types of neurosis. (cf. 3, 253) But it does not mean that such symbols refer to the past. (Compare the fact that an unwitting remembrance which one takes to be truly creative does not involve one's referring to or designating the past — see the example concerning a painter in Martin and Deutscher [64] and Shope [18]).

When Freud discussed his sense of the expression, "mnemic symbol," he explained it as labelling something beyond a residue, and as covering a broad genus that includes physical monuments, such as London's Monument to the Great Fire. (11, 16-17) Apparently, mnemic symbols *arise* as part of an *activity* of remembering (cf. 2, 95), in contrast to merely being left over from a past experience (in the way that a concept learned during an experience might be, or a mere *memento* might be, e.g., a brick from a building destroyed in the Great Fire). The symptoms in question often arise later than the trauma, as the patient is consciously remembering the earlier scene, thereby forming part of the patient's "life" of memories. (*2*, 144; cf. 133, 168-69, 173)

(3) Conscious ideas in free associations and symptoms are "in the nature of" an allusion and "like" a representation of the repressed in indirect speech, and they may be compared to allusions made in a joke. (*11*, 30-31)

However, Freud warns that we cannot expect to find in jokes the very same characteristics of the ideas in free association, and only says that they involve a common "motive" for not producing the unspoken idea. (*11*, 31) He goes on to say that the conscious idea in free association is in an indirect fashion "dependent on" the repressed material. (*11*, 32)

(4) A mnemic symbol "may be replaced by a discourse – a pain in the leg, for example, may be equivalent to a linguistic expression of the relation between the patient's desire and the paternal figure." (Ricoeur [59], 299) This translation is like interpreting a dream by assigning a meaning to it, in Freud's words, "replacing it by something which fits into the chain of our mental acts as a link having validity and importance equal to the rest." (*4*, 96)

But in my earlier discussion (Shope [63]) I pointed out that to say a symptom is a stand *in*, i.e. something that occurs because a wish is not consciously admitted, or, in Ricoeur's words, something that occurs in place of "what the desire would say could it speak without restraint" ([61], 15), is not to say that the symptom stands *for* the (content of) the wish in the sense of referring to it.

There I extracted from Freud's works four main characterizations of what it is for y to be the meaning of x (where x is a conscious or manifest state): (i) x occurs at least partly because y is not fully conscious or manifest (i.e., x is a substitute for y); (ii) y is the combination of the intention(s) or purpose(s) which x serves and x's place in some sequence of mental states; (iii) the same as (ii) and it is true that x is significant (i.e., its occurrence and nature is intelligible relative to certain theories or types of explanations); (iv) y is the (set of) motive(s) for x (in the sense of exciting, instigating causes of x). The referents of "y" will be the same in all these characterizations, given the same value for x. (Shope [63]) So the characterizations may be regarded as indicating either four concepts of meaning that Freud interchanges or aspects of a single, complex concept of meaning. (See Rubinstein [65] regarding non-Freudian concepts of meaning.)

What remains to be clarified is Freud's exact thought when speaking in (ii) of desires or purposes "served" by x. This is the point at issue in many of the discussions I have been considering and is not decided by Ricoeur's citations of Freud's remarks on meaning.[5]

Ricoeur says that displacement and condensation do not unfold within "the milieu of discourse," but are "mechanisms" tempting us to use energic and quasi-physical metaphors to describe them because they concern unconscious processes that are "desymbolized by the situation of repression." ([59], 303) But even if the deepest links in these processes only involve what Freud calls "thing presentations" rather than "word presentations," Ricoeur emphasizes that they do involve ideational content and at least fall within a semiotic or semiological system, "if by this we understand everything concerning relations of internal dependence between signs or components of signs." ([62], 86) But in order to present Freud's viewpoint as operating within a "space of phantasy," Ricoeur needs to keep condensation and displacement as clase as possible to linguistic phenomena, e.g., comparing the former to "a form of abbreviation (lacanism)" and the latter to issues concerning "the distribution of elements as a function of a central point or a focal idea." ([59], 303-304) This treatment of condensation does not succeed in distinguishing a dream containing separate images of separate facial features, say, of various relatives, from a dream image containing a single composite of those features. Nor does the description of displacement account for the fact that the content of a fetish may be something the person simply happened to see in childhood simultaneously with glimpsing the parental genitals. It is not clear how the conscious misremembering in the Signorelli incident when the names "Botticelli" and "Boltrafio" come to Freud's mind involves imagination or phantasy. Nor does Freud's failing to remember the proper name lend itself to such a description.

Indeed, Ricoeur seems to acknowledge the difficulty of treating these mechanisms semiotically when he says that what they "achieve is less a distinct relating than a confusion of relations," and he goes on to discuss a dream that "plays upon the homophony" of various words. ([61], 405)

A link involving homophony is one of those connections that Breuer described as involving lowered critical powers, and which Freud says is sometimes the only way to account for the full details of a conscious manifestation, e.g., the Rat-man's focus on his thickness (*dick*) in his obsessive thought rather than on some other content. One might be inclined to understand such an example in the light of Saussure's view of the signifier as an acoustic image, and to say that in the example there are two concepts attached to a single signifier. However, I have discussed (Shope, [33]) a dream modelled on one that Freud describes as involving transition from a latent thought concerning primitive man (*Urmensch*) to a manifest dream image involving the dreamer's father counting off the quarter hours. Freud says that the dreamer made her father into a clock-man (*Uhrmensch*). What is important is that these are Freud's words, not the dreamer's. So neither the dream image nor the dreamer's report of it is a pun. Rather, we have an example that does not comfortably fit into a semiological model concerning indirect reference, but instead some type of model concerning the causal activity of registrations of associated intentional contents (see Section 4, below).[6]

Thus, Ricoeur is forced back onto the fundamental argument that in passages such as the one concerning the id with which we began, Freud applies the same term, "*Repräsentanz*," not only to various derivatives as representatives of repressed desires and memories, and to unconscious desires as representatives of biological instincts, but even to the instincts as representatives of separate bodily sources or processes of stimulation. Ricoeur says that representing is an "irreducible" and "primitive" relation of "standing for" something else, an "intentional connection" that involves "a signifying power that is operative prior to language." ([61], 134-35, 150, 398) I have argued (Shope [63]) that Ricoeur overlooks the alternative possibility of construing Freud's concept of representation in terms of causal mediation among a chain of factors. (Also see Schimek [66], 177n.) (Although I do not concur with all its details, an interesting discussion of causal aspects of representation is found in Stampe [67].) Such a reading meshes with Freud's claims to be developing a science and spares us the obscure notion of one biological state's having an intentional relation to another when neither is even the registration of intentional contents.[7]

Roy Schafer, influenced by Sartre and various British philosophers, notably Ryle, has recently maintained [4, 5] that Freud never relied upon his metapsychological concepts in clinical writings, and did not even need to use substantives such as "desire" and "strength of desire." Without loss of meaning, Freud's explanations are to be recast in a less misleading "action language," referring to one's activities of thought, feeling, and behavior, or sets of such activities, as the person observes rules having the form of Kantian maxims, e.g., 'To do x' or 'To bring about x by doing y.' (cf. [4], 54, 64) Only active verbs (with modifying adverbs for modes of action, e.g., "preconsciously," "unconsciously") are to be used in order to acknowledge responsibility for all one's parapraxes, symptoms, and dreams. For Freud supposedly showed that people "are far more creators and stand much closer to their gods than they can bear to realize." ([5], 153)

Schafer's program suffers from significant internal difficulties. He translates Freud's talk about repressed or inhibited impulses into talk about "conditional actions," saying that "an impulse is an action a person would do were he not effectively refraining from doing it." ([5], 137; cf. 324) But applications of this paraphrase do not coincide with Freud's ascriptions of impulses, such as a desire to kill one's father. The paraphrase commits three fallacies: the *ceteris paribus* fallacy, the fallacy of irrelevant conditionals, and the conditional fallacy. (Shope [69]) The first fallacy occurs because father might successfully resist the attempt to kill him, and because one cannot kill an already deceased father. We may uncover the second fallacy by attending to Cioffi's objection [48] to Wisdom's dispositional view of motivation; Cioffi in effect asks what conditional actions Freud could have attributed to Dora when he ascribed to her a wish for a penis. Schafer's translation commits the third fallacy because there are cases where the truth of the antecedent of the conditional would account for the consequent's being false, e.g., when paralyzing anxiety would occur with the dropping of defense or the patient would repudiate the wish. Elsewhere, Schafer says that a conditional action is an action that "one would perform under other circumstances or at least one anticipates that one would." ([5]), 366) But did Dora believe, even unconsciously, that there were circumstances in which she would beg, borrow, or steal a penis for her very own? (Schafer distinguishes a conditional action from mere fantasizing of the action (cf. [5], 137).)

A second difficulty is that Schafer disregards certain aspects of what Freud meant by speaking of the "sense" of a "mental act." The relevant issues emerge when we notice that even Schafer must admit that actions can stand in relations which are not themselves aspects of actions. For he allows that knowledge or skills may be needed before one can perform certain actions. Consider, then, the exact temporal relation that a performance of one of the latter actions bears to some randomly designated earlier action. This temporal relation need not be intentionally controlled by the person. So other relations, notably causal ones, might occur between past actions and aspects of a present one, e.g., the Rat-man's inclusion of the concept *dick* in his obsessive thought. The connotation that Freud gives to the phrase "mental act" allows this possibility. (Shope [63])

Moreover, I have shown (Shope [70]) that in some parapraxes the interfering intention or desire is what Anscombe [71] calls a "mental cause." Some psychoanalysts have found this interpretation of Freud to be problematic because Anscombe thinks that this type of causation cannot be integrated with more standard conceptions. But we shall see that the details of Freud's account reveal a way of overcoming Anscombe's reservations.

In my earlier discussion (Shope [70]), I emphasized that Freud considers a continuum of parapraxes, one end of which involves everyday examples of fully conscious sources of parapraxes, where the examples are drawn from non-psychoanalytic investigators. In these examples, the following sequence occurs: (a) thinking about or intending or desiring to do one thing; (b) suppressing the desire or thought or reversing or suppressing the intention; (c) deviating from completely or smoothly carrying out some (other) intention, e.g., making a verbal slip. I suggested that when Freud says that the agent will single out (a) as what produced the slip, he is indicating that the agent spots (a) as its mental cause, and cites it in answer to the Anscombian question, "What produced this action or thought or feeling on your part?"

I would now add that (b) involves more than the agent's being aware of (a). It also involves special *attention* focused on (a), often because expressing (a) or carrying it out would conflict with some further concern of the person. Indeed, Anscombe's own examples of mental causes have the property of being something that catches one's attention, or both catches and holds it for a while (cf. Anscombe [71], 15-16). The effects in all her examples involve a shift of content, that is, they involve behavior, feelings, or thoughts whose content or manner is discontinuous with immediately prior behavior. But throughout life the person has witnessed a high correlation between shifts of attention and ensuent discontinuities in the content of the person's thoughts, feelings or behavior.[8] Such statistics are evidence of causal connections (cf. Shaffer [72]).

This offers the beginning of a reply to Skinnerian attacks on so-called "mentalism" in the philosophy of mind. Skinner suggests that when introspection reveals intentions prior to action, one is aware of a probability state, which is a natural phenomenon inside the organism. (Skinner [73], 52, 57, 224) But he challenges us to provide evidence that there is a causal connection between the intention and the ensuent behavior. Whether intentions are objective propensities or instead the activities of which Schafer speaks. Freud has provided such evidence drawn from everyday introspective contexts, where the deviant behavior often is partly identical with the content of the interfering factor.

A third difficulty in Schafer's account concerns his belief that self-deception is involved in all of the special phenomena that Freud purports to explain. In the parapraxes we have just been describing, Schafer would need to add a belief on the part of the person that the deviant aspects of (c) will achieve or satisfy or express (a). But because of the high degree of distortion often involved in the connections of content between (a) and (c), such a belief would be quite irrational and would have to be construed as unconscious. But Freud never says that such a belief becomes conscious (Shope [33]), nor does any strategy of concealing the belief from oneself.

Mischel [56] attempts to interpret defense and repression as intentional activity. He does not settle on a single articulation of his view because he equivocates on the term "conflict." Sometimes he means being distressfully *concerned about* some fact of form f: the content of or circumstances surrounding various emotions, desires, and valuations make it impossible to act on or in accordance with all of them. Accordingly, Mischel says that defense may "resolve" or "avoid" a conflict (233, 235) since concern about f requires at least preconscious awareness of f. However, in a more usual psychoanalytic sense of the term "conflict" (cf. Schafer [4], 98-99), Mischel speaks of the members of the set of emotions, desires, and valuations as forming the conflict even when they are unconscious. This leads him to speak of "fending off" conflict ([56], 235, 249, 253) or impulses (230) or consciousness of anxiety-provoking impulses (249). Most generally, he speaks of an intention to protect oneself from great anxiety that would arise from consciousness of a conflict. (236) Thus, Mischel seems to be attributing to the neurotic the intention: 'To avoid extreme anxiety by taking steps toward not being conscious of various matters,' where the matters in question are elements of a conflict in the standard psychoanalytic sense, and the steps toward such a goal are the various defensive maneuvers.

Mischel again provides various descriptions of additional unconscious beliefs that Freud supposedly attributes to the neurotic (cf. 230-35), but perhaps we may unite them in ascribing a single, complex unconscious belief to the neurotic, roughly, (B_1) 'I would (probably) not be able to resolve concern about some fact of form f before an expression of one of the involved desires, feelings or valuations led to thwarting one of the other ones,' for example, thwarting a desire to avoid castration. In order to deal with "signal anxiety," Mischel will need to speak of a belief (B_2) that certain feelings of anxiety indicate of certain impulses (*de re*) what belief B_1 says of them (*de dicto*).

It is crucial that Mischel will also need to attribute to the neurotic beliefs which are so surprising as to warrant our seeking a different reading of Freud. Mischel quotes freud as speaking of "the intentional reproduction of anxiety as a signal of danger." ([1] *20*, 137-38) Mischel comments that this anxiety "alerts the

ego to an expected danger against which it must defend itself."
([56], 231) This implies that one has intentionally brought about
signal anxiety because one believes it will lead to belief B_2. But
the point of doing this would be to arrive at the shorter belief
mentioned in the description of B_2 regarding the danger related
to certain impulses, feelings or valuations. Yet the latter information was already contained in belief B_1 that helped to initiate the
signal of anxiety. Thus, only a break in the intentionality of this
context at some point could save Mischel's interpretation from incoherence.

It would be too complex to consider here how many of the
forms of defense can be described as forms of self-deception utilizing techniques found in normal thinking. Mischel points out
that Fingarette's view [74] that defense involves refraining from
"spelling something out" will not cover all defense, and he invokes Hamlyn's discussion [75] for a broader perspective.

Neither Mischel's nor Schafer's approaches mesh with the interpretation of Freud's account of phobia formation given above.
Nor do they add any further contributions toward clarifying or
defending the view that dreams, for example, are "archaic, iconic
ways" of saying something which constitutes "a coherent, sensible
statement even if predicated on some fantastic infantile assumptions." (Schafer [4], 41-42)

We may conclude this section by considering Schafer's view
that when Freud said that dreams are the dreamer's responsibility
he based his assertion on an action model of responsibility. (Schafer [5], 233-34) What Freud actually held to be the dreamer's
responsibility was the latent dream, consisting of preconscious
thoughts and repressed wishes. (*19*, 133) The fact that I am the
person who must deal most directly with these wishes does not
entail that their "acting" is my action in the sense of an intentional attempt to guide myself by a maxim.

3. THE NOUMENAL EMPHASIS

Matte Blanco [76] seeks to summarize in non-energic terminology
the principles governing the manner in which the reality of our
psyche manifests itself in primary process thinking, and then to

use these "laws" as grounds for a description of the metaphysical nature of that reality, extending to its manifestations in less irrational phenomena which are not assigned to the id. He takes this to be a return to Freud's view that the unconscious is the "true psychical reality" ([1], *4/5*, 613), a noumenon behind the appearances.

Matte Blanco suggests that this essence of the mental, which he prefers to call "symmetrical being," is never manifested in pure form; each manifestation is also a manifestation of a more rational, "asymmetrical" mode of being that is governed by ordinary logic. The set of "laws" governing thought processes that manifest symmetrical being is the combination of ordinary logic with the following two principles, which he maintains that Freud implied but never openly and systematically states: (I) *The Principle of Generalization*: Treat an individual thing (person, object, concept) as if it were a member or element of a set or class which contains other members; treat this class as a subclass of a more general class, and so on; (II) *The Principle of Symmetry*: Treat asymmetrical relations as if they were symmetrical. ([76], 38)

For example, if I already have the thoughts, (1) "Prison windows have bars," and (2) "The windows of my room have bars and my pyjamas have stripes like the bars of the prison," then the symmetrical mode of being may manifest itself in my inferring or coming to have the thought, (3) "I am in prison." (162) In accordance with (I), both the prison windows and my pyjamas have been treated in thought as members of the class defined by the propositional function, 'x has bars.' And in accordance with (II), the asymmetrical relation 'being a member of' or 'belonging to,' which holds between items in this class and the class itself has been treated as symmetrical. As a result, the class is treated as identical with each member and each member treated as identical with every other. This leads to (3).

Matte Blanco concludes that in its manifestations the symmetrical mode of being never deals with individuals *as* individuals but only with classes. Moreover, because of the identity of the class with each of its members, he argues that the classes in question are infinite sets (which Matte Blanco is not concerned to distinguish from classes), due to Dedekind's definition of an infinite set as one that can be put in bi-univocal correspondence with a proper part of itself. (147)

Not only does this make psychoanalysis a science like no other, but surprising metaphysical consequences supposedly follow. Matte Blanco insists that when Freud attributed timelessness to the unconscious, as he did in our initial quotation concerning the id, timelessness should be understood in a very strong sense, namely, as absence of temporal process. For "the existence of a succession of moments requires serial ordination; and if symmetrical relations are barred [because of principle (II)], according to symbolic logic there can be no such ordination. In other words, succession disappears," and in the unconscious there is literally "no time." (42) Analogous reasoning supposedly shows that symmetrical being is "spaceless," because (II) prevents relations of contiguity between parts of a whole. (40-41)

However, this attempt to extract metaphysical insights from (I) and (II) fails because these "laws" speak only of potential sequences of mental contents and say nothing about the nature of the source of these sequences.

Matte Blanco comes close to admitting this when he points out a certain difficulty in his characterization of the unconscious as infinite sets. Because a member of a set is included in the set, (II) implies that the set is included in the member, "which is not the case in the relation between the whole and the proper part in infinite sets." (147) His solution to this difficulty is to admit that the proper part does not become the whole class but that in describing symmetrical being from the outside we see the proper part "treated as though" it were the whole, and see that the whole and the part are "treated as" infinite sets. (149) But then we also ought not to say that symmetrical being is timeless and spaceless but simply that its manifestations *do not explain* temporal and spatial aspects of (the intentional content of) mental phenomena. In other words, the (contents of the) mental phenomena are "treated as though" they do not concern sequences oriented toward real time and space. The latter aspects are, as it were, ignored.

Matte Blanco initially describes symmetrical being as ineffable and homogenous, because internal differentiations would involve asymmetrical relations. But because (I) and (II) describe "permissible, but not obligatory" ways in which thought sequences may

be affected by symmetrical being (41), he subsequently says that
the unconscious is not homogeneous but is capable of differentiating between sets (as required by (II)), and says that (II) rules
within the set or class. (150) He claims that this ledas to "levels"
of the unconscious, dealing with broader and broader classes in
relation to (I). But it seems to me that this once again conflates
a description of the supposed noumenon with a description of its
presumed appearances.

According to Matte Blanco, (I) and (II) help to explain various
clinical phenomena, such as the extreme terror that may be
evoked in reaction to certain fantasies. For example, because of
the identification of part and whole, a tearing fantasy contains
infinitely many potential realizations of the action of tearing.
(175, 207-208) Since we "directly experience" symmetrical being
even though consciousness cannot contain more than a few of its
manifestations at any moment, these fantasies have tremendous
impact on a patient. However, if each minor tearing possibility
is identified with each extreme one, Matte Blanco's reasoning
allows us equally to say the reverse, and we might just as well
expect patients to remain unperturbed because of a levelling tendency. This difficulty arises because Matte Blanco wishes to
speak of identity without providing suitable means for capturing
the distinction between thoughts of the form, 'If Wagner were
Verdi...,' and 'If Verdi were Wagner...'

Finally, it must be noted that Freud might not have accepted
Matte Blanco's principles as a proper summary of primary process
associative potential (cf. Gill [77]). Matte Blanco admits that a
through-going application of (I) and (II) results in saying that any
conscious content can be linked to any repressed content. For
there will always be some class to which the respective contents
both belong. (106) However, Freud may have rejected such extreme flexibility when he said: "the imagination does not admit
of long, stiff objects and weapons being used as symbols of the
female genitals, or of hollow objects, such as chests, cases, boxes,
etc., being used as symbols for the male one." ([1] *4/5*, 359)

4. THE CAUSAL/INTENTIONALISTIC EMPHASIS

Some of the causal consideration in previous sections can be combined with an understanding of timelessness that Freud confirmed in a letter to Löwenstein: "unconscious wishes remain active until they are brought into consciousness where through the process of thought associations they can be correlated with reality testing." (Panel [78], 131; cf. Freud [1] *6*, 274-75) Similarly, as indicated in the previous section, it is real spatial relations to which the wishes are unresponsive, e.g., even if the patient's father is six feet under the ground, the patient's wish to put him there may persist.

We may expand this approach in order to understand some central threads in Freud's metaphysics of the mind by taking note of his relation to Brentano. Stanescu [79] has suggested that this connection should be explored, and has remarked that Brentano was the only one of Freud's philosophy instructors who is discussed very much in Freud's letters to his young friend, Silverstein. I believe that Freud extended Brentano's conception of mental states as having intentionally inexistent objects by understanding the latter as states of affairs of which there can be "registrations" that partly constitute the presence of wishes, thoughts, and fantasies in the psychic apparatus. This understanding may be significant for those who seek to relate psychoanalysis to information theory (e.g., Basch [13]), or to computer simulation (e.g., Boden [80]), or, perhaps, to Chomskian linguistics (e.g., Edelson [81]).

Suppes and Warren [82] suggest that we may use the concept of *propositions* to discuss the unconscious "within the framework of the use of mathematical models in psychology," so that we may speak of propositions as "representing" thoughts, impulses, or feelings. (405) They point out that in discussing paranoia Freud ([1] *12*, 63 ff.) once "represented unconscious contents by propositions, specifically of the form subject-verb-object," e.g., *I (a man) love him (a man)*. At some points (405-406, 408), they speak as if propositions themselves are in the unconscious and undergo transformations when entering consciousness. At other points, they suggest instead that something which represents a proposition is what is present in the unconscious, for example, they say that a proposition may be "extracted from, or represented by, a memory of a visual scene, or a memory of a sequence of events, with the events being held in memory in terms of visual or auditory but not linguistic expression" (407) But we should not ignore the distinction between propositions and states of affairs (Slote [83]), nor equate either with a trace of an actual state of affairs. I have argued (Shope [18]) that we also should not assume, as many do (e.g., Martin and Deutscher [64]; Thickstun and Rosenblatt [14]), that a trace must be internally a structural analogue of the related state of affairs, but should regard the concept of a trace more broadly, in terms of functional relations. This point may be extended to the more general concept of the "registration" of states of affairs, even those which are not actual states of affairs. (Also see the discussion of registration in Bennett [84].)

This approach may help to explain Freud's autumnal comment that, in spite of his efforts, the essence of the mental remains obscure ([1] *23*, 163), and that entities within the unconscious are something "of which we are totally unable to form a conception..." (*23*, 197) For Brentano's point of view allows us to speak of the *content* of a mental state, yet requires that it be the content of some *type* of state, e.g., a memory, a wish, a fantasy. Freud was able in therapy to follow the threads leading from content to content without ever being quite sure, and perhaps for therapeutic purposes not needing to be sure, what type of mental states possessed each content (see his suggestion that primal fantasies might actually be inherited memories, or his early confusion of seduction fantasies with memories). Nor could he regard his energic speculations as clear enough to characterize the exact causal nature of the various registrations.

Thus, just as Kant said that we can think some concepts, e.g., causality, in relation to his noumenal realm but not flesh them out with a sensory material, so Freud can think unconscious states in terms of their intentional content without thereby delineating their full mental or causal dimensions. At best, Freud achieved only partial gratification of his metaphysical passion: "My life work was aimed at one goal only: to deduce or to guess how the psychic apparatus is constructed and what forces interplay and counteract in it" (quoted in Bernfeld [85]).

218   *R.K. Shope*

NOTES

1. Nagel cites a passage in which Freud expresses the hope of eventually replacing certain psychological terms by physiological or chemical ones.
([1] *18*, 60) But the passage only concerns replacement of phrases
describing *instinctual* changes, and we shall see that Freud envisions a
rather different role for instincts than for desires, thoughts, and affects.
(also see *14*, 78.)
2. Similar sophistication about reference is shown in Freud's treatment of
the philosophical view that what is mental is by definition something
conscious (cf. [1] *8*, 161-62; *19*, 13-14; *23*, 282-83). The possibility
of radical conceptual change that Freud allows concerning what we in
an everyday sense call "mental" is some ways anticipates Rorty's views
on that issue. (see Rorty [10], [11]; for discussion see Shope [12].)
3. Occasionally, Ricoeur says that a symbol designates another "experience" ([61], 13, 19), which might lead to interpretation (ii) above.
4. Ricoeur [59] connects this axiom with Freud's statement that dreams
concern themselves "with attempts at solving the problems with which
our mental life is faced." ([1] *5/6*, 507n) But Freud actually attributes
this concern to the preconscious problem-solving thoughts in the day
residue, and denies that such concern is always present in dreams. (579n)
5. Regarding the dream as a "rebus," see Shope [63].
6. Difficulties for a semiological reading are implicit in Ricoeur's argument
that deep unconscious links are not related in a linguistic system because
in the id there is no negation, doubt or degree of certainty; these characteristics "bear the mark of nonmeaning [*du non-significant*]." ([61],
148) The links connect the "presignifying and the nonsignifying" states
which are constituted by "desire as desire" and which involve "the *sum*
of the Cogito." (454)

    For a discussion of the relevance of Freud to the Cogito and self-
knowledge, see Ricoeur [61], 419 ff., [62], 99 ff.
7. Ricoeur's more recent work [68] seems to move in a causal direction.
See his remarks about the relation of symbols to power, efficacy, and
force, 59-63.
8. Freud says that we can often explain why one detail of a trauma is preserved as the mnemic symbol by pointing out that it caught or held the
patient's attention at some point during the scene, e.g., it was an odor
which broke through a loss of sense of smell due to a heavy cold, or was
a bodily location that got persistently rubbed. (*2, 107, 116, 175)*

BIBLIOGRAPHY

Alexander, P. [45] Rational Behaviour and Psychoanalytic Explanation.
Mind 71 (1962): 326-341. Reprinted in Wollheim [86].

Alston, W. [51] Logical Status of Psychoanalytic Theories. In *The Encyclopedia of Philosophy* 6, pp. 512-516. New York 1967.

Anscombe, G. [71] *Intention*. Ithaca, New York 1963.

Applegarth, A. [25] Comments on Aspects of the Theory of Psychic Energy. *Journal of the American Psychoanalytic Association* 19 (1971) 379-416.

Audi, R. [42] Psychoanalytic Explanation and the Concept of Rational Action. *Monist* 56 (1972): 444-464.

Basch, M. [13] Theory Formation in Chapter VII: A Critique. *Journal of the American Psychoanalytic Association* 24 (1976): 61-100.

Bennett, J. [84] *Linguistic Behaviour*. Cambridge 1976.

Bernfeld, S. [85] Freud's Earliest Theories and the School of Helmholtz. *Psychoanalytic Quarterly* 13 (1944): 341-362.

Bloor, D. [6] Is the Official Theory of Mind Absurd? *British Journal for the Philosophy of Science* 21 (1970): 167-183.

Boden, M. [80] Freudian Mechanisms of Defense: A Programming Perspective. In *Wollheim* [86], pp. 242-270.

Brandt, R., and Kim, J. [37] Wants as Explanations of Actions. *Journal of Philosophy* 60 (1963): 425-435.

Brenner, C. [49] *An Elementary Textbook of Psychoanalysis*. New York 1955.

Carella, M. [50] Psychoanalysis and the Mind-Body Problem. *Psychoanalytic Review* 61 (1974): 53-61.

Cheney, J. [40] The Intentionality of Desire and the Intentions of People. *Mind* 87 (1978): 517-532.

Cioffi, F. [48] Wishes, Symptoms and Actions. *Aristotelian Society Proceedings*, Supplement 48 (1974): 97-118.

– [53] Wollheim on Freud. *Inquiry* 15 (1972): 171-186.

Collins, A. [41] Unconscious Belief. *Journal of Philosophy* 66 (1969): 667-680.

Davidson, D. [9] The Material Mind. In P. Suppes et al. (Eds.), *Logic, Methodology and Philosophy of Science* 4, pp. 709-722. Amsterdam 1973.

Dilman, I. [46] Is the Unconscious a Theoretical Construct? *Monist* 56 (1972): 313-342.

Edelson, M. [81] *Language and Interpretation in Psychoanalysis*. New Haven 1975.

Fingarette, H. [74] *Self-Deception*. New York 1969.

Fox, M. [47] On Unconscious Emotions. *Philosophy and Phenomenological Research* 34 (1973): 151-170.

Freud, S. [1] *Standard Edition of the Complete Psychological Works*. London 1953-1966.

– [54] *The Origins of Psychoanalysis*. New York 1954.

Galatzer-Levy, R. [7] Psychic Energy: A Historical Perspective. *Annual of Psychoanalysis* 4 (1976): 41-61.

Gill, M. [2] Metapsychology is Not Psychology. In M. Gill and P. Holzman (Eds.), *Psychology versus Metapsychology: Psychoanalytic Essays in Memory of George S. Klein*, pp. 71-105. New York 1976.

– [20] Psychic Energy Reconsidered. *Journal of the American Psychoanalytic Association* 25 (1977): 581-597.

– [77] The Primary Process. In R. Holt (Ed.), *Motives and Thought: Psychoanalytic Essays in Honor of David Rapaport*, pp. 260-298. New York 1967.

Hamlyn, D. [75] Self-Deception. *Aristotelian Society Proceedings*, Supplement 45 (1971): 45-60.

Holt, R. [29] Beyond Vitalism and Mechanism: Freud's Concept of Psychic Energy. In B. Wolman (Ed.), *Historical Roots of Contemporary Psychology*, pp. 196-226. New York 1968.

Horowitz, M. [26] The Quantitative Line of Approach in Psychoanalysis: A Clinical Assessment of Its Current Status. *Journal of the American Psychoanalytic Association* 25 (1977): 559-579.

Klein, G. [3] Two Theories or One? In *Psychoanalytic Theory: An Exploration of the Essentials*, pp. 41-71. New York 1976.

– [28] Peremptory Ideation: Structure and Force in Motivated Ideas. In R. Holt (Ed.), *Motives and Thought. Psychoanalytic Essays in Honor of David Rapaport*, pp. 80-128. New York 1967.

Lacan, J. [60] *Ecrits I.* Paris 1966.

MacIntyre, A. [43] *The Unconscious.* London 1958.

Martin, C., and Deutscher, M. [64] Remembering. *Philosophical Review* 75 (1966): 161-196.

Matte Blanco, I. [76] *The Unconscious as Infinite Sets.* London 1975.

Mischel, T. [55] Concerning Rational Behaviour and Psycho-analytic Explanation. *Mind* 74 (1965): 71-78. Reprinted in Wollheim [86].

– [56] Understanding Neurotic Behavior: From 'Mechanism' to 'Intentionality'. In *Understanding Other Persons*, pp. 216-259. Totowa 1974.

Mullane, H. [44] Psychoanalytic Explanation and Rationality. *Journal of Philosophy* 68 (1971): 413-426.

– [52] Unconscious Cleverness. *Scientia* 101 (1966): 329-338.

Nagel, T. [8] Freud's Anthropomorphism. In Wollheim [86], pp. 11-24.

Panel [78] On the Psychoanalytic Theory of Thinking. *Journal of the American Psychoanalytic Association* 6 (1958): 143-153.

Pribram, K. [23] The Neuropsychology of Sigmund Freud. In A. Bachrach (Ed.), *Experimental Foundations of Clinical Psychology*, pp. 442-468. New York 1962.

Radden, J. [39] *Unconscious Wisdom.* Unpublished D. Phil. Thesis, Oxford University 1976.

Ricoeur, P. [58] *The Rule of Metaphor.* Toronto and Buffalo 1977.

– [59] Image and Language in Psychoanalysis. In J. Smith (Ed.), *Psychoanalysis and Language*, pp. 293-324. New Haven and London 1978.

– [61] *Freud and Philosophy: An Essay on Interpretation.* New Haven and London 1970.

– [62] *The Conflict of Interpretations: Essays on Hermeneutics.* Evanston 1974.

– [68] *Interpretation Theory: Discourse and the Surplus of Meaning.* Fort Worth 1976.

Rorty, R. [10] Mind-Body Identity. Privacy, and Categories. *Review of Metaphysics* 19 (1965): 24-54.
– [11] Incorrigibility as the Mark of the Mental. *Journal of Philosophy* 67 (1970): 399-424.
– [16] Realism and Reference. *Monist* 59 (1976): 321-340.
Rubinstein, B. [31] Explanation and Mere Description: A Metascientific Examination of Certain Aspects of the Psychoanalytic Theory of Motivation. In R. Holt (Ed.), *Motives and Thought. Psychoanalytic Essays in Memory of David Rapaport*, pp. 18-77. New York 1967.
– [65] On the Possibility of a Strictly Clinical Psychoanalytic Theory: An Essay in the Philosophy of Psychoanalysis. In M. Gill and P. Holzman (Eds.), *Psychology versus Metapsychology: Psychoanalytic Essays in Memory of George S. Klein*, pp. 229-264. New York 1976.
Schafer, R. [4] *Language and Insight: The Sigmund Freud Memorial Lectures 1975-1976 University College London*. New Haven and London 1978.
– [5] *A New Language for Psychoanalysis*. New Haven and London 1976.
– [22] *Aspects of Internalization*. New York 1968.
Schimek, J. [66] A Critical Re-examination of Freud's Concept of Unconscious Mental Representation. *International Review of Psycho-Analysis* 2 (1975): 171-187.
Schur, M. [24] *The Id and the Regulatory Principles of Mental Functioning*. London 1966.
Schaffer, J. [72] *Philosophy of Mind*. Englewood Cliffs 1968.
Shope, R., [12] Eliminating Mistakes about Eliminative Materialism. *Philosophy of Science* 46 (1979): 590-612.
– [18] Remembering, Knowledge, and Memory Traces. *Philosophy and Phenomenological Research* 33 (1973): 303-322.
– [30] Physical and Psychic Energy. *Philosophy of Science* 38 (1971): 1-12.
– [33] The Psychoanalytic Theories of Wish-Fulfilment and Meaning. *Inquiry* 10 (1967): 421-438.
– [34] *Wish-Fulfilment and Psychic Energy in Psychoanalytic Theory*. Unpublished Ph.D. Thesis, Harvard University 1966.
– [38] Dispositional Treatment of Psychoanalytic Motivational Terms. *Journal of Philosophy* 67 (1970): 195-208.
– [63] Freud's Concepts of Meaning. *Psychoanalysis and Contemporary Science* 2 (1973): 276-303.
– [69] The Conditionsl Fallacy in Contemporary Philosophy. *Journal of Philosophy* 75 (1978): 397-413. Reprinted in *The Philosopher's Annual* 2 (1979): 173-190.
– [70] Freud on Conscious and Unconscious Intentions. *Inquiry* 13 (1970): 149-159.
Skinner, B. [73] *About Behaviorism*. New York 1974.
Slote, M. [83] *Metaphysics and Essence*. Oxford 1975.
Smythe, T., [36] Unconscious Desires and the Meaning of 'Desire'. *Monist* 56 (1972): 413-425.
Solomon, R. [35] Freud and 'Unconscious Motivation'. *Journal for the Theory of Social Behaviour* 4 (1974): 191-216.

— [17] Freud's Neurological Theory of Mind. In Wollheim [86], pp. 25-52.

Stampe, D. [67] Show and Tell. In B. Freed et al. (Eds.), *Forms of Represen-tation*, pp. 221-245. Amsterdam, Oxford, New York 1975.

Stanescu, H. [79] Young Freud's Letters to His Rumanian Friend, Silber-stein. *Israel Annals of Psychiatry and Related Disciplines* 9 (1971): 195-207.

Suppes, P., and Warren, H. [82] On the Generation and Classification of De-fence Mechanisms. *International Journal of Psycho-Analysis* 56 (1975): 405-414.

Swanson, D. [21] A Critique of Psychic Energy as an Explanatory Concept. *Journal of the American Psychoanalytic Association* 25 (1977): 603-633.

Thalberg, I. [19] Freud's Anatomies of the Self. In Wollheim [86], pp. 147-171.

Thickstun, J., and Rosenblatt, A. [14] *Modern Psychoanalytic Concepts in a General Psychology*. New York 1977.

— [15] A Study of the Concept of Psychic Energy. *International Journal of Psycho-Analysis* 51 (1970): 265-277.

— [27] Energy, Information, and Motivation: A Revision of Psychoanalytic Theory. *Journal of the American Psychoanalytic Association* 25 (1977): 537-558.

Wallerstein, R. [32] Psychic Energy Reconsidered: Introduction. *Journal of the American Psychoanalytic Association* 25 (1977): 529-535.

Wollheim, R. [57] *Sigmund Freud*. New York 1971.

— [86] *Freud: A Collection of Critical Essays*. Garden City 1974.

Brentano's philosophy of mind

BURNHAM TERRELL
University of Minnesota, Minneapolis

Despite fluctuations of doctrine and style and the apparent fragmentation of the philosophical enterprise into discrete fields of specialization, topical or temporal boundaries within philosophy continue to be arbitrary. The purpose to be served by this volume establishes at least a rough definition of the period to be covered. My report on Brentano's philosophy of mind will consider books and articles that have appeared in print during the years 1966 through 1978.

All of the primary material most important to an understanding of Brentano's philosophy of mind has been published during this span of years. Indeed, even though the period commences just short of fifty years after Brentano's death in 1917, some of it appears for the first time. The story of the preservation of the large collection of Brentano's unpublished manuscripts, lecture notes and correspondence has been told by his son, the late J.C.M. Brentano, in [1]. Professor Franziska Mayer-Hillebrand of the University of Innsbruck, who took on the chief responsibility for continuing the editorial work of Alfred Kastil after his death, has drawn on this collection and other sources for several important volumes. The most important of them is *Die Abkehr vom Nichtrealen* [2], in which she has gathered together a comprehensive group of selections, including much previously unpublished material, that are essential to an understanding of Brentano's *Reismus*, a sweeping denial of irreal entities and consequent reinterpretation and clarification of the major problems of metaphysics. It is impossible to appreciate the full significance of the

Contemporary philosophy. A new survey. Vol. 4, pp. 223–247.
©*1983, Martinus Nijhoff Publishers, The Hague/Boston/London.*

reistic phase for the notions familiarly attached to Brentano's psychological theories — intentional inexistence, intentional object, mental content, and the like — or for the relationship between philosophy of mind and other departments of philosophical inquiry without a careful study of the material Mayer-Hillebrand has assembled in this volume. Her 100-page long introduction chronicles Brentano's dismantling of the ontological structures that had evolved during the last decade or so of the nineteenth century and his ultimate adoption of reism in the twentieth century.

Mayer-Hillebrand published in 1970 a new edition of Brentano's epistemological writings originally edited by Kastil in *Versuch über die Erkenntnis* [3]. She carried out Kastil's intention to include in the new edition a number of briefer studies in epistemology. The 1970 edition is consequently a significantly expanded version of the original, with an emphasis on the clarification of the theory of evidence. Several of the added essays bear directly on the philosophy of mind, primarily on the distinction between inner and outer perception, the evidence of the former and the non-evidence of the latter, and on the allegation of psychologism that had been directed against Brentano's theory of knowledge.

A minor historical item selected from the *Nachlass*, *"Was an Reid zu loben"* [4] completes the list of Brentano's previously unpublished writings that have appeared during the years covered by this report. It offers some interesting comparisons between his theses in the philosophy of mind and Thomas Reid's.

Several of the new editions of volumes published earlier differ only in the replacement of Oskar Kraus's highly polemical and consequently somewhat dated introductions. So far as the philosophy of mind is concerned, Vol. III of the Psychology, titled *Vom sinnlichen und noetischen Bewusstsein* [5], is especially important. Its principal subject is the distinction between sensory and noetic consciousness. Most of the themes of Brentano's philosophy of mental phenomena are represented: inner and outer perception, perception and apperception, modes of presentation and perception, the theory of abstraction and the thesis that the intentional reference characteristic of all mental phenomena is always a general reference, varying in degree of generality, never reference to a specific individual. Mayer-Hillebrand has added an index as well as her brief introduction and has brought the references in Kraus's notes up to date.

Even where publications are reprints of an earlier text without any significant changes, deletions or additions whatsoever, they are of real value. The unfortunate history of the uniform edition of Brentano undertaken by F. Meiner's *Philosophische Bibliothek* under the editorship of Kastil and Oskar Kraus is in part responsible for the blurred understanding of Brentano's thought that has prevailed even up to the present. The interruptions caused by political disorder and war, and especially the destruction in the bombing of Leipzig of Meiner's stock of books made the works already published during the 20s and 30s difficult to obtain. That impediment to accurate scholarly appraisal of Brentano's philosophy based on primary sources has now been removed. Reproductions of previously published volumes that appeared between 1966 and 1978 include Volumes I and II of *Psychologie vom empirischen Standpunkte* [6 and 7], *Vom Ursprung sittlicher Erkenntnis* [8], *Wahrheit und Evidenz* [9], *Kategorienlehre* [10], *Vom Dasein Gottes* [11], and *Die Grundlegung und Aufbau der Ethik* [12] (of which Part Three is on freedom of will). An early work, not in the *Philosophische Bibliothek*, has also been made available again in photoreproduction, *Die Psychologie des Aristoteles* [13]. It is a historical study, of course, focusing on the Aristotelian notion of *nous poetikos*, but Brentano's investigation of that topic and the Aristotelian doctrine of the soul generally should not be neglected by anyone interested in the full development of his philosophy of mind over a span of more than fifty years. *Aristoteles und seine Weltanschauung* [14] treats some of the same topics more superficially in a broader context.

English translations of the standard German editions of Brentano's works first became available during the period, beginning with a translation of the third edition (1934) of *Vom Ursprung sittlicher Erkenntnis* [15], published in 1966. An Italian edition [16], translated by Adriano Bausola, was also published the same year. Other volumes more directly pertinent to the study of philosophy of mind have followed: translations of *Wahrheit und Evidenz* [17], Vols. I and II of the *Psychologie* [18], Vol. III [19], of *Grundlegung und Aufbau der Ethik* [20], and of *Die Psychologie des Aristoteles* [21]. The last has a brief and illuminating preface by the editor and translator, Rolf George, in which he defines the relevance of the work to Brentano's own philosophical ideas. George has also published a translation of Brentano's first book on Aristotle [22] and together with R. Chisholm a translation of *Aristoteles und seine Weltanschauung* [23].

Book-length discussions of Brentano have been few. Srzednicki [24] published an account of Brentano's analysis of truth that should not go unmentioned although it falls barely outside our temporal boundaries and is not of great value as a source of information about Brentano's philosophy of mind. Rancurello [25] is quite useful for an understanding of Brentano's place in the history of psychology but is not very penetrating, nor even consistently accurate in its account of the philosophical reaches of Brentano's thought. It does contain a valuable and comprehensive annotated bibliography. The primary concern of Bausola [26] is with Brentano's ethical theory, but the first two parts, devoted respectively to intentionality, truth and evidence and to the classification of mental phenomena take up topics clearly within the philosophy of mind. They emphasize the views Brentano defended during the nineteenth century and the relation between Brentano's doctrine of intentionality and Thomistic philosophy. Very little attention is given to the implications for philosophy of mind of Brentano's denial of *entia irrealia*, although the emergence of the reistic thesis in the twentieth century is noted.

Several collections of articles on Brentano, all containing material pertinent to our topic, appeared between 1966 and 1978. Those are the publication dates of the *Revue internationale de Philosophie* number devoted to Brentano and of the volume of *Grazer Philosophische Studien* in which the proceedings of the international conference on Brentano held in Graz in 1977 were published. The papers presented at the Brentano Colloquium held during the XIVth International Congress of Philosophy in Vienna in 1968 are published in Vols. I and VI of the Proceedings. A volume edited by McAlister [27] is an especially useful source on Brentano's philosophy generally. It includes articles judiciously selected from the *Revue Internationale* and the Brentano Colloquium and other sources, some in English translation for the first time, several of them not readily available heretofore. The collections edited by Castañeda [28] and Marras [29], although not specifically directed to Brentano, contain sufficient material relevant to his philosophy of mind to deserve notice here. A few articles in Pivčević [30] are pertinent.

There are several brief summaries of Brentano's philosophy that include useful accounts of his philosophy of mind. Spiegelberg [31] is excellent on Brentano's role in the phenomenological movement, but its value is not limited to that connection. H. Bergman [32], R. Chisholm [33], L. Gilson [34] and F. Mayer-Hillebrand [35] are all written from a standpoint sympathetic to Brentano and represent his ideas with care and accuracy. Sections VI-IX in Bergman [32] are especially good on philosophy of mind. E. Morscher [36] is another useful brief summary, somewhat more critical.

The last work I shall mention in this survey is the only all-out attempt at a thorough and penetrating critique of Brentano's philosophy, by a writer both critical and knowledgeable, that appeared during the period we are considering: Part III of Gustav Bergmann's *Realism* [37]. It is exasperating in style and nearly impossible to read without extreme frustration. The author's frequent stage whispers distract from the tortuous argumentation, and it is I believe fundamentally misguided in its interpretation of Brentano; but it is a serious and painstaking effort that for all its flaws puts to shame the shallow and facile treatment Brentano has received at the hands of many others.

The concentration of literature by and about Brentano makes the imposition of temporal boundaries somewhat less arbitrary than it might otherwise be. The choice of appropriate boundaries around the topic itself presents special problems. Assuming a narrow interpretation of philosophy of mind, conceiving it as that branch of philosophy devoted to questions about mental or spiritual substance, there has been very little discussion of Brentano's views. Nor is there extensive discussion of them in his own writings, at least in the ones that have received the most attention. In the *Psychologie vom empirischen Standpunkte*, Brentano accepts the definition of psychology as the science of mental phenomena and consequently the possibility of a "psychology without a soul," despite his own belief in a spiritual substance that is immortal. The substantial soul or mind, the subject of mental phenomena, is not the defining object of psychological science, which Brentano would prefer to see pursued unencumbered by metaphysical controversy. In considering Brentano's philosophy of mind, we must adopt a broader understanding of the scope of "philosophy of mind."

Philosophy of mind can encompass everything that can be called "the mental," whether it be mental substance or mental phenomena, mental events, mental properties, mental states, or whatever else can be designated "mental." Most of the discussions of Brentano have been devoted to his philosophy of mind in this broader sense, particularly to his account of the nature of mental phenomena as contrasted with physical phenomena. Indeed for many philosophers that is what defines and exhausts Brentano's philosophy of mind. The greater danger, then, lies not in confining the consideration of Brentano's philosophy of mind to his theory of mental substance, but in limiting it to what he had to say about intentionality and the distinction between mental and physical phenomena.

From the perspective of Brentano's own philosophical development, there is an even greater risk that his philosophy of mind might engulf almost every other aspects of his philosophy. Philosophy of mind, extended to include whatever has to do with the mental, according to the looser interpretation recommended above, threatens in the later Brentano to break through all topical boundaries. Ontology, epistemology, ethics, logic all cease to be separate fields of investigation and are reduced to provinces of the philosophy of mind. To recognize such a tendency in Brentano's philosophical evolution is not to accept Gustav Bergmann's charge in [37] that Brentano is a "structural idealist." It is misleading to interpret a move from the material mode of speech to the formal mode as the substitution of words for things. It is rather the substitution for questions and statements that seem to be about non-linguistic things of questions and statements that are about words. The same is true of the move from the ontological mode to the psychological mode as it does occur in Brentano's philosophy. What is important about it, is its implications for the boundaries of our topic. If questions about truth and knowledge, about fact, being, the right and the good are all to be converted into questions about judgment, love and hate, or whatever mental phenomena may be adduced, then philosophy of mind has been extended far beyond the limits that would ordinarily be imposed on the study of mind or the mental.

I shall keep my discussion within the boundaries of philosophy of mind as understood less narrowly than to be confined to mental substance, less broadly than to encompass every topic in philosophy that in some way has psychological foundations according to Brentano's treatment of it. I shall begin by considering several topics that surely count as "philosophy of the mental" if not necessarily of the mind as mental substance. Most of the discussion of Brentano has focused on this set of topics. They include (1) the distinction between mental and physical phenomena; (2) intentionality, specifically as a criterion of the mental, as irreducible, and with attention to a variety of ontological problems that attach themselves to the notion of intentionality; (3) the classification of mental phenomena, (4) the distinction between inner perception and inner observation and related issues; and (5) the distinction between descriptive and genetic psychology, especially the epistemological status of the deliverances of descriptive psychology.

A second group of topics belongs to philosophy of mind in the strict and narrow sense. They have to do with the distinction between mental and physical substance, mind and body and the relationship between them, the unity of consciousness, and the immortality of the soul. They have received much less attention than the problems relating to mental phenomena. A more peripheral topic is the contribution of philosophy of mind to theology and philosophy of religion by way of the so-called psychological proof of the existence of God.

For the past quarter century the dominant influence on the appreciation and interpretation of Brentano's philosophy of mind has been Roderick M. Chisholm's, beginning with the presentation (in 1955) of an early version of [38]. The effect of his indispensable contribution has been ambivalent, however. His primary interest has been not in the elucidation of Brentano's position as much as in the exploration of the problem of intentionality and its relation to the distinction between the mental and the material. He rightly acknowledges his debt to Brentano for this constellation of themes, but his treatment of them does not attempt to, nor does it profess to adhere faithfully to Brentano's. As a consequence, there is some uncertainty even about the selection of appropriate literature to be considered here. Many who responded to Chisholm's publications on Brentano and intentionality did so with no recognition of the difference. Articles begin with an almost ritualistic invocation of the lines in which Brentano asserts that mental phenomena are characterized by "what the Scholastics of the middle ages referred to as the intentional (also the mental) inexistence of the object," as quoted by Chisholm at the beginning of [39]. What follows may have little to do with Brentano, however. Field [40] is an extreme example of the distorting consequences of equating Brentano with Chisholm. This is a long paper (of considerable *philosophical* merit) intended to defend materialism against two problems it must overcome: the problem of *experiential* properties and the problem of *intentionality*. He identifies the latter as "Brentano's problem" and devotes more than half of his discussion to it. The bibliography includes no primary source material of Brentano's and none of the secondary sources listed in the bibliography appended to this report with the exception of Chisholm [39]. He states "Brentano's problem" in these terms: "...*since* [Brentano] *saw no alternative to viewing belief and desire as relations to propositions*, he concluded that materialism must be false." (p. 9, my italics). But this has no basis in Brentano. It is not Brentano's problem.

The path from Chisholm's modification of Brentano to Field's misappropriation of Brentano's name for someone else's problem is readily explained. Reviewing current issues in the philosophy of mind, Dennett [41] catches Chisholm's turn of thought neatly and succinctly:

> (using the tactic of semantic ascent to great effect) [Chisholm turned Brentano's notion of intentionality] into a feature of *language*: the sentence[s] we typically use to talk about mental events have certain peculiarities of logic. (p. 257)

Dennett goes on to acknowledge that intentionality "does mark an important divide in our conceptual scheme, though not quite the divide Brentano supposed." He next identifies intentional idioms as "roughly those Russell called the idioms of propositional attitude," then concludes: "*Roughly*, again, the intentional idioms are those idioms in our language that relate people, their parts, their acts, their artifacts to *propositions*." The slippage from Brentano's notions of intentional reference and intentional object to Russell's idioms of propositional attitude (or their extra-linguistic counterparts in Frege's *Gedanken* and Meinong's *Objektiven*) is a phenomenon frequently encountered. Dennett is aware that this account of intentionality represents a departure from Brentano, who ultimately denied that mental phenomena were relational at all, and had never thought of them as relations to propositions. Field, and others, have not been so careful.

The presence of Brentano's name together with problems about intentionality and the notions of mental and material is no guarantee that the discussion has to do with Brentano's philosophy of mind. The absence of Brentano's name can also be misleading. It is absent, for example, from the index and the main text of Sellars [42]. (His correspondence with Chisholm on intentionality, another influential publication from the late 50s, can be read in Chisholm [43].) Chapter III, however, is on *Intentionality* and Chapter 4, on *Truth*. We read in the Preface (p. ix): "I attempt to show, *in the spirit of the latter Brentano* (my italics), that the appearances discriminated by careful phenomenology in the Platonic tradition can be saved without too much affront to 'extensionalistic', 'nominalistic' and 'naturalistic' sensibilities." It would be rewarding to work out in these two chapters the respects in which "the spirit of the latter Brentano" exerts its influence and assess the extent to which they could appropriately be counted as part of the ongoing discussion of Brentano's philosophy of mind. It is not possible to do so here.

Chisholm's *Encyclopedia of Philosophy* article on "Intentionality" [44] is organized in terms of two theses he distinguishes in Brentano. According to the *ontological thesis*, there are *intentional objects* with a peculiar ontological status, *intentional inexistence*. The *psychological thesis* is the claim that *intentional reference* is the distinguishing feature of the mental or psychological as against the physical. In this and other articles published during the 60s, however, Chisholm has been preoccupied with a subsidiary problem that emerges naturally out of his linguistic treatment of the psychological thesis. He turns directly from Brentano's thesis to a search for satisfactory logical criteria of intentionality.

Chisholm begins [45] with the comment: "every proposed mark of intentionality has turned out to be a mark, more generally, of intensionality (or nonextensionality)." (The marks in question are mainly those he had proposed himself in [38] and [39]. They are "existential indifference" or the failure of existential generalization in intentional contexts, nonextensional occurrence, and referential opacity.) He offers three versions of more satisfactory criteria. The first, in [44], is that "a simple sentence prefix, M, is *intentional* if, for every sentence p, $M(p)$ is logically contingent." The second (ibid. and throughout [45] and [46]) is more complex. The notion of a modal prefix is introduced and then four statement forms are distinguished by inserting the modal prefix before or immediately after the quantifier in a universally or an existentially quantified statement form. Specifically intentional prefixes are distinguished from other nonextensional forms by the patterns of logical relationship that hold among the statements so constructed. The third criterion, proposed in [47], also uses logical relations between quantified expressions as a mark of intentionality. A relationship, represented by R, is intentional if for some individual term that may occupy the place of a neither of the two statements below implies the other and no well-formed sentence that is part of (1) is noncontingent:

$$(1) \quad (Ex)\,(Ey)\,(y = a \ \& \ xRa)$$
$$(2) \quad (Ex)\,(Ey)\,(y = a \ \& \ xRy).$$

Chisholm proposes this criterion as an improvement on existential indifference and deems it "more faithful to Brentano's intention."

Although these new criteria of intentionality seem far removed from anything to be found in Brentano, Chisholm's motivation in developing them is the preservation of Brentano's psychological thesis. His problem is: How can we distinguish that variety of intensionality (nonextensionality) which can serve to distinguish the psychological? We need to isolate within the intensional, which extends beyond the bounds of the mental, just that segment which coincides with the psychological. Whatever does that for us is intentionality. Criteria of intentionality are thus satisfactory only if they succeed in marking a feature that makes the distinction. For Chisholm, Brentano's psychological thesis, that intentionality is the distinguishing feature of the mental, has become a tautology.

L.J. Cohen [48] considers both Chisholm's earlier criteria of intentionality and his later proposals, defending Chisholm (with some modifications, including an abandonment of the psychological thesis) against an extended critique of the earlier criteria in Urmson [49]. O'Connor [50] is critical of Chisholm's earlier tests of intentionality in [39] both as to method and result. Chisholm's account of intentional language, he argues, is not sufficient to establish any interesting philosophical consequences apart from other claims, particularly irreducibility. But Chisholm's linguistic tests do not even accomplish their primary purpose, to draw the line between intentional and nonintentional idioms, effectively. Lycan [51] discusses Chisholm's later criteria using inference-patterns in a way essentially sympathetic to Brentano's point of view. Sleigh [52] and [53] and Luce [54] are critical of later tests. Chisholm [55] and [56] were prepared as responses to their criticisms. Sanford [59] briefly discusses the later criteria as well as the earlier ones and objections raised to them, with particular attention to the significance of irreducibility.

In [45], Chisholm briefly alludes to yet another aspect of intentionality, viz. the indeterminacy of the intentional object. While he refers only to Chisholm's earlier criteria of existential indifference and referential opacity, R. Wollheim [56] has some interesting comments on degrees of generality and specificity in intentional contexts.

The psychological thesis was a permanent fixture of Brentano's philosophy of mind. The ontological thesis was abandoned with the adoption of Reismus. The relationship between the two theses is crucial and problematic. The ontological thesis as Chisholm states it posits an intentional *object* with intentional *inexistence* as its ontological status. On Chisholm's interpretation of intentional *reference* the intentional object *need* not exist at all. If it does exist, it exists in a perfectly ordinary way as a perfectly ordinary object. Therefore, the psychological thesis that mental phenomena have intentional reference appears to be separable from the ontological thesis about peculiar entities in a peculiar status.

Chisholm's opinion is that before and after the reistic turn, Brentano's treatment of the ontological thesis generates difficulties for the psychological thesis. In [47, p. 11], he correctly points out that according to Brentano the object of thought is a thing, not a thought-of thing. The thought of a horse is directed upon the horse, not a thought-of horse. Diogenes is looking for an actual honest man, not an intentionally inexisting one. The latter he already has. "The ontological use of the word 'intentional' ... seems to undermine its psychological use. Intentionally inexistent objects were posited in the attempt to understand intentional reference, but the attempt did not succeed – precisely because the objects so posited *were* intentionally inexistent."

The abandonment of the ontological thesis does not bring new strength and stability to the psychological. If the ontological thesis itself seems to undermine the psychological, the arguments advanced against the ontological thesis have an equally devastating impact on the latter. While the ontological thesis ran, the word 'object' was ambiguous, meaning on one occasion an object of thought as such, an intentionally inexistent object, and on another occasion an ordinary object upon which a thought was directed. According to the linguistic analysis characteristic of Brentano's reistic period, there is only the second meaning. "Object of thought as such" and similar expressions mimic meaningful words, but do not really have meaning of their own. They are merely synsemantical fragments of larger expressions that do have meaning. Chisholm takes this account to hold of ordinary words as they occur in intentional contexts as well. Thus the word "horse" is meaningful in ordinary contexts, but when it is inserted into a context such as "John is thinking of horses," it ceases to have independent meaning. It is part of an adjectival complex that is supposed to describe the subject, John. It has not shifted its meaning from ordinary horses, it has lost any meaning of its own entirely. If that is so, Chisholm concludes, there is no accounting for any logical relationship between describing someone as believing there are horses and asserting that there are horses. Unless 'horses' preserves something of its usual significance, there is no accounting for the feature of thought crucial to the psychological thesis: that the thought of horses should be directed upon — horses.

The same problem, the relationship between the psychological and the ontological features of Brentano's account of the intentionality of mental phenomena, emerges from the consideration of his historical antecedents as well. H. Spiegelberg argues in [31] and [59] that the Scholastic notion of intentional inexistence is distinct and separable from intentional reference or "directedness upon an object." Marras [60] disagrees, holding that immanent objectivity must be the mode of existence of an intention and that directedness is essential to it. Such a view is compatible with a realistic epistemology, he observes, only if we take care to distinguish the object of the intentional reference from the *intentio* in the mind that, like a word, carries our reference to the object. McAlister [61] complicates matters by requiring a distinct special ontological status for each. Mental contents are immanent; intentional objects have intentional inexistence. Thought-of objects, correlates of the act of thinking that come into being whenever we think of something, must not be identified with the object of thought. The latter may have intentional inexistence only or it may have both actual and intentional status. In neither case is it or its status identical with the thought-of object or its status.

In this way, McAlister attempts to resolve an apparent conflict between Brentano's later pronouncements about his earlier theory and what he had actually written. He can correctly deny, as he does in a passage included by Kraus in [9, p. 87 = 17, p. 77] and by Mayer-Hillebrand in [2, pp. 119-21], that he had ever held that the object of thought was a thought-of object as such. The two editors both note that Brentano is just mistaken about his earlier position; Chisholm follows their interpretation. Translating *vorgestelltes Objekt* as "object of thought," he is inhibited from making the distinction required by the McAlister interpretation between the "thought-of object" or immanent thought correlate and the intentionally inexistent "object of thought."

McAlister has made a persuasive case for the need to make such a distinction and its compatibility with Brentano's original doctrine. It is not so easy to find a clear statement of it in Brentano's texts. We can best find a place for it by reading Brentano backwards, interpreting the earlier theory, ambiguous and obscure as it is on this point, in the light of the latter. According to Brentano's mature views, a thing enters into a thought in each of the two modes, *modo recto* and *modo obliquo*. The doctrine of inner perception requires that the same mental phenomenon include a presentation of itself, in which the object of thought is present *modo obliquo*. Thus *its* object is present in inner perception *as* object of thought, whereas the primary object of thought is presented without any essential reference to thought. Since the descriptive psychologist is thinking about the mental phenomenon, the primary object of the intentional reference which is his object of investigation enters into his consciousness *modo obliquo*, i.e., as object of his subject's thinking. It is not present to the subject's thinking in that way, however, except by way of the secondary reference of inner perception. The object enters into the subject's consciousness in two ways, then, *modo recto* as object of primary reference, *modo obliquo* as object of the object of inner perception, and enters in still another way into the psychologist's consciousness, *modo obliquo* as object of the object of his primary reference. In the reistic period, Brentano treats the use of the word 'object' in all of these contexts as synsemantical. The psychologist exists, as a person thinking of the subject's thought about something. The subject exists, as a person thinking of something and aware of his thinking about it. If the psychologist takes 'object' in these contexts to be autosemantic, to name something, he will find in his subject's mind two references for which correlative objects can be invented. The object of the subject's primary reference (if he is thinking of a unicorn) is just a unicorn, not a thought-of unicorn, and Brentano is correct in insisting that he never thought otherwise. The psychologist thinks of it as an object of thought, *modo obliquo*, however, because he is not thinking of a unicorn, but of someone else thinking of a unicorn. On the other hand, the psychologist, in thinking of such a person, is thinking of someone who is aware of his own thinking, aware in inner perception of his thought of a unicorn and in that capacity referring *modo obliquo* in secondary consciousness to a unicorn as object of the thought of which he is aware. It is appropriate to call the object of the subject's thought as his thought is present in inner perception a thought-of object, because insofar as we can think of him as thinking about a unicorn at all in this context, he is thinking of a unicorn *modo obliquo* as object of the thought of which he is aware, i.e., thinking of it as thought about. Thus the unicorn as primary object *modo recto* is the reified correlate invented by the psychologist to accompany the primary reference, a psychologist who must also devise a status such as intentional inexistence to accomodate it. The unicorn as object *modo obliquo* in inner perception serves as correlate of inner perception, in which it is present as object of thought only, existing only in that respect as thought-of object, ceasing to exist when the thought of it ceases.

"What the subject is thinking of" (= "the subject's object of thought as such") and "What the subject is aware of himself as thinking of" (= "the object of the mental phenomenon of which the subject is aware in inner perception") are both equally syn-semantica according to reistic analysis. They are different syn-semantica. A question formulated in terms of the former expression can be answered fully by, say, "unicorn." A complete answer to a parallel question formulated with the latter could be answered without distortion by "a unicorn as thought-of." The difference between the two in the pre-reistic period is reflected by the two different versions of the ontological thesis distinguished by Mc-Alister, with the consequent ambiguity in "object as such" and the confusion between "object of thought" and "thought-of object." Taken in this way, with the later analysis as interpretive background to understanding the earlier ontological thesis, the transition from one to the other is easy to understand. To deny independent meaning to expressions that seem to identify objects as correlates of mental references is to repudiate in this strong sense *both* the correlate as object *modo recto* of the primary reference and as object *modo obliquo* in inner perception.

McAlister has lately proposed in [62] a modified interpretation of Brentano on intentionality which she thinks more accurate, but the interesting ontological complexities of the earlier piece that link it to the controversy between Marras and Spiegelberg and the scholastic background receive less attention. The new interpretation is critical of Chisholm's emphasis on the existential indifference of mental phenomena. Her emphasis now is not on the ontological status of the object, but on the peculiar feature of the intentional relationship essential to mental phenomena. In this relationship, sensible qualities (physical phenomena) never take objects at all, even existing ones; they can only *be* objects. In other relations, they can occupy either subject or object place.

Other discussions of the ontological thesis with some attention to historical background deserve at least brief mention. K. Hedwig [63] takes up the question about Brentano's use of scholastic sources as it had been posed by Spiegelberg. R. Aquila [64], J. Deely [65] and [66] and A. Lisska [67] discuss Brentano on intentionality from a Thomist perspective. W. Kneale [68] and A.N. Prior's response in [69] range over a wider variety of logical, ontological and historical topics, including allusions to Frege and Wittgenstein as well as the Aristotelian and Scholastic background. Prior [70] places Brentano on intentionality in a somewhat different historical context, Reid's theory of perception.

D. Føllesdal [71] sees the problem of accounting for the directedness of mental phenomena as one which Brentano never solved. He calls attention to Husserl's proposal of the *noema* as a solution. The *noema*, like the thought-of correlate object on McAlister's robust ontological account of Brentano, is distinct from the object and accounts for the reference to it. D. Carr [72] suggests that many of the problems we have had to consider were perceived by Husserl and that he made his solutions to them the basis of phenomenological method. Husserl's own discussion of Brentano is now available in an English version (Husserl [73]).

R. Scruton [74] offers a detailed critique of "the Brentano property," considered mainly as a property of grammatical contexts, and concludes that there is no useful grammatical concept of intentionality. R. Arnaud [75] rejects the notion of "Brentanist relations" (relations in which only one term needs to exist) as incoherent.

Intentionality was not the only distinguishing characteristic of mental phenomena that Brentano identified. H. Bergman [32] restates Brentano's summary of distinguishing characteristics. At least four must be cited. Intentionality is pre-eminent among them, but the others are judged to be sufficient to mark the distinction. (Kraus and Husserl, in a battle of footnotes, disagree on the degree of pre-eminence.) In addition to intentionality, there are these criteria of mental phenomena: they are presentations or phenomena based on presentations, objects of inner perception; and phenomena that present themselves as a unity. (Brentano's own summary cites another, that mental phenomena are the only phenomena that have actual as well as intentional existence. Bergman seems to consider it subsidiary to inner perception.) Morrison [76] identifies eight differentiations in Brentano's text. He adds the following criteria: all mental phenomena are acts; they are evident; they are "private." C.T. Kim [77] finds six, adding the fact that mental phenomena appear unextended, which Brentano had rejected as a useful criterion. R. Solomon [78] examines the attempt to distinguish psychological predicates and properties as pertaining to persons or to sentences and concludes that the solution to the difficulties he sees can be found in the "semantic space" between the phenomenological or descriptive psychological method and linguistic analysis, "in the *use* of sentences to ascribe psychological properties to people."

To the thesis that all mental phenomena are characterized by intentional reference Brentano added the claim that the fundamental classification of such phenomena must be according to the different ways in which they refer, the mode of reference. He proposed three fundamental classes, presentation, judgment and emotional attitude. There were originally no further distinctions among presentations besides differences as to object. (The distinction between presentation *modo recto* and *modo obliquo* and others were introduced later.) An affirmative and a negative mode were distinguished within the other two classes, affirmation and rejection, love and hate. Even when Brentano admitted peculiar entities with peculiar ontological status, the basic classification of mental phenomena was not by reference to different sorts of object, but according to different modes of referring.

There has been little attention given to Brentano's classification of mental phenomena, in comparison with the wealth of material on intentionality. D. Hamlyn [79] has criticized Brentano's subsumption of all emotional attitudes under "Phenomena of love and hate," in large part because he chooses to understand Brentano's intentions much too literally and specifically. E. Anscombe's contribution to the Brentano conference in Graz [80] attacks Brentano's thesis that feeling and will belong to one basic class. B. Terrell [81] has defended his way of differentiating

between presentation and judgment and has attempted to demonstrate the dangers of too uncritical a reliance on linguistic models
in interpreting Brentano's classification.

All mental phenomena include an awareness of themselves
according to Brentano's doctrine of inner perception or secondary
consciousness. Inner perception as a component feature of a mental phenomenon must therefore be distinguished from any mental
act, including so-called introspection, that has another such phenomenon as its primary object of reference. Introspection in the
sense of contemporaneous observation of one's own mental states
Brentano declares to be impossible. There has been relatively little
examination of this aspect of Brentano's philosophy of mind that
goes beyond either the mere restatement of the doctrine or an expression of despair of understanding it. A noteworthy exception
is G. Küng's critique of inner perception and *Evidenz* in [82].

One of the implications of the distinction between inner perception and introspection is that Brentano's conception of descriptive
psychology cannot be identified as another form of ordinary
introspective psychology. Descriptive psychology, which Brentano
began to distinguish sharply from genetic (or explanatory) psychology in the late 1880s, has received considerable attention as a
consequence of Chisholm's focus on it in his presentation [83] to
the Brentano Colloquium in 1968. A number of the other contributions to the Colloquium were responses to Chisholm. They
included T. de Boer [84], J. Findlay [85], K. Fischer [86],
L. Landgrebe [87] and B. Terrell [88]. A later discussion, comparing descriptive psychology and Husserl's transcendental phenomenological psychology, is J. Golomb [89]. Quinton [90] has
a like purpose.

Brentano's distinction between mental and physical phenomena
has often been mistaken for a distinction between mental and
material substance. M. Adler [91], for example, scolds Brentano
for having neglected the Aristotelian-Scholastic distinction between sense-perception, which is a function of a material organ,
and abstract conception, an act of the immaterial soul. Therefore,
Brentano is mistaken in taking intentionality, which is characteristic of both, as coincident with and distinctive of immateriality.
Adler is not familiar either with Brentano's writings on Aristotle
or the quite separate distinction he draws between two kinds of

substance. The distinction between the sensitive and the intellectual soul in Aristotle is prominent in Brentano [13 and 21]. The distinction between mental and material can be found in Brentano [10] and [11].

Acceptance of intentionality as a pre-eminent criterion of the mental is compatible with a nondualistic metaphysics, at least with an identity theory on the mind-body relation. J. Kim [92] calls attention to this compatibility, as does D. Dennett in [93] and [94]. The same point is indicated in R. Aquila [95]. The argument for a distinction between material and spiritual entities is based on the unity of consciousness, which requires that the subject of mental phenomena be a nulldimensional and not a three-dimensional entity. Nulldimensionality, not intentionality, is the distinguishing feature of minds. Brentano's views on the unity of consciousness are considered in C.-T. Kim [72] and B. Mijuskowic [95]. The latter is at some pains to demonstrate that Kant was a major influence on Brentano, without considering Brentano's antipathy to his alleged source.

That Brentano ultimately took refuge from the implications of his earlier views (as elaborated by Meinong especially) in an extreme ontological parsimony that has come to be known as *Reismus* has been emphasized in our discussion of the ontological aspects of intentionality.

The effective instrument of that development was a sort of linguistic analysis or *Sprachkritik*. Besides the articles that have already been mentioned, attention should be drawn to R. Haller [97], T. Kotarbinski [98], F. Mayer-Hillebrand's long introduction to Brentano [2], J. Srzednicki [99] and B. Terrell [100]. S. Körner in [101] and [102] discusses some of the logical features of *Reismus*, especially the distinction between the relational and the "relation-like" (*relativliche*). Especially valuable on the comparison between Brentano and Meinong are R. Grossmann [103] and K. Wolf [104]. The latter includes extensive discussion of other features of Brentano's philosophy as well. Grossman [105] is also pertinent, as a review article on the Brentano issue of the *Revue Internationale de Philosophie* and on G. Bergmann [37].

G. Bergmann's book just cited, *Realism: A Critique of Brentano and Meinong*, deserves special mention despite the failings noted earlier. It is the only substantial attempt at a profound evaluation of Brentano's ultimate ontological commitments and especially of the complications that attach to his philosophy of mind. He recognizes the significance of aspects of Brentano that others have ignored, e.g., the peculiar features of his treatment of substance and accident. He fails, however, to take note of some essential distinctions, which are set out in R. Chisholm [106]. Bergmann's conclusion is that Brentano is ultimately committed "structurally" to idealism and that his obdurate attempt to defend reism against all difficulties finally fails. Whether this estimate is correct or not, Bergmann's effort has set an example, in substance if not in style, for future interpreters of Brentano's philosophy.

BIBLIOGRAPHY

Adler, M. [91] Intentionality and Immateriality. *The New Scholasticism* 41 (1967): 312-344.

Anscombe, E. [80] Will and Emotion. *Grazer philosophische Studien* 5 (1978): 139-148.

Aquila, R.E. [64] The Status of Intentional Objects. *The New Scholasticism* 45 (1971): 427-456.

— [95] Brentano, Descartes, and Hume on Awareness. *Philosophy and Phenomenological Research* 35 (1975): 223-239.

Arnaud, R.B. [71] Brentanist Relations. In K. Lehrer (Ed.), *Analysis and Metaphysics*. Dordrecht 1975.

Bausola, A. [26] *Conoscenza e Moralitá in Franz Brentano*. Milan 1968.

Bergman, H. [32] Franz Brentano. *Revue international de Philosophie* 78 (1966): 349-372.

Bergmann, G. [37] *Realism: A Critique of Brentano and Meinong*. Madison (Wis.) 1966.

Brentano, F. [2] *Die Abkehr vom Nichtrealen*. Edited with an introduction by F. Mayer-Hillebrand. Bern and Munich 1966.

— [3] *Versuch über die Erkenntnis*. Hamburg 1970. Enlarged edition with a new introduction by F. Mayer-Hillebrand.

— [4] Was an Reid zu loben. Über die Philosophie vom Thomas Reid. *Grazer philosophische Studien* 1 (1975): 1-18.

— [5] *Psychologie vom empirischen Standpunkt*, Vol. III: *Vom sinnlichen und noetischen Bewusstsein*. Hamburg 1974. Revised edition with introduction by F. Mayer-Hillebrand.

— [6] *Psychologie vom empirischen Standpunkt*, Vol. I. Hamburg 1973 (1924).

— [7] *Psychologie vom empirischen Standpunkt*, Vol. II: *Von der Klassifikation der psychischen Phänomene*. Hamburg 1971 (1925).

- [8] *Vom Ursprung sittlicher Erkenntnis*. Hamburg 1969 (1934).
- [9] *Wahrheit und Evidenz*. Hamburg 1974 (1930).
- [10] *Kategorienlehre*. Hamburg 1974 (1933).
- [11] *Vom Dasein Gottes*, Hamburg 1968 (1929), pp. 417-435 (Der psychologische Beweis).
- [12] *Die Grundlegung und Aufbau der Ethik*. Hamburg 1978 (1952).
- [13] *Die Psychologie des Aristoteles*. Mainz 1967 (1867).
- [14] *Aristoteles und seine Weltanschauung*. Hamburg 1977 (1911).
- [15] *The Origin of Our Knowledge of Right and Wrong*. London 1969. Translation of [8] by E. Schneewind and R.M. Chisholm.
- [16] *Sull' origine della conoscenza morale*. Brescia 1966. Translation of [8] by A. Bausola.
- [17] *The True and the Evident*. London 1966. Translation of [9] by R. Chisholm.
- [18] *Psychology from an Empirical Standpoint*. London 1973. Translation of [6] and [7] by L. McAlister, A. Rancurello and B. Terrell.
- [19] *Sensory and Noetic Consciousness*. London 1979. Translation of [5] by L. McAlister and M. Schättle.
- [20] *The Foundation and Construction of Ethics*. London 1973. Translation of [12] by E. Schneewind.
- [21] *The Psychology of Aristotle*. Berkeley 1977. Translation of [13] by R. George.
- [22] *On the Several Senses of Being in Aristotle*. Translation by R. George of *Von den mannigfachen Bedeutungen des Seienden nach Aristoteles* (1862). Berkeley 1975.
- [23] *Aristotle and His World View*. Berkeley 1978. Translation of [14] by R. George and R.M. Chisholm.
- *The Theory of Categories*. Translation of [10] by R.M. Chisholm and N. Guterman. The Hague 1981.

Brentano, J.C.M. [1] The Manuscripts of Franz Brentano. *Revue internationale de Philosophie* 78 (1966): 477-482.

Carr, D. [72] Intentionality. In E. Pivčević (Ed.), *Phenomenology and Philosophical Understanding*, pp. 17-36. Cambridge 1975.

Castañeda, H.-N. (Ed.) [28] *Intentionality, Minds and Perception*. Detroit 1967.

Chisholm, R.M. [33] Franz Brentano. In P. Edwards (Ed.), *Encyclopedia of Philosophy*, Vol. 1, pp. 365-368. New York 1967.

- [38] Sentences About Believing. In Marras [29], pp. 31-51.
- [39] Intentional Inexistence. In McAlister [27], pp. 140-150.
- [43] The Chisholm-Sellars Correspondence on Intentionality. In Marras [29], pp. 214-248.
- [44] Intentionality. In P. Edwards (Ed.), *Encyclopedia of Philosophy* 4, pp. 201-204. New York 1967.
- [45] On Some Psychological Concepts and the "Logic" of Intentionality. In Castañeda [28], pp. 11-57.
- [46] Notes on the Logic of Believing. In Marras [29], pp. 75-84.

– [47] Brentano on Descriptive Psychology and the Intentional, Essay 1. In M. Mandelbaum and E. Lee (Eds.), *Phenomenology and Existentialism*. Baltimore 1967.

– [55] Rejoinder (to Sleigh [52]). In Castañeda [28], pp. 46-57.

– [56] Believing and Intentionality: A Reply to Mr. Luce and Mr. Sleigh. In Marras [29], pp. 91-96.

– [83] Brentano's Descriptive Psychology. *Proceedings of the XIVth International Congress of Philosophy*, Vol. I, pp. 164-174. Vienna 1968. Reprinted with slight modification in McAlister [27], pp. 91-100.

– [106] Brentano's Conception of Substance and Accident. *Grazer philosophische Studien* 5 (1978): 197-210.

Cohen, L.J. [48] Criteria of Intensionality. *Proceedings of the Aristotelian Society*, Supp. Vol. LXII, pp. 122-142. Vienna 1968.

De Boer, T. [84] The Descriptive Method of Franz Brentano: Its Two Functions and Their Significance for Phenomenology. In McAlister [27], pp. 101-107. Translation by McAlister and M. Schättle of the German original in *Proceedings of the XIVth International Congress of Philosophy*, Vol. I. Vienna 1968.

Deely, J.N. [65] The Immateriality of the Intentional As Such. *The New Scholasticism* 42 (1968): 293-306.

– [66] The Ontological Status of Intentionality. *The New Scholasticism* 46 (1972): 220-233.

Dennett, D.C. [41] Current Issues in the Philosophy of Mind. *American Philosophical Quarterly* 15 (1978): 49-61.

– [93] The Problem of Intentionality. In *Content and Consciousness*, pp. 19-32. London 1969.

– [94] Intentional Systems, Essay 1. In *Brainstorms*, pp. 3-22.   Ann Arbor 1978.

Field, H. [40] Mental Representation. *Erkenntnis* 13 (1978): 9-61.

Findlay, J.N. [85] Comments and Questions raised by Professor Chisholm's Paper on Brentano's Descriptive Psychology. *Proceedings of the XIVth International Congress of Philosophy*, Vol. I, pp. 200-203. Vienna 1968.

Fischer, K. [86] Discussion of Roderick M. Chisholm's "Brentano's Descriptive Psychology". *Proceedings of the XIVth International Congress of Philosophy*, Vol. I, pp. 204-208. Vienna 1968.

Føllesdal, D. [71] Brentano and Husserl on Intentional Objects and Perception. *Grazer philosophische Studien* 5 (1978): 83-94.

Gilson, L. [34] Franz Brentano on Science and Philosophy. In McAlister [27], pp. 68-79. Translation by L. McAlister and M. Schättle of the French text in *Revue internationale de Philosophie* 78 (1966): 416-433.

Golomb, J. [89] Psychology from the Phenomenological Standpoint of Husserl. *Philosophy and Phenomenological Research* 36 (1976): 451-471.

Grossman, R. [103] *Meinong*. London 1974.
– [105] Non-existent Objects: Recent Work on Brentano and Meinong. *American Philosophical Quarterly* 6 (1969): 17-32.
Haller, R. [97] Brentanos Sprachkritik oder dass "Man unterscheiden muss, was es (hier) zu unterscheiden gibt". *Grazer philosophische Studien* 5 (1978): 211-224.
Hamlyn, D.W. [79] The Phenomena of Love and Hate. *Philosophy* 53 (1978): 5-20.
Hedwig, K. [63] Der scholastische Kontext des Intentionalen bei Brentano. *Grazer philosophische Studien* 5 (1978): 67-82.
Husserl, E. [73] *Logical Investigations*. Translated by J.N. Findlay. Investigation V, Vol. II, pp. 533-659, and Appendix, pp. 852-69. London 1970.
Kim, C.-T. [77] Brentano on the Unity of Mental Philosophy. *Philosophy and Phenomenological Research* 39 (1978): 199-207.
Kim, J. [92] Materialism and the Criteria of the Mental. *Synthese* 22 (1971): 323-345.
Kneale, W. [68] Intentionality and Intensionality. *Proceedings of the Aristotelian Society*, Supp. Vol. XLII, (1968): 73-90.
Körner, S. [101] On the Logic of Relations. *Proceedings of the Aristotelian Society N.S.* 77 (1967-77): 150-163.
– [102] Über Brentanos Reismus und die extensionale Logik. *Grazer philosophische Studien* 5 (1978): 29-43.
Kotarbinski, T. [98] Franz Brentano as Reist. In McAlister [27], pp. 194-203. Translation by L. McAlister and M. Schättle of the French original in *Revue Internationale de Philosophie* 78 (1966): 459-476.
Küng, G. [82] Zur Erkenntnistheorie von Franz Brentano. *Grazer philosophische Studien* 5 (1978): 169-81.
Landgrebe, L. [87] *Das Problem der phänomenologischen Psychologie bei Husserl*. *Proceedings of the XIVth International Congress of Philosophy*, Vol. I, pp. 151-163. Vienna 1968.
Lisska, A. [67] Axioms of Intentionality in Aquinas' Theory of Knowledge. *International Philosophical Quarterly* 16 (1976): 305-322.
Luce, D. [54] On the Logic of Belief. In Marras [29], pp. 85-86. Excerpt from *Philosophy and Phenomenological Research* 25 (1964-65): 259-269.
Lycan, W.G. [51] On "Intentionality" and the Psychological. In Marras [29], pp. 97-111. From *American Philosophical Quarterly* 6 (1969): 305-311.
Marras, A. (Ed.) [29] *Intentionality, Mind and Language*. Chicago 1972.
– [60] Scholastic Roots of Brentano's Conception of Intentionality. In McAlister [27], pp. 128-139.
Mayer-Hillebrand, F. [35] Franz Brentano's Einfluss auf die Philosophie seiner Zeit und der Gegenwart. *Revue internationale de Philosophie* 78 (1966): 373-394.
– [95] Introduction to [2], pp. 1-99.

McAlister, L. (Ed.) [27] *The Philosophy of Franz Brentano*. London 1976.
- [61] Franz Brentano and Intentional Inexistence. *Journal of the History of Philosophy*, 1970.
- [62] Chisholm and Brentano on Intentionality. In McAlister [27], pp. 151-159. From *Review of Metaphysics* XXVIII (1974): 328-338.
Mijuskovic, B. [96] Brentano's Theory of Consciousness. *Philosophy and Phenomenological Research* 38 (1978): 315-324.
Morrison, J.C. [76] Husserl and Brentano on Intentionality. *Philosophy and Phenomenological Research* 31 (1970): 27-46.
Morscher, E. [36] Brentano and His Place in Austrian Philosophy. *Grazer philosophische Studien* 5 (1978): 1-9.
O'Connor, D.J. [50] Tests for Intentionality. *American Philosophical Quarterly* 4 (1967): 173-178.
Pivčević, E. (Ed.) [30] *Phenomenology and Philosophical Understanding*. Cambridge 1975.
Prior, A.N. [69] Intentionality and Intensionality. *Proceedings of the Aristotelian Society*, Supp. Vol. XLII, pp. 91-106. 1968.
- [70] Ch. 8: Intentional Attitudes and Relations, In P.T. Geach and A.J.P. Kenny (Eds.), *Objects of Thought*. London 1971.
Quinton, A. [90] The Concept of Phenomenon. In Pivčević [30], pp. 1-16.
Rancurello, A. [25] *A Study of Franz Brentano*. New York 1968.
Sanford, D. [57] On Defining Intentionality. *Proceedings of the XIVth International Congress of Philosophy*, Vol. I, pp. 216-221. Vienna 1968.
Scruton, R. [74] Intensional and Intentional Objects. *Proceedings of the Aristotelian Society N.S.* 71 (1971): 187-207.
Sellars, W. [42] *Science and Metaphysics*, Chs. III: Intentionality and IV: Truth, pp. 60-115. London 1968.
Sleigh, R. [52] Comments on Roderick Chisholm's Paper. In Castañeda [28], pp. 36-45.
- [53] Notes on Chisholm on the Logic of Believing. In Marras [29], pp. 87-91.
Solomon, R. [78] Psychological Predicates. *Philosophy and Phenomenological Research* 36 (1976): 472-493.
Spiegelberg, H. [31] Franz Brentano (1838-1917): Forerunner of the Phenomenological Movement. In *The Phenomenological Movement*, Part 1, pp. 27-50. Third rev. and enl. edition. The Hague 1982.
- [59] "Intention" and "Intentionality" in the Scholastics, Brentano and Husserl. In McAlister [27], 108-127. Translation, with modifications by the author of the German original in *Philosophische Hefte* 5 (1936) and reprinted in *Studia Philosophica* 29 (1970): 189-216. Also (with Supplement 1979) in *The Context of the Phenomenological Movement*, pp. 3-26. The Hague 1981.
Srzednicki, J. [24] *Franz Brentano's Analysis of Truth*. The Hague 1965.
- [99] Some Elements of Brentano's Analysis of Language and their Ramifications. *Revue internationale de Philosophie* 78 (1966): 434-445.

Terrell, B. [81] Quantification and Brentano's Logic. *Grazer philosophische Studien* 5 (1978): 45-65.

– [88] Descriptive Psychology and the Nomology of Mind. *Proceedings of the XIVth International Congress of Philosophy*, Vol. VI, pp. 527-532. Vienna 1971.

– [100] Brentano's Argument for Reismus. In McAllister [27], pp. 204-212. From *Revue internationale de Philosophie* 78 (1966).

Urmson, J.O. [49] Criteria of Intensionality. *Proceedings of the Aristotelian Society*, Supp. Vol. XLII, pp. 107-122. 1968.

Wolf, K. [104] Ernst Mallys Destruktion des Meinongschen Gegenstands. *Proceedings of the XIVth International Congress of Philosophy*, Vol. VI, pp. 584-591. Vienna 1971.

Wollheim, R. [56] Thought and Passion. *Proceedings of the Aristotelian Society N.S.* LXVIII (1968): 1-24.

Husserl's philosophy of mind

DAVID WOODRUFF SMITH
University of California, Irvine

The last ten or fifteen years have seen considerable research on Husserl's philosophy of mind and in particular the emergence of a second major interpretation of Husserl's theory of intentionality. Husserl's overall philosophy involves many strands and multiple purposes, but our concern here is restricted to his account of the nature of mind or consciousness, principally his theory of intentionality, which is the foundation of his phenomenology. Husserl took over from his teacher Brentano the view that consciousness is intentional, or directed toward something. For Husserl, the directedness of an act of consciousness consists in its correlation with a "noema" or meaning (*Sinn*). As of the mid-1960s, the dominant interpretation of Husserl's theory of intentionality and its central notion of noema was the interpretation well articulated by Aron Gurwitsch, dating from 1929. The Gurwitschian interpretation of the noema was taken for granted in the works of such eminent phenomenologists as Dorion Cairns, Alfred Schutz, Rudolf Boehm, and Eugen Fink (so reports Hubert Dreyfus [1], pp. 136-137). But as the 1960s moved into the 1970s, a competing interpretation took root, initiated by Dagfinn Føllesdal. It will be our principal purpose here to lay out Føllesdal's interpretation and compare and contrast it with the orthodox, Gurwitschian interpretation.

Crudely, the contrasting interpretations are these. On Gurwitsch's reading, the noema or Sinn of an act is the "intended" object *as* it is intended, the object *under* the aspect presented, especially the object as it appears perceptually; and the object

Contemporary philosophy. A new survey. Vol. 4, pp. 249–286.
©*1983, Martinus Nijhoff Publishers, The Hague/Boston/London.*

itself is the unity of such Sinne consisting of the object as it would be intended in various other acts. Thus, for Gurwitsch, Husserl's position is somewhat like phenomenalism with "noemata" substituted for the latter's "sense-data". On Føllesdal's interpretation, by contrast, the noema or Sinn of an act is a conceptual entity like Frege's Sinn, and the object intended is (typically) of a very different kind. If one sees a tree and what one sees exists, the object of one's perceptual act is the tree, while the Sinn of one's act is a conceptual entity that prescribes such a tree. The Sinn is an abstract "meaning", while the tree is a physical thing and in no way a unity of Sinne. We might put the contrast thus: on Gurwitsch's reading, the noema or Sinn is an "intentional" object and the object is an infinitely complex intentional object including the Sinn as a limited part; while on Føllesdal's reading, the noema or Sinn is an "intensional" entity like a concept and the object is a thing of a different kind that satisfies the noema as a thing satisfies a concept.

Gurwitsch's absorption with Husserlian phenomenology traces back to his doctoral dissertation of 1929. (See Embree's "Biographical Sketch of Aron Gurwitsch" in Embree [2]. After phenomenology, Gestalt psychological theory was the second great influence on Gurwitsch. Gestalt theory is felt in Gurwitsch's understanding of Husserl insofar as the perceptual noema is considered an "appearance" of the object perceived, and of course Gestalt theory is a strong component of Gurwitsch's own position in his Husserl-inspired phenomenology of perception. (See Gurwitsch [3].) A mature statement of Gurwitsch's reading of Husserl's theory of noema and intentionality is Gurwitsch's "Husserl's Theory of Intentionality in Historical Perspective" [4]. This essay is particularly well-suited to our purpose of comparing and contrasting Gurwitsch's and Føllesdal's readings of Husserl.

Føllesdal's interpretation is presented succinctly in his "Husserl's Notion of Noema" [5]. In a letter to the present author dated 4 December 1979, Føllesdal described the evolution of his reading of Husserl:

> In my M.A. thesis *Husserl und Frege* (1958) [6], I did not yet have the idea that Husserl's notion of noema was a generalization of Frege's notion of Sinn. ... I concentrated

on the transition from *Philosophy of Arithmetic* to *Logical Investigations* and claimed that Frege in all likelihood was a main mover in Husserl's transition from psychologism to phenomenology. ...

The important new idea in Husserl is that he generalizes the notion of Sinn to that of noema. This I did not discover until the late fifties, when I wrote an article on Husserl in Norwegian ... ("Edmund Husserl", in *Vestens tenkere* (Thinkers of the West), Vol. III, pp. 157-177. Oslo: Aschchough, 1962). The interpretation of Husserl that I gave in this article was the basis for the lectures I gave on Husserl at Harvard in the early 1960's and at Stanford since the latter 1960's. After I had taught this course once at Harvard, I also presented the idea in a lecture in a special lecture series at Harvard in July 1962 which I decided to publish many years later ("An Introduction to Phenomenology for Analytic Philosophers" [7]). Hubert Dreyfus, who had been following my course, explained my interpretation to Gurwitsch, who did not agree with it, and Dreyfus brought us together in order to discuss our differences. This was in 1963 or early in 1964, and it seems to me that Gurwitsch's 1967 article [4] may in part be looked upon as an attempt to see how much of a Fregean interpretation of Husserl he could accommodate in his own.

If the speculation in the final sentence is correct, then Gurwitsch's 1967 piece is indeed the work to compare and contrast with the Føllesdalian interpretation. In any event, we shall focus on the 1967 essay by Gurwitsch [4] and the 1969 essay by Føllesdal [5].

The interpretation of Husserl that Føllesdal has presented in his course at Harvard and Stanford will appear before too long as a book on Husserl. The Harvard lectures influenced the doctoral dissertation of Dreyfus (1963) [8], and the lectures at Stanford influenced dissertations of Ronald McIntyre (1970) [9], David Woodruff Smith (1970) [10], John Lad (1971) [11], and Izchak Miller (UCLA, 1980) [12]. In the 1970s there have appeared a number of articles arguing the Føllesdalian interpretation of Husserl, by Dreyfus, McIntyre, and (Woodruff) Smith, as well as related articles by Harrison Hall, Guido Küng, J.N. Mohanty, and

Barry Smith and related books by Richard Aquila and Robert Tragesser. The dissertations of McIntyre and (Woodruff) Smith as well as a joint book [13] published in 1982 also connect the theory of Husserl with modern possible-worlds semantic theory, especially the work of Jaakko Hintikka on belief and perception; and Hintikka has responded to the Husserlian work with ideas from his own approach to intentionality. (All these works are cited in the Bibliography below.)

Addressing recent work on Husserl's theory of mind, we have chosen to focus our efforts on the emergent, Føllesdalian interpretation of Husserl and its differences from the traditional, Gurwitschian interpretation. Here we seek to understand, not to evaluate, the two approaches. We shall consider proposals linking Husserlian doctrine with doctrines of Frege, Bolzano, Meinong, and Twardowski and also proposals about Husserl's theory of perception. We shall also remark on Jacques Derrida's prominent critique of the *Logical Investigations* (his [14]) and on Ernst Tugendhat's notable work on the concept of truth in Husserl (and in Heidegger) [15], insofar as these works interpret Husserl's doctrine of noema and intentionality.

We cannot do justice here to all that has been written in recent years with relevance to Husserl's theory of mind. But some further works surely command mention: David Carr's study of the late Husserl [16], J.N. Findlay's introduction to his invaluable English translation of the *Logical Investigations* [17], D.M. Levin's thorough study of Husserl's epistemology [18], the English translation of Emmanuel Levinas' work on Husserl's theory of intuition [19], Eduard Marbach's study of the self in Husserl's phenomenology [10], Maurice Natanson's award-winning [21], Edo Pivčević's concise and accurate portrait of Husserl's phenomenology [22], (the English translation of) Paul Ricoeur's study of Husserl [23], and Robert Sokolowski's wide-ranging [24]. Other works are cited in the Bibliography below, and many more still in the Bibliography in Elliston and McCormick [25]. In [25] Frederick Olafson's article on Husserl's theory of intentionality should especially be noted.

I. GURWITSCH'S INTERPRETATION OF HUSSERL'S THEORY OF INTENTIONALITY

We begin with Gurwitsch's interpretation as set out in his fine article, "Husserl's Theory of Intentionality in Historical Perspective" [4]. Gurwitsch stresses the continuity of Husserl's theory of intentionality with the history of modern philosophy. Descartes posed the seminal problem by arguing that the immediate and certain objects of human knowledge are one's own mental states, "ideas" in the subsequent terminology of the British empiricists, which for Descartes represent external objects. Berkeley and Hume concurred that ideas are the objects of knowledge but held that objects of nature are not represented by but merely are ideas. Hume further stressed the problem of consciousness of identity (how on his theory to explain our tendency to think that the same object is considered in successive moments of consciousness). Husserl responded to Descartes' problem with a very different solution. For Husserl, consciousness grasps objects such as trees, it is not confined to its own constituent states. Thus, consciousness is "directed" toward, or "intends", something other than itself. Intentionality is just this directedness. The key notions in Husserl's theory of intentionality are "noesis" and "noema". A noesis is a mental act (p. 47), while a noema is a nonmental entity, a "meaning" aligned with the object intended "as" it is intended.

For the sake of comparison with Føllesdal's [5], we shall impose on Gurwitsch's essay a format similar to that of Follesdal's essay, which lays out a series of twelve theses attributed to Husserl. Accordingly, we shall extract from Gurwitsch's essay thirteen theses attributed to Husserl. Then, as we lay out Føllesdal's theses in the next section, we can compare his unfolding interpretation thesis-by-thesis with the interpretation we shall have extracted from Gurwitsch's article. The theses we extract from Gurwitsch's reading follow forthwith.

1. Every act of consciousness is intentional, or directed. (Cf. p. 43.)
2. Directedness is a purely phenomenological feature of an act. (p. 43.)

3. The object toward which an act is directed is distinct from the act itself. (Cf. pp. 25-43.)

Thus, the objects of consciousness are not restricted *à la* Berkeley and Hume to ideas, the states or events of consciousness themselves. Theses 1-3 are the starting point of Husserl's theory, as discussed above.

4. Correlated with every act is a noema or meaning (Sinn), that is, exactly one noema or meaning. (pp. 45-46, 49.)

In understanding a linguistic utterance, one grasps a meaning, which aligns with the object or state of affairs referred to "under" a particular aspect. Similarly, in perception one entertains a "meaning" which aligns with the thing perceived "under" a certain aspect. And, in general, every act has a noema which is a kind of meaning that corresponds to an object under a certain aspect. (We shall return to this characterization of meaning.)

5. The notion of noema is a generalization of the notion of linguistic meaning: as there is correlated with every linguistic act a meaning, so with every act of consciousness there is correlated a meaning, generally called a noema. (p. 47.)
6. Different acts may have the same noema, or meaning. (pp. 46-46.)

For the same object may be presented under the same aspect in different acts. And since the same object can be presented to consciousness under different aspects, acts with different noemata or meanings may present the same object. Thus:

7. Different meanings may refer to the same object. (pp. 45-46.)
8. The noema or meaning of an act is distinct from the object intended in the act. (p. 45.)

This is a corollary of thesis 7.

9. Noemata, or meanings, are ideal, or abstract. (p. 46.)

They are aspatial, atemporal, acausal (p. 46). Thus, they are abstract entities of a special kind. If the object intended is a tree, the object, unlike the meaning, is located in space and time and enters into causal relations.

10. The same noematic "nucleus", or meaning, may be accompanied by different noematic "characters". (p. 48.)

For instance, what is seen under a certain aspect may later be remembered under that same aspect. Then the same meaning is accompanied by the noematic character of perception in the one act and by the character of memory in the other act. We might infer, as Føllesdal makes explicit, that the noema of an act includes not only a meaning as nucleus but also a noematic character.

11. An act is essentially correlated with its noema and importantly distinguished by it.

"...it is only with reference to the [noema] that the act is qualified and characterized as that which it is, e.g., that particular perception of the house as seen from the front" (p. 48).

12. An act is directed to an object if and only if its noema includes references to further noemata incorporating different manners of presentation of that same object. (p. 50.)

Perception, in particular, presents an object only one-sidedly, from one perspective, under one aspect. But the same object can be presented differently, from different perspectives, under different aspects. And this fact must be reflected in the perceptual act's noema.

13. The meaning of an act is the object intended *as* it is intended. (pp. 45, 47.)

This is the key thesis in Gurwitsch's interpretation. The "object which is intended" is dintinguished from the "object *as* it is intended", the latter being the meaning. (p. 45.)

> 14. The object intended in an act is nothing but the system of noemata presenting the same object. (p. 53.)

Thus, "the thing perceived also proves to have noematic status. As a noematic system it is a noema itself, but a noema of higher order, so to speak." (p. 54.) Indeed:

> 15. The relation of a noema to the object it refers to is a relation of part to whole. (p. 53.)

Theses 13-15 seem to form a kind of idealism — what Husserl called "transcendental idealism", if Gurwitsch's interpretation is correct. For Husserl, consciousness grasps "the thing itself" (p. 52), which is neither an idea (noesis) nor a bundle of ideas, as Berkeley and Hume had held, to this extent, Husserl was not an idealist. But consciousness grasps objects only one-sidedly, under one aspect (p. 52), in short, noemata. And yet the object itself is nothing but a unity of noemata, objective but merely "intentional" in its being. This seems to be a sort of idealism albeit non-Berkeleyan: "noemalism", if you will. Moreover, since Gurwitsch stresses primarily perceptual noemata, objects under perceptual aspects, the object of a perceptual act is a system of perceptual aspects or "appearances". And this is a view not unlike subsequent forms of phenomenalism.

The unity of noemata that constitutes an object is an intentional unity: a unity of noemata or meanings which by virtue of their own structure cohere as "the same object". This, Gurwitsch holds, is the twist that solves Hume's problem of how identity is given in consciousness. Thus, intentionality consists not merely in the correlation of noema with noesis (as theses 4 and 11 require — cf. p. 49). Intentionality consists in this correlation being such that the correlated noema includes references to further noemata (as 12 requires), a system of noemata constituting "the same object" (as per 13-15). Only with this reference to further noemata is a transcendent object intended. (Cf. pp. 43, 54.)

In sum, Gurwitsch understands an act's noema or meaning as what is sometimes called an "intentional object". an object that is intended independently of whether it actually exists and is exactly and only "as" it is intended (having just those properties it is intended as having). Indeed, Husserl often calls the noematic Sinn the "intentional object" as well as the "object as intended". Further, Gurwitsch understands the object "which" is intended to be merely an intentional object comprising not only the given aspect but all other aspects "the same" object might have. (The "existence" of an object consists in its having a place in a system of objects appropriately related to one another, this system prescribed by the relevant system of noemata: cf. Gurwitsch [26], p. 123.) Importantly, it seems that on Gurwitsch's reading the Sinn, the object as intended, is *intended*. It is not the object *which* is intended but is that part of the object that is in a strict sense apprehended in the act. The full object is intended as the indeterminate completion of the object as intended.

II. FØLLESDAL'S INTERPRETATION OF HUSSERL'S THEORY OF INTENTIONALITY

In "Husserl's Notion of Noema" (1969) [5], Føllesdal proceeds by laying down a series of theses he holds are fundamental to Husserl's theory of intentionality. We shall recite the theses in Føllesdal's own words and compare and contrast them with Gurwitsch's interpretation.

"The general theme of phenomenology, according to Husserl," Føllesdal begins, "is intentionality, that is, the peculiarity of consciousness to be consciousness *of* something." Føllesdal stresses Husserl's response to Brentano, his acceptance of Brentano's thesis that consciousness is essentially intentional and his avoidance of Brentano's theory of intentionality. "The directedness has nothing to do with the object's being real, Brentano held; the object is itself contained in our mental activity, intentionally contained in it" (p. 241). Evidently, Brentano held a theory akin to the theory of ideas, that the proper and immediate objects of consciousness are somehow contained in consciousness itself. But Husserl held a very different view:

> Although every act is directed, this does not mean that there always is some object toward which it is directed. According to Husserl, there is associated with each act a *noema*, in virtue of which the act is directed toward its object, if it has any. When we think of a centaur, our act of thinking has a noema, but it has no object: there exists no object of which we think. Because of its noema, however, even such an act is directed. To be *directed* simply is to have a noema. [p. 242]

Thus, Føllesdal would agree with Gurwitsch that for Husserl every act is intentional, intentionality is a phenomenological feature of acts, and the object of an act is distinct from the act itself; these were Gurwitsch's first three theses. Clearly, the key notion in Husserl's theory of intentionality, according to both Gurwitsch and Føllesdal, is the notion of noema.

Føllesdal's main thesis about the noema in Husserl's theory is:
> "1. The noema is an intensional entity, a generalization of the notion of meaning (Sinn, Bedeutung)."

Gurwitsch's thesis 5 holds the same. But Føllesdal says thesis 1 "and its consequences go against the usual interpretations of Husserl" (p. 242). The difference, to which we shall return, lies in what Føllesdal and Gurwitsch take meanings to be.

> "2. A noema has two components: (1) one which is common to all acts that have the same object, with exactly the same properties, ... regardless of the 'thetic' character of the act, i.e., whether it be perception, remembering, imagining, etc., and (2) one which is different in acts with different thetic character."

The first component, Føllesdal notes, Husserl calls "noematischer Sinn". This thesis is pretty explicit in Gurwitsch's 10.

> "3. The noematic Sinn is that in virtue of which consciousness relates to the object."

Gurwitsch could agree with this, as stated, but his account of this point would be very different because the relation of Sinn to object is different on his account.

> "4. The noema of an act is not the object of the act (i.e., the object toward which the act is directed.)"

Here we have Gurwitsch's 8. The point is crucial.

> "5. To one and the same noema, there corresponds only one object."
> "6. To one and the same object there may correspond several different noematic Sinne, and hence several different noemata."

Gurwitsch would surely accept 5, and 6 is Gurwitsch's 7.

> "The noemata help to individualize the acts," Føllesdal says, "in that":

> "7. Each act has one and only one noema."

This is Gurwitsch's 4 and the remark is similar to Gurwitsch's 11.

> "8. Noemata are abstract entities."

This is Gurwitsch's 9.

Gurwitsch's 12 said directedness requires a noema to include references to further noemata incorporating different manners of presentation of that same object. Føllesdal too recognizes this feature of intentionality for Husserl:

> That seeing is intentional, object-directed, means that the near side of the thing we have in front of us is regarded only as a side of a thing, and that the thing we are seeing has other sides and determinations which are co-intended to the extent that the full thing is regarded as something more than one side. ... The noema is a complex system of such determinations ... which make a multitude of visual,

tactile and other data be appearances of one object. [p. 249]

Thus:

"12. This pattern of determinations, together with the Gebenheitsweise, is the noema."

(The *Gegebenheitsweise* is the noema component including the thetic character and other "ways of givenness".)

Highlighting our comparison so far, we find Føllesdal and Gurwitsch in agreement on the following fundamentals of Husserl's theory of intentionality. An act is (in most cases) directed toward something other than itself. Correlated with the act is a noema, including in particular a Sinn. The act is directed toward an object in virtue of its noema, in particular, its Sinn. Different acts may have the same noema, and different noemata or Sinne may be related to the same object. A noema predelineates other noemata related to the same object, presenting that same object under different aspects. The noema or Sinn is not the object. The noema or Sinn is an abstract entity. Indeed, Sinn is a generalization of meaning.

Thus, Føllesdal and Gurwitsch are in agreement on a great deal: on Gurwitsch's theses 1-12 and Føllesdal's theses 1-8 and 12. Where do they differ? They differ primarily in what they take the noema to be and hence on its role in intentionality. The Sinn, says Gurwitsch, is for Husserl the object *as* intended; and the object is but a system of Sinne, the Sinne being parts of the objects, the object "under" various aspects. These are Gurwitsch's theses 13-15, and Føllesdal could not accept them. Specifically, on Gurwitsch's reading, the Sinn, the object *as intended*, is apparently *intended* – though it is distinguished from the full object *which* is intended, of which it is only a part. In particular, the object as perceived is perceived, for it is an appearance of the object. (Cf. Dreyfus [1], pp. 153 ff.) Føllesdal explicitly denies this, holding:

"9. Noemata are not perceived through our senses."

Føllesdal also holds:

> "10. Noemata are known through a special reflection, the phenomenological reflection."
>
> "11. The phenomenological reflection can be iterated."

Now, thesis 9 is surely in conflict with Gurwitsch's interpretation. But Gurwitsch would doubtless agree with 10: the phenomenological reduction surely yields the "object as intended", and not the object itself. However, what is obtained, what the Sinn is, differs from Føllesdal to Gurwitsch. So the agreement, on Føllesdal's 10 and indeed on his 1 and 3, is agreement in words only: they mean to say different things with the words. And Gurwitsch could not agree with thesis 11; in fact, on the Gurwitschian reading, 11 makes little sense — having bracketed the object to yield the object as intended, one cannot bracket that (to yield the object as intended as intended?).

Gurwtisch holds that the Sinn is an abstract entity, as Føllesdal requires. But this point raises a problem for Gurwitsch's view of the Sinn and the object. For Gurwitsch, the Sinn is the intended object under an aspect, a sort of part of the object, while the object is a unity of Sinne and thus itself has "noematic status". Yet, as Føllesdal quotes Husserl (p. 246, citing *Ideas*, § 89), the tree that is perceived can burn away but the perceived tree as such, the tree as perceived, cannot burn away: it is ideal, abstract. Now, if the object that is intended is itself a noematic unity, how can it burn away? Similarly, Dreyfus says ([1], p. 246), "If the noema is ... [an] ideal entity in Husserl's sense, there is no way to understand how a system of such entities could ever be said to *be* a perceptual object." And if the Sinn is the object *as* intended, the object restricted to an aspect, a sort of part of the object, how can this exist when the object has burned away? At the least, it is difficult to see how to make sense of the position Gurwitsch ascribes to Husserl on this point.

On the other hand, Husserl explicitly characterizes the Sinn of an act as the "object as intended", and Føllesdal's position must be reconciled with this characterization of Husserl's. Dreyfus takes up this need ([1], pp. 153 ff). The phrase 'the "object as intended"' appears already in *Logical Investigations*, Dreyfus observes, where it is used as a way to distinguish linguistic meaning from the object referred to. "[T]o clear up the ambiguity in the phrase 'what is meant,'" Drefus writes (p. 157), "Husserl quite naturally chooses to call the object 'what is meant' and to call the sense of the expression 'the meant as such,' i.e., what is purely and essentially meant." Here, according to Dreyfus, Husserl is dealing with a theory of linguistic meaning like Frege's. This notion is extended to perception and other kinds of acts in the later Investigations. Then in *Ideas* the notion of noematic Sinn is explicitly assumed as a generalization of the notion of linguistic meaning to all acts: Dreyfus and Føllesdal both quote *Ideen* III, p. 89, "the noema is nothing but a generalization of the notion of meaning to the total realm of acts." And Husserl continues to use this counter-intuitive expression 'the "intended as such"' or 'the "object as intended"' to characterize noematic Sinn in general. However, the Føllesdalian should say, this is not to specify what the Sinn *is*, viz., as Gurwitsch takes it, the object restricted to an aspect, especially what is purely given of the object, rather, it is to specify the Sinn, understood in a Frege-like way, as opposed to the object — and so to signal the turn from object to Sinn.

Føllesdal's reading attributes Husserl the following broad picture of intentionality. The directedness of an act consists in the correlation with the act of a noema, which includes a Sinn. The Sinn is a conceptual entity that prescribes an object having various properties. If there is such an object, an object satisfying the Sinn, then that is the object of the act. If there is no such object, then the act has no object, though it remains as if directed successfully toward an object. Sinne are abstract entities generically of a kind with linguistic meanings. When I see a tree, the Sinn of my perceptual act is an entity of a completely different kind than the tree, if such tree exists. The Sinn prescribes only an aspect of the tree; thus, the perception is a one-sided presentation of the tree, presenting only an aspect and in particular a side of the tree. But the Sinn is in no way a part of the tree, and the tree is a physical thing and in no way a unity of Sinne. Correlated with the tree is a system of Sinne that present that same tree, and the act's Sinn somehow calls these further Sinne into play. But the tree is something of a completely different kind. The relation of Sinn to object is in no way one of part to whole, it is the relation of a conceptual entity to the object satisfying it. This is the relation on which semantics is based in the tradition of Frege. Thus, where for Gurwitsch's Husserl the Sinn is an "intentional" object and the object a "higher-order" intentional object, for Føllesdal's Husserl the Sinn is an "intensional" entity and the object is in no way an intensional entity but rather a physical thing of a different ontological category. Gurwitsch agrees that the notion of noematic Sinn is a generalization of the notion of linguistic meaning, but he takes meaning or Sinn to be a very different sort of entity.

III. HUSSERL AND FREGE ON *SINN*

Fundamental to the Føllesdalian approach to understanding Husserl has been an assimilation of Husserl to Frege. Husserl's distinction between act, Sinn, and object (*Gegenstand*) — or noesis, noema, and object — "exactly parallels" Frege's distinction between idea, sense, and reference (*Vorstellung, Sinn*, and *Bedeutung*) in "Über Sinn und Bedeutung" (1892) [27], Dreyfus says in [28] (p. 198; from his dissertation [8]). "The only change Husserl made in Frege's analysis was terminological," he continues; "Husserl proposes to use 'object' (*Gegenstand*) for 'reference' (*Bedeutung*), and *Bedeutung* and *Sinn* interchangeably for 'sense' (*Sinn*)" (p. 199).

In his [5], Føllesdal notes some "striking similarities between Husserl's notion of noema and Frege's notion of Sinn" (p. 248): Husserl and Frege both hold that a Sinn illuminates an aspect of the object it determines; both hold that there corresponds to a physical object an infinity of Sinne and no Sinn can exhaust the object (i.e., illuminate every aspect of it); and both recognize an infinite hierarchy of Sinne leading from an object to Sinne of that object to Sinne of each such Sinn and so on (here Føllesdal quotes Husserl's unpublished manuscript *Noema und Sinn*). More than the similarities of Sinn, Føllesdal has stressed in his lectures that an important way to understand Husserl's theory of intentionality is by analogy with Frege's theory of sense and reference. On Frege's theory of linguistic reference, an expression refers to an object just in case it expresses a sense that determines that object; and if no (existing) object answers to the sense, then nothing is referred to, though the expression still is meaningful insofar as it has a sense. Similarly, on Husserl's theory of intentionality, an act is directed toward an object just in case it has a noema or Sinn that determines that object, and if no (existing) object answers to the Sinn, then nothing is intended, though the act still has the character of being as if directed toward an object insofar as it has a noema. Both theories are founded on a sharp distinction between sense and object referred to or intended. It is assumed senses prescribe or determine objects, and in the case of physical objects there is a sharp difference in ontological kind between the object and the sense that determines it. For the sense is abstract, while the object is concrete. A sense determines an object by appeal to a limited aspect of the object, but the sense is in no way — as Gurwitsch held — the object itself limited to that aspect. And the sense is in no way referred to for Frege or intended for Husserl, as Gurwitsch held.

Smith and McIntyre's "Intentionality via Intensions" [29] pursues the parallel between Husserl's theory of intentionality and Frege's theory of reference in some detail. But the authors further stress Husserl's structuring of the Sinn component of the noema into an "X" and a complex of "predicate-senses", a structure not found in Frege's theory of Sinn. The X is an item of sense that Husserl stresses in *Ideas*, § 131, distinguishing it from predicate-"content"; where the X stands for the object "simpliciter" or "in abstraction from" its properties, the predicate-senses in the Sinn prescribe the properties the object is intended as having, the aspect under which it is presented. Thus, the authors write:

> This abstract meaning entity, the noematic Sinn in a noema, does two things, through its two components. Through its predicate-meanings (collectively, its content), a Sinn prescribes what it is that one experiences about an object given in an act through this Sinn, what properties the object is given as having. And through its X — though probably together with some of its predicate-meanings — the Sinn serves to pick out *which* object is given, to *individuate* it.

The role of X's in noematic Sinne is most clearly evident

> ... in the *co-directedness* of acts, the directedness of differ-
> ent acts to numerically the same object. [pp. 555-556]

We may observe that the X plays the crucial role required of the noema by both Gurwitsch and Føllesdal, that of invoking the multiplicity of noemata related to the same object. The authors also note that Husserl's notion of noema and his theory of intentionality via noematic Sinn, understood as similar to Frege's theory of reference via sense, preclude identifying the object intended with a system of noematic Sinne (as Gurwitsch held); on their reading, Husserl is a realist and not an idealist (of the sort Gurwitsch proposed).

In [28] Dreyfus sketches the development of Husserl's account of Sinn in supporting the proposal that Husserl took over Frege's doctrine and generalized it. The sixth of Husserl's *Logical Investigations* offers Husserl's first phenomenological analysis of perception, which *Ideas* carries further. The sixth Investigation depends on results of the first Investigation, which deals with expression and meaning. There Husserl distinguishes the signifying act, the intentional content or ideal meaning (Bedeutung), and the object referred to. It is this distinction that is generalized in the sixth Investigation and in *Ideas* becomes the distinction between act, noema, and object.

In "Husserl's Identification of Meaning and Noema" [40], McIntyre and Smith pursue a stronger line, that Husserl's notion of noema is not only similar to, a generalization of, the notion of linguistic meaning but is identical therewith. Husserl, the authors hold, held a strong version of the classical theory that language expresses thought. The meanings expressed in language just are the noematic Sinne of underlying acts of thought; and noematic Sinne are in principle always expressible in language. (There are certain limitations on expressibility: certain "Gegebenheitsweise", or "ways of givenness", are not expressible directly; these include clarity, attentiveness, and especially intuitional fullness.) Thus, meanings and noematic Sinne are the same things, for Husserl. And intentionality is not only analogous to reference in being mediated by Sinn. Husserl's theory of reference, which is essentially the same as Frege's but stressed speaker's over word's reference, is based on his theory of intentionality: a person's referring to an object by uttering a given expression is founded on his underlying intention of that object, and the meaning expressed is the noematic Sinn of that intention.

Robert Solomon too has sought to assimilate Husserl and Frege in "Sense and Essence: Frege and Husserl" [30]. Solomon too assimilates Husserl's notion of meaning or Sinn to Frege's, but he also identifies Husserl's notions of Sinn and essence (*Wesen*) and identifies these with Frege's notion of Sinn. But, J.N. Mohanty has argued in his [31], Solomon has gone too far. Husserl's notion of Sinn is indeed close to Frege's: as Solomon observes, the differences might be seen as differences in theory about the same assumed entities (p. 269). But essences and Sinne are not the same thing for Husserl. Essences are abstract, or ideal, entities including especially properties; senses are abstract, or ideal, entities but not properties, or essences, of objects. In the *Investigations* Husserl did take senses to be "intentional" or "semantic" essences of acts, but he was careful to distinguish the essence Red that belongs to red objects from the sense "red" that is an essence belonging to acts of thinking of red objects. In *Ideas*, though, Husserl no longer takes senses to be essences of acts, evidently, they are a special class of abstract entities other than act-essences. (Cf. Aquila [32], pp. 108 f, 115 f.)

Obviously, the affinities between Husserl and Frege are of conceptual importance for understanding Husserl's theory of intentionality on the Føllesdalian interpretation. If there were actual historical influences between the thinkers, this would lend support to the interpretation. In his [6] Føllesdal hypothesized that Husserl was led from psychologism to anti-psychologism, and ultimately phenomenology, by criticism from Frege. Føllesdal's reasoning is summarized by Mohanty in opening his "Husserl and Frege: New Look at Their Relationship" [33]:

> Husserl's explicit rejection of psychologism ... and his advocacy of a conception of pure logic as a science of objective meanings were first expounded in the *Prolegomena to Pure Logic* (1900) of *Logical Investigations*, and Husserl tells us that the *Prolegomena*, in its essentials, is a reworking of lectures he had given at Halle in the year 1896. Føllesdal, in his careful study of the relation between Frege and Hus-

serl during these years, asks the question, at what point of time between 1890 (the year of publication of the *Philosophie der Arithmetik*) and 1896 did this change in Husserl's mode of thinking take place? The papers published during 1892-93 do not, according to Føllesdal, bear testimony to any such change. In the paper "Psychologische Studien zur elementaren Logik" of the year 1894, Husserl is still found to believe that the foundations of logic can be clarified with the help of psychology. Accordingly, the change must have occurred between the years 1894 and 1896. Frege's famed review of the *Philosophie der Arithmetik* appeared in the year 1894. Føllesdal therefore conjectures that it is Frege's review which must have led Husserl to a complete revision of his prior mode of thinking. [p. 51]

Dreyfus in [28] (pp. 198-199) and Solomon in [30] (pp. 260-261) follow suit, holding that Frege's critical review in 1894 turned Husserl to the act/sense/object doctrine of *Logical Investigations* and *Ideas*, and to his developed theory of intentionality. But Mohanty in his [33] finds Husserl's distinction between *Vorstellung* (psychic act, representation, idea), *Sinn* or *Bedeutung*, and object (*Gegenstand*) already in Husserl's 1891 review of Schröder's *Vorlesungen über die Algebra der Logik*. On the basis of letters exchanged between Husserl and Frege, Mohanty observes that both Husserl and Frege held threefold distinctions between Vorstellung, Sinn, and object already in 1891 — before Frege's "On Sense and Reference" [27] and before Frege's critical 1894 review. Mohanty thus hypthesizes that both Husserl and Frege had arrived at similar distinctions independently of one another by 1891.

It may be that the historical connections between Husserl and Frege have been overemphasized. Though Frege's review no doubt played a major role in moving Husserl from psychologism to anti-psychologism and hence to phenomenology, Husserl's distinction among act, content or noema, and object was not simply taken over from Frege's distinction among idea, sense, and referent. In the letter of 4 December 1979, to the present author, Føllesdal reports:

In my M.A. thesis (1958) ... I ... showed that Husserl had studied all of Frege's writings very carefully before he started developing phenomenology. This includes ... the distinction between the sense and reference of linguistic expressions. However, I make no major point of this latter distinction. I mention briefly that Husserl in LU II[I], p. 47 ff, makes a similar distinction and that in a footnote in LU II[I], p. 53, he criticizes Frege's choice of terms for this distinction. The reason that no major point should be made of the occurrence of the distinction in Husserl, is that this and similar distinctions have a long tradition in philosophy and that Husserl knew the distinction also from, e.g., Bolzano's *Wissenschaftslehre*. In some of my papers I mention various other philosophers with similar ideas, from the stoics on. In my course on Husserl I go into some of these, notably Bolzano, to whom, as you know, I devote several lectures.

If Føllesdal is right, then influences on Husserl other than Frege should be considered too.

IV. HUSSERL AND BOLZANO, TWARDOWSKI, AND MEINONG

In his *Wissenschaftslehre* (1837), Bernard Bolzano had drawn a distinction among subjective idea (Vorstellung), objective idea, and object — a distinction very like Frege's later distinction. In *Logical Investigations*, Husserl refers to Bolzano frequently and positively; indeed, he says, "Logic as a science must ... be built upon Bolzano's work" (Prolegomenon, Appendix to § 61). And a few years later Brentano says in a letter to Husserl in 1905, "You praise Bolzano as your teacher and guide" (in Solomon [34]). Evidently, Bolzano's distinction was a strong influence on Husserl's act/content/object distinction in the *Investigations* and his later noesis/noema/object distinction. Judging by the references in the *Investigations*, Husserl would seem to have been more strongly influenced by Bolzano's distinction than by Frege's distinction among idea, sense, and reference. Notice that an assimilation of Husserl's distinction to either Bolzano's or Frege's aligns more closely with the Føllesdalian than the Gurwitschian reading of Husserl. We might say the Føllesdal reading stresses Husserl's affinity for prior doctrines in *logical* theory, whereas the Gurwitsch reading stresses Husserl's affinity for prior doctrines in *epistemological* theory. But both interpreters would surely agree on the other stress as well.

Another influence on Husserl, it has been suggested, may have been Kasimir Twardowski's *On the Content and Object of Presentations* [35], which Husserl reviewed in 1896. This work was published in the same year as Frege's critical review of Husserl's *Philosophy of Arithmetic*. Twardowski frequently cites Bolzano, and Husserl cites Twardowski's book several times — somewhat critically — in *Logical Investigations*. Thus, Husserl's doctrine of act, content, and object may have been reinforced by reading the works of Bolzano, Frege, and Twardowski. But since Frege, Twardowski, and Husserl all produced similar distinctions in about the same years, and since the general sort of distinction had a long tradition in logical theory before their time, a tradition not only including Bolzano and Mill in the mid-1800s but tracing into Medieval times, it is most likely that all these thinkers were developing their own versions of a general idea that was widely known and commonly discussed in their time.

J.N. Findlay says (in Pivčević [36]) that it was from Twardowski that Husserl "took over" the doctrine of [reell] content in *Logical Investigations* (that which in *Ideas* became noesis). In 1977 there appeared an English translation [35] by Reinhardt Grossmann of Twardowski's book including a lengthy introduction with Grossman's own perspective on Twardowski, Meinong, and Husserl. Grossmann further assumes that Husserl acquired his act/noema/object distinction from Twardowski, who carefully distinguished act, content, and object. Meinong, it is known, explicitly adopted the distinction from Twardowski; Husserl did too, Grossmann assumes. (Grossmann does not explicitly say this, but his discussion imples this, as when, for example, he writes of "Twardowski and his followers", Meinong and Husserl.) Findlay's and Grossmann's assumption conflicts with Føllesdal's hypothesis and with Mohanty's evidence in letters between Husserl and Frege in 1891 that Husserl already held a distinction between Vorstellung, Sinn, and Gegenstand. Grossmann offers no textual support for either the historical assumption or the conceptual assimilation; his introduction is offered as a philosophical discussion of the relevant issues. Still, the assimilation Grossmann draws between Husserl and Twardowski and Meinong is of conceptual interest.

Grossmann's understanding of Husserl is essentially Gurwitsch's, and Grossmann sees the same theory of intentionality in Husserl, Twardowski, and Meinong. Recalling "Moore's famous example of the inkstand of which, so Moore claims, he can never see the whole," Grossmann writes:

> We must ... carefully distinguish [for Twardowski] between the *intention* of an idea and the *object* of the idea. ['Intention' in this use is Grossmann's, not Twardowski's.] The intention of an idea comprises just those properties, features, aspects, or parts of an object which are presented by means of the idea and its parts. ... The object of the idea, on the other hand, is an "infinitely" complex bundle of properties and relations. This bundle is so complex that it can never be the intention of a single idea. What our ideas intend, therefore, are never the "real" perceptual objects, but, at best, certain properties, features, aspects, or parts of them. ...
>
> Both Meinong and Husserl reach the same conclusion as Twardowski, and essentially along the same line: There are no adequate ideas of objects. Both Meinong and Husserl, therefore, must also distinguish between the intentions of ideas and their objects. Meinong calls these intentions "incomplete objects," while Husserl speaks of "noemata". And both of these philosophers hold that objects can only be given to a mind *through* the intentions of our ideas; they themselves can never be intentions. ... [pp. xxv-xxvi]

The coincidence of this view of Husserl with Gurwitsch's should be clear.

Grossmann sees no significant difference between Husserl's phenomenology and Meinong's theory of "entities" (or objects: *Gegenständen*):

Meinong's theory of entities and Husserl's phenomenology rest on the same two basic theses. According to the first thesis, every mental act has an intention [or intentional object] , the second thesis states that intentions have properties and stand in relations irrespective of their ontological status. The theory of entities is simply the theory of intentions, and so, of course, is phenomenology. ... Twardowski ... defends both of these theses. [p. xi]

Even if the alignment between Meinong and Husserl (i.e., Husserl *à la* Grossmann and Gurwitsch) is not perfect, the assimilation is of considerable help in grasping the Gurwitschian Husserl's position. For Meinong's view is sharply put by Meinong himself and succinctly summarized here by Grossmann. Meinong's great early expositor, J.N. Findlay, too, sees a great parallel of endeavors between Meinong and Husserl, though he does not articulate the isomorphism Grossmann sees. (Cf. [37] , pp. viii-ix.)

For Meinong, objects are assumed as whatever can serve as an object of thought, regardless of whether it exists or has being. And an object has properties regardless of whether it exists or has being. Some objects are "incomplete", or incompletely determined; these are objects that have only a certain number of properties and neither have nor lack any other property: thus, *the golden mountain* has just the properties of being golden and being mountainous. Existing physical objects are complete (either having or lacking every appropriate property), and lie beyond the grasp of the human mind. Thus, what are intended in mental acts are only incomplete objects. These are, on one important construction, "objects under aspects", as Gurwitsch says noematic Sinne are. Even complete objects are of a kind with incomplete objects, i.e., they have the status of objects of thought even though they lie beyond actual human thought; their existence or nonexistence is another matter. This point would explicate the Gurwitschian claim that the object itself has "noematic" status. The principal tension between this "Meinongian" reading of Husserl and the Gurwitschian reading would seem to be that Gurwitsch stresses that the complete physical object is intended — it is the "object *which* is intended" as opposed to the "object as intended".

Grossmann rejects the Føllesdalian assimilation between Husserl and Frege. Noting the need to distinguish along Fregean lines between a "description" (whatever is expressed by a linguistic expression of form 'the ...') and what is described, Grossmann writes:

> ... Meinong and Husserl had already arrived, independently of any consideration of descriptions, at a distinction between incomplete and complete objects. Nothing may seem therefore more natural, at least on first glance, than to identify incomplete objects with descriptions and complete objects with the entities described by descriptions. Indeed, there are some recent articles in which it is claimed that Husserl's noemata (incomplete objects, in Meinong's terminology) are really Fregean senses. [Footnote cites Dreyfus' and Føllesdal's articles discussed above.] But even though Husserl — and Meinong as well — talks at times as if noemata are what Frege calls senses, an identification of these two kinds of entity is not at all plausible. The relation between an incomplete object and "its" complete object is that of part to whole, the incomplete object is a constituent of the complete object. The relation between a description [or sense] and what it describes [or refers to], on the other hand, is quite obviously not of this sort. [p. xxi]

The Føllesdalian's response is clear: Meinong's incomplete objects are indeed quite sifferent from Frege's senses, but Husserl's noemata or Sinne align with Fregean senses and not Meinogian incomplete objects. (For a critique of the Meinongian position from such a perspective, cf. Smith [38].) Nor is Husserl's motivation of his Sinn/object distinction initially, primarily, or exclusively the need — as Grossmann holds — to account for the fact that we apprehend physical objects only under limited aspects, as opposed to the Fregean need to distinguish sense and referent because two descriptions may have the same referent but have different senses. The Fregean motivation is in fact Husserl's motivation in the first of the *Logical Investigation*. Dreyfus observes:

The need for this distinction between the real object and the ideal content [or meaning] of the act will become clear, Husserl claims, when we notice that ... several expressions may have different meanings (*Bedeutung*) and all have the same object (*Gegenstand*). [Husserl, LU 47] To conceptualize these relationships we must distinguish in a threefold way: the meaning-conferring act, the meaning of the act, and the object meant. [28], [p. 198]

As we noted earlier, Dreyfus has observed that Husserl generalized his initial account of meaning and object from acts of linguistic expression to acts of consciousness generally. In the sixth Investigation Husserl addressed perception, and in *Ideas* he stressed perception and other acts much more than linguistic acts. He did increasingly stress the problem of the object being given only "one-sidedly" in perception, which Grossmann stresses. But he also stressed the Fregean problem that the same object can be given under different aspects. At root, the problems are the same: an object can be given only *under* a *limited* aspect.

V. TUGENDHAT AND DERRIDA ON HUSSERL

Among prominent recent works on Husserl are Ernst Tugendhat's *Der Wahrheitsbegriff bei Husserl und Heidegger* (1967) [15] and Jacques Derrida's *Speech and Phenomena* [14] (English translation, 1973; title essay, 1967). Tugendhat's interpretation lines up fairly precisely with the orthodox Gurwitschian; it coincides with the Føllesdalian up to the point where Føllesdal and Gurwitsch diverge. Derrida's understanding of Husserl's theory of intentionality is harder to pin down; he stresses the ideality of sense and noema for Husserl, which is consonant with Føllesdal, but he seems to think Husserl identifies being with intuitive presence, an interpretation aligning with Tugendhat and with some idealist readings of Husserl.

Tugendhat's concerns with the concept of truth in Husserl's philosophy lie tangential to our concerns with Husserl's theory of intentionality. But Tugendhat's study includes a careful, recent reading of Husserl's theory of intentionality and of Sinn and noema. In contrast with the psychological position of Brentano and the object-theoretic position of Meinong, he holds, the central theme of Husserl's "phenomenology" is that of "ways of givenness" (*Gegebenheitsweisen*) (p. 30).

Where Brentano distinguished act from object and where Twardowski distinguished act-content from act-object (from whence Meinong went on to his theory of objects), Tugendhat observes, Husserl distinguished intentional content from real (*reell*) content. The real content of an act is a part of the stream of consciousness, whereas the intentional content is instead something correlated with the real content (p. 33). But 'intentional content' can mean either the intentional object or the intentional Sinn (pp. 34-45). Thus the "object *which* is intended" is distinguished from the "object *as* it is intended"; or, in the terms of *Ideas*, the "object simpliciter" is distinguished from the "object in the manner of its determinations" (p. 35). These same distinctions are observed in both *Logical Investigations* and in *Ideas*; what is called "matter" in the *Investigations* is called "Sinn" in *Ideas*, though 'Sinn' is consistently applied to a part of the intentional content in *Ideas* whereas 'matter' was sometimes applied to the corresponding part of the real content. These basic distinctions are of course observed by both the Gurwtischian and Føllesdalian interpretations. But further points align Tugendhat with Gurwitsch.

The distinction between "object simpliciter" and "object in the manner of determinations" is a distinction within the Sinn, according to Tugendhat. And this claim falls directly in line with Gurwitsch and against Føllesdal:

> Therein lies a decisive step beyond Brentano and Meinong: To be sure, every act is directed "through" its Sinn and always upon one or more objects (*Ideen* 316), but the full correlate of the intentionality, that "whereof" the act has a "consciousness", is not an object but rather Sinn (*Ideen* 218 f). [p. 36, in translation]

So, on Tugendhat's reading, the Sinn is intended in the act and is the proper object or intentional correlate of consciousness.

The full noema includes the intentional object (p. 38) (the Sinn as "object in the manner") and the components representing positing characters. These distinctions too fit either Gurwitsch's or Føllesdal's interpretation, except that the intentional object, or object intended, is not for Føllesdal a part of the noema.

Ideas brings a new theory concerning the status of the object of an act, according to Tugendhat. Underlying the various adumbrations (*Abschattungen*) of "the same" spatial object, as perceived from different orientations, is a unifying rule. And

> the thing "itself" ... is indeed nothing other than this unifying rule (Ideen II 86). As that which is showing itself in manifold perspectives in different orientations as "the same", holding itself as identical, the thing itself *is* also nothing other than the synthetic unity of the perspectives, in which it is "constituted" not only for us but essentially. [p. 77, in translation]

This reading bears a resemblance to but does not yet entail Gurwitsch's understanding that the object of a perception is itself a systematic unity of noemata, especially those consisting of the object as it would appear from different perspectives. Tugendhat will differ from Gurwitsch *if* Tugendhat clearly distinguishes the thing-unity from the noematic unity. At issue is Husserl's phenomenological idealism.

If Husserl's theory of intentionality is set within a form of transcendental or phenomenological idealism, as Gurwitsch and Tugendhat could agree, then Husserl's philosophy should include a theory of truth different from the naive realist's view of truth as correspondence of thought with an independent reality. Tugendhat has supplied a careful interpretation of Husserl laying out such an alternative theory of truth. Tugendhat unfolds several related concepts of truth in Husserl, including: truth as the objective (noematic) correlate of adequation, which is the synthesis of coincidence between a positing or signitive intention and the corresponding perception or intuition; truth as correctness (*Richtigkeit*), which is the property of an intention (especially a judgment) that holds where the object of the (signitive) act is identical with that of the corresponding intuitive act; truth as a property of the intended situation (*Sach*) itself, holding where this situation is the object of a judgment and coincides with the object of an intuition.

Briefly, then, truth comes with "evidence", with intuition, with the "self-givenness" of a situation. And such a theory of truth fits nicely with an idealist reading of Husserl.

In *Speech and Phenomenon* [14], Jacques Derrida offers a critique of Husserl's philosophy focussed usually on Husserl's theory of linguistic expression. The critique does not directly address Husserl's theory of intentionality, but along the way Derrida does address some of the issues we have isolated in Husserl's theory of intentionality.

Derrida observes Husserl's essential distinction among expression, meaning (*Bedeutung*), and object; and he observes that different expressions may have different meanings but the same object (p. 91). He observes Husserl's distinction between Sinn and Bedeutung, or sense and linguistic meaning, and notes Frege's different distinction using the same terms (pp. 18-19). Although Derrida's focus is on expression, he does address the acts of consciousness whose senses or noemata are brought to expression, and it seems clear he would recognize the fundamental distinction among act, noema or sense, and object as well as the fundamental doctrines that different acts may have the same noema or sense and that different acts may have different senses and yet have the same object. (Cf. Derrida [39], pp. 70-71.) These fundamentals are shared with Føllesdal's reading and Gurwitsch's 1967 essay [4].

Derrida stresses that a noema or sense or meaning is an ideal entity, the same entity repeatable on different occasions (like a Platonic form) (pp. 6, 9, 33, 52). This stress on the ideality of noemata agrees with Føllesdal's reading. Gurwitsch too in his 1967 piece [4] recognizes the atemporal, aspatial character of noemata; there is no suggestion in Derrida, however, that the noema or sense is the proper object of consciousness, as Gurwitsch and Tugendhat hold. (Note that Derrida does not observe the difference between sense as ideal act-species in *Logical Investigations* and noema as a different kind of ideal entity in *Ideas*.)

Derrida focuses on the *Logical Investigations*, insisting that Husserl's philosophy in all later works, even the *Crisis*, is but the natural unfolding of principles in the *Investigations* (p. 3). The continuity of Husserl's earlier and later thought is also urged by Føllesdal. But most who read Husserl's philosophy in *Ideas* and later works as straightforwardly idealist — in accord with the Gurwitschian interpretation — see a very sharp discontinuity after the *Investigations* (cf. Findlay's "Husserl's Idealism" in Pivčević [36]).

Derrida's concern is expression and its implications for phenomenology in general. Evidently he sees Husserl's general notion of sense (Sinn) as developing out of the notion of linguistic meaning (Bedeutung), as Husserl moves from the first to the later *Investigations* and on to *Ideas*. Hence, Derrida's reading would accommodate Føllesdal's observation (quoting from Husserl) that the notion of Sinn is but a generalization of the notion of linguistic meaning. Aligning with the Føllesdalian interpretation, McIntyre and Smith [40] stressed that noematic Sinn and linguistic Bedeutung are the same thing, though some elements of some noemata cannot properly be expressed. In "Form and Meaning" (in [14]), Derrida lays out pretty much that same interpretation. What's more, the heart of Derrida's critique of Husserl's theory of mind is the assumption that the sense of an act is the meaning of an "interior monologue", the "voice" of "phenomenological silence", the mind speaking to itself without words (pp. 32-48).

In Derrida's eyes, Husserl was the apotheosis of the Western tradition of "metaphysics of presence" (pp. 5 ff, 101 ff). "Presence" for Husserl is the immediate presence with which objects are given in intuition. This is a phenomenological trait of intuitive or self-evident acts and the epistemological foundation for a radical intuitionism and foundationalism. Husserl's "principle of all principles" holds that objects of each "region" of being are knowable through some type of intuition. Derrida says this *epistemological* principle is the basis of a *metaphysics* in Husserl; indeed, he says theory of knowledge is really metaphysical (p. 5). And in the closely related work "Form and Meaning" (in [14]), Derrida says phenomenology has proceeded "only on the basis of conceiving being as *self-presence*" (p. 128). In this Derrida is perhaps consonant with Tugendhat's reading of Husserl as taking truth to be self-givenness. However, Derrida stresses primarily the "self-presence" of an act to itself on Husserl's account and the intuitive presence of a noema or sense in phenomenological reduction according to Husserl. The latter is Husserl's doctrine that the mind knows its own meanings with absolute certainty in transcendental reflection; and it is a common reading of Husserl that such knowledge is the foundation for Husserl's entire philosophy.

So Derrida understands noema or sense in the Føllesdalian, not the Gurwitschian, way. And he separates object and noema *à la* Føllesdal, rather than construing the object as a unity of noemata *à la* Gurwitsch. But he reads the being of something as consisting in its intuitive presence to the mind, which contrasts with the realist stance of the Føllesdalian reading where the being of things in the natural world are concerned.

VI. HUSSERL ON PERCEPTION

Although Husserl's theory of intentionality was meant to be general, Husserl focussed strongly on the special case of perception. And perception involves the special topic of sensation. Perception was also Gurwitsch's main focus, and Gurwitsch offered the principal traditional study of Husserl's view of perception and sensation. Recently, Føllesdal has argued a reading of Husserl on perception that distinguishes Husserl from "sense-datists". Also, Dreyfus has focussed the debate between the Gurwitschian and Føllesdalian interpretations of noema on the case of perception. These three pieces of work we discuss.

In *Ideas*, §§ 84-85, Husserl recognizes in an act of perception two distinct phases: a hyletic phase of "sensation", or "data of sensation", and a noetic phase of "apprehension" – the "matter" and the "form" of the perception. In *The Field of Consciousness* [3], Gurwitsch explains Husserl's "dualistic" theory of perception:

> Under the heading of Hylé, Husserl comprises sense-impressions as well as impressions of pain, pleasure, tickling ... Devoid of intentionality in themselves, hyletic data serve as materials to operating factors by which they are "animated" and receive meaning. Such factors are denoted by Husserl as intentional or noetic forms or *noeses*. [pp. 265-266]

> ... The perceptual noema is the intentional correlate of the
> act of perception as a whole, including hyletic data and
> noetic forms. Interpreted and apperceived, sense-data enter
> as *components* or *constituents* into the perceptual sense or
> noema, that is, the perceived object as it presents itself
> through the given act of perception. [p. 269]

Gurwitsch held that Husserl's dualistic theory of perception is
based on the "constancy hypothesis", that *"sense data ... depend
exclusively and exhaustively on local stimulation*: When a sense
organ is stimulated in the same way, the same sensation is bound
to arise" (quoted from a letter to Embree in Embree's anthology
[2], pp. xix-xx). But the constancy hypothesis should have been
bracketed with the phenomenological reduction, Gurwitsch argued, because it assumes sensation is a causal result of physical
stimulation of the sense organs (Gurwitsch [3], pp. 270-271).
Gurwitsch admitted, however, that he was never able to convince
Husserl that the doctrine of hyletic data contains the unexamined
assumption of the constancy hypothesis (Embree reports on p. xxi
of his [2]).

Indeed, in "Phenomenology" [41], Føllesdal defends Husserl
against Gurwitsch's charge of assuming the constancy hypothesis:

> Aron Gurwitsch ([in *Studies in Phenomenology and Psy-
> chology*] 1966) criticizes Husserl for holding that hyletic
> data "remain really unchanged with regard to the different
> noeses operating upon them". Gurwitsch argues that "data
> devoid of all articulation, hyletic data in the strict sense,
> do not exist at all. What is given depends on the structural
> connections within which it appears." [Gurwitsch, 1966,
> p. 256]

However, Husserl was well aware of this difficulty. In Husserl
[*Ideas*], (1913), § 85), he characterizes the hylé-noesis schema as
provisional, and in a manuscript dating from between 1918 and
1921 he writes:

> We cannot place side by side two components in intuition, sense and filling. We can only obtain the difference by contrasting the empty and the filled sense, that is, through a synthesis of intuition and empty consciousness. ... [*Analysen zur passiven Synthesis* (The Hague, 1966)]
>
> There are hence no noesis-independent hyletic data that can be reidentified from one act to another. The hyle can perhaps only be characterized as something ego-foreign that enters into our acts and limits us in what we can experience. [p. 383]

Thus, hyletic data are not themselves discernible in phenomenological reflection, unarticulated sensuous experiences awaiting noeses. Rather, Føllesdal holds, hyletic data are "boundary conditions" that limit the range of noemata that may by noeses be present in a perceptual act. (This idea is discussed in Izchak Miller's doctoral dissertation [12].)

The sensuous and intuitive character of perception is the theme of Dreyfus' "The Perceptual Noema" (in Embree [2]). Dreyfus observes two conflicting interpretations of Husserl's notion of the perceptual noema: "Dagfinn Føllesdal interprets the perceptual noema as a concept, while Aron Gurwitsch takes it to be a percept" (p. 135). Dreyfus argues that Føllesdal has Husserl more nearly correct, but that Gurwitsch's own views on the perceptual noema, which influenced Merleau-Ponty, are an important improvement on Husserl's. What Husserl needs, Dreyfus says, is an "incarnate meaning, a meaning which is not abstractable from the intuitive content which it informs" (p. 147). And it was Gurwitsch's work, Dreyfus urges, that moved to fill this need.

VII. INTENTIONALITY AND INDIVIDUATION: HORIZON AND POSSIBLE WORLDS

For Husserl, Gurwitsch held, intentionality *requires* that an act's noema include reference to other noemata presenting the same object under further aspects. This is a feature not much stressed by Føllesdal. Often it is stressed under the theme that the same object can be given in a multiplicity or manifold of acts with varying noemata. (Cf. Sokolowski [24], Ch. 4.) Gurwitsch assimilated this theme of Husserl's to Hume's concern with consciousness of identity. But how is this consciousness of identity achieved according to Husserl? An account has emerged from work by Smith and McIntyre.

Husserl's notion of X is of that noema component that merely stands for the object intended "in abstraction from all predicates" (as stressed in Smith and McIntyre [29] and [13]). Now, different acts are directed toward *the same* object insofar as their noematic Sinne include the same (or "coinciding") X's. (Cf. *Ideas*, § 131, stressed in Smith and McIntyre [29].) So the crucial item of noematic structure grounding co-directedness of acts, and hence consciousness of identity, is the X.

The X and predicate-senses making up a noematic Sinn reflect Husserl's doctrine of substrata, as studied in Smith [10]. For Husserl, an object is not reducible to its properties. Husserl further distinguished temporal stages of an enduring object, holding that the enduring substratum is a complex entity comprising partial substrata, being temporal phases of the enduring substratum. (Cf. the manuscripts on individuation in B III, of Husserl *Zur Phänomenologie des inneren Zeitbewusstsein* (Martinus Nijhoff, The Hague, 1966), discussed in Smith [10], Ch. 3.)

Co-directedness requires not only coincidence of X's but also "harmony" of the predicate-contents of Sinne (*Ideas*, § 131). This is the basis of synthesis of identification (*Cartesian Meditations*, § 18) and hence the "predelineation" of the "horizon" of an act (§ § 19 ff). The crucial notion of horizon, best formulated in the *Meditations*, is extensively studied in two chapters of Smith and McIntyre [13]. The horizon of an act Husserl defines as the range of possibilities left open by the act, or alternatively the range of possible acts (especially perceptions) that further "determine" the intended object. At the ideal limit, these acts make up the "manifold" of all acts directed toward the same object. This maximal horizon is predelineated in the given act on the basis, evidently, of background beliefs making up the subject's basic conception of the relevant sort of individual. (Different notions of horizon are distinguishable in Husserl; here we deal with the "horizon" of possibilities concerning the object as intended in an act and with the correlative "horizon" of possible acts codirected with the given act.)

One of the dominant motifs in recent philosophy is the role of "possible worlds" in metaphysics and epistemology, deriving from their role in the logic of modalities and propositional attitudes such as belief. Husserl's notion of horizon leads to a similar view, as demonstrated in Smith and McIntyre [10] (the essentials are already found in their dissertations of 1970). The possible-worlds approach to belief and perception was developed by Hintikka in his [42] and [43] (with origins in earlier work). For Hintikka, the role of possible worlds is indicated by the tautological equivalence: a believes that p if and only if in every possible world compatible with what a believes, it is the case that p. Similarly, a sees that x is φ — or, more properly for Husserl, a sees x as φ — if and only if in every world compatible with what a sees, x is φ. The connection with Husserl's notion of horizon is now very close. The range of possible worlds in which x is φ is but a certain gerrymandering of the range of possibilities concerning x in which x is further determined than as being φ. And this range of possibilities is what Husserl calls the horizon of the perception.

Hintikka has made much of the distinction between *de re* and *de dicto* mental acts, i.e. acts about a definite object and acts about "the φ, which ever that be". Once this distinction is pursued, it becomes clear that Husserl has restricted his theory, apparently unwittingly, to *de re* acts. For, if as Gurwitsch holds Husserl requires an act's noema to include references to other noemata presenting the same object, Husserl has evidently assumed that a definite object is presented, i.e. the act is *de re*. (The limitation is noted in McIntyre's and Smith's writings and in Hintikka [43], p. 212.)

Another connection with possible-worlds theory accrues to Husserl's theory of intentionality, concerning not horizon but meaning. The notion of meaning has been analyzed, in the fashion started by Carnap (cf. Hintikka [43], Ch. 5), so that a meaning is identified with the function that assigns to each possible world the referent picked out in that world by the meaning. When this notion of meaning is brought to Husserl's theory of intentionality via sense, it is natural to see intentionality as directedness via a meaning toward an object in a possible world. Thus, with meaning understood in this Carnapian way and with horizon understood in the preceding Hintikkian way, we find a close assimilation of Husserl's full theory of intentionality with the modern-day possible-worlds approach to intentional acts. The assimilation is drawn in McIntyre's and Smith's dissertations [9[and [10] and developed in their [13]. Hintikka has addressed the connection between his own work and Husserl's in his [43] (Ch. 10). There, in particular, he criticizes Husserl and Frege for taking senses to be individuals; senses, Hintikka holds, should be functions, functions from worlds to referents.

BIBLIOGRAPHY

Ameriks, K. Husserl's Realism. *The Philosophical Review* 86 (1977).

Aquila, R.E. [32] *Intentionality: A Study of Mental Acts.*University Park: Pennsylvania State University Press; and London, 1977.

Carr, D. [16] *Phenomenology and the Problem of History: A Study of Husserl's Transcendental Philosophy*. Evanston: Northwestern University Press, 1974.

Derrida, J. [14] *Speech and Phenomena: And other Essays on Husserl's Theory of Signs*. Translated with an introduction by David B. Allison, preface by Newton Garver. Evanston: Northwestern University Press, 1973. Title essay *La Voix et la Phenomene* published in 1967 by Presses Universitaires de France.

— [39] *Edmund Husserl's Origin of Geometry: An Introduction*. Translated by John P. Leavey, edited by David B. Allison. Stony Brook, N.Y.: Nicolas Hays, Ltd., 1978.

Dreyfus, H.L. [1] The Perceptual Noema: Gurwitsch's Crucial Contribution. In Embree [2].

— [8] *Husserl's Phenomenology of Perception*. Doctoral dissertation, Harvard University, 1963.

— [28] Sinn and Intentional Object. In Solomon [34]; a reprinting of pages 1-17 of Dreyfus [8].

Elliston, F., and McCormack, P. (Ed.), [25] *Husserl: Expositions and Appraisals*. Notre Dame: University of Notre Dame Press, 1977.

Embree, L.E. (Ed.) [2] *Life-World and Consciousness: Essays for Aron Gurwitsch*. Evanston: Northwestern University Press, 1972.

Findlay, J.N. [17] Introduction to his translation of Edmund Husserl. *Logical Investigations*. London: Routledge and Kegan Paul, 1972.

— [37] *Meinong's Theory of Objects and Values*. Oxford:University Press, 1963; first edition, 1933.

Føllesdal, D. [5] Husserl's Notion of Noema. *The Journal of Philosophy* LXVI/20 (October 16, 1969): 68--687. Reprinted in Solomon [34]; page references in text are to Solomon pagination.

- [6] *Husserl und Frege*. Oslo: Aschehoug, 1958.
- [7] An Introduction to Phenomenology for Analytic Philosophers. In R.E. Olson and A.N. Paul (Eds.), *Contemporary Philosophy in Scandinavia*. Baltimore: The John Hopkins Press, 1972.
- [41] Phenomenology. In E.C. Carterette and M.P. Friedman (Eds.). *Handbook of Perception*, Vol. 1, Ch. 21. New York: Academic Press, 1974.
- Brentano and Husserl on Intentional Objects and Perception. *Grazer philosophische Studien* 5 (1978): 83-94.

Frege, G. [27] On Sense and Reference. In P. Geach and M. Black. Transl.), *Translations from the Philosophical Writings of Gottlob Frege*. Oxford: 1966. Basil Blackwell, 1966. German original: Über Sinn und Bedeutung. *Zeitschrift für Philosophie und philosophische Kritik* NF 100 (1892).

Gurwitsch, A. [3] *The Field of Consciousness*. Pittsburgh: Duquesne University Press, 1964.
- [4] Husserl's Theory of Intentionality in Historical Perspective. In E.N. Lee and M. Mandelbaum (Eds.), *Phenomenology and Existentialism*. Baltimore: The John Hopkins Press, 1967.
- [26] *Studies in Phenomenology and Psychology*. Evanston: North-western University Press, 1966.

Hall, H. Idealism and Solipsism in Husserl's Cartesian Meditations. *Journal of the British Society for Phenomenology*, Vol. 7, No. 1 (Jan. 1976).

Hintikka, J. [42] *Models for Modalities*. Dordrecht: Reidel, 1969. See Semantics for Propositional Attitudes *and* On the Logic of Perception.
- [43] *Intentions of Intentionality and other New Models for Modalities*. Dordrecht and Boston: Reidel, 1975. See The Intentions of Intentionality.

Kung, G. The World as Noema and as Referent. *The Journal of the British Society for Phenomenology* III (1972): 15-26.
- Noema and Gegenstand. In R. Haller (Ed.), *Jenseits von Sein und Nichtsein*. Graz: Akademische Druck- und Verlagsanstalt, 1972.
- Husserl on Pictures and Intentional Objects. *Review of Metaphysics* XXVI (1973): 670-680.

Lad, J.F. [11] *On Intuition, Evidence, and Unique Representation*. Doctoral dissertation, Stanford University, 1972.

Levin, D.M. [18] *Reason and Evidence in Husserl's Phenomenology*. Evanston: Northwestern University Press, 1970.

Levinas, E. [19] *The Problem of Intuition in Husserl's Phenomenology*. Translated by Andre Orianne. Evanston: Northwestern University Press, 1973.

Marbach, E. [20] *Das Problem des Ich in der Phänomenologie Husserl's*. The Hague: Martinus Nijhoff, 1974.

McIntyre, R. [9] *Husserl and Referentiality: The Role of the Noema as an Intensional Entity*. Doctoral dissertation, Stanford University, 1970.
- and Smith, D. Woodruff [40] Husserl's Identification of Meaning and Noema. *The Monist* 59/1 (1975): 115-132.

Miller [12] *The Phenomenology of Perception: Husserl's Account our Temporal Awareness*. Doctoral dissertation, UCLA, 1979.

Mohanty, J.N. [31] On Husserl's Theory of Meaning, *Southwestern Journal of Philosophy* 5 (1974): 229-244.

— [33] Husserl and Frege: A New Look at their Relationship. *Research in Phenomenology* IV (1974): 51-62. Reprinted in Mohanty, 1977.

— *Edmund Husserl's Theory of Meaning*. The Hague: Martinus Nijhoff, 1964; third edition, 1976.

— *The Concept of Intentionality*. Warren H. Green, Inc., 1972.

— Frege-Husserl Correspondence, translated with notes. *Southwestern Journal of Philosophy* 5 (1974): 83-95.

— (Ed.), *Readings on Edmund Husserl's Logical Investigations*. The Hague: Martinus Nijhoff, 1977.

Natanson, M. [21] *Edmund Husserl: Philosopher of Infinite Tasks*. Evanston: Northwestern University Press, 1973.

Olafson, F., Husserl's Theory of Intentionality in Contemporary Perspective. *Nous* ^ (1975): 73-83. Reprinted in Elliston and McCormack [25].

Pivčević, E. [22] *Husserl and Phenomenology*. London: Hutchinson, 1970.

— (Ed.) [36] *Phenomenology and Philosophical Understanding*. Cambridge: Cambridge University Press, 1975.

Ricoeur, P. [23] *Husserl: An Analysis of his Philosophy*, translated by Edward G. Ballard and Lester Embree. Evanston: Northwestern University Press, 1967.

Sokolowski, R. [24] *Husserlian Meditations: How Words Present Things*. Evanston: Northwestern University Press, 1974.

Solomon, R.C. [30] Sense and Essence: Frege and Husserl. *International Philosophical Quarterly* 10/3 (1970). Reprinted in Solomon [34].

— (Ed.) [34] *Phenomenology and Existentialism* New York: Harper and Row, 1972.

Smith, B. Frege and Husserl: The Ontology of Reference. *The Journal of the British Society for Phenomenology* 9 (1978): 111-125.

Smith, D. Woodruff [10] *Intentionality, Noemata, and Individuation: The Role of Individuation in Husserl's Theory of Intentionality*. Doctoral dissertation, Stanford University, 1970.

— and McIntyre, R. [13] *Husserl and Intentionality: A Study of Mind, Meaning, and Language*. Dordrecht and Boston: Reidel, 1982.

— and McIntyre, R. [29] Intentionality via Intensions. *The Journal of Philosophy* LXVIII 18 (September 16, 1971): 541-561.

— [38] Meinongian Objects. *Grazer philosophische Studien* 1 (1975): 43-71.

Tragesser, R.S. *Phenomenology and Logic*. Ithaca: Cornell University Press, 1977.

Tugendhat, E. [15] *Der Wahrheitsbegriff bei Husserl und Heidegger*. Berlin: Walter de Gruyter & Co., 1967.

Twardowski, K. [35] *On the Content and Object of Presentations*. Translated with an introduction by Reinhardt Grossmann. The Hague: Martinus Nijhoff, 1977. German original, *Zur Lehre vom Inhalt und Gegenstand der Vorstellungen*, 1894.

Heidegger's philosophy of mind

THOMAS SHEEHAN
Loyola University of Chicago

The period after World War Two saw the emergence both of the so-called later Heidegger and of the corresponding problem of the unity of his thought. Although his major work, *Sein und Zeit*, 1927, (= SZ) had announced Heidegger's intention of working out the meaning of being (*Sein*), his publications up through 1943, with the exception of the brief *Vom Wesen der Wahrheit*, presented only his preparatory analysis of human being (*Dasein*). However, Heidegger's post-war publications emphasized being itself (the history of being, being as language, pre-Socratic notions of being, the withdrawal of being in the modern world) and indeed almost seemed to hypostasize being into an "other" with a life of its own. This state of affairs, combined with Heidegger's announcement in 1953 that SZ would be left a torso, gave rise to such questions as whether his later thought was still phenomenological, how it might be continuous with his earlier writings, and how, if indeed at all, it was to be understood.

A first wave of scholarly engagement with the later Heidegger issued in a number of important writings which, because they were published before 1966, fall outside the scope of the present essay. H.-G. Gadamer's *Wahrheit und Methode* (1960), while based on Heidegger, opened up original new paths into hermeneutics and its application to literary as well as philosophical texts. Significant interpretations appeared in German (Allemann, Demske, von Herrmann, Löwith, Marx, Pöggeler, Pugliese, Schulz, Volkmann-Schluck, Wiplinger), French (Biemel, Birault, Chapelle, Guilead, Levinas, Wahl), English (King, Kockelmans, Langan, Richardson,

Contemporary philosophy. A new survey. Vol. 4, pp. 287–318.
©*1983, Martinus Nijhoff Publishers, The Hague/Boston/London.*

Seidel, Spiegelberg, Vycinas), Italian (Chiodi, Vattimo) and Dutch (IJsseling). Secondary literature on Heidegger from 1945 through 1965 ran to almost 1800 titles.

From 1966 until his death in 1976 Heidegger published some essays, a seminar and a lecture course [1-8], but, most importantly, he began the publication of his *Gesamtausgabe*. Among the most significant works that will appear in this Collected Edition are the heretofore unpublished texts and notes from his lecture courses and seminars from 1923 through 1944. Some of these have recently appeared [9-18], but the entire project will require some years to be completed.

The present report is devoted exclusively to Heidegger's own publications between 1966 and today, and particularly to the topics of (1) the development of his early thought in dialogue with Husserl and Aristotle and (2) the unity of his thought around the notion of *Ereignis* (appropriation), for these two topics come to the fore most clearly in Heidegger's latest publications. The secondary literature on Heidegger continues to expand (almost 2000 titles since 1966), and some of these works are listed in the bibliography at the end. Inevitably, some very good studies had to be omitted for lack of space.

A word about the title of this essay is in order. One cannot speak of a "philosophy of mind" in Heidegger without serious and major qualifications. The center of his thought remained, in the broadest sense, the correlation between being and human nature. Thus he considered the issues of mind, consciousness, and knowledge — in short, subjectivity — to be two steps removed from "the thing itself," first because they were derived problematics in relation to *Dasein*, and secondly because *Dasein* in turn received its meaning from the nature of being itself. It is true that the question of intentionality ("mind") served as Heidegger's *entrée* to working out the meaning of human nature, but in the process Heidegger shifted the weight from intentionality to what he called transcendence. Nonetheless, with the qualifications that will emerge below, we may try to gain access to Heidegger's own topic via the problematic of mind. The first step is to locate, by way of a schematic overview, the general lines of Heidegger's central issue.

I. THE QUESTION OF THE MEANING OF BEING

Heidegger began philosophy in 1907 with the reading of Franz Brentano's 1862 dissertation, *Von der mannigfachen Bedeutung des Seienden nach Aristoteles* [2, p. 81]. He learned that the Greek particle *on* has both a gerundive sense (to-be-in-being: *sein*) and a substantive sense (that-which-is-in-being: *das Seiende*). From that was born his question: If that-which-is-in-being has several senses, what is the meaning of being itself in its analogical unity?

The question seems to coincide with that of traditional metaphysics, viz., the investigation of entities in their common being (ontology) and of being in its highest instance (theology). But on the way to SZ Heidegger transformed the question of being in two ways, one which we may call "phenomenological" and the other "kinetic."

The phenomenological transformation. Being for Heidegger is always the being of entities, but he interprets it not as the raw existence of entities but as their meaningful disclosure to human experience. Whereas entities may exist apart from whether or not man exists, being as the meaningful givenness of entities never "is" apart from human experience. Moreover, the question of the *meaning* of being concerns how it happens that being (not just entities) is given to human experience. That question shifts the emphasis from the relation of intentionality between experience and entities to the relation of transcendence between experience and being itself. As we shall see below, Heidegger's phenomenological transformation of traditional ontology entailed an ontological transformation of traditional phenomenology.

The kinetic transformation. Heidegger allows that the tradition did discuss the being of entities in more or less explicit correlation with human experience, but he claims that metaphysics failed to see that being is intrinsically kinetic, i.e., an ontological movement of disclosure that is bound up with the ontological movement of man himself. Thus metaphysics interpreted the being of entities as one or another form of stable presentness in conjunction with man as a stable subject. Heidegger's kinetic transformation of the being-question entailed (1) working out the meaning of *kinesis* in Aristotle as an ontological presence-by-absence; (2) determining man's nature as an ontological movement of presence-by-absence (transcendence); and (3) interpreting being as an ontological movement that renders entities present by remaining itself in relative absence (*a-letheia*). As we shall see below, Heidegger's kinetic transformation of the being-question entailed the retrieval or articulation of what Aristotle and the Greeks left unsaid.

In their unity, Heidegger's two transformations of traditional ontology point to a single issue: the correlation between being's pres-ab-sential movement that issues in present entities and man's pres-ab-sential movement that is called transcendence. The name Heidegger gave that correlation is itself a kinetic term, *Ereignis* or appropriation, which is Heidegger's interpretative translation of *kinesis* in Aristotle. In the last section of this essay we shall see how appropriation is the unifying issue of Heidegger's thought.

II. THE POLEMIC WITH HUSSERL

In recent publications [8, 14, 17] Heidegger has clarified for the first time explicitly and at length his debts to and disagreements with Husserl. By analyzing how Heidegger's own thought grew out of and yet away from Husserl, we shall see how Heidegger began to transform phenomenology from a philosophy of mind into a philosophy of appropriation.

A. *Heidegger's debts to Husserl*

Phenomenology was born of the effort to gain an *a priori* science of mind as the foundation for scientific philosophy and ultimately for philosophically grounded empirical sciences. The first step in that direction was Franz Brentano's *Psychologie vom empirischen Standpunkt* (1874). Brentano methodically bracketed the metaphysical claim of the existence of mind as a substance in order to focus presuppositionlessly on mental experiences just as they directly reveal themselves to immanent apperception. The goal of his empirical-descriptive (as contrasted with an experimental-genetic) psychology was first to describe the essential structure of mental experiences and then to arrange and classify them according to their natural order. Inner apperception — not to be confused with a supposed introspection — reveals that the common characteristic of all mental experiences is directedness toward or reference to a meant object (*Beziehung auf ein Objekt; intentionale/mentale Inexistenz eines Gegenstandes*), whether or not that object actually exists in the world. The essence of mental experience is intentionality — the minding-of-the-meant.

Whereas Brentano only showed *that* intentionality characterizes mental experience, Edmund Husserl's *Logische Untersuchungen*, 1900/01, (= LU) worked out the essence of intentionality, at least in its logical performances, with regard to: its bivalent structure of *intentio* and *intentum*; the way the *intentum* is had, viz., in the "how" of its being-intended; the possibilities of empty and fulfilled intention; and the nature of truth as an intentional identity-synthesis of the meant and the perceived.

But as far as Heidegger was concerned, the major achievement of LU was the discovery that the being of entities can itself be rendered present as a phenomenon through categorial intuition. Taking expressed language as his clue, Husserl showed that not all parts of an assertion can find intuitive fulfillment in sensuous perception. For example, in the statement "The paper is white," the intentions represented by "paper" and "white" can indeed be filled in by the corresponding sense perceptions, but the state of affairs corresponding to "is" (the paper *as being* white) does not appear to sensuous intuition. It remains a surplus over and above the content of sensuous intuition and so requires another act, founded on sensuous intuition, to render it immediately present: the categorial intuition. The dimension of the categorial corresponds to what the tradition called "being." More specifically, it is the "being-as" dimension of phenomena (X *as* Y = X *is* Y). Therefore, by freeing being from its mere status as a copula and by seeing it as a directly given phenomenon, Husserl showed that the full range of phenomenological immediacy covers not just entities but entities-in-their-mode-of-being, entities *as being* such or so. Intentionality in its full range is intrinsically ontological, a disclosure of entities in their being.

Heidegger's debts to LU were chiefly three and concerned the goal, the theme, and the method of philosophy.

1. *The goal: The meaning of being.* By discovering that the being of entities is an immediately given phenomenon, Husserl,

unbeknownst to himself, had opened the way to a phenomeno-logical solution of the traditional being-question. If all intentional comportment has its *intentum* in the "how" of its being intended, then categorial intuition likewise sees being in the "how" of *its* being intended or revealed. To Heidegger this suggested a question that went beyond Husserl: What is the nature of the empty in-tention that can be "filled in" by being? Or: What is the relative absence from out of which being is disclosed as presence?

2. *The theme: The being of intentionality*. Husserl had demon-strated that the essence of all comportment is intentionality, in-deed as a movement (directedness to) that reveals (renders pres-ent). To Heidegger this suggested the need to think out the unity of movement and revelation in terms of presence-and-absence. In Aristotle, movement (*kinesis*) is the momentary presence that an entity has on the basis of its stretch towards the privatively absent; and revelation (*aletheia*) is the becoming present of what was here-tofore absent. But the intention of being is a stretch into relative absence (empty intention) that allows being to come from absence to presence (fulfilled intuition). Thus the goal and the theme of philosophy came together in the one issue of pres-ab-sence: man's intentional movement (presence by absence) as correlative with the revelation of being (presence from out of absence).

3. *The method: Phenomenology*. Husserl's investigations into logical comportment provided the model that should characterize all phenomenology, viz., rigorous analytic description of the *a priori* (i.e., the being) of the various modes of intentionality. For Heidegger phenomenology was a method for letting intentionality show itself (*legein* as *apophainesthai*) just as it shows itself to be (*phainesthai*). Phenomenology was the ontology of intentionality. And since intentionality itself is intrinsically ontological, the phenomenology of intentionality could lead to solving the ques-tion of the meaning of being in its analogical unity. The goal, the theme, and the method of philosophy thus form a unity. Husserl bequeathed to Heidegger a descriptive method for analyzing the kinetic-disclosive essence of intentionality for the sake of raising and answering the question about the absence that allows the being of entities to become present.

B. *Heidegger's transformation of phenomenology*

Heidegger's debts to LU were transformed into tasks insofar as Husserl's later works (1) failed to follow up the ontological implications of the discovery of categorial intuition, (2) overlooked everyday intentionality in order to study pure consciousness, and (3) legislated the reductions as the necessary means for moving from the natural attitude to transcendental consciousness. In Heidegger's eyes these shortcomings were due to Husserl's inadequate pre-grasp (*Vorgriff*) of the task of philosophy.

Heidegger's topic was the traditional being-question, phenomenologically transformed: how man "minds being" in its various instantiations and its analogical unity. Husserl's ultimate interest, on the other hand, was the relatively modern one, traceable to Descartes, of building a pure logic or *mathesis universalis* on the foundation of pure consciousness. This ultimate goal prescribed the penultimate theme of his philosophy: the epistemological clarification of pure consciousness insofar as it can become the object of universally valid statements in an *a priori* psychology. And just as the goal prescribed the theme, so the theme dictated the method: that of bracketing intentionality in the natural attitude so as to reach transcendental consciousness.

We may spell out Heidegger's disagreements with Husserl in three areas: the field of phenomenology, its theme, and its method.

1. *The field: Everydayness vs. theoretical comportment.* For Heidegger intentionality was primarily operative in the realm of ordinary habitual experience − e.g., work, conversation, history, religion − and it deserved to be treated on its own terms and not, as Husserl would have it, by analogy with or from the viewpoint of theoretical comportment. Heidegger maintained that Husserl's logical-theoretical interests not only prevented him from seeing everydayness as the basic field of intentionality, but also led him to read the natural attitude from a prejudicial natural-scientific viewpoint. His analyses of perception, for example, tended to interpret perception as a mere "staring" at objects (cf. his descriptions of the famous cube on his desk) rather than realizing that man first of all has the things of his world in pragmatic concernful dealings (*Umgehen mit*) and "perceives" any single thing only within a totality of other useful things (a hammer with nails,

shingles, etc.). Moreover, Husserl tended to see man in the natural attitude, e.g., the empirical ego, simply in connection with psychophysical and neurological processes, hence as a thing-entity of nature. In that regard, Heidegger considered the "natural attitude" in Husserl to be not natural enough.

In Heidegger we may speak of a transposition of the ontological as-factor from the theoretical dimension that Husserl discussed in terms of the categorial intuition to the practical dimension of everydayness. In ordinary experience man lives in his concerns and projects and thus already has a practical, if unthematic, understanding (*hermeneia*) of the being of himself, other people, tools and nature. For example, when he employs tools for purposes, he knows the tool *as for* something, and this pragmatic as-factor indicates that man already understands the being-dimension of the tool (X as *being for* Y). In fact, Heidegger claims that the Greeks basically experienced being in this practical modality, as evidenced by their appropriation of the word *ousia* — which refers to things of practical concern, like tools and houses — for "being." For Heidegger man gives evidence that he is a living understanding of the being of things (= the "hermeneutical as") whenever he performs a task (using a hammer to nail) or spells out a pragmatic concern ("Give me the lighter hammer"). Theoretical statements with their categorial or "apophantic" as-factor ("This hammer weights two kilos") are, for Heidegger, derivations from and a levelling down of the primary practical way that man understands being.

2. *The theme: Facticity vs. pure consciousness.* Heidegger claimed that Husserl, fascinated by his rediscovery of the ideal content of logical acts and in keeping with his epistemological and logical interests, neglected the ontological question of the being of real intentional acts (and more generally, the question of the meaning of being as such) in order to focus on pure consciousness. Heidegger, on the other hand, influenced by Dilthey, found historical existence (facticity) to be "the point where all philosophical inquiry arises and to which it returns." We may note four points of difference between Heidegger's reading of facticity and Husserl's characterization of pure consciousness.

(a) *Worldliness vs. immanence.* For Husserl consciousness is immanent being, i.e., self-transparent in such a way that its direct intentional acts are interior to reflective intentional acts. For Heidegger, man in his lived, factical intentionality is being-in-the-world, i.e., always "outside" the supposed immanence of consciousness and concernfully absorbed in worldly contexts of meaning: the use-world of implements, the co-world of sociality, and, running through both of these, the self-world of concern for his own interests. Evidence of his worldliness is the fact that man always finds himself in moods, that is, "tuned in" to a given worldly context.

(b) *Fallenness vs. apodictic self-givenness*. For Husserl apodictic self-givenness is the index of the presence that direct intentional acts have for second-order reflective acts; the self-givenness of consciousness is in contrast with the givenness of transcendent entities which may not be as they appear and indeed may not be at all. For Heidegger man as being-in-the-world is so absorbed in his intentional interests and in public opinions (*das Man*) that his true nature is usually hidden from him (fallenness), and he knows himself not directly but by reflection (*Relucenz*) from his projected concerns (*Praestruktion*). Far from being a negative factor that would argue against intentionality in everyday life, fallenness testifies that man is so utterly intentional as to be lost in his interests. It also indicates the need to "wrest" self-givenness from everyday absorption, but not by a reduction to some disengaged consciousness. Rather, intentionality can thematize itself *from within* its own movement, e.g., by the breakdown of tools or especially by the "call of conscience."

(c) *Thrownness vs. self-position*. For Husserl consciousness is absolutely self-positing (so much so that the annihilation of the world leaves it untouched) and as such is absolutely constitutive of the meaning of transcendent reality. For Heidegger man in his facticity does not posit himself over against the world and then constitute it presuppositionlessly from some supreme vantage point. Rather, he finds himself already posited ("thrown") into possibilities, which possibilities in turn constitute the meaningfulness or being-dimension of the things he meets in the world. As an already posited project (*geworfener Entwurf*), man is already appropriated (*vereignet*) by possibility, and he attains authentic selfhood, not self-position, by personally reappropriating his appropriation.

(d) *Mineness vs. pure consciousness.* For Husserl "consciousness" is finally "pure consciousness," seen in its eidetic whatness apart from concretization in a corporeal individual. For Heidegger factically lived intentionality is always individuated as one's own (*Jemeinigkeit*), is known only in "having oneself" in historical situations (*Mich-Selbst-Haben*), is bodily and emotively determined (*Befindlichkeit, Stimmung*), is always co-existing with others (so much so that for the most part "everyone is the other and no one is himself"), and in the final analysis is projected towards the ultimate personal possibility that is one's death. In short, "We ourselves are the entities to be analyzed." Moreover, factical man can never be reduced to an atemporal eidetic whatness, for his essence *is* his very temporal existence, the need to become the projected possibility that he already is.

3. *The method: Hermeneutical induction vs. phenomenological reduction.* Method in phenomenology is not a technique imposed on the subject matter but simply a way of seeing the issue – intentionality – in its being. If, following Husserl, we speak of intentionality as "constitution" ("the property of an act which makes the object present"), then phenomenological method is the interpreter's way of re-seeing how intentional acts constitute modes of presence. As such, phenomenological method entails looking away from the thematically intended object so as to see its "how" or mode of presence, i.e., its being.

For Husserl intention or constitution is performed by the absolutely self-positing transcendental ego. Therefore the moment of "looking away" becomes a radical bracketing of the entire natural attitude (with its already operative understanding of the being of entities) so as to see how entities are intended by pure consciousness (phenomenological-transcendental reduction), indeed in their essential whatness freed from individuating characteristics (eidetic reduction).

But for Heidegger everyday intentionality already understands being, and therefore phenomenological method is simply the thematization of ordinary life. That does entail a "looking away" from the thematic objects of intentional acts. However, this is not a reflective "looking back" to pure consciousness, but rather a thematic "looking ahead" into the realm of projected possibilities that is the practical being-dimension of entities, their way of being present. Phenomenological method for Heidegger is not *re-duction* but *induction* (*epagoge*: cf. *Physics* A, 2, 185 b 13), a second-order hermeneutics that explicitates the first-order hermeneutical understanding of being that man already is. By "induction" Heidegger does not mean reasoning from particulars to universals but rather re-seeing (*Hinführung zu*) the being-dimension one has already seen, bringing it into explicit view, and reading entities in terms of it. When the entity to be analyzed is oneself, then hermeneutical induction is "resolve": consciously seeing and reappropriating the appropriation-by-possibility that one already is. In 1921 Heidegger called this "*die Wiederholung des Lebens.*"

This brief presentation of Heidegger's disagreement with Husserl with regard to the field, the theme and the method of phenomenology has merely sketched out the parameters within which Heidegger intended to work out, in a phenomenological way, the question of the analogical unity of being. He filled in that area with his study of Aristotle.

III. THE RETRIEVAL OF ARISTOTLE

Heidegger was convinced that Aristotle's treatises constituted an implicitly phenomenological philosophy of everydayness without the obscuring intervention of a philosophy of subjectivity. But it was also clear that Aristotle moved within the Greek horzion of being as the stable presentness of entities. Heidegger's reading of Aristotle, therefore, had two tasks: that of explicitating what Aristotle said about the appearance of being in everyday life and that of retrieving what Aristotle did not say about movement as the condition of that appearance.

Aristotle described wisdom as "philosophizing about truth" (*Meta.* A, 3, 983 b 2), not about the concept of truth but about the presentation process that lets entities be seen as what and how they are. We may follow out Heidegger's examination of that presentation process in Aristotle under three headings: the place and kinds of truth; the structure of linguistic truth; and the kinetic condition of truth. Heidegger worked out these questions in his 1925-26 course on logic [10].

A. *The place and kinds of truth*

The tradition has generally appealed to Aristotle as the source of its double claim that the proper locus of truth is the judgment or assertion and that the essence of truth consists in the correspondence of a judgment with an objective state of affairs. Apart from the problems inherent in the position itself (e.g., how mental representations can accord with worldly facts), Heidegger challenges the claim that this doctrine can be found in Aristotle.

Heidegger finds in the Aristotelian treatises a hierarchy of the "places" of truth:

1. entities as autodisclosive (*on alethes*)
2. man as disclosive of entities (*psyche* as *aletheuein*)
   a. in intuition (*aisthesis, noesis*)
   b. in composition (*logos*)
      i. preverbal: disclosive comportment (*episteme* and *sophia*; *phronesis* and *techne*)
      ii. verbal: disclosive speech (*logos apophantikos*).

Four remarks about this hierarchy are in order.

1. For Aristotle the primary and proper locus of truth (disclosure) is not man at all but entities themselves. In *Meta*. IX, 10, a text which Heidegger defends as authentic, Aristotle says that the most proper characteristic of entities insofar as they are encountered by man is their self-disclosure in their whatness and howness (*eidos*). The being of entities is their appearing, and man is revelatory in a secondary sense, i.e., insofar as he takes things just as they reveal themselves to be (1051 b 6-9).

2. When Aristotle considers truth or disclosure as a performance of man, he asserts that its primary locus is not judgment (*logos apophantikos*) but intuition, whether sensuous or, above all, noetic. Because judgment is by nature a synthetic and dia-logistic disclosure of a complex state of affairs (*legein*: to bind together; *dialegein*: to say one thing through another), it has the possibility of falsehood as well as of truth and so is not the primary mode of human disclosure.

3. Intuition is the primary mode of disclosure because it immediately presents its object without the possibility of falsehood.

Sensuous intuition always aims at its proper object (*to idion*) and in that sense is always true (*De An.*, III, 3, 427 b 11). Noetic intuition discloses its proper object by just "seeing" or "touching" (*thigein*) it. It discovers and never covers over (*pseudesthai*); at worst it is not error but simply non-seeing (*agnoein*, 1052 a 1-4).

4. Moreover, when Aristotle in *Nicomachean Ethics* VI considers man insofar as he "has *logos*" (*to logon echon*), he considers *logos* in its prelinguistic or preverbal function of disclosive comportment [18]. He first distinguishes the two parts of *logos* — the theoretical, ordered to the eternal and unchanging, and the practical, ordered to the changeable — and then asserts that the function of both parts is disclosure. The theoretical modes of disclosure are *sophia* (wisdom) and *episteme* (discursive knowledge), whereas the practical modes are *phronesis* (prudence or circumspect insight: *umsichtige Einsicht*) and *techne* (know-how about the being of what is to be produced: *Sichauskennen*). These four modes of composite-relevatory behavior are called *hexeis*, ways that man essentially "has himself" as disclosive in preverbal comportment. For Aristotle the best of these modes (*beltiste hexis*) was wisdom, whereas for Heidegger, with his practical and historical interests, the best is prudence. But since man as prudential is always posited in a world, Heidegger combined the two practical disclosive virtues into his notion of concern: man ultimately acts for his own good (*phronesis*) and to that end carries out practical projects (*techne*).

The results of Heidegger's reading of the place and kinds of disclosure in Aristotle are: first, the location of disclosure primarily in entities themselves, i.e., in their being, and, secondly, the unfolding of a panoply of modes of disclosure in man, with judgment or assertion being the last. Within the *logos*-modes of disclosure Heidegger emphasizes the preverbal over the verbal: *logos* is a preverbal "reading" (*Rede*) of the world *as* such and so, before it is ever spoken out in language. And within the preverbal he emphasizes — against Aristotle — the practical over the theoretical. This shift, of course, was basic to his own treatment of concern, tool-use, and the worldhood of the world in SZ.

B. *The structure of linguistic disclosure*

In order to work out a phenomenology of disclosure in man's linguistic or verbal comportment, Heidegger turned to Aristotle's *De Interpretatione*, a treatise on intelligibility (*hermeneia*) both in the broad sense of reference and in the narrow sense of assertion (*apophansis*). Here above all Heidegger's effort was to retrieve from Aristotle a heretofore unarticulated phenomenology of facticity. The following presents in rough fashion Aristotle's schematization of language in the treatise, with help from *De Anima*.

Sound
(psophos)

<table>
<tr>
<td rowspan="5">Non-referential
(psophos monon)</td>
<td colspan="7" align="center">Referential
(phone semantike)</td>
</tr>
<tr>
<td colspan="2" align="center">Simple utterance
(phasis)</td>
<td colspan="5" align="center">Complex utterance: talk
(logos)</td>
</tr>
<tr>
<td rowspan="3">Noun
(onoma)</td>
<td rowspan="3">Verb
(rhema)</td>
<td rowspan="3">Non-presentative
(ouk apophantikos)</td>
<td colspan="4" align="center">Presentative
(apophantikos)</td>
</tr>
<tr>
<td colspan="2">Affirmation
(kataphasis)</td>
<td colspan="2">Negation
(apo-
phasis)</td>
</tr>
<tr>
<td>true</td>
<td>false</td>
<td>true</td>
<td>false</td>
</tr>
</table>

According to this diagram, the structure of disclosive language consists of: (1) sounds that refer (2) to complex states of affairs, (3) in such a way that they present something *as* something (4) with the claim that it is or is not the case, (5) with the possibility that the claim may be either true or false (correct or incorrect). Heidegger first explains this position and then "retrieves" what it leaves unsaid.

1. *Reference*. Whereas animals make sounds, only man can make an utterance, i.e., a meaningful or referential sound (*phone semantike*). Aristotle delineates the characteristics of reference

in five interconnected ways.

(a) The sound must be *meta phantasias* (*De An.*, II, 8, 420 b 33), that is, about an *eidos*, not as some "species" in the sense of a "mental representation" but about something that can show itself in the world of human possibility [19].

(b) A referential utterance is found only *hoti genetai symbolon* (*De Interp.*, 16 a 27), only when there is a binding together (*syn + ballein*) of man and the being of a worldly entity.

(c) Meaningful sounds are *hermeneia* (420 b 19) in the broad sense, i.e., *delousi ti* (cf. *De Interp.*, 17 a 18): they create a circle of intelligibility by showing something, even if they do not yet show it from itself (*apo-phainesthai*).

(d) Referential utterances are not *physei* but *kata syntheken* (17 a 1): they do not arise from nature but from convention, i.e., by the historical actions and social intercourse of men.

(e) Finally, referential utterances are intrinsically social (cf. *ho akousas eremesen*, 16 b 21), oriented towards others with whom the speaker shares the world, and directed to effecting the hearer's agreement.

In summary, for Heidegger the referential character of language shows that man is: in the world; transcendent to the being of entities; hermeneutical, i.e. caught up in intelligibility; historical; and social.

2. *Mere utterance vs. talk*. While all utterances are referential, not all referential utterances constitute talk (*logos*). Nouns and verbs, for example, are indeed referential sounds, but, taken by themselves, they are only namings (*phaseis*). A noun names a thing without reference to time; a verb has a reference to time and to synthesis (*legomenon kat' heteron*, 16 b 5), yet it posits neither the time nor the synthesis but remains only a sign (*semeion*) of such positing. Talk requires synthesis with regard to time.

3. *Mere talk vs. apophantic talk*. While all talk refers to complex states of affairs in a temporal synthesis, not all talk is presentative (*apophantikos*) of a state of affairs so as to let it be seen from itself. According to Aristotle prayers, commands, wishes, definitions and the like are indeed talk but not apophantic talk, not talk which can be either true or false. Aristotle refers discussion of mere talk to the *Poetics* and the *Rhetorics* (17 a 7), and in that latter treatise Heidegger found the basis for his own dis-

cussion of "mere talk" (*Gerede*) in SZ [19].

4. *Apophantic talk: Two levels of disclosure.* Insofar as apophantic or presentative talk does put something forth to be seen, it is always true or disclosive in the broad sense of bringing something out of hiddenness; the opposite of *to alethes* in this wide sense is *to lanthanomenon*, that which does not appear. However, within this broad revelatory function, apophantic talk can be either true or false in the narrow sense of correctness/incorrectness. The first level of disclosure has no counterpart of falsehood: it is a simple tendency to disclose. This primary presentational disclosure is man's dianoetic participation in noetic intuition; Heidegger calls it "the disclosive having of an entity" (in its being), or more simply, the pre-having (*Vorhabe*). The second level of truth is embedded within primordial disclosure and runs the risk of presenting something incorrectly as well as correctly. The basis of predicative truth-or-falsehood is prepredicative presentational disclosure.

5. *Disclosure in affirmation and denial.* Assertoric or categorial talk, whether affirmation or denial, presumes the prepredicative appearance of the phenomenon and then speaks from (*apo-*) the phenomenon so as to show it (*-phainesthai*) as such and so or as not such and so, with the possibility that such showing may be correct or incorrect. What constitutes the possibility of correct assertoric talk is the same as what constitutes the possibility of incorrect assertoric talk: the structure of composing and dividing (*synthesis, diairesis*). Aristotle says that falsehood (and therefore truth in the narrow sense of correctness) is possible only where there is *synthesis* (*De An.*, 430 b 1), and he adds that *synthesis* in itself is also a *diairesis*. It is not the case that affirmative judgments compose the subject and predicate whereas negative judgments divide them. Rather, composition and division both occur in every judgment, whether affirmative or negative, whether true or false. Hence, *synthesis* and *diairesis* are two names for a single bivalent phenomenon. The unity of *synthesis* and *diairesis*, whatever that might be, is the condition for the possibility of both correctness and incorrectness.

Aristotle did not question "below" the composing-dividing structure of assertoric talk to the underlying condition of its possibility. Heidegger's retrieval of Aristotle finds that underlying phenomenon to be movement in the form of what he calls the "hermeneutical as."

C. *Movement as the ontological condition of truth*

Heidegger's articulation of linguistic disclosure in Aristotle had two major results: first it showed that apophantic *logos* has a moment of primordial disclosure with no counterpart of falsehood; secondly, it showed that, within that primordial disclosure, affirmation and denial can be either true or false because of the unified structure of *synthesis-diairesis*. In his retrieval of the unsaid in Aristotle's position, Heidegger brought these two insights together and (1) interpreted the unity of *synthesis and diairesis* in terms of the primordial disclosure in *logos*, and (2) interpreted the primordial disclosure in terms of movement.

1. *Primordial disclosure as the hermeneutical as.* To know an entity is to know it as being such and so. And in the practical mode of comportment, that entails knowing the entity as "being for" such and such a purpose. Indeed, the "as-for" dimension (*Wozu*) is what is priorly known when one knows an entity. That is, man can get involved with an entity only by being already beyond it, by having already understood it as being for something. This primordial, unthematic, prepredicative understanding of an entity's being is what Heidegger called the "hermeneutical as." This is the underlying structure that makes possible assertoric composition of a subject with its logically distinguishable predicate: *synthesis* and *diairesis*. To synthesize is to distinguish, and the assertoric synthesis-distinction (the "apophantic as") rests on the prepredicative synthesis-distinction (the "hermeneutical as") of entities and what they are for.

2. *Primordial disclosure as transcendence.* Heidegger interprets man, insofar as he already knows the being-dimension of entities, as "transcendence" to that dimension, i.e., as being beyond entities and disclosive of the possibilities in terms of which entities can be understood. This kinetic exceeding of entities he calls man's *Immer-schon-vorweg-sein*, his "always already being out ahead" of entities. This movement is disclosure in the primordial sense; Heidegger calls it "world-disclosure," and it

corresponds to the *diairesis*-moment of the hermeneutical as. In his lecture course, *Die Grundbegriffe der Metaphysik* (Feb. 27, 1930 [20]) Heidegger said that *diairesis*, seen as man's transcendence, "pulls him asunder, as it were, and grants him a stretching-ahead, takes him away into the possible...." But at the same time man returns *from* that transcendence *to* entities so as to know them in terms of possibility, i.e., "so as to allow the possible — as what empowers the actual — to speak back to the actual in a binding way..., binding or bonding it: *synthesis*." Clearly the unity of *diairesis* as transcendence to the being of entities and *synthesis* as the return to entities in their being constitutes the *kinetic structure of the hermeneutical as*, which in turn makes possible truth and falsehood in assertions. Man is nothing other than this disclosive movement of transcendence and return: excess to being and access to entities.

Heidegger's study of Husserl and Aristotle transformed the traditional question of being by putting it on a phenomenological and a kinetic base. Husserl provided Heidegger with a method for analyzing the intentional disclosure of being; Aristotle let Heidegger see the kinetic basis for that disclosure. Disclosure and movement came together in the answer Heidegger gave to the question of the meaning of being: *Ereignis* or appropriation.

IV. THE UNITY OF HEIDEGGER'S THOUGHT: APPROPRIATION

Heidegger scholarship is haunted by a tendency to hypostasize being into an autonomous "other," separate from entities and from man. Often Heidegger's own way of speaking about being seems to abet this misunderstanding. But it is sure that being is not a thing or event off by itself (cf. *Physics* B, 1, 193 b 5: *ou choriston on*) but rather is only the disclosive structure of entities, distinguishable from entities but neither separate from nor reducible to them. Moreover, it is distinguishable only by man (cf. ibid., *all' e kata ton logon*), specifically through his kinetic structure of transcendence-and-return. When Heidegger speaks of the meaning of being (or equally: the time-character of being, the truth of being, the clearing of being [8]), he is simply naming the *analogical unity of the disclosive structure of entities insofar as it can be experienced by man.* Thus, when we speak below about "being as appropriation," we are simply referring to the analogical unity of the ways that entities are disclosed to man — or equally, that man experiences entities — in the various regions of human awareness.

At the beginning of SZ Heidegger stated a threefold program that he filled out over the next fifty years: (1) the analysis of the kinetic structure of man with regard to disclosure, (2) the analysis of the kinetic structure of disclosure in its analogical unity, and (3) a reinterpretation of the history of metaphysics in the light of the kinetic structure of disclosure. In order to see the unity of Heidegger's thought around the notion of appropriation, we shall follow this threefold program.

A. *The kinetic structure of man*

A recent publication of Heidegger's [9] allows us to see the simplicity and unity of the analyses of man's kinetic structure as worked out more densely in SZ. To state it schematicatically: man as transcendence (existentially-factically ahead of himself in possibilities) holds open the world within which he can have meaningful access to entities. As an "excess" that has "access" to entities, man is called the "there," the open area of intelligibility. The kinetic structure that holds this area open is called "care." The first division of SZ works out the bivalent structure of care, while the second division defines that structure in terms of movement.

1. *The bivalent structure of care.* We have already seen that the structure that makes for man's practical disclosive activity (e.g., in using tools) is his transcendence-and-return, his excess-and-access. SZ spells out the excess-dimension in terms of existentiality and facticity (or project and positedness) and spells out the access-dimension as presence-to (*Sein bei*). By existentiality and facticity, taken as a unity, Heidegger means that man is posited or thrown into his proper condition of living ahead of himself in possibility, and specifically in the possibilities that constitute given worldly contexts. By presence-to-entities Heidegger means that man understands entities, relates to them, and is usually ab-

sorbed in them (fallenness). The definition of care is: "Being-already-out-ahead-in-possibilities as being-present-to-entities." It merely articulates Heidegger's understanding of the unity of *diairesis-synthesis*.

2. *The "temporal" structure of care*. The second division of SZ first of all shows that the ultimate term of man's already-aheadness is death, not in the sense of a future demise but as his ever-present finitude that is concretized in his dying. "Being *towards* death" is not to be understood as a directionality towards a moment that has not yet come. Rather, it means that, as finite, man is always "at the point of death." Secondly, division two discusses how man might appropriate his essentially finite condition. The "call of conscience" is the radical awareness of one's essential finitude; when heeded, that awareness issues in a decision to accept and affirm what one already is. This "resolve" is disclosure of oneself to oneself in the form of a "retrieval" of oneself.

The analyses of finitude and self-disclosure round out the proper wholeness of man's kinetic structure and allow it to be defined in its "temporal" structure. By "temporality" Heidegger means nothing chronological or linear but rather the way in which man's essential movement is generated (*zeitigt sich*).

(a) As ahead of himself, man is always *becoming* his proper possibility, death. This becoming or coming-towards (*Zukommen*) constitutes what is called the existential "future" (*Zukunft*).

(b) However, what man is becoming is what he already and essentially is: his finitude concretized in his dying. In the existential scheme, the "past" as something by-gone is replaced by the "already-essential" or "alreadiness" (*Gewesenheit*). This is Heidegger's interpretation of Aristotle's *to ti en einai* (he translates: *das jeweils schon voraus Wesende*), and it points to the *a priori* determination that is registered in man's facticity. The existential "future" and existential "alreadiness" belong together: man is becoming what he already is.

(c) The unified movement of becoming one's alreadiness gives man his proper "present moment" or situation, within which he can authentically understand himself and properly render entities present instead of just being absorbed in them.

The upshot of SZ is that the bivalent structure of care finds it meaning in "temporal" movement. Again, excess (becoming what one already essentially is) makes possible access (the meaningful presence of entities.) The next question is how "time is the original essence of being" ([16] lecture of February 24, 1931).

B. *The kinetic structure of disclosure*

In the late 'twenties Heidegger had hoped to read off the analogical unity of the disclosure of entities, as itself kinetic, from the kinetic nature of man as world-disclosive. His recently published work, *Die Grundprobleme der Phänomenologie* [9], was a failed attempt in that direction. In the 'thirties Heidegger tried a different approach to the problem of the kinetic unity of disclosure: through interpretations of Hölderlin [15] and above all Aristotle [1, pp. 239-301].

1. *Movement in Aristotle*. Whereas his earlier analyses of *De Interpretatione* read movement simply in terms of man's transcendence-and-return, Heidegger's later interpretations of *Physics* II and III studied movement in terms of the self-disclosure of entities. In both cases, however, *kinesis* is an ontological affair. It is the kind of being that characterizes moving entities. A moving entity is one that does not fully appear (is not completely present) and yet does appear in its incompletion. Its presence is always fraught with absentiality: a not yet and a no longer, a coming into and a going from presence. But such relative absentiality is precisely what lets the entity *be* a moving entity. Therefore, to know a moving entity as what it truly is means to keep present to mind not only the *present entity* but also the *presence of the absentiality* that makes it a moving entity. The presence-of-its-absentiality is the moving entity's being-structure. We may call it "pres-ab-sentiality."

Aristotle's word for the pres-ab-sentiality of moving entities is *dynamis*, a word for "being." It does not mean "mere possibility" but rather "imperfect presence" or "movement into presence." As Heidegger interprets it, it means the same as *kinesis*. Indeed, he translates both words coequally as *Eignung* and *Ereignung*: "the appropriation into presence of what is not fully present," an entity's coming into presence from out of absence. It is crucial to note that the absential dimension of an entity's emergence into presence is *itself present in its own way*, viz., as "privative presence," and therefore can be experienced. (Examples: anticipation of the future of an entity or retention of its past [2, p. 13].)

Dynamis and *kinesis* are the origin of Heidegger's term *Ereignis*. This word describes a moving entity's disclosive structure, its being. Since being is always and only the disclosive structure of entities, "appropriation" does not name a separate hypostasis but only the common way that all moving entities disclose themselves.

2. *Appropriation in Heidegger*. Aristotle held that, properly speaking, only natural entities — as contrasted with artifacts — have their being as movement. However, Heidegger maintains that all entities, insofar as they are autodisclosive phenomena, have their being as movement into appearance. They may come from complete unknownness into knownness, or from distortion into clarity, or from forgottenness into remembrance. All of these are modes of appropriation, ways an entity comes into presence. Thus, to see an entity as disclosed is to see it as kinetic. And that means not only seeing the present entity but also (indeed priorly) co-seeing the being of the entity, its pres-ab-sentiality.

We can distinguish two moments in that being: the presential and the absential. The presential dimension is, of course, the entity itself as currently present in the flesh: visible, understandable, usable. The absential dimension is the same entity as not fully present or knowable or controllable. Thus within the entity's disclosive structure there is a character of non-appearance (*lethe*) as well as appearance (*aletheia*), of un-appropriatedness (*Enteignis*) as well as appropriation (*Ereignis*), of absence as well as presence. But it must be remembered that these negative dimensions are privative modes of presence. Heidegger calls them the recess-dimension (*Entzug*) of an entity's autodisclosure. Following Heraclitus (Frag. 123: "being moves to hide"), Heidegger says that this privative dimension is intrinsic to an entity's being-structure. Thus it cannot be rendered present the way entities are present but rather must be recognized in its own privative presentness, its pres-ab-sentiality. Knowing the essential finitude of an entity's autodisclosure is essential to knowing the entity as what it properly is.

Since disclosure characterizes entities only insofar as they can be experienced by man, appropriation has an essential relation to man's kinetic being. The being of man is itself a mode of appropriation: he knows himself as here-and-now-present by co-knowing his own pres-ab-sentiality, by "becoming his alreadiness." Awareness of his privative presence ("future" and "alreadiness") allows him to know himself authentically and to know entities authentically, i.e., in terms of their appropriation.

Thus there is a correlation between the self-disclosive structure of man and the autodisclosive structure of entities. Man's transcendence (his relative absentiality) is correlative to the privative dimension of the disclosure of entities (their relative absentiality); and man's return from transcendence (his relative presentiality) is correlative to the positive dimension of the disclosure of entities (their relative presentness). The conjuncture of the relative absence of man and the relative absence of entities allows the relative presentness of entities. The correlativity of excess and recess allows man's access to entities.

Heidegger's unfortunate tendency to hypostasize being can be seen in the following statement in which he summarizes his thought: "Being itself recedes, but, as this recess, being is precisely the pull that claims man's being as the place of being's own arrival" (*Nietzsche*, II, p. 368). Translated, that means: the disclosure of entities has a privative dimension that is registered in man's transcendence in such a way as to allow the disclosure of entities. That is: the analogical unity of the being of entities is their disclosive movement conjoined with, and indeed initiating, the self-disclosive movement of man.

C. *Metaphysics and appropriation*

Heidegger undertook what he called a phenomenological deconstruction of traditional ontology in order to show that, ever since classical Greek thought, the meaning of being has been interpreted in terms of time, but only one moment of time. He found evidence of this in the fact that Plato and Aristotle named being with the words *ousia* and *parousia*, "presentness." Thus entities were understood as presently disclosed, but the kinetic pres-absential disclos*ing* of entities was overlooked. Correlative with this interpretation was the understanding of man's *logos* as a rendering *present* of entities. The one-dimensional "temporality" of man was correlative with the one-dimensional temporality of being. In fact there is no temporality here but rather an attempt to read presentness in terms of, and to reduce it back to, the eternal. Time and movement were seen as indices of the weakness, the relative non-being, of the world. In his reinterpretation of metaphysics, Heidegger sought to use the kinetic-disclosive meaning of being as a clue to unpacking traditional ontology so as to show the kinetic source of its categories. He meant neither to "destroy" metaphysics nor to ground it, but rather to find the ground from out of which metaphysics arose. That ground turns out to be no "ground" at all but rather the movement of appropriation, which Heidegger, citing Heraclitus, calls a "game" (cf. Frag. 52: *paizon*). And man's highest calling is to "play along" with that game, i.e., to realize and accept his own kinetic involvement with appropriation.

Heidegger's deconstruction of metaphysics entailed an analysis of (1) pre-metaphysical Greek thought, (2) metaphysics from Plato to the present, and (3) the possibility of overcoming metaphysics.

1. *The pre-Socratics*. Heidegger claims that the archaic Greek thinkers did in fact experience the disclosure of entities in both its positive and privative dimensions (*a-letheia*) but did not thematize either the privative dimension itself (*lethe*) or its conjunction with man's transcendence. In Anaximander, Parmenides and Heraclitus he finds the same topic addressed: the openness of things (*aletheia*), indeed the *emergence* of things into openness (*physis*) in such a way that things bring with them an intrinsic absentiality [13]. As Heidegger reads them, the pre-Socratics were aware of the privative dimension of presence and named it (e.g., *kyrptesthai philei*, Heraclitus, Frag. 123), but did not investigate it for itself. It remained, as it were, in their penumbral vision as they focused on the emergent, radiant entities that were the issue of this pres-ab-sentiality. For Heidegger, the very implicitness of the appropriation process is what constituted the beauty and the enchanting naïveté of the archaic Greek world and made possible their celebration of the up-front-ness of things in their poetry, art and reli-

gion. The archaic Greeks were, so to speak, "all eyes," caught up in seeing the world as resplendently "there" without the mediation of subjectivity or anthropocentrism. They lived the everyday natural attitude at its best — the experience of the emergent openness of things — while the archaic thinkers preserved in word the privative presence that lets things be open.

Heidegger's purpose was not to "restore" ancient Greece but to explicate what it left implicit and to articulate what it left unsaid, i.e., *lethe* and man's transcendence. Because privative presence is intrinsically privative (and thus "loves to hide"), it lends itself to being overlooked, and when it is overlooked, man becomes absorbed in entities as presently disclosed and forgets the pres-ab-sentiality that lets them be. The emergence of man as the "measure of all things" in fifth-century Greece heralded the end of the penumbral awareness of appropriation and the beginning of what would become metaphysics: the understanding of the world — the realm of human possibility — as the correlation between stably disclosed entities and stably disclosive man.

2. *Metaphysics as the "forgetting" of being.* The appropriation process (*physis, aletheia*) is an entity's movement into appearance. According to Heidegger it was with Plato that the bi-dimensionality of appropriation (movement, appearance) was forgotten, with the result that only one moment of it was seen, the eidetic appearance of entities as what they are: *eidos.* The *eidos* loses its reference to the entity's emergence into disclosure and becomes instead that-as-which an entity presents itself for possible intellectual viewing by man. As *physis* and *kinesis* (privative presence) drop out of the picture, any hope of grasping the corresponding kinetic nature of man is lost. The being of entities is interpreted as stable disclosedness, and man is understood as the one who renders entities meaningfully present in that stable appearance. And since only what is unmoving and eternal is, for Plato, truly stable, only the eternal shows itself as true being (*ontos on*). Temporal, moving entities are relegated to the status of *me on*, not-really-in-being. Concomitantly, a new term emerges to designate the being of entities: *ousia*, "presentness-in-reality," and the proper formation (*paideia*) of man consists in his ability to see eidetic presentness in a correct (*orthotes*) vision. Thus, according to Heidegger, truth comes to be understood not as the pres-ab-

sential disclosure of entities but as man's intellectual correspondence with entities in their disclosed presentness.

Aristotle effects a decisive shift away from Plato's emphasis on *idea/eidos*, but without recovering the original Greek sense of kinetic disclosure. To be sure, for Aristotle an entity that is still moving and becoming is no longer, as it was for Plato, a *me non*; rather, it is the primary instance of *ousia*. It is a stable thing (*hypostasis*) that is in the process of being brought forth (*morphe*) into what it is (*eidos*). In short, it is an *ergon*, a "work" in the unique Greek sense of that which appears as being brought forth and rendered stable. Its being is *energeia*, presentness as an *ergon*, or (since *telos* means the same as *ergon*) *entelecheia*. While this vision of entities does regain some of the archaic sense of movement, it falls short of the pre-Socratic insight precisely to the degree that is follows after and is to some extent controlled by Plato's *idea/eidos*. *Kinesis* in Aristotle is entirely for the sake of appearance and presentness, so much so that the absential dimension of disclosure is not seen as intrinsically privative (*kryptesthai philei*) but as *not-yet*-in-appearance. *Ousia* dominates in Aristotle as much as in Plato, and although Aristotle gives priority to *prote ousia* (that which is in *ousia*: existence) over *deutere ousia* (that *as which* something is in *ousia*: essence), nonetheless the controlling viewpoint is still *ousia*, presentness. The emergent character of appropriation which issues in *ousia* lies back behind both existential and essential *ousia* and is not recovered by Aristotle.

From classical Greece onwards, metaphysics would continuously manipulate the whatness and thatness of *ousia* by giving primacy to one or another of them (ontology) and in turn would trace *ousia* back to its highest instance in a self-present God (theology). But all such "ousiology," according to Heidegger, does not raise the question of the kinetic process that lies behind stable presentness. (Even Aquinas' *esse entium* and *ipsum esse subsistens* is, for Heidegger, only an existence-oriented modality of ousiology.) The forgetting of pres-ab-sentiality has its source not in some psychological defect of man but rather in the intrinsically privative (self-concealing) nature of pres-absentiality itself. Man's fallenness or absorption in entities-as-present is thus a normal consequences of the very nature of disclosure. The fact that metaphysics thematizes the presentness of entities and traces it back to God does not break out of fallenness but in fact reinforces fallenness by elevating it to the level of a thematic science. The history of metaphysics consists in the various transformations of the understanding of the presentness of entities. For Heidegger the fullest form of such forgetting of pres-ab-sentiality is the widespread contemporary attitude of *Technik*, which interprets entities as totally disclosed or disclosable for man's use.

3. *Overcoming metaphysics: The "turn."* The much discussed and frequently misunderstood *Kehre* [12, p. 201] or "turn" in Heidegger's thought refers neither to a shift in Heidegger's language and style in the 'thirties, nor to the supposed emergence of a new topic (*Ereignis*) in his thought, nor to his abandonment of the "transcendental" standpoint of SZ. The turn, rather, is what Heidegger means by the overcoming (*Überwendung*) or surpassing of metaphysics' forgetting of appropriation. As early as 1920, in a course on the phenomenology of religion, Heidegger called this *die Umwandlung der Philosophie*, i.e., the transformation of man's philosophical awareness into a recognition of the privative dimension of disclosure and of the corresponding structure of human transcendence. This "turn" was the goal of Heidegger's thought from the early 'twenties onward. In SZ it was discussed in a preliminary way as "resolve" (*Entschlossenheit*), man's acceptance of himself as ordered to the appropriation process; in later writings it is talked about in terms of *Gelassenheit*, letting oneself go along with the appropriation process. The *Kehre* is man's turn towards (his recognition of) the pres-absentiality that is already operative both in his own kinetic structure and in the kinetic structure of disclosure but that is obscured by fallenness, metaphysics and the attitude of *Technik*. To "take the turn" is to awaken to the privative dimension of disclosure. This means getting "behind" the historical formations of presentness (*idea, energeia, esse*, etc.) which make up the history of metaphysics, thus getting "to" the kinetic source of all such formations: appropriation. In that sense Heidegger can say that appropriation "gives" the various forms of presentness in metaphysics while being itself "withheld" in the double sense of being intrinsically privative (self-concealing) and thus overlooked (forgotten). To awaken to appropriation, therefore, means to overcome the history of forgetfulness and to enter into the true movement that is disclosure, not so as to extinguish

the privative dimension of disclosure (an impossibility) but rather to recognize and to accept it in its pres-ab-sential bivalence [2, pp. 44 f.] . In short, the "turn" — the unifying goal of Heidegger's thought — means re-appropriating the structure of appropriation.

We have seen that Heidegger's latest publications reveal the unity of his thought precisely by revealing its genesis. His philosophy is not an existential anthropology and not a philosophy of "mind." It is not a metaphysics and least of all a study of some platonically separate thing called "being." Rather it is a phenomenology of movement or appropriation: the analysis of man's experience of the pres-ab-sential disclosure of entities in its analogical unity.

BIBLIOGRAPHY

PRIMARY LITERATURE, 1966-1980

Heidegger, M. [1] *Wegmarken*. Frankfurt 1967; 2nd. expanded ed., Fr.-W. von Herrmann, 1976.
— [2] *Zur Sache des Denkens*, Tübingen 1969.
— [3] *Die Kunst und der Raum*. St. Gallen 1969.
— [4] *Heraklit*, with E. Fink. Frankfurt 1970.
— [5] *Schellings Abhandlung über das Wesen der menschlichen Freiheit (1809)*, ed. H. Feick. Tübingen 1971.
— [6] *Erläuterungen zu Hölderlins Dichtung*, 4th expanded ed., Frankfurt 1971.
— [7] *Frühe Schriften*. Frankfurt 1972; 2nd expanded ed., Fr.-W. von Herrmann, 1978.
— [8] *Questions IV*. Gallimard 1976; in part = *Vier Seminare*, trans. C. Ochwadt. Frankfurt 1977.
— [9] *Die Grundprobleme der Phänomenologie*, ed. Fr.-W. Herrmann. Frankfurt 1975.
— [10] *Logik. Die Frage nach der Wahrheit*, ed. W. Biemel. Frankfurt 1976.
— [11] *Phänomenologische Interpretation von Kants Kritik der reinen Vernunft*, ed. I. Görland. Frankfurt 1977.
— [12] *Metaphysische Anfangsgründe der Logik im Ausgang von Leibniz*, ed. K. Held. Frankfurt 1978.
— [13] *Heraklit. 1. Der Anfang des abendländischen Denkens. 2. Logik. Heraklits Lehre vom Logos*, ed. M. Frings. Frankfurt 1979.
— [14] *Prolegomena zur Geschichte des Zeitbegriffs*, ed. P. Jaeger. Frankfurt 1979.

— [15] *Hölderlins Hymnen "Germanien" und "Der Rhein,"* ed. S. Ziegler. Frankfurt 1980.
— [16] *Hegels Phänomenologie des Geistes,* ed., I. Görland. Frankfurt 1980.
— [17] *Der Beginn der neuzeitlichen Philosophie,* ed. Fr.-W. von Herrmann. Frankfurt, forthcoming.
— [18] *Platon: Sophistes,* ed. I. Schüssler. Frankfurt, forthcoming.
— [19] *Aristoteles: Rhetorik.* Frankfurt, forthcoming.
— [20] *Die Grundbegriffe der Metaphysik. Der Weltbegriff,* ed. Fr.-W. von Herrmann. Frankfurt, forthcoming.

SECONDARY LITERATURE 1966-1976

Research tools

Feick, H. *Index zu Heidegger "Sein und Zeit",* 2nd. ed. Tübingen 1968.
Sass, H.-M. *Heidegger-Bibliographie.* Meisenheim 1968.
— *Materialien zur Heidegger-Bibliographie 1917-1972.* Meisenheim 1975.

General collections

Ballard, B., and Scott, C. (Ed.), *Martin Heidegger in Europe and America.* The Hague 1973.
Beaufret, J. *Dialogue avec Heidegger.* Paris 1973-1974. 3 vols.
Frings, M. (Ed.), *Heidegger and the Quest for Truth.* Chicago 1968.
Gadamer, H.-G. *Kleine Schriften,* various volumes. Tübingen 1967.
Klostermann, V. (Ed.), *Durckblicke.* Frankfurt 1970.
Pöggeler, O. *Heidegger. Perspektiven zur Deutung seines Werks.* Köln 1969.
Sallis, J. (Ed.), *Heidegger and the Path of Thinking.* Pittsburgh 1970.

Overviews and introductions

Biemel, W. *Martin Heidegger in Selbstzeugnissen und Bilddokumenten.* Reinbeck bei Hamburg 1973.
Courturier, F. *Monde et être chez Heidegger.* Montréal 1971.
Fløistad, G. *Heidegger.* Oslo 1968.
Franzen, W. *Martin Heidegger.* Stuttgart 1976.
Mehta, J.L. *The Philosophy of Martin Heidegger.* New York 1971.
Vattimo, G. *Introduzione a Heidegger.* Bari 1971.

On "Being and Time"

Antoni, C. *L'existenzialismo di Martin Heidegger.* Napoli 1972.
Fløistad, G. On Understanding Heidegger: Some Difficulties. In R.E. Olson and A.M. Paul (Eds.), *Contemporary Philosophy in Scandinavia,* pp. 431-454. London 1972.

Gelven, M. *A Commentary on Heidegger's "Being and Time"*. New York 1970.
Guzzoni, G. *Considerazioni intorno alla prima sezione di "Sein und Zeit"*. Urbino 1969.
Herrmann, Fr.-W. von. *Subjekt und Dasein*. Frankfurt 1974.
Macdowell, J.A. *A Gênese da Ontología Fundamental de Martin Heidegger*. São Paulo 1970.
Schmitt, R. *Martin Heidegger on Being Human*. New York 1969.

On language and hermeneutics

Ihde, D. *Hermeneutic Phenomenology*. Evanston 1971.
Kockelmans, J. (Ed.), *On Heidegger and Language*. Evanston 1972.
– Language, Meaning, and Ek-sistence. In F.J. Smith (Ed.), *Phenomenology in Perspective*, pp. 94-121. The Hague 1970.
McCormick, P. *Heidegger and the Language of the World*. Ottawa 1976.
Palmer, R. *Hermeneutics*. Evanston 1969.
Pöggeler, O. (Ed.), *Hermeneutische Philosophie*. Munich 1972.
– Hermeneutische und mantische Phänomenologie. In O. Pöggeler (Ed.), *Heidegger* (cf. supra), pp. 321-357.
Sallis, J. Towards the Showing of Language. *Southwestern Journal of Philosophy* 4 (1973): 75-83.
Sini, C. *Semiotica ed ermeneutica in De Saussure, Husserl, Heidegger, Pierce*. Milano, 1976. See his *Semiotica e Filosofia*. Bologna 1978.
Stassen, M. *Heideggers Philosophie der Sprache in "Sein und Zeit" und ihre philosophisch-theologischen Wurzeln*. Bonn 1973.
Volkmann-Schluck, K.H. Das Problem der Sprache. In J. Beaufret et al. (Eds.), *Die Frage Martin Heideggers*, pp. 50-61. Heidelberg 1969.

On Heidegger and metaphysics

Bucher, A. *Martin Heidegger. Metaphysikkritik als Begriffsproblematik*. Bonn 1972.
Jaeger, P. *Heideggers Ansatz zur Verwindung der Metaphysik in der Epoche von "Sein und Zeit"*. Frankfurt 1976.
Laffoucrière, O. *La destin de la pensée et "La mort de Dieu" selon Heidegger*. The Hague 1968.
Magnus, B. *Heidegger's Metahistory of Philosophy*. The Hague 1970.
Regina, U. *Dal nichilismo alla dignità dell'uomo*. Milano 1970.
Severino, E. *L'essenza del nichilismo*. Brescia 1972.
Vitiis, P. de. *Heidegger e la fine della filosofia*. Firenze 1974.
Wiplinger, F. *Metaphysik*, ed. P. Kampits. Freiburg 1976.

On Heidegger and other thinkers

Bartels, M. *Selbstbewusstsein und Unbewusstes. Studien zu Freud und Heidegger*. Berlin 1976.

Boehm, R. Chiasma. Merleau-Ponty und Heidegger. *Durchblicke* (supra), pp. 369-393.

Caputo, J. Meister Eckhart and the Later Heidegger. *Journal of the History of Philosophy* 12 (1974): 479-494; 13 (1975): 61-80. See his *The Mystical Element in Heidegger's Thought*. Athens, Ohio 1978.

Declève, H. *Heidegger et Kant*. The Hague 1970.

Dufrenne, M. *Heidegger et Kant*. The Hague 1966.

Fløistad, G. The Concept of World in Existentialism. *Revue International de Philosophie* 135 (35e anne 1981): 28-40.

Harries, K. Wittgenstein and Heidegger. *Journal of Value Inquiry* 2 (1968): 281-291.

Krell, D. Toward *Sein und Zeit*. Heidegger's Early Review of Jaspers' "Psychologie der Weltanschauungen." *Journal of the British Society for Phenomenology* 6 (1975): 147-156.

Langan, T. Heidegger Beyond Hegel. *Filosofia* 19 (1968); 735-746.

Lévinas, E., *En découvrant l'existence avec Husserl et Heidegger*. Reissued, Paris 1967.

Lotz, J.B. *Heidegger und Thomas von Aquin*. Pfullingen 1975.

Penso, G. *Friedrich Nietzsche nell'interpretazione heideggeriana*. Bologna 1976.

Schürmann, R. *Maire Eckhart ou la joie errante*. Paris 1972.

Sherover, C. *Heidegger, Kant and Time*. Bloomington, Ind. 1971.

Starr, D. *Entity and Existence*. New York 1976.

Taminiaux, J. Le regard et l'excédent. Remarques sur Heidegger et les "Recherches logiques" de Husserl. *Revue philosophique de Louvain* 77 (1975) 74-100. Also in Taminiaux, *Le Regard et l'Excédent*. The Hague 1977.

— Finitude et absolue. Remarques sur Hegel et Heidegger, interprèts de Kant. *Revue philosophique de Louvain* 71 (1969): 190-215. Also in Taminiaux, *Le Regard et l'Excédent*. The Hague 1977.

Verra, V. Heidegger, Schelling et l'idealismo tedesco. In *La Filosofia della Storia della Filosofia*, pp. 51-71. Padova 1974.

Volpi, F. *Heidegger e Brentano*. Padova 1976.

Various topics in Heidegger

Axelos, K. *Einführung in ein künftiges Denken: Über Marx und Heidegger*. Tübingen 1966.

Allemann, B. Martin Heidegger und die Politik. *Merkur* 21 (1967): 962-976.

Cousineau, R.H. *Humanism and Ethics*. Louvain 1972.

Doherty, J. *Sein, Mensch und Symbol*. Bonn 1972.

Frings, M. *Person und Dasein*. The Hague 1969.

Gethmann, C.F. *Verstehen und Auslegung*. Bonn 1974.

Gethmann-Siefert, A. *Das Verhältnis von Philosophie und Theologie im Denken Martin Heideggers*. Freiburg 1975.

Herrmann, Fr.-W. von. *Bewusstsein, Zeit und Weltverständnis*. Frankfurt 1971.

IJsseling, S. Het zijn en de zijnden: Een studie over de ontologische Differenz bij Martin Heidegger. *Tijdschrift voor Filosofie* 28 (1966): 3-51.

Kisiel, T. The Happening of Tradition. *Man and World* 2 (1969): 358-385.

— On the Dimension of a Phenomenology of Science in Husserl and the Young Dr. Heidegger. *Journal of the British Society for Phenomenology* 4 (1973): 217-234.

Macomber, W.B. *The Anatomy of Disillusion*. Evanston 1967.

Marx, W. *Vernunft und Welt*. The Hague 1970.

Nicholson, G. Heidegger on Thinking. *Journal of the History of Philosophy* 13 (1975): 491-503.

Noller, G. (Ed.), *Heidegger und die Theologie*. Munich 1967.

Palmier, J.-M. *Les écrits politiques de Heidegger*. Paris 1968.

Perrotti, J. *Heidegger on the Divine*. Athens, Ohio 1974.

Pöggeler, O. *Philosophie und Politik bei Heidegger*. Freiburg 1972.

— Heideggers Topologie des Seins. *Man and World* 2 (1969): 331-357.

— "Historicity" in Heidegger's Late Work. *Southwestern Journal of Philosophy* 4 (1973): 53-73.

Richardson, W.J. Heidegger's Critique of Science. *New Scholasticism* 42 (1968): 511-536.

— Heidegger's Quest for Freedom. *Theological Studies* 28 (1967): 286-307.

Ricoeur, P. The Critique of Subjectivity and Cogito in the Philosophy of Martin Heidegger. In *Heidegger and the Quest for Truth* (supra), pp. 62-75.

Rosales, A. *Transcendenz und Differenz*. The Hague 1970.

Schrag., C. Heidegger on Repetition and Historical Understanding. *Philosophy East and West* 20 (1970): 287-296.

Schwan, A. *Die politische Philosophie im Denken Heideggers*. Köln 1965.

Tugendhat, E. *Der Wahrheitsbegriff bei Husserl und Heidegger*. Berlin 1967.

Vail, L. *Heidegger and the Ontological Difference*. London 1972.

Vitiello, V. *Heidegger. Il nulla e la fondazione della storicità*. Urbino 1976.

Zimmermann, M. Heidegger's New Concept of Authentic Selfhood. *The Personalist*, 76 (1976): 198-212. See his *The Eclipse of the Self*. Athens, Ohio 1980.

Wittgenstein's philosophy of mind

BARRY STROUD
University of California, Berkeley

The teaching and writings of Ludwig Wittgenstein were largely responsible for bringing the philosophy of mind into its central position in philosophy in the English-speaking countries in the 1950s and 1960s. But other works which were thought to derive from his ideas often exerted a more immediate and a more specific influence on the topics discussed and on the way the subject was pursued. Gilbert Ryle's *The Concept of Mind* [1] was perhaps predominant. It determined both the form and the content of most treatments of particular issues in the philosophy of mind in Oxford and therefore in Britain and in much of America for more than a decade after its appearance in 1949. What came to be called "Wittgensteinian" positions, like those of Norman Malcolm in his accounts of the problem of other minds [2] and of dreaming [3], were also widely discussed, if less widely believed. Chapter Three of P.F. Strawson's *Individuals: an Essay in Descriptive Metaphysics* [4] was also extremely influential throughout the 1960s in its emphasis on the primacy of the person over the body or the mind and on the special character of psychological predicates.

The indirectness of Wittgenstein's influence also had a significant, and not always beneficial, effect on the interpretation of his writings. If certain theses about behaviourism, or about the "criteria" for the ascription of psychological states, or about the relation between intentions and actions, for example, were at the centre of philosophical debate within the Anglo-American tradition, and if Wittgenstein was known to be a formative influence

Contemporary philosophy. A new survey. Vol. 4, pp. 319–341.
© *1983, Martinus Nijhoff Publishers, The Hague/Boston/London.*

on the philosophy of mind as it was then pursued, then it went without saying that his writings must contain discussions and defences of such theses, or at least attempted answers to the problems then current. And that is how Wittgenstein was read. It was presumably this state of affairs that Anthony Kenny was reporting on when he said in his chronicle in *Contemporary Philosophy* in 1969 that "during the decade 1956-66 the philosophy of mind was dominated by the ideas of Wittgenstein" ([5], p. 258).

To what extent it was Wittgenstein's actual ideas, as opposed to what it was widely believed his ideas must be, that so dominated the subject at that time is still an open historical question. But it is clear that neither his ideas nor the interpretation of his ideas, nor even the ideas that were thought to be his, have dominated the philosophy of mind since the middle 1960s. When Norman Malcolm declared Wittgenstein to be "easily the most important figure in the philosophy of mind" ([6], p. xi) in 1970, he might have been making a correct assessment of the true value and importance of Wittgenstein's philosophy, but I do not think he was giving an accurate report of Wittgenstein's influence on what was actually going on in the most active parts of the subject at that time or on what continues to go on today.

In the last ten or fifteen years the philosophy of mind in the English-speaking tradition has concentrated on the relation between mind and body, in particular the identity or non-identity of physical and psychological states, or their "functional" equivalence; on the status of desires, intentions, etc., and their causal or non-causal role in the production and explanation of action; on intentionality and the nature of "propositional attitudes" such as believing, asserting, and so on, and on related issues bordering on both the philosophy of language and cognitive psychology and the computing-machine model of the mind. Although all these topics include issues which Wittgenstein discussed and brought to prominence in philosophy, his work exerts very little influence on the ways in which the questions are now discussed.

Wittgenstein's reputation at the moment is largely in eclipse. That is not because his main ideas have been appreciated and absorbed into a tradition now busily engaged in extending them in new directions. Quite the contrary. Recent philosophy of mind is in many ways more uncongenial to Wittgenstein's way of thinking than even the prevailing philosophies of Wittgenstein's own time had been. One key to understanding the significance of his philosophy is to appreciate his lifelong opposition to scientism. But even logical positivism, which was a form of scientism, was still sufficiently Kantian to see philosophy as a special discipline, separate and subservient to science, to be sure, but still a distinct intellectual activity which must somehow be fitted in to a scientific world-view. The more empirical, "naturalistic" turn in the approach of many contemporary philosophers, their search for "theories" and their appeal to general "theoretical" considerations apparently continuous with natural science, deny any real distinction between philosophical and scientific problems. That puts the dominant philosophy of the 1970s farther from the Kantian tradition than any other twentieth-century philosophy, and therefore farther from the spirit as well as the letter of Wittgenstein's conception of philosophical problems. He thought that "philosophers constantly see the method of science before their eyes, and are irresistibly tempted to ask and answer questions in the way science does. This tendency is the real source of metaphysics, and leads the philosopher into complete darkness" ([17], p. 18). Recent philosophers confess, even proclaim, their immersion in "scientific" metaphysics. A report on the main activity in the philosophy of mind in the period since 1966 would therefore be a report of activity within what Wittgenstein would regard as "darkness"; it would not be a report of developments and extensions of his own ideas during that period.

The exposition and interpretation of the writings of Wittgenstein, on the other hand, has been anything but dormant since 1966. In one respect there has been some decline even in that area; fewer people, and fewer of the best young philosophers, are working on Wittgenstein today than was true fifteen or twenty years ago. But a number of excellent books and papers on Wittgenstein have appeared and continue to appear, putting us now in a much better position for a dispassionate study of the real meaning of Wittgenstein's philosophy and an accurate understanding of its sources and implications. During our period much more of Wittgenstein's own writing has been published — *Zettel* [8] in 1967, "Notes for Lectures on 'Private Experience' and 'Sense-Data'" [9] in 1968, *Philosophische Grammatik* [10] and *On Certainty* [11] in 1969, and *Remarks on Colour* [12] in 1978. Of these, the first two include the most material directly relevant to the philosophy of mind (although it is unwise to think of Wittgenstein as dealing with separate, isolated subjects in philosophy in a way that this remark might suggest).

Since 1966 some of the best books containing discussion of issues more-or-less directly relevant to Wittgenstein's philosophy of mind have been David Pears [13] (1970), an excellent introduction, emphasizing the Kantian or "critical" orientation of Wittgenstein's philosophy; James Bogen [14] (1972), primarily an account of the change in Wittgenstein's philosophy of language from his earlier to his later work; P.M.S. Hacker [15] (1972), a resourceful exploration of many parallels to and constrasts with Wittgenstein's views in Kant, Schopenhauer, Frege, and Russell, with special concentration on solipsism and first-person psychological sentences; Anthony Kenny [16] (1973), a clear and very helpful account of Wittgenstein's main ideas at each of the different stages of his development; Robert Fogelin [17] (1976), a sympathetic, plain-speaking exposition and explanation of some of Wittgenstein's main problems and lines of solution; Stanley Cavell [18] (1979), an extremely wide-ranging intellectual excursion, including a complex and illuminating account of Wittgenstein on language, on privacy, and on the problem of other minds. Scholars of Wittgenstein will be indebted for many years to come to Garth Hallett [19] (1977), an industrious compendium of passages and references to passages in the entire Wittgenstein corpus and elsewhere, put to the service of interpreting all of the sections of the *Philosophical Investigations*. The commentary of G. Baker and P.M.S. Hacker will be equally indispensable. The first volume [20] has just appeared, but too late to be commented on here.

Hundreds of articles on Wittgenstein's philosophy of mind have been published since 1966, and it is not possible to survey them all, or even to indicate the main trends of the discussion. They have tended to concentrate on quite general issues about the nature of the mind, rather than on particular mental states like belief, thought, emotion, etc.

To explain Wittgenstein's philosophy of mind, even as it applies to such general issues, would not be to explain his philosophical theory of the nature of the mind and its place in the physical world. Rather it would be to explain the point and the effect of Wittgenstein's philosophizing about the mind, and to show how it fits in to his philosophical work in general. The distinction is important because the basic idea behind all his philosophizing, both early and late, is that we are naturally, almost inevitably, led, often by the form of our language, to misunderstand or to fail to understand many of the things we most want to understand about ourselves and the world. Philosophy for Wittgenstein is a battle against that "bewitchment" ([21], § 109); it is the attempt to gain a "perspicuous representation" (*übersichtliche Darstellung*) of our use of words ([21], § 122) rather than a theoretical or scientific explanation of what puzzles us. But simply speaking a natural language, even if we do so perfectly, would not in itself give us the kind of "representation" Wittgenstein has in mind; "every sentence in our language 'is in order as it is'" ([21], § 98), but "our grammar is lacking in this sort of perspicuity" ([21], § 122). He thinks we must first fall prey to the temptations we are naturally prone to; only then can we appreciate the illumination provided by an accurate description of the actual workings of language. Such a description, which is what Wittgenstein hopes to provide in his philosophizing, "get its power of illumination — i.e. its purpose — from the philosophical problems" ([21], § 109); it would have no such power on its own. Philosophical problems are solved when we gain an insight into the workings of our language *in spite of* or *in the face of* an urge to misunderstand them ([21], § 109). The urge is as important as the insight that quells it. It is the "bumps that the understanding has got by running its head up against the limits of language" that make us see the value of uncovering the nonsense that a successful descriptive philosopher reveals ([21], § 119).

To understand Wittgenstein's philosophy of mind it is therefore important to understand and perhaps even to be tempted by the sorts of confusions, puzzles, and misunderstandings which we are naturally led to in thinking about the mind or about mental or psychological states and processes. One could then try to see how Wittgenstein attempts to avoid or dissolve the puzzles in a way that gives us the proper or appropriate understanding of such things. Most commentators have emphasized only the second of these two essential elements of Wittgenstein's philosophy. Confident about what the problems of mind are or must be, they have concentrated on what they take to be Wittgenstein's solutions to them.

Greater emphasis on the nature of the misunderstandings which are said to give rise to philosophical problems would also perhaps have led commentators to concentrate more on the unique form and arrangement of Wittgenstein's writings, and on the question of why he presented his thoughts in just the way he did. It is well known that he composed those works he prepared for publication by careful juxtaposition and continual re-arrangement of the separate *Bemerkungen*, so there is presumably much to be gained from following the thoughts in the order in which Wittgenstein presented them and in pondering the reasons for the particular transitions from one to another. G.E.M. Anscombe [22] briefly redirected attention to this issue, and Hallett explicitly discusses the composition and structure of *Philosophical Investigations* for ten pages or so of his General Introduction to [19], but, on the whole, commentators have mentioned or otherwise paid lip-service to the special form of Wittgenstein's writings, but have then gone on to expound and interpret him as if he were doing philosophy in the conventional way. His "theories", "views", and "arguments" for his "theses" are identified and criticized as if there were no question about the presence of such standard philosophical items in his work, and so the striking look or shape of his writing then seems like little more than an eccentricity on his part or, worse, perhaps even wilful obscurantism. I think this way of reading Wittgenstein might well be responsible for some of the hostility that has undoubtedly been directed towards him as a philosopher. It makes it look as if, for some reason, he simply will not come right out and say what he thinks about the nature of language, or of meaning, or of the mind, and so it therefore seems left up to his commentators to extract his theories from the messy text. Many commentators have obliged the hostile critics by eventually finding the theories after complicated detective-work, thereby confirming the original impression of disingenuousness. This might in turn help to explain the relative neglect of Wittgenstein in recent philosophy, but there are no doubt deeper reasons for that state of affairs to be found in the development of Anglo-American philosophy and of twentieth-century culture generally.

A great deal that has been written about Wittgenstein's philosophy of mind in *Philosophical Investigations* treats it in isolation even from his own discussions of meaning and understanding in the earlier sections of that book, as well as from his discussion of other topics, such as the philosophy of mathematics. He spent at least as much time and effort throughout his life on the philosophy of mathematics as he did on the philosophy of mind. It would not be surprising to find similar approaches and similar treatment – perhaps even similar problems – in each. More exploration of this connection is to be hoped for in the future.

It would be difficult to deny that misunderstandings of how our language works can lead us into confusion or consternation about the mental or the psychological. Frege thought the same was true with respect to mathematics. He thought that we can easily come to think of some things as mental or psychological which are not – numbers, for example, or operations such as addition and mulipication. For Frege the main source of this confusion is our asking for the meaning of a word in isolation, forgetting about its role within the whole sentences in which it can appear. Failure to appreciate the fact that a word has meaning only in the context of a sentence almost inevitably forces us to accept an idea or a mental picture or an act of the mind as the meaning of the word, and hence to think of the number one, for example, as something psychological [23]. Frege was aware that the significance of this important point is not restricted to mathematics, but he himself never undertook the task of applying it in other areas. The idea, or a descendant of it, is one of the main themes at the heart of Wittgenstein's work, and in particular at the heart of his later philosophy of mind.

Misunderstanding the way language works can lead us not only to think of certain things as mental or psychological which are not, but also to misunderstand how it is possible for us to talk about those things that really are mental or psychological, and thereby to misconstrue their nature in a way that leads to philosophical problems about the mind. Even Frege, despite his admirable maxim about meaning and his anti-psychologism in mathematics, might perhaps have been regarded by Wittgenstein as still under an illusion about the nature of the psychological in this respect, in his belief in "ideas" or "sense-impressions" or in an incommunicable content of psychological acts or states which is not capturable in the "objective meaning" of our words ([23], pp. 35-36; [24], pp. 26-38). It is the purpose of Wittgenstein's philosophy of mind to expose the source of such illusions.

There has been a wide consensus among Wittgenstein's commentators that his most important and most characteristic contribution to the philosophy of mind is what is usually called his "argument" against the possibility of a "private language" — a language the words of which refer to what can be known only to the speaker, his "immediate private sensations" ([21], § 243). More articles have been written on one or another aspect of that topic than on any other issue connected with Wittgenstein's philosophy — indeed perhaps more than all the other writings on Wittgenstein's later philosophy combined. Even if it is no longer a topic of such "hot debate" as Kenny reported it to be in 1969 ([5], p. 258), there continues to be a great deal written about something called "the private-language argument", and a considerable proportion of that total even connects the discussion more or less directly with Wittgenstein.

Although it is conceded that Wittgenstein discusses only sensations in those sections of *Philosophical Investigations* in which "the private-language argument" is to be found, the conclusion he arrives at is thought to be easily generalizable to all mental events, processes and states. He is thought to be advancing a quite general philosophy of mind which he illustrates by considering the kind of mental phenomenon (viz., sensation) for which his opponents' view has the greatest plausibility.

The "private-language argument" is, at least in part, of negative philosophical significance. It is said or believed by most commentators to constitute an attack on a whole tradition of thinking about the mind, most characteristic perhaps of traditional empiricism, but also to be found in Descartes and other rationalists and even, as I have suggested, in an attenuated form in Frege himself. Kenny, for example, finds that the question of the possibility of a private language is interesting and important, not so much in its own right as because of its far-reaching consequences for epistemology and philosophy of mind. Any empiricist theory according to which we can know only our own experiences and can do so without relying on any acquaintance with the physical world or with other minds is committed to a possibility which Wittgenstein is said to argue is no possibility at all. "One point of the private-language argument is to refute this version of empiricism with its attendant scepticism" ([16], pp. 179-180). I think this expresses what has almost universally come to be thought of as the point or significance of what is now called "the private-language argument". Hacker is perhaps only putting the same understanding of it in another way when he says its purpose is "to extend and elaborate the Kantian dictum that intuitions without concepts are blind" ([15], p. 216) (although it is not clear what it would be to *extend* that dictum).

Given the great importance of "the private-language argument", so understood, it is somewhat disappointing to find considerable disagreement among commentators about exactly what the argument is, how it is supposed to lead to its conclusion, and even where it is to be found in Wittgenstein's text. In general it is agreed that discussion of the topic begins at *Philosophical Investigations* § 243 where Wittgenstein asks whether we could imagine a language of a certain sort, it is agreed also that the language in question is specified more precisely in § 256, and that the most telling questions about it are raised in § 257 and § 258. But many expositors of the "argument" find some of its crucial steps expressed as late as § 265 or § 270, and some would extend it at least as far as § 293.

Disagreement about the textual location of the "argument" is perhaps not surprising, given the equally wide disagreement about what the "argument" actually is. It is rare that a commentator is so bold as to identify a set of fairly uncontroversial premisses from the conjunction of which the desired conclusion can with some plausibility be said to follow, and each one of which can be shown, on the basis of what is asserted or implied in the text, to have been believed by Wittgenstein. Of course, the very form of Wittgenstein's writing makes that a daunting prospect. Many expositors therefore proceed dialectically by constructing a developing interchange between Wittgenstein and an imaginary opponent, during which the opponent finds himself with less and less to say. That is much closer to the form of what Wittgenstein actually wrote, but correspondingly farther from the presentation of a plausible *argument* to a definite and devastating conclusion, and even farther from a *proof* of the impossibility of something.

A further reason for the difficulty in identifying, let alone assessing the validity of, the "argument" is uncertainty about exactly what its conclusion is supposed to be. For one thing, as Cavell seems to have been the only person to point out, Wittgenstein never goes so far as to *say* that there can be no private language ([18], p. 344). And it is easy to fall into formulating the alleged conclusion of the "argument" in a way that either simply denies the obvious or seems to be more-or-less explicitly denied by Wittgenstein himself.

It would obviously be incorrect, for example, to say that there can be no language or code which only a single speaker understands. And it would therefore be equally wrong to say that there could be no such language in which the speaker talks about his sensations. Similarly, it would be absurd to say that Wittgenstein has shown that it is impossible for us to refer to or talk about our sensations; we do it every day, as he himself points out ([21], § 244). Even to say that what is to be established is that the sensations and other mental phenomena which we undoubtedly talk about are not "private" would hardly guarantee that we had identified something that Wittgenstein could be supposed to have proved. What would such a conclusion amount to? If it meant that it is not possible for only one of several people in a room to be in pain and for the others not to know that anyone in that room is in pain, then again it would simply deny the obvious. Wittgenstein himself grants that something true might well be expressed by saying "Sensations are private", viz., that it always makes sense to say of other people that they doubt whether I am in pain, but not to say it of myself ([21], § 246). And he says "The proposition 'Sensations are private' is comparable to 'One plays patience by oneself'" ([21], § 248), so whatever Wittgenstein's attitude towards the proposition "Sensations are private" is said to be, it cannot be that he simply regards it as false, let alone as necessarily false. Many commentators resort to what they call "logical privacy" (an expression Wittgenstein never uses) and find that the "argument" establishes the impossibility of a "logically private language". That is meant to convey the idea of a language in which it is "logically impossible" for anyone but the speaker to know what his words refer to, but very little has been said, either in general or in this particular case, to explain what 'logically impossible' means.

Pears in [13] describes the target of Wittgenstein's attack as a "necessarily unteachable" language. Any philosophical theory of the mind that implies that our language for sensations and other mental phenomena would be necessarily unteachable would be refuted if it were shown that no such language is possible. Wittgenstein's argument, according to Pears and many other commentators, rests on the very strong premiss that "it is an essential feature of any language that there should be effective rules which a person using the language can follow and know that he is following" ([13], p. 169). A necessarily unteachable language would be a language in which no effective rules could possibly be taught or transmitted from one person to another, so it would be a language which at best it is possible for only one person to speak. But Pears holds that, for any given statement one might try to make, either one would be under the impression that that statement is true or one would be under the impression that that statement is false. And in a necessarily unteachable language there is said to be no possible check on the correctness of one's impression, no detectable difference between being under the correct impression and being under the incorrect impression, and therefore no effective rules. "Anything you said would do" ([13], p. 169). So it would not be a language.

This conclusion, which appears to be a quite general thesis about language, can be applied to any philosophical theory of the mind which says that sensations and other mental phenomena are "private" in the sense of being completely inaccessible to everyone except the person who has them or completely detached from the physical events we normally suppose to cause them or to "express" them. If sensations and other mental phenomena, so understood, could be talked about at all, it would seem that the words for them would have to acquire their meanings only through the speaker's fixing his attention on them and attaching names to them, as Pears thinks we can in fact do in the case of material objects. Attaching the name directly to a sensation in this way would be required because of the absence of links between the sensation so named and any publicly observable material objects, including the speaker's own body. With no such links, all the external stimuli operating on the speaker and all the subsequent behaviour which others could observe would be irrelevant to the meaning or application of the appropriate sensation-word. But it would therefore be impossible for anyone to teach others or to be taught by others the meanings of such words, and so the philosophical theory in question is committed to a "necessarily unteachable" language for sensations and other mental phenomena. If such a language is impossible, for the general reasons given earlier, then that traditional philosophical theory of the mind is refuted.

This reading of Wittgenstein, or something very much like it, is widely shared among commentators on Wittgenstein and other philosophers of mind. If it is correct, it is easy to see why "the private-language argument" is thought to be of more than negative significance. It would seem to imply that sensations *can* be talked about (as of course they can be) only because the application of sensation-words is in some way governed by conditions which everyone can observe and be guided by — external stimuli and the subsequent behaviour of the person in question. That is why Kenny thought "the private-language argument" was at the same time "a proof of criterionism", Wittgenstein's "middle stance between dualism and behaviourism" according to which "the bodily expression of a mental process was a *criterion* for that process" in the sense that "it was part of the concept of a particular mental process ... that certain types of behaviour counted as direct and non-inductive evidence for its occurrence" ([5], p. 258). The "private-language argument" was supposed to have shown that if that were not true of the concepts of mental processes then they would be inapplicable and would make no sense to us. On this interpretation, if we can talk of the mind at all, "criterionism" must be true.

This immediately raises three questions. Precisely *what* connection holds between the mental process and the behaviour or bodily expression of it when the latter is said to be a "criterion" of the former? How can it be established that that "criterial" relation does hold between the two sorts of things? Does the "private-language argument" in particular establish that that relation holds between a mental process and some piece of behaviour which "expresses" it?

Considerable attention has been focussed on one form or another of the first question, much of it quite independently of Wittgenstein's alleged views on the subject (for a survey of some of it see Lycan [25]). Nevertheless, the general issue raised in the second question has not been much discussed. As for the third question, there are at least two good objections to the "private-language argument" as formulated above. Pears himself and a number of other commentators have raised similar objections to what they take to be Wittgenstein's position. If the objections succeed, the argument does not prove anything like what it purports to prove.

The first objection is that the traditional philosophical theory of the mind need not adopt as crude a semantic theory as the one "refuted" by the above argument. Even if sensations cannot be simply dubbed or named in complete isolation from all material objects, on pain of necessary unteachability, there is a slightly more subtle account of the meaning of sensation-words according to which one simply fixes one's attention on one's sensation and gives it the name, say, 'pain', thereby meaning by 'pain' something like "sensation of a type which has such-and-such connections with observable material objects". Other people could then learn the meaning of 'pain', so understood, since they would have access to those observable material objects which figure essentially in the specification of the meaning of 'pain'. Although the word would not then be unteachable, it still could refer to something completely inaccessible to everyone except the person who has it. In fact, it could refer to something completely different from person to person, even though it retains the same meaning for all. If sameness of meaning from one person to another does not guarantee sameness of reference, there would seem to be room for something inaccessible or private to each person even though the words used to talk about it were publicly intelligible and teachable. The "private-language argument" as described so far would not rule out such a possibility and therefore would not refute the traditional theory of the mind.

The second objection is directed towards that step of the argument which says that in a necessarily unteachable language there is no possible check on one's impression that one is using an expression correctly, so there are no effective rules. If it had been established, both by oneself and by others, that one had a generally reliable memory when speaking of publicly observable material objects, why could not that same kind of reliability be inductively inferred to be present in one's speech about one's own private inner states as well? Inductive support for the presence in one area of a capacity which can be conclusively verified to be present in other areas is often all we have to go on in ordinary life, and it would seem to be all we (and the speaker) would need to be assured that a speaker is using correctly the words he has attached to inner states with which it is impossible for the rest of us to be acquainted. So the "private-language argument" as described so far would be inconclusive in another way. It would not establish the impossibility even of the cruder of the two kinds of language for sensations.

Kenny accepts the force of the first of these two objections. He thinks it is precisely because of the possibility of a distinction between the meaning and the reference of words for sensations that a special "private-language argument" must be added to Wittgenstein's attack on bare ostensive definition earlier in *Philosophical Investigations* and elsewhere. If Wittgenstein was right in denying that "bare ostension without training in the use of words could constitute the teaching of a language" ([16], p. 180), then the names of sensations could not be learned simply by acquaintance with the sensations which the names are supposed to name. But that still leaves open the possibility that they might be learned by "some private analogue of training in the use of words" and thereby come to refer to private sensations in a way that escapes Wittgenstein's earlier attack. So the possibility of a position like the one appealed to in the first objection is regarded by Kenny as the very reason why a special "private-language argument" is needed.

Kenny declares the second objection irrelevant, since he thinks the reliability of memory is not at issue in the argument. The question Wittgenstein asks about the putative sensation-language he considers is not "When the speaker next wants to apply the word 'S' in the same way as he originally resolved to use it, how can he know that he is applying it correctly?", but rather "Can the original private ostensive definition of the word 'S' confer meaning on 'S'?". It seems to me that Kenny is quite right to insist on this point. If the alleged act of meaning itself is what Wittgenstein finds questionable, then he is not to be understood as raising a sceptical objection to memory. Kenny interprets him as arguing that the "stage-setting" that is needed for an act of naming to succeed in a public language is not available in a "private" language, and so no meaning can be "privately" conferred on the putative sensation-word.

That too seems to me promising, but at a crucial point in his elaboration of Wittgenstein's criticism, Kenny seems once again to fall back on an appeal to the possible unreliability of memory. The reason he gives for saying that the original private ostensive definition cannot confer meaning on the sensation-word 'S' is that in subsequent uses of 'S' the speaker either would be simply dubbing his later sensations, whatever they happened to be, with that same name, and so would not be saying anything about them that could be true or false, or else he would be trying to apply 'S' to sensations of the same kind as those to which he had applied it in the past. And, Kenny argues, either it is possible for him to remember his past sensation wrongly, or it is not. If it is not possible, then 'S' would mean whatever happens to occur to him in connection with the word 'S', and so "whatever seems right is right". And if it *is* possible to misremember, he would "not really know what he means" ([16], p. 194); and so (can this be Kenny's reasoning?) he has not conferred any meaning on 'S'. If Kenny was right about the irrelevance of questions about the reliability of memory to Wittgenstein's scrutiny of the original act of conferring meaning on the sensation-word, as I think he was, then his curious reliance on just such questions here strongly suggests that he has not given the proper account of Wittgenstein's reasons for denying that the original ostensive ceremony can confer meaning on 'S'. That could be because even he fails to connect the later discussion of sensation-words closely enough with the more general treatment of meaning, ostension, rule, interpretation, and practices that appears earlier in *Philosophical Investigations*.

Robert Fogelin [17] is excellent in this respect. He shows clearly how sensations and the "privacy" of experience are discussed at § § 243 ff. as potential counter-examples to the points made earlier about the need for general practices or customs in the "solution" to the "paradox" about rules and interpretations described in § § 201-202. The later passages are best seen not as a direct attack on, or disproof of, the possibility of a "private" language, but as an exposure of those misunderstandings which make a "private" use of language seem possible. "A misunderstanding of our everyday sensation talk combined with a misunderstanding of how meanings are fixed conspire to generate the image of a private language" ([17], pp. 155-156).

Fogelin explains how Wittgenstein's exposure of the second misunderstanding involves showing that the meaning of a word cannot be fixed by the ceremony of ostensive "definition" or "attachment" alone. For a word to have any meaning at all, it must also be applicable outside the situation of the ostensive definition, and its wider applicability is not fixed by what occurs in the ostensive ceremony. This is a quite general point about meaning; it is not specifically tied to names for sensations or other mental phenomena. And Fogelin, like Pears and Kenny, finds that it does not immediately imply that a "private" language of sensations is impossible. He therefore puts more stress on Wittgenstein's claim that "it is not possible to obey a rule 'privately'; otherwise thinking one was obeying a rule would be the same thing as obeying it" ([21], § 202). And he interprets that remark as saying that in "private" rule-following there could be no *independent* justification of the application of a word. Even an appeal to memory would be to no avail, since there would be no way to distinguish a correct memory report or impression from one that only seems to be correct; "whatever is going to seem right to me is right" ([17], p. 162).

Fogelin regards Wittgenstein's argument on this point as completely unsatisfactory, and it seems to me that what he says about the kind of argument he considers is correct. It is a sceptical argument which is completely general in form; it exploits the distinction between 'seems' and 'is', and argues that there is no way to determine whether the application of a word is in fact correct, or only seems to be. Since it appears to rest on nothing more than the general failure of implication from 'seems' to 'is', the argument, if successful, would show not just the impossibility of a special "private" language of sensations, but of any language at all, even a language about public material objects. From the fact that an application of a particular word to a material object seems to me to be correct it does not follow that it is correct, even if it also seems correct to everyone else or it seems to me that everyone else regards it as correct. No *special* conclusion about only a particular form of language or only a restricted range of facts can be derived from such a *general* sceptical argument.

I think Fogelin is right on this important point, and it applies to most of the arguments attributed to Wittgenstein by his many interpreters, but it does not follow that Wittgenstein has failed to show what he wants to show. The most that follows is that when Wittgenstein remarks that if one were obeying a rule "privately" then "thinking one was obeying a rule would be the same thing as obeying it" or "whatever is going to seem right to me is right", what he says would have no special force against the possibility of a "private" language of sensations *if* those remarks are understood as exploiting or in any way relying on a general sceptical distinction between 'seems' and 'is'. If Wittgenstein has something else in mind he might still succeed in exposing some natural or far-reaching misunderstandings of our everyday talk of sensations and of the way in which meanings are fixed.

All interpretations of Wittgenstein on this point which attribute to him a reliance on the impossibility of distinguishing the way things are from the way they seem tend to concentrate on a stage in the attempted development of a "private" language which comes later than the original ostensive ceremony to which Wittgenstein primarily directs his attention. They raise a question about whether, in the attempt to apply the words of one's "private" language, something *is* being done correctly or only *seems* to be being done correctly. But more care is needed in specifying *what it is* that is supposed to be being done correctly. To apply the word 'S' correctly is to apply it in the same way on this occasion as it was applied earlier, or to use it in accordance with the meaning given to it on the first occasion of its attachment to that of which it is supposed to be the name. But in the attempt to give 'S' a meaning which Wittgenstein considers, *is* there such a thing as "the way it was applied" on the first occasion, or such a thing as "the meaning given to it on the first occasion of its attachment to that of which it is supposed to be the name"? Wittgenstein's attack on the notion of a purely ostensive fixing of meaning or reference is intended to cast doubt on that idea.

The best understanding and explanation of this fundamental point that I know of in the published literature is in Goldberg

[26]. He shows convincingly that, even if we concede that a speaker has direct acquaintance with an item he wishes to name, and he calls that thing S and undertakes to use the word 'S' in the future to stand for anything that is exactly like that one, nothing at all has been determined so far about how 'S' is to be applied the next time. Any object that can be named belongs to many different classes of things, so from the original starting-point of the particular item and the word "attached" to it, as described so far, an indefinite number of completely different paths lead off, each one of which, if followed, would represent a way of applying 'S' *in the same way* or to things *exactly like* the original item.

The difficulty in "applying 'S' correctly" is not that one must remember what the original item was like and be sure to apply the term only to things that are like it; rather the difficulty is that it has not been determined by the original ceremony alone which of the many possible paths is the one to be followed, and so there is so far nothing to be correct or incorrect about. "What could it mean to say that I have made a mistake except that my application of 'S' conflicts with what was established concerning the range of its application. But since nothing was established concerning its range of application there is nothing for my use of 'S' to conflict (or agree) with" ([26], p. 88). Even an infallible memory would not help, since "nothing that happened, nothing that *could be* remembered, has determined whether or not 'S' is to be applied" ([26], p. 89). Goldberg shows that the basic point Wittgenstein relies on or exploits has nothing to do with the alleged fallibility of memory; it is simply the fact that "for any two objects, there is no (unique) determinate answer to the question concerning whether or not they are the same ([26], p. 89).

The point holds quite generally, for material objects as well as for sensations and everything else. If there is to be such a thing as the correct (or incorrect) use of a word, it must be determined, somehow or other, which of the many possible paths one is supposed to follow in applying it. This might suggest that the speaker of a "private" language can confer a particular kind of meaning on 'S' by attaching it ostensively to a certain sensation he has and resolving to use it as a word for a *sensation* of that particular kind. But, even leaving aside the indeterminateness of "that kind", it is not clear what it is to make such a resolution. The word 'sensation' is, after all, a word in English, our common language, so if 'S' is to be a sensation-word it must be used as sensation-words are used in our common language. All of us speak and understand that language; it is not a language whose words are intelligible to the speaker alone. In an attempt to give 'S' a meaning which only the speaker can understand, it would not help to eschew the use of the word 'sensation' and to say that "it need not be a *sensation*; that when he writes 'S', he has *something* – and that is all that can be said. "Has" and "something" also belong to our common language. – So in the end when one is doing philosophy one gets to the point where one would like just to emit an inarticulate sound." But even that would not help, since "such a sound is an expression only as it occurs in a particular language-game, which should now be described" ([21], § 261).

The exact description of the use of sensation-words, or of psychological expressions generally, free of the misunderstandings we are naturally prone to, is all Wittgenstein thinks there is to appeal to in gaining the kind of understanding of the mind which we seek. In his *Zettel* ([8], § § 472, 488) he sketches what he calls a "plan for the treatment of psychological concepts", and nowhere in that plan is there any mention of "criteria" for the ascription of psychological states and processes, or of the problem of characterizing some special "non-inductive" evidential relation which "behaviour" is supposed to bear to them. If that were the key to Wittgenstein's philosophy of mind it would be surprising that he does not at least mention it. But it would not be surprising if the kind of interpretation I have been outlining above were on the right track. Wittgenstein's exposure of the natural misunderstandings of "privacy" and of the language we use to describe and express our thought and experience, and his more general discussion of the need for customs or practices for the possibility of intelligible thought and talk about the mind or about anything else, seem to promise little in the way of a more-or-less precise philosophical conclusion about a quasi-logical relation holding in general between a "criterion" and a mental state or process of which it is the "criterion" and on the basis of which the mental state or process is ascribed to someone. The conditions under which psychological concepts are actually applied to human beings are extremely various, as they are for non-psychological words as well. Our language provides us with a rich and highly flexible network for speaking of and making sense of things, and what in one context is all we need to "go on" in ascribing a particular mental concept to someone is in a quite different context no good at all as a "basis" for such an ascription.

Why should it be supposed that for every psychological word there is, let alone must be, some special "criterial" relation between observable "behaviour" and the psychological state or process referred to by that word? And why is it so widely believed that Wittgenstein thought there was, or must be, such a relation? The voluminous literature on Wittgenstein's philosophy of mind, it seems to me, has not adequately answered these questions on the basis of anything Wittgenstein actually wrote. And to say that there must be a "non-inductive" or "quasi-necessary" connection between something called "behaviour" and something else called a "mental state or process" seems to me to invoke precisely the kind of distinction between two different things or two different realms which Wittgenstein's whole treatment of psychological concepts is meant to bring into question. For him, the nature of the mental or the psychological is to be illuminated, not by discovering or inventing a special relation holding between otherwise puzzling "mental" things and relatively unproblematic "physical" things, which might help bring the two sorts of things closer together, but rather by an understanding of what psychological concepts are actually like, and how they work.

The *Zettel* plan begins:

> Plan for the treatment of psychological concepts. Psychological verbs characterized by the fact that the third person of the present is to be verified by observation, the first person not.

> Sentences in the third person of the present: information. In the first person present: expression. ((Not quite right.))

The first person of the present akin to an expression. ([8], § 472)

It seems to be Wittgenstein's idea that these asymmetries between first- and third-person uses are one of the definitive characteristics of psychological concepts, part of what makes a concept a "psychological" one, so they are obviously of central importance for the study of the nature of mind. And understanding the special peculiarities of first-person psychological sentences — how they are possible, and in what ways they are "akin" to "expressions" and in what ways not — can be expected to take us a long way towards understanding the source of traditional difficulties about "other minds". There has been relatively little exploration of Wittgenstein's discussion of this topic in recent years (see Hacker [15], Malcolm [27]).

But for Wittgenstein the description of the actual workings of psychological concepts in all their complexity still derives its philosophical significance or gets its "power of illumination" only from the philosophical problems we are naturally led into in thinking about the mind. At one point he asks how what he calls "the philosophical problem about mental processes and states and about behaviourism" arises, and he answers:

> The first step is the one that altogether escapes notice. We talk of processes and states and leave their nature undecided. Sometime perhaps we shall know more about them — we think. But that is just what commits us to a particular way of looking at the matter. For we have a definite concept of what it means to learn to know a process better. (The decisive movement in the conjuring trick has been made, and it was the very one we thought quite innocent.) ([21], § 308)

The step that is said to "escape notice" here is a step which has long since been taken by those who look for a special "criterial" relation between "behaviour" and an inner process or state. Wittgenstein suggests that as soon as we ask, for example, "What is pain?" or "What is this particular pain?" we have gone wrong. He intimates that any answer we give to such questions will be, or will lead to, a misunderstanding. There has not been enough discussion of this idea by Wittgenstein's interpreters. Malcolm [28] touches on it briefly. Wittgenstein tries to express the right view of the matter by saying that the sensation "is not a *something*, but not a *nothing* either" ([21], § 304). That remark gets whatever sense it might possess only from the discussion of which it forms a part. It has not been adequately interpreted so far.

Physicalism — the view that pain, or at any rate the state of being in pain, is a metter of being in a certain (as yet not fully specified) physical state —would appear to answer in one way the sorts of questions which Wittgenstein thinks lead us astray. It is not clear how the obscure remark to the effect that the sensation is "not a something" accord with that sort of position. In a very interesting paper [29], Hopkins has explored the extent to which Wittgenstein's account of psychological concepts is compatible with the kind of physicalism which has become so fashionable in recent years. He does not explicitly discuss whether physicalism makes what Wittgenstein regards as the first, unnoticed step towards philosophical perplexity. That is an area that needs more exploration, as does the more general question of the relation between physiological and other scientific investigation and our understanding of psychological concepts and the nature of the mind.

The careful and sympathetic interpretation of the writings Wittgenstein has left us, although still very much needed, would not be sufficient for this latter task. It would be fully in the spirit of Wittgenstein's philosophy to continue, quite independently of textual exegesis, the exposure of those philosophical pretensions so frequently advanced for otherwise respectable scientific theories about one or another aspect of *homo sapiens*.

BIBLIOGRAPHY

Ameriks, K. [30] Recent Work on Wittgenstein and the Philosophy of Mind. *New Scholasticism*, 1975.

Anscombe, G.E.M. [22] On the Form of Wittgenstein's Writing. In Klibansky [32].

Baker, G., and Hacker, P.M.S. [20] *Wittgenstein: Understanding and Meaning*. Oxford 1980.

Bogen, J. [14] *Wittgenstein's Philosophy of Language*. London 1972.

Cavell, S. [18] *The Claim of Reason: Wittgenstein, Skepticism, Morality and Tragedy*. New York 1979.

Fogelin, R. [17] *Wittgenstein*. London 1976.

Frege, G. [23] *Foundations of Arithmetic*, tr. J.L. Austin, Oxford 1953.

— [24] The Thought. In Strawson [31].

Goldberg, B. [26] The Linguistic Expression of Feeling. *American Philosophical Quarterly*, 1971.

Hacker, P.M.S. [15] *Insight and Illusion: Wittgenstein on Philosophy and the Metaphysics of Experience*. Oxford 1972.

Hallett, G. [19] *A Companion to Wittgenstein's 'Philosophical Investigations'*. Ithaca, N.Y. 1977.

Hopkins, J. [29] Wittgenstein and Physicalism. *Proceedings of the Aristotelian Society*, 1974-75.

Kenny, A. [5] Philosophy of Mind in the Anglo-American Tradition. In Klibansky [32].

— [16] *Wittgenstein*. London 1973.

Klibansky, R. (Ed.) [32] *Contemporary Philosophy*. Firenze 1969.

Lycan, W.G. [25] Non-Inductive Evidence: Recent Work on Wittgenstein's 'Criterion'. *American Philosophical Quarterly*, 1971.

Malcolm, N. [2] Knowledge of Other Minds. *The Journal of Philosophy*, 1958.

— [3] *Dreaming*. London 1959.

— [6] *Problems of Mind: Descartes to Wittgenstein*. New York 1971.

— [27] Wittgenstein's Conception of First-Person Psychological Sentences as Expressions. *Philosophical Exchange*, 1978.

— [28] Wittgenstein on the Nature of Mind. In *Thought and Knowledge*. Ithaca, N.Y. 1977.

Pears, D. [13] *Ludwig Wittgenstein*, New York 1970.

Ryle, G. [1] *The Concept of Mind*, London 1949.

Strawson, P.F. [4] *Individuals: an Essay in Descriptive Metaphysics*, London 1959.

— (Ed.) [31] *Philosophical Logic*, Oxford 1967.

Wittgenstein, L. [7] *The Blue and Brown Books*. Oxford 1958.

— [8] *Zettel*. Oxford 1967.

— [9] Notes for Lectures on 'Private Experience' and 'Sense-Data'. *Philosophical Review*, 1968.

— [10] *Philosophische Grammatik*. Oxford 1969.

— [11] *On Certainty*. Oxford 1969.

— [12] *Remarks on Colour*. Oxford 1978.

— [21] *Philosophical Investigations*. Oxford 1953.

Merleau-Ponty's philosophy of mind

HARRISON HALL
University of Delaware

There are two problems that arise as soon as one attempts to specify Merleau-Ponty's position on any of the standard problems or within any of the major problem areas of philosophy. The first of these is that his view on a particular issue or set of issues is almost never self-contained or self-sufficient, but depends on other parts of his general theory of human experience, not simply for the evidence of its correctness, but for its intelligibility as well. The second problem is that on almost any question, although it is quite easy to identify a number of answers which Merleau-Ponty takes to be clearly wrong, it is almost impossible to specify very clearly that answer which he takes to be correct. With these problems in mind, this essay will be divided into two main sections. In the first of these I will present enough of Merleau-Ponty's basic philosophical view to provide the needed background for a discussion of his philosophy of mind. In the second section I will take up a number of issues in the philosophy of mind, attempting not only to locate Merleau-Ponty vis-à-vis the alternatives he rejects, but also to give as clear an account as possible of the positive theory which is to replace them.

I. MERLEAU-PONTY'S PHILOSOPHY

Merleau-Ponty stands squarely within the existential tradition. His philosophical position is at the end of a line of progression which can be traced back through the Heidegger of *Being and Time* at

Contemporary philosophy. A new survey. Vol. 4, pp. 343–361.
© *1983, Martinus Nijhoff Publishers, The Hague/Boston/London.*

least to Kierkegaard. He shares two characteristics with the other members of this tradition. The first of these is a desire to understand human existence as it is lived from the 'inside' rather than as it is observed or thought about from the 'outside,' to capture our 'first-personal' rather than 'third-personal' sense of what it is to be an existing human being. The second is a belief that there is something fundamentally paradoxical or contradictory about being human which makes such an understanding very difficult to achieve and virtually impossible to conceptualize. What separates Merleau-Ponty from the rest of this tradition is the particular form these characteristics assume within his philosophy. I will approach Merleau-Ponty's unique version of existentialism by way of a discussion of two fundamental tenets of his thought, namely, that the lived body is the proper subject of experience, and that, within experience, perception must be understood as primary.

1. *The lived body as subject*

In the last work published during his lifetime, Merleau-Ponty refers to the role of the lived body in experience by describing it as "the sentinel standing silently at the command of my words and acts" (1964a: 13). Unfortunately, no brief description captures very much of what Merleau-Ponty has to say about the lived body. We will need no retrace briefly the route Merleau-Ponty follows in *Phenomenology of Perception* (1962), in order to arrive at the theory behind such descriptions. This requires that we first make clear just what the lived body is not.

The sense we have of our bodies as we live them is not that of an object. This is not to say that our bodies never play the role of objects within our experience — we can, of course, see and touch parts of ourselves — but rather that they play no such role essentially. For most of our experience our own bodies do not function as objects of our awareness. They are, if anything, on our 'side' of experience, but function transparently enough so that Sartre, for example, is able to miss them entirely when he looks for the experiencing subject. There is a price to be paid for such an oversight, however, and Merleau-Ponty's conception of the lived body aims at avoiding this penalty. I will return to this shortly.

To say that the lived body is not primarily an object entails the following for Merleau-Ponty. First, the lived body is not to be identified with that entity which the physiologist studies. The command we have of our bodies as active subjects is not experienced by us as a command of the physiological processes which underlie our activity. The practical know-how employed in our bodily behavior neither includes nor depends upon any knowledge of physiological theory. Second, the lived body is not the blind reactive mechanism described by unsophisticated versions of stimulus-response psychology. The world as we interact with it cannot be adequately understood as an array of physical properties, but must be treated instead as a system of significant contexts or situations whose meaning depends not simply upon their physical constituents but upon our biological, social and cultural nature, interests and goals as well. And the unity which must be recognized by an adequate theory of human behavior is not a unity of mechanical reaction, but rather a unity of meaning or style which joins actions by virtue of their sharing a common biological, social or cultural significance for the humen agents involved.

The peculiar mobility and spatiality of the body also serve to distinguish it from objects. We do not need to locate the various parts of our bodies in objective space in order to have them at our command; and we do not, in the course of skillful bodily activity, move our bodies from place to place in the way that we move objects. It is much closer to the sense of our experience to say with Merleau-Ponty that our bodies move themselves, or that we *are* our bodies. Our bodies as lived are the vehicles, not the objects, of our motor intentions. These intentions do not originate elsewhere and then come to animate the body as the puppeteer animates a puppet. Our motor intentions are embodied from the start, pre-possessed of that tacit understanding of the body's place and potential which is self-knowledge in act.

Finally, the special unity of the body as lived helps to assimilate it to the experiencing subject. Just as, in general, our sense of ourselves is that of a single, undivided subject, so our sense of our lived bodies is that of a unified potential for perceptual and motor activity. We do not need to gather together the parts of our bodies in order to employ them in skillful activity. Nor is the process of coordinating the various functions of the body experienced as made up of parts or as a summative phenomenon. We are in undivided possession of our bodies, and our natural coordination as embodied subjects extends across the diverse sensory and motor functions of the lived body.

The lived body, for Merleau-Ponty, is the subject's sense of him/herself as a unified "I can" and the world is experienced correlatively as a unified field of potential sensory-motor activity. It is features of this bodily "I can" which allow Merleau-Ponty to account for those aspects of human subjectivity which remain mysterious if we try, as does Sartre, to treat human consciousness as not essentially embodied. Pure consciousness could not, for example, form habits which would serve in any way to guide its decisions and actions. The result is the implausible Sartrean explanation of all habitual modes of thought and activity in terms of an elaborate attempt at self-deception ("bad faith") so as to hide from ourselves the truth about our total lack of content. For Merleau-Ponty on the other hand, what Sartre describes as bad faith is simply part of the definition of concrete human consciousness. Since we are essentially embodied, our behavior is to be understood on the model of bodily activity. Proficiency in bodily activity requires the development of bodily skills, and bodily skills simply are habitual modes of activity employed almost automatically in response to situations perceived as similar. The lived body is a natural acquirer of habitual skills, just as it is naturally unified and coordinated. We do not learn the ability to acquire bodily habits or to act as a single embodied subject of our intentions. These are the conditions for learning on the basis of which we learn particular bodily skills and coordinate more elaborate bodily behavior in our unified interaction with the world.

2. *The primacy of perception*

Merleau-Ponty's theory of perception follows from his understanding of the lived body or body-subject described above. And just as certain basic features of the experiencing subject cannot be understood independently of the lived body, so the basic features of the experienced world of objects must be understood in terms of their correlation with the functioning of the body-subject of that world. The subject is the ensemble of skills which actively involve him in the world, and the structure of the world is a function of the subjects being 'at home' in it. At the perceptual level, the lived body is a synergic system of habitual sensory-motor skills with which certain features of the perceived world are to be understood as strictly correlative. These bodily skills or powers are at once both specific and general, the ability to perform a particular operation and the general capacity to perform a broad range of operations which for the body, as a coordinated system of equivalences across the various sensory modalities and motor circuits, count as the same by virtue of their filling the same role in the overall activity of the embodied agent. Every bodily skill thus amounts to the ability to perform not only those tasks through which the skill was acquired, but an indefinite number of similar tasks as well. Correlatively, objects apprehended through the skillful employment of the body are apprehended not only as specific individuals but as members of a family of objects which would fit in the same way into a certain general pattern of skillful bodily activity.

Since the body's skills are habitual rather than explicitly formulated and arrayed before a mind in perfect possession of itself, the correlative perceptual meanings are essentially opaque and ambiguous rather than perfectly transparent and fully determinate. Perceived objects are encountered as partially determined and further determinable; but the process of perceptual disambiguation is incompletable in principle.

The natural synergy of the body, the ability to unite all parts and functions of the lived body in a single sensory-motor project directed toward the world, results correlatively in object's being perceived as wholly present in each of their profiles, rather than hidden indefinitely behind them. Because the individual senses and motor skills, rather than working independently, function together in the perceiver's unified exploration of the world, the perceived characteristics of objects are not limited to those which could mechanically affect the appropriate parts of the objective body but extend across the various senses and beyond the momentarily given as a correlate of the motility and inter-sensory potential of the lived body. The inter-sensory nature of the perceived object, its wholeness, and the unity of the entire perceptual field are a function of the unity of the active body-subject. Within the functional unity of the lived body there is, however, an important distinction to be drawn. At any particular time there is a particular skill or skills actively employed against a background of potentially employable skills. Correlatively, within the unity of the perceptual field, there is a distinction between the explicitly given figure and the background from which it stands out. Just as the background skills are implicitly given in the active employment of any particular skill as able to be brought to the fore by a shift in sensory-motor project, so the perceptual background is implicitly given with the figure as a source of other figures attendant upon further bodily exploration. The horizonal givenness, for example, of the 'unseen' parts of an object or of the perceptual field is a correlate of the sensory-motor potential to 'go and see' on the horizon of any particular visual project.

To summarize the foregoing, the body as lived is a natural acquirer of habits or potentials for skillful activity. In skillful activity the body-subject is naturally unified and coordinated. And the structure of the experienced world is correlative with the nature and functional organization of the active body. But all of that is only part of the story of the body and, hence, of perception. The body is not simply the subject of experience and active; it is also a thing among other things in the experienced world and acted upon by them. Merleau-Ponty believed the paradoxical relationship between the lived or subjective body and the body as object to be one which no other philosopher (including himself in the earlier part of his career) had understood or appreciated fully, and at the same time one which held the key to understanding the whole of human existence and the human world. He characterized the relation between the two aspects of the body as an "overlapping" or an "intertwining" in his later works, and I will have to examine these notions very carefully when I take up the mind-body problem in the next section. For my present purposes, it will suffice to indicate the way in which this very special relation enables Merleau-Ponty to round out his account of perception.

The correlation between the structure of the world and the characteristics of the active body-subject allows Merleau-Ponty to capture Husserl's sense of our contributing meaning or structure to experience. Nothing enters into human experience whose meaningful structure can be understood as entirely independent of human subjectivity. And because the subject responsible for the organizing or structuring of experience is an embodied subject and bodily activity habitual by nature, Merleau-Ponty is able to make sense of the development of habits of meaning-giving or meaning-constituting which, as Sartre pointed out, are at best mysterious on Husserl's theory, being attributed by Husserl to a disembodied transcendental subject. The most important advantage of Merleau-Ponty's concept of the lived body for his theory of perception is that is makes possible the incorporation of the Gestalt psychologists' insight into the real passivity as well as the real activity within perceptual experience. In addition to being active or interpretive as perceivers, we are also responding to solicitations already present in our experience. Perceptual meaning is thus to be understood as the product of a kind of discovery rather than the product of a free bestowal of sense. We are active or interpretive, but always in response to a structure or organization which is already there. To the extent to which he took it into account at all, this original passivity of perception was simply labelled by Husserl and treated as a brute fact. And in the final analysis, even Husserl's "pasive constitution" is to be understood as a sense-bestowing rather than a sense-receiving. Merleau-Ponty uses the special relation of the lived to the objective body to explain the interrelation of activity and passivity in perceptual experience. Since the body is an object among objects, it is natural for it to be affected by them. Merleau-Ponty sometimes employs the metaphor of inscribing. Things inscribe a kind of ambiguous 'sense' upon the objective body. And since the body-subject is so intimately related to the objective body, the 'meanings' which things inscribe upon the latter have their immediate equivalents in the experience of the former. Merleau-Ponty refers to the two terms of this intimate relationship by means of the notions of "obverse" and "reverse." The lived body is the "other side" of the objective body, and vice versa. They are the obverse and the reverse of each other, and together form a single indivisible being, in spite of the problems this raises for objective thought -- philosophic or scientific. Merleau-Ponty's account of the actual functioning of the two 'sides' of the body in perception is as follows. Things offer to the body a pre-objective and indeterminate significance which is primarily motor in nature. With respect to this significance the role of the body is that of passive recipient. In response to this preobjective motor significance, the body moves itself so as to reveal a sensible object with determinate properties. As the earlier discussion of the unity of the lived body indicated, the meaning of the perceptual object is inter-sensory and sensory-motor in nature and always incompletely determined, open to further determination.

This brief sketch of Merleau-Ponty's theory of perception is sufficient for my present purpose, which is an explanation of Merleau-Ponty's thesis of the primacy of perception (for a more complete account, see Hall, 1977). To say that perception is primary means, for Merleau-Ponty, that all the meanings and structure of human experience are either perceptual or to be understood as elaborations or outgrowths of the structure of perceptual experience. The implications are numerous, and I will mention only a few here. First, in every area of human experience there will be an interplay of activity and passivity similar to that found in ordinary perception. At no time is human consciousness purely active, and hence, as will be discussed in detail in the next section, at no time are human beings absolutely free. Second, all human experience must be understood as situated. There is no part of human existence in which consciousness can be understood as at the world from outside it. We are always already situated, already involved. Our choices are choices of response to more or less open situations, not choices of whether or not to be situated. Our actions are selected from a field of possible activity whose outline is determined by our situation and which is never entirely of our own making. We take up and transform or preserve our situation; we do not produce it from nothing. Third, our situatedness throughout the entire range of human experience is to be understood on the model of our actual embodiment. Thus for each sphere or region of experience there must be at least an analog of the human body with its subjective and objective sides.

II. PHILOSOPHY OF MIND

Merleau-Ponty's philosophy of mind represents a fairly direct application of his views concerning the role of the body and the primacy of perception in human experience. The relationship between mind and body cannot be understood along the lines of traditional dualism if the mind is really the "other side" of the body. Nor can either be reducible to the other as either substance is traditionally understood. What Merleau-Ponty seeks is a new understanding of the mind compatible both with his theory of the body and with his view of the intimate relation between mind and body. The result is a theory of the mind which makes it *necessarily* embodied, and an extended argument designed to show that certain features of our experience require this theory. Similarly, human freedom is embodied, not by chance, but by its very nature. This places conditions upon human freedom which restrict its scope but which by no means eliminate it.

1. *The mind-body relation*

Merleau-Ponty's account of the body as we live it already takes us well beyond the ordinary conception of the body as a physical thing and nothing more. Similarly, the account he gives of the subject of perception leaves us well below the ordinary conception of the mind as a locus of explicit ideas or representations. And, in fact, a good first approximation of Merleau-Ponty's view of the relation of mind to body is to think, not in terms of the traditional opposition of incompatible substances, but rather in terms of a continuum of functions and a 'substance' capable of supporting that entire continuum. Given the thesis of the primacy of perception, the best way to flesh out this view is to explore the functioning of mind and body in perceptual experience.

Although the body is in part a physical thing inserted into the system of things which constitute the physical world, it is certainly not reducible to that. The body possesses a kind of natural 'understanding' of the structure of things. Below the level of our awareness, this understanding guides the movement of the eyes from blurred image toward focus, adjusts the movement of the hands toward that speed and pressure which will give us the feel of things, and sets general threshold levels which serve as the background against which the sensory features of things can be perceived. The body solves the perceptual equivalent of Plato's problem of knowledge without the myth of reincarnation. It is able to 'know' in some sense what we are looking for perceptually, and without this tacit knowledge perception would not succeed in finding anything. So that finally if we try to maintain a clear distinction between mind and body we are forced to say with Merleau-Ponty that there is a "mind of the body."

Conversely, there is a "body of the mind." Just as at the perceptual level we find the body possessed of something analogous to mental powers (a kind of tacit 'knowledge' or 'understanding'), so at the level of thought we find the mind encumbered by something analogous to the body. And in neither case is the conjunction of the bodily and the mental accidental. Without bodily 'foreknowledge', perception would be impossible; and without a mental analog of the body, thought would lack its necessary conditions. In view of the latter, it is misleading to speak of the mind as encumbered, the temptation to do so brought on by belief in the 'mythical' possibility of pure thought, unsituated and unconditioned.

What fills a role analogous to that of the body within conceptual experience is the system of implicit beliefs and habits *according to which* we think. Merleau-Ponty uses Husserl's notion of "sedimentation" to describe the process by which such a system develops. The personal and cultural history of the individual, the dominant scientific, social and artistic views, all contribute toward the formation of something like mental 'habits' and a mental 'perspective.' The effect is to make certain modes of thought, certain ways of sorting the important from the trivial, the problematic from the taken-for-granted, preferred or natural for the individual. We might speak of these as second nature to the individual, and Merleau-Ponty wants us to take that very literally. There is a second nature of the individual, a sediment of his personal and cultural past, some of which is embedded in the language and in the conceptual scheme which he inherits, and all of which is crystallized in his own peculiar variants of them. And his insertion into this 'second nature' is perfectly analogous to his insertion into the 'first' — we are situated or embodied in the mental as well as in the physical dimension. At every level of human experience we have something very like the embodiment of the perceptual subject; and at no level do we have a situation in which it is descriptively useful to think of the subject as essentially physical in nature, essentially mental in nature, or essentially split with the two halves of his nature in absolute opposition to each other.

How should we describe the relation of mind and body? I have already suggested, somewhat metaphorically, a description of each as the "other side" of the other. In his first book, *The Structure of Behavior* (1963; see pp. 188 ff.), Merleau-Ponty in effect offers this same description non-metaphorically. He claims that all of the relations within perceptual experience, including that between the mind (perceptual consciousness) and the body, can be understood in terms of the relation between the perspectival aspect and the thing perceived. Since the claim that the mind is literally the other side of the body also appears in his last book, *The Visible and the Invisible* (1968; see, for example, pp. 259 ff.), it is certainly to be taken seriously and suggests a natural approach to Merleau-Ponty's view of the nature of mind and body and the relation between them. This approach is through a more careful analysis of the unity of the perceived object. In the previous section the unity of the perceptual thing was described as a correlate of the functional unity of the perceiving subject. I will try to make as clear as possible Merleau-Ponty's view of the correlative unity of the subject's perceptual and motor functions on the one hand, and the unity of the aspects of the perceived object on the other, before attempting to assimilate to these the general unity of the subject's body and mind. The advantage of this approach to the problem is that, at least initially, the relationships between aspects of an object or between functions of the subject (for example, sight and touch, perception and movement) do not seem as mysterious or as troublesome as that between body and mind.

Merleau-Ponty describes the unity of sight and touch or of perception and movement as a unity by "transgression" or "encroachment." I am able to engage my whole being in any single project so that, at least from the standpoint of self-description, the sense of each of my acts is that I do them, rather than that part of me does them. To talk about my power of movement as horizonally present in, or part of the background of, a particular visual project, for example, is not, for Merleau-Ponty, simply to say that it is waiting in the wings to be employed if needed; but rather that it is somehow already engaged along with my power of sight. And the same is true of the relation of movement to any of the sensory functions or of any one sense to another. The result is that none of our sensory-motor powers are confined within their 'proper' spheres, but rather that each is to be viewed as encroaching upon or transgressing the boundaries of the others. Correlatively, there is a single experienced world, with the 'worlds' of my particular sensory and motor projects encroaching upon or transgressing the boundaries of each other. The point of these somewhat cryptic claims is the following. Those aspects of things not strictly perceivable at a given time which are the correlates of my other sensory powers and of my motor potential to explore further, to move so as to make them perceivable in the strict sense, acquire some element of sensory presence by virtue of which all of an object is perceptually present in each of its perspectives, rather than broken up into perspectival parts only one of which can ever be recovered in any perceptual act. The direct perception of depth, solidity and mass — without which we would not perceive objects as objects — is made possible by the bodily system of equivalents which 'translate' the elements of the sensory and motor fields into each other, producing a single world. Correlative with the body-subject's ability to engage his entire sensory-motor being in a single perceptual act is the 'ability' of the sensory and motor significances of things to be all there at once in perception.

Merleau-Ponty conceives of this ability to coordinate and unify functions, to translate the 'givens' of one sphere of experience into those of any other so that each is complete or total and yet opens upon or implicates all the rest, as the defining characteristic of the lived body. It is this ability which accounts for the fact that every perceptual act is both sensory-motor and intersensory in nature. And since the significance things have within my experience is correlative with the structure of my experiencing, the perceptual significance of things will also be sensory-motor and inter-sensory in nature. The sense of things correlative with my power of movement will be inscribed, for example, within their visual profiles, as will the sense of things correlative with my power of touch. Like the unseen but see-able aspects of things, their hardness or softness, roughness or smoothness, even their heat and cold will have some visual equivalent, will possess some element of sensory presence within the visual field as a result of the unified structure of perceiver and perceptual world. This theory seems to accord well with the phenomenal facts that even from the front houses look different to us than do façades, that mountains can look cold, that objects made of metal can look hard or heavy, and so on. And Merleau-Ponty's fascination with painting is closely related to this feature of his theory of perception. The painter captures the visual equivalents of the proper objects of all of our sensory and motor powers to make visible much more than what can be seen in the strict sense. But the resources he draws on explicitly are the same as those which function implicitly throughout ordinary perception.

This notion of the lived body as a natural system of equivalences which translate the worlds of each of our senses and even of our motor potentials into one another both overcomes the naive view of the distinction and separation of each of our sensory and motor powers and gives us a way to understand the unusual unity which is characteristic of their normal functioning. The unity of the subject is not a unity accomplished by joining distinct parts or pieces to each other until they add up to the whole. Each 'part' is, in Merleau-Ponty's words, a total part. Each includes all of the others by a kind of translational overreaching, each maps onto all the others to produce a single range of activity. The loss of one of our senses, for example, does not so much result in a gap in the subject's field of activity as it does in a loss of structure or integration within a field which remains, nonetheless, complete. One might think of the 'worlds' of the various senses — in Merleau-Ponty's language, the 'maps' of our visual, tactile, etc., projects — as overlayed upon one another, so that each one covers the entire world and yet adds structure to it so that something would be lost by its removal. And Merleau-Ponty's metaphors frequently suggest just this model. What needs to be added, though, is that no layer of the experienced world is independent of the others. Removing one of the overlays does not leave the others unchanged. The visual world, for example, would not be the same if it did not contain through a kind of quasi-presence the tactile significances of things and a reference to the tactile world proper within its own internal structure.

For Merleau-Ponty, the mental and physical 'worlds' map onto each other in much the same way and allow the relation of mind and body to be characterized in the same terms as the relations between the near side (properly visual) and the whole (properly motor, a correlate of the potential to move so as to make visible) of an object, the look (properly visual) and the feel (properly tactile) of a thing, or between the powers of sight and touch themselves. We are mental-physical in the same way that we are sensory-motor or inter-sensory, by a kind of transgression or encroachment of one 'world' into another, an immediate translation via the lived body of the language of one into that of the other. The physical world is complete, not just in the sense of having no gaps, but in the sense of containing, through a kind of quasi-presence, the mental world as well in much the same way that the visual 'world' contains the tactile. The subject as subject, not just as object, has a 'place' in the physical world, registers upon the map of the physical in the same way that the hardness of things can be registered upon the map of the visible. And, conversely, the physical effects of the world upon the objective body have their immediate equivalents in the universe of thought. So, for example, a human being can look angry as easily as a mountain can look cold, and a certain pressure on the tips of the fingers can *mean* the hardness or softness of a thing without the intervention of thought or inference. Through the medium of the body as a translational system of equivalences, the lived and the objective aspects of our being are pulled together and intertwined as closely, as tightly, as are the visual and tactile features of things or our powers of sight and touch. The real message is that we are in undivided possession of ourselves across the physical-mental distinction just as we are across the various senses or across the division of our sensory and our motor powers. There are whole persons and a single world from which, with certain reservations, their various aspects can be abstracted. But it is not by adding together the abstract pieces that the original experiencing subject and experienced world are built up. Nor is it by analyzing these 'parts' in isolation from their concrete integrated context that an adequate understanding of the natural unity of their ordinary functioning, of their true interrelatedness, will be achieved.

There is, for Merleau-Ponty, a kind of limited truth to traditional dualism. Dualism fails to capture both the unified structure of the embodied subject and the special relation which in normal functioning leads to an "overlapping" or "intertwining" of the mental and physical aspects of the subject's embodied being — a relation which is certainly not the ordinary relation of cause and effect. However, there are cases of breakdown or disintegration of the subject's normal functioning and structure in which mind and body approach the level of independent substances externally related to each other (see Merleau-Ponty, 1963: 209-210). Sometimes, for example, as a result of 'mechanisms' built up in the past, the body mimicks intentions which the subject no longer has. And sometimes, in timidity for example, the subject is unable to find in the body an adequate vehicle for his intentions. But such cases do not reveal the true nature of either term of the normal relation, nor do they show anything but the extreme limits of a single functional structure which includes inseparably both aspects of the subject's being. What they invite us to do by their strangeness, their lacking of something present in the usual case (in much the same manner as do Heidegger's examples in the early chapters of *Being and Time*) is to conceive very differently the nature of the mental and the physical within human being so as to understand a structure which approaches the traditional conceptions of mind and body only at its extreme limits.

2. Human freedom

Philosophical discussions of human freedom are typically dominated by concerns about the compatibility of an adequate deterministic account of human behavior with the central features of moral life — duty, responsibility, praise, blame, and so on. The usual problem raised by the analysis of freedom of choice and action is that of finding a conception of human freedom which will allow both a complete causal account of human behavior in physical terms and the application to the subjects of that behavior of a reasonable range of moral predicates. With respect to such discussions, Merleau-Ponty's account of human freedom is clearly atypical. The argument of the whole of *The Structure of Behavior*, which is continued in the first part of *Phenomenology of Perception* (Chs. 1-5), leads to the conclusion that no causal theory which is mechanistic or physicalistic in nature can provide an adequate account of human behavior. (There is no space to reproduce the argument here.) And this is not because such theories would leave no room for morality, but rather because such theories would lack the necessary resources for an adequate explanation of human behavior according to the standard criteria for scientific theories. As a result of Merleau-Ponty's taking this fact to be established, the discussion of freedom in the last chapter of *Phenomenology of Perception*, and in all of his subsequent writing, does not take determinism to be a tenable scientific theory, and hence does not take the standard problem of freedom of the will at all seriously. What is taken seriously is the opposite extreme, namely, the thesis that human freedom is absolute or unlimited, and human responsibility total. Here Merleau-Ponty's (frequently silent) interlocutor, of course, is Sartre.

According to Sartre, human consciousness gives meaning to its world via the choice of a project through which it aims at a particular future. Since this choice is itself a completely free one and the meaning of the world entirely a product of such choosing, human consciousness becomes totally responsible for its world, and external restriction becomes, at best, a kind of illusion. And because human consciousness is, at each instant, totally free to choose as if its past choices had never been made or been made very differently, that is, totally free of its past choosings, internal content or restriction becomes equally impossible and is to be viewed as a kind of comforting self-deception. For Merleau-Ponty, too, human consciousness gives meaning to its world. His problem is to explain how this meaning-giving can be restricted, can be anything other than totally free. The pieces of that explanation are to be found, as usual, in his theory of perception and the functioning of the lived body within perceptual experience.

For Merleau-Ponty (1962: 438), "The idea of an initial choice involves a contradiction." (See also p. 439, where Merleau-Ponty concludes that "there is no freedom without a field.") Perception and action always take place within a pre-given field, on the basis of previous perception and commitment. Human consciousness never has the divine privilege of creating its world, its situation, its field of activity from nothing. To the extent that Sartre's theory requires an unsituated choosing or projecting which brings a situation into being out of nothing, the theory overlooks the essential nature of perceptual consciousness — its necessary situatedness or embodiment in the widest sense — and the presence within all levels of human consciousness of the basic field structure of perceptual experience. The subject of explicit choice and decision is also the subject of the entire range of human experience. As we focus upon the more basic perceptual levels of that range, Sartre's description of a consciousness which is totally transparent (without internal resistance) and purely active becomes less and less plausible. The perceiving subject is passive as well as active according to MerleauPonty, and the meaning-giving which is characteristic of perception is restricted by the nature, the culture, and the individual development of the human subject. And if we take seriously Merleau-Ponty's model for our insertion into each of these, we are no more free of our cultural and individual histories than we are of our bodies and their natural development. This is not to say that the contents of our experience are strictly determined by features of our embodiment, but simply that experience is always situated within a field whose structure is never entirely up to us and whose influence is, like that of the lighting with respect to the appearance of the visible thing, implicit and inaccessible in principle.

In my earlier discussion of Merleau-Ponty's theory of perception, I indicated that the initial stage of ordinary perception is one with respect to which the subject is essentially passive. At this stage we simply register a significance which is largely indeterminate and essentially motor in nature, and then move in response to it so as to reveal a sensible thing with its relatively determinate properties. But there is another kind of passivity which extends well beyond this initial phase of perceptual experience. It is the passivity associated with habitual modes of thought and activity, and is present throughout perception in conjunction with each level of embodiment of the perceiving subject. At the lowest level, the natural subject gives meaning to his experience by imposing habitual 'forms' so basic that they constitute universal structures of human experience. Merleau-Ponty characterizes the set of such structures as a species *a priori*. This set of structures accounts for those favored forms or natural groupings which seem to hold across individuals and cultures, and includes such things as the basic tendency to group things together within the perceptual field on the basis of differential proximity. This natural level underlies all of our perceptual experience, and though we are, even at this level, active in the sense of bringing a structure to bear or giving meaning, we are not active with respect to the choice of that structure or meaning. Everything occurs within perception as though such choice were always already made, and this places them outside of the sphere within which human freedom operates.

At the cultural and personal levels there are also favored forms and groupings which become sufficiently habitual to restrict the range of meanings effectively available to human consciousness in a given situation. There may even be something like a cultural, and perhaps even an individual, *a priori*, which would hold across all the individuals within a given culture in the former case, and across all the experiences of a particular individual in the latter. But although we do speak of habitual traits which serve to identify an individual either as a member of a particular culture or simply as himself, these traits are not quite on a par with the basic invariant structures of human perception. There are at least two reasons for this. The first is that cultures and individuals are not nearly as fixed or static as are species. There is a kind of constant exchange between groups within a culture which instantiate it in different ways, and between cultures and individuals who instantiate their cultures more or less completely or accurately. Individual and social change and development are constant and complex products of these exchanges. The second reason, which serves to explain the first, is that these traits or habits, unlike those included in our species *a priori*, are, at least in principle, within the purview of human freedom. We can and do, occasionally, make *some* of them explicit, bringing them to the level of self-consciousness and then choosing to maintain them, to modify them, or to break them entirely.

Still, for any particular individual and time, there will be pre-ferred patterns of thought, perception and action, some of them explicitly chosen by him in the past, others appropriated almost automatically from his family, his social group, or his broader cultural context, and all of them functioning much more like habitual skills than explicit beliefs. It is this system which con-stitutes his personal and cultural embodiment, and, integrated with the system of habitual skills which make up the natural subjective body, lays down the total field within which all ex-perience takes place and to which the individual's freedom must be geared if it is to find a foothold in the human world. In short, and this is Merleau-Ponty's bottom line, Sartre would be right about human reality if perception, thought, decision and freedom — that is, human consciousness in all its functions — were not in every sense embodied.

BIBLIOGRAPHY

Hall, H. (1977). The Continuity of Merleau-Ponty's Philosophy of Percep-tion. *Man and World* 10 (4): 435-447.

Merleau-Ponty, M. (1962). *Phenomenology of Perception*. London: Rout-ledge and Kegan Paul.

— (1963). *The Structure of Behavior*. Boston: Beacon Press.

— (1964a). *L'oeil et l'esprit*. Paris: Gallimard.

— (1964b). *The Primacy of Perception and Other Essays*. Evanston: North-western.

— (1968). *The Visible and the Invisible*. Evanston: Northwestern.

— (1970). *Themes from the Lectures at the Collège de France 1952-1969*. Evanston: Northwestern.

American pragmatism

PETER SKAGESTAD
Williams College, Massachusetts

INTRODUCTION

Pragmatism originated in Cambridge, Massachusetts, in the 1870s. Conceived in the womb of the informal Metaphysical Club, from seeds sown by Charles Darwin and Alexander Bain, it first saw the light of day in Charles Peirce's articles in Popular Science Monthly in 1877 and 1878, and burst full-blown upon the stage of educated public opinion through the lectures and writings of William James from 1898 onwards. Originally a Harvard-born-and-bred theory of meaning, truth, and knowledge, pragmatism was adopted by the Chicago School led by John Dewey, and transformed into a social and political philosophy which was eventually to be put in the service of the New Deal and the New Frontier. Under the aegis of Oliver Wendell Holmes Jr., himself a member of Peirce's Metaphysical Club, pragmatism made its debut in the field of constitutional law, where its hallmark can be found on Supreme Court opinions even to the present day. Meanwhile, back at Harvard, the purer strain of pragmatism continued its academic career through the teaching of Clarence Irving Lewis, and has been transmitted to contemporary philosophy by his brilliant successors including Quine and Goodman.

Today, while the word 'pragmatism' has become common coin, there is no clearly defined, self-consciously pragmatist movement in American philosophy. A recent commentator, H.S. Thayer ([20], p. 435), has suggested that, from the viewpoint of the original pragmatists, this fact constitutes a vindication of prag-

Contemporary philosophy. A new survey. Vol. 4, pp. 363–386.
©*1983, Martinus Nijhoff Publishers, The Hague/Boston/London.*

matism. "To have disappeared as a special thesis by becoming infused in the normal and habitual practices of intelligent inquiry and conduct is surely the pragmatic value of pragmatism." So far Thayer. James and Dewey might have been surprised at this pronouncement, but Peirce would undoubtedly have agreed. To him, pragmatism meant, among other things, the dissolution of philosophical schools and movements and the emergence of philosophy as a cooperative venture of impartial inquiry, after the model of the empirical sciences. To the extent that this has come to pass, the disappearance of pragmatism as a distinct movement would count, in the eyes of its founder, as a signal victory. The chronicler of recent American pragmatism, on the other hand, cannot be content to share this euphoria. He is faced with the problem of how to identify his subject-matter, and, in the absence of a self-conscious, articulated pragmatist movement, he is aware of having to delimit his subject in a somewhat arbitrary manner. The solution chosen for the purposes of the present paper is deliberately eclectic. American philosophical discussion of the last decade has seen two developments of special interest to the student of pragmatism. In the first place, ideas and perspectives originally proposed by the classical pragmatists have reemerged with increasing frequency in contemporary discussions of metaphysics, epistemology, and the philosophy of language — often accompanied by acknowledgements of indebtedness to the earlier pragmatists. In the second place — whether as cause or as effect of the former development — volumes of scholarly writings about the classical pragmatists have appeared, writings which straddle philosophy and the history of ideas in so far as they frequently combine historical exposition with either criticism or further development of ideas originally proposed by Peirce, James, Royce, Dewey, and Lewis, among others. The present survey will focus chiefly on the former development, although the latter development will also be taken account of.

Little is gained, I think, by setting out from a definition of the word 'pragmatism'. Any formula which would be acceptable to all the major pragmatists would necessarily carry vagueness to an extreme. Peirce, James, and Dewey would probably all have agreed that thought is intimately related to action, and that it can be fully understood only through its relation to action. As the Russians say, "America has been discovered!" Rather than adopt such a vapid definition of 'pragmatism', I shall take the word to refer to that frequently discordant family of doctrines associated with the names Peirce, James and Dewey.[1] The degree of pragmatism to be found in the thought of present-day philosophers will be measured by their explicit or implicit references to these paradigm cases.

PRAGMATISM IN METAPHYSICS AND EPISTEMOLOGY

In the 1950s and 60s, while pragmatic themes were pursued by a small, but distinguished number of academic philosophers, pragmatism was widely regarded as part of an historical past, rather than as a live philosophical option. To the extent that metaphysics and epistemology have taken a pragmatic turn in recent years, it is in no small measure due to the influence of Willard V.O. Quine. Already in 1951, when pragmatism had for some time been largely eclipsed by logical empiricism, Quine ([22], p. 46) published his now-classic 'Two Dogmas of Empiricism,' concluding with the words:

> Each man is given a scientific heritage plus a continuing barrage of sensory stimulation, and the considerations which guide him in warping his scientific heritage to fit his continuing sensory promptings are, where rational, pragmatic.

What is significant is not, of course, that Quine used the innocuous adjective 'pragmatic'. What links him with the classical pragmatists is his characterization of scientific rationality as the most convenient adjustment of old ideas to novel sensory stimuli — a conception which is nowhere more clearly set forth than in James' *Pragmatism* ([23], pp. 59-61). More importantly yet, the main thrust of Quine's article was the criticism of the two dichotomies of analytic vs. synthetic and theoretical vs. observational (dubbed by Quine "the dogma of reductionism"). Both dichotomies were central to twentieth-century positivism, and both had been combatted by the pragmatists.

This is not the place to review Quine's contributions to philosophy during the 1950s and 60s, for the period here under consideration an appropriate angle of approach can be found in his *Ontological Relativity* [1]. The title essay of this book opens with a strong affirmation of intellectual kinship with John Dewey:

> With Dewey I hold that knowledge, mind, and meaning are part of the same world that they have to do with, and that they are to be studied in the same empirical spirit that animates natural science. There is no place for a prior philosophy. ([1], p. 26)

One might be tempted to construe this statement as an obligatory courtesy, prompted by the circumstance that 'Ontological Relativity' originated as the first of the John Dewey Lectures at Columbia University. The fact is, though, that the statement faithfully records several deeply held convictions shared by Dewey and Quine. Quine has long stressed that there is no *a priori* vantage point from which to philosophize, that philosophy and science are continuous activities, that language is part of the world of experience and therefore amenable to empirical investigation, and that relations such as meaning, synonymy, and reference are relations *in* the world and hence knowable in no other way than anything else in the world. These views were indeed central to Dewey's pragmatism; Quine could also have found them in certain writings by Charles Peirce, whose kinship he has, however, been more reluctant to acknowledge.[2]

The thesis of ontological relativity may perhaps be popularized as follows ([1], esp. pp. 51 ff.). There is no absolute distinction to be drawn between a theory, its linguistic expression, and its ontology, i.e. the world of objects which the theory is about. So long as we are operating within a given theory, we can state our theory only by uttering the sentences comprising the theory, and we can talk about the objects of the theory only by using the words belonging to the theory. Within a suitable meta-language we may distinguish between the sentences comprising the theory, the things satisfying its predicate letters, and the values of its bound variables — the ontology of the theory. But the sentences in the meta-language by which we make these distinctions are themselves interpretable only in the same manner, so the distinctions between language, theory, and ontology have been made only relatively to our meta-language and its underlying ontology.

The role of meta-language has been discussed by earlier thinkers; Quine's novel contribution may perhaps be said to consist in his explanation of ontological relativity by means of the notion of "inscrutability of reference," most vividly illustrated by the "indeterminacy of translation." In 'Ontological Relativity,' Quine illustrates the indeterminacy of translation with an example made famous through his earlier *Word and Object* ([2], pp. 30-34). The field linguist who repeatedly hears the natives use the word 'gavagai' in the presence of rabbits, may conclude that 'gavagai' *means* 'rabbit'. Now, for one thing, this claim of likeness of meaning depends upon empirical hypotheses about the natives' responses to the actual presence of rabbits; so, while ostensibly an assertion merely about words, it is as much an assertion about people and rabbits. More importantly, though, the claim also depends upon the hypothesis that the natives are employing *our* ontology. Whenever we are in the presence of a rabbit, we are also in the presence of a set of undetached rabbit parts, as well as a temporal stage of a rabbit. Hence 'gavagai' might mean either 'rabbit', 'undetached rabbit part', or 'rabbit stage', and the choice among these translations is not determined by observation of the natives' linguistic behavior. Questions about empirical facts, about the meaning of words, and about ontology are not, then, distinct questions which can be tackled separately; in deciding what 'gavagai' means, we must also decide both what are the actual stimuli to which the natives are responding, and what is their ontology. Nor is this indeterminacy restricted to translation between language. Within English, when I hear someone use the words 'cool', 'square', or 'hopefully' in ways which in *my* idiolect would be absurd, I infer the meaning of his words by means of the supposition that he intends to say something not absurd, along with a number of suppositions about what is or is not absurd to assert ([2], p. 46). Hence reference within a language is inscrutable in the same way that translation between languages is indeterminate.

Another important essay in the same volume is called 'Epistemology Naturalized.' The cardinal tenet of this essay is that the time has come to give up the ambitious project which dominated traditional epistemology from Descartes to Carnap, namely, the project of "strictly deriving the science of the external world from sensory evidence ([2], p. 75). Of all the traditional epistemologists, Carnap came closest to carrying out this project, in the "construction" attempted in his *Aufbau*. Carnap failed, however, and there is little reason to believe that anybody else will succeed. Does this mean that epistemology as such will have to be given up? Not quite; what it does mean, in Quine's view, is that epistemology must be "naturalized", that is to say, it must be itself understood as a *part* of natural science, rather than as a supra-scientific justification of natural science. Peirce's alternative to Cartesianism — "Dismiss make-believes!" — is repeated almost verbatim by Quine as an alternative to logical empiricism:

> But why all this creative reconstruction, all this make-believe? The stimulation of his sensory receptors is all the evidence anybody has had to go on, ultimately, in arriving at his picture of the world. Why not just see how this construction really proceeds? Why not settle for psychology? ([2], p. 75)

The use of psychological evidence in epistemology, Quine concedes, would be circular if the validation of the scientific worldview were the goal of epistemology. However, once we give up the attempt at validation and try instead merely to understand what this world-view is, the charge of circularity collapses. It should be added that Quine has not confined himself to the *advocacy* of naturalistic epistemology. Already in 1960, he made a beginning at implementing this programme, through the behavioral account of meaning, synonymy, and reference proposed in *Word and Object* [2]. More recently, *The Roots of Reference* [3] represents a further development of this naturalistic programme.

So far, Quine appears as a thinker in the mainstream of the pragmatist tradition — closest, perhaps, to Dewey, but also developing certain themes of central concern to Peirce and James. In one respect, however, Quine, to the best of my knowledge, stands alone among American pragmatists, to wit, in respect of his physicalism, summed up in the thesis: "There is no difference in the world without a difference in microphysical states."[3] Without advocating a logical reduction of other sciences to physics, Quine has repeatedly affirmed the pre-eminence of contemporary physics, as providing the fundamental conceptual framework within which he philosophizes (cf. [2], p. 4, and [1], p. 25). This idea, which plays a significant role within Quine's philosophy, is alien not only to his predecessors in the pragmatist tradition, but also to his Harvard colleagues Nelson Goodman and Hilary Putnam, themselves distinguished contributors to present-day pragmatism.

Over the last four decades Nelson Goodman has left his signature on logic, the philosophy of science, and the philosophy of art. His most recent work, *Ways of Worldmaking* [4], encompasses all of these fields and addresses itself to the project of constructing a metaphysics which is appropriate to both scientific and aesthetic experience, and which is subject to the most rigorous requirements of logic. In Goodman's view, there is no such thing as *the* world; there are many worlds — many *actual* worlds. Moreover, as the title of the book implies, worlds are made, not found. As Goodman puts it with his characteristic dry wit, what is before me is what I make of it, what is given is what is taken, and facts are fabricated, not found. This does not mean that anything goes, that we are entitled to believe what we please; on the contrary, worldmaking is difficult, and it requires hard work. Hence Goodman ([4], p. x) initially describes his outlook as "a radical relativism under rigorous restraints."

What exactly is meant by this paradoxical expression? Something like the following. Our experience encompasses numerous versions of 'the world', presented to us by, e.g., science, perception, and art. These versions are mutually incompatible, and even within art we encounter different and incompatible versions: Van Gogh's version cannot be reduced to Canaletto's, Constable's version cannot be reduced to James Joyce's, and none of these can be reduced to the version of physics. This does not mean that each version is necessarily a right version — right on its own terms, as it were. In physics, two incompatible theories present us with alternative world-versions, of which one is true and the other false. The role played by truth in physics is a special case of the role played by *rightness* in worldmaking in general. Just as a physical theory may be true or false, so any world-version — such as a work of art — may be right or wrong. Now the rightness of a version cannot be determined by comparing it with something called 'the world'. The world confronts us only through its versions; hence, if the rightness of a version consists in its correspondence with the world, there will be as many worlds as there are mutually incompatible right versions:

> Yet doesn't a right version differ from a wrong one just in applying to the world, so that rightness itself depends upon and implies a world? We might better say that 'the world' depends upon rightness. We cannot test a version by comparing it with a world undescribed, undepicted, unperceived, but only by other means that I shall discuss later. ([4], pp. 4-5)

What Goodman discusses later — what takes up the bulk of his book — are the tools, techniques, and rules by which science, perception, and art construct their multiplicity of world-versions. This discussion, in effect, constitutes Goodman's metaphysics: the criteria for "rightness of rendering" tell us what a right version is and, hence, what actual worlds there are.

Like Quine — indeed, like all pragmatists — Goodman disclaims an *a priori* vantage point from which to philosophize. In his view, we can do the metaphysics only of those worlds which we have actually made; there are no merely "possible" worlds. Unlike Quine, Goodman ([4], p. 102) does not accord any primacy to physics; the worlds of art are not reducible to the world of physics, and so an adequate metaphysics must incorporate a philosophy of art, as well as of science and of perception. In spirit, if not in method, Goodman appears closer to James than to any other of the classical pragmatists. This kinship appears both in Goodman's pluralism and in his insistence that worlds are made not found — a generalization of James' insistence that truth is made not found. Where Goodman most strongly contrasts with James, is in his unequivocal rejection of the "anything-goes" attitude which James at times certainly appeared to endorse.

Though still productive, both Quine and Goodman are now professors emeriti; the tradition of "Harvard pragmatism" is being carried forward by their younger colleagues, among them Hilary

Putnam. In recent years, Putnam has shown himself so profilic and versatile that a brief sketch cannot hope to do justice to the range of his interests. I shall content myself with giving a couple of glimpses of his philosophy of language and of science, starting out from his article 'Is Semantics Possible?' [24] from 1970.

Putnam starts out by challenging the traditional view that the meaning of a common noun consists of a conjunction of properties, which can be specified in an analytic definition. The most obvious defect of this view is that some common nouns are used to refer to natural kinds, which may have abnormal members. 'Green' is not one of the properties by which we may define the word 'lemon'; yet: "a green lemon is still a lemon — even if, owing to some abnormality, it *never* turns yellow" ([24], p. 103). The traditional view of meaning is, of course, one which Quine has combatted at least since 1951. Quine concluded by taking a dim view of the notion of 'meaning'; to say what I mean by the word 'lemon', in Quine's view, would be simply to assert all the sentences which I believe to be true of lemons. Putnam agrees with Quine that the meaning of a word like 'lemon' cannot be specified in an analytic definition; it can be conveyed only by conveying certain facts about lemons. However, it is neither possible nor necessary to convey *all* the facts there are about lemons. "Natural-kind terms" like 'lemon', 'tiger', 'gold', etc. have certain "core facts" associated with them, facts which are taken to characterize the normal members of each kind. To convey the meaning it is sufficient to convey these core facts. The core facts are not, however, the defining properties of the term. The belief that normal lemons are yellow is an *empirical* belief; it may turn out that normal lemons are blue and that we have been growing an atypical variety all along. In such an eventuality we would not conclude that there are no lemons, but rather that we had been mistaken in our belief that 'lemon' means a fruit which, among other things, is normally yellow — when ripe. That is to say, we may discover empirically (through botanical inquiry) that we have been wrong about the *meaning* of the word 'lemon'.

In the article 'Meaning and Reference' ([5], pp. 124-125), Putnam attacks the two notions that meanings are "in the head" — consist in psychological states — and that the reference of a term is fixed by its meaning. His arguments are extremely subtle, and I can here do no more than give a couple of his more vivid illustrations. Suppose I cannot tell a beech from an elm; in that case my *concept* of a beech may be exactly the same as my concept of an elm, and my psychological state will then be precisely the same whether I am thinking of a beech or of an elm. Yet, when I use the word 'beech' I certainly do not *mean* 'elm'. Secondly, by the word 'gold' I intend to refer to the same thing that metallurgists refer to by this word, but I do not know their criteria for determining whether something is gold. My own criteria for using the word 'gold' are of a more rough and ready kind; hence the metallurgist and I have different concepts of 'gold'. All the same, we use the word to refer to the same thing; when I want a gold wedding ring, I want a ring which metallurgists would recognize as gold, not merely one which *I* would recognize as gold. Putnam draws, *inter alia*, two interesting conclusions. In the first place, whether a term refers, and what it refers to, are empirical questions, which cannot be settled by an inspection of the definition of the term. In the second place, in a vast number of cases (as in the case of 'gold') the possibility of reference depends on a division of linguistic labor, which in turn depends on the social division of non-linguistic labor ([5], p. 125). In thus affirming both the empirical character of semantic questions and the social nature of meaning and reference, Putnam affirms two tenets which were integral to the pragmatism of both Peirce and Dewey.

The affinity with Peirce is seen even more clearly in Putnam's 1976 John Locke Lectures, now published as *Meaning and the Moral Sciences* [6]. Central to Putnam's discussion here is the distinction between reference and understanding. I understand a word when I possess criteria for its use, and the concept of reference contributes nothing to the analysis of language-understanding. Yet I cannot explain the contribution which language-use makes to the success of my total activity without the notion of objects to which words refer. Language is in this respect similar to any other tool: I can use electric light simply by knowing how to flip the switch and without knowing the first thing about electricity — nor would knowledge of electricity make me a better switch-flipper. But I cannot explain how my switch-flipping produces light, without invoking the notion of electricity. Comparing Wittgenstein's early theory of language as a picture with his later theory of language as use, Putnam concludes that they may both be correct, though for different purposes. The picture theory was right as a theory of language functioning; the use theory was right as a theory of understanding: "Talk of use and talk of reference are part of the total story, just as talk of switch-flipping and talk of electricity flowing through wires are parts of a total story." ([6], p. 100)

From the point of view of this distinction — which was drawn in almost exactly the same manner by Peirce (cf. Skagestad [25], Ch. 4) — Putnam, again like Peirce, has gone on to embrace realism as an empirical hypothesis which explains such facts as convergence of opinion and increased predictive success in the history of science. The familiar Kuhnian objection that the meanings of scientific terms are incommensurable across scientific revolutions is met with the reply (earlier made by Israel Scheffler ([26], esp. p. 61) that the reference of these terms may still remain constant, so that it still makes sense to regard our theories as better descriptions of *the same* reality that our scientific ancestors attempted to describe. If, in the future, our descendants are forced to conclude that none of our scientific terms refer to anything, realism will have been empirically refuted (Putnam [6], p. 25). Hence it is a respectable — and so far highly confirmed — empirical hypothesis. At the same time, Putnam emphatically rejects what he calls "metaphysical realism", and in recent, as yet unpublished, writings he directs the battery of his criticisms chiefly against realism in its metaphysical version (e.g., in 'Models and Reality,' Presidential Address to the Aristotelian Society, 1978).

A fourth Harvard philosopher who must be said to belong within the pragmatist tradition, is Israel Scheffler. His numerous writings in the philosophy of science fall outside the time-span here under consideration; our attention will focus only on one recent article which bridges psychology and epistemology in a manner which would surely have won the approval of William James. Scheffler's 'In Praise of the Cognitive Emotions' [27] argues persuasively that there is no sharp line to be drawn between the emotive and the cognitive realms. The author ([27], p. 171) states at the outset that his aim is not reductive: "I am concerned neither to reduce emotion to cognition nor cognition to emotion — only to show how cognitive functioning employs and incorporates diverse emotional elements — these elements themselves acquiring cognitive significance thereby." Scheffler first addresses himself to the various ways in which the emotions in general are put in the service of cognition. There are *rational passions* — such as a love of truth and a contempt of lying — without which science as a human activity could hardly be sustained. There are *perceptive feelings*, such as the feeling of fear which signifies the presence of danger even when we have no independent evidence of such danger. And there is the *theoretical imagination*, involving "boldness, verve, speculative daring," without which scientific method would remain barren.

In addition to the cognitive role played by the emotions in general, Scheffler takes note of a special class of emotions, which he terms "cognitive emotions". By calling an emotion cognitive, Scheffler ([27], p. 179) means "not simply that it presupposes the existence of a factual claim but that the claim in question specifically concerns the nature of the subject's cognitions (and, in cases of interest, is epistemologically relevant to them)." Scheffler instances two such emotions: the joy of verification, and the feeling of surprise. These play a cognitive role different from that of the emotions mentioned above. Fear, for instance, is cognitively significant because the feeling of fear presupposes the factual claim that the subject's environment contains dangerous features. The joy of verification presupposes a factual claim of a different kind, namely, the claim that the subject was right in his expectation. Conversely, the feeling of surprise presupposes the claim that something has occurred contrary to the subject's expectation. So, whereas fear signifies danger, whether or not danger has been anticipated, the cognitive emotions signify to the subject the validity or invalidity of his previous cognitions. The significance of the cognitive emotions is seen from the fact that one may block the progress of knowledge not only by refusing to acknowledge novel facts, but also by cultivating an emotional attitude of "epistemic apathy", which shuts out all occasions for surprise and thereby robs the novel facts of their epistemic significance. Such epistemic apathy may take the form of either scepticism or gullibility. The sceptic is not surprised by a novel fact, since he never expected anything to the contrary; the gullible person is not surprised, since he fully expected anything and everything to happen. Neither of them needs to take the discovery of the novel fact as an occasion for revising his previous beliefs; novel facts can serve as such an occasion only for the person who cultivates an attitude which lays him open to surprise through the formation of definite expectations.

Quine, Goodman, Putnam, and Scheffler are the obvious intellectual heirs of the original Harvard pragmatists. Their writings abound with pragmatic themes, frequently accompanied by explicit acknowledgements of intellectual indebtedness. Yet none of them has identified himself with pragmatism to the extent of attempting a general formulation or defense of pragmatism as a philosophical outlook. This project has been undertaken, and carried in very different directions, by Nicholas Rescher and Richard Rorty. The former's *Methodological Pragmatism* [7] provides the most explicit statement of his position.

In factual inquiry of every kind, Rescher notes, our goal is to find factual truths, which in turn we want for a variety of non-cognitive purposes. While truth is not identical with that which works for non-cognitive purposes, yet our methods or procedures of inquiry are chosen with the final *telos* — eventual application — in mind. It is trivially true that methods are appropriate objects of a pragmatic justification; there is no other criterion for the goodness of a method than its utility. Now the immediate goal of a method of inquiry is to produce factual truth, but the method cannot in practice be evaluated on the score of its utility in this respect. What we recognize as factual truths are just those statements which have been validated by our methods of inquiry, and a method cannot without circularity be evaluated on the basis of its success in validating those statements which it does validate. The circularity vanishes, however, if we take success in the implementation of the results of inquiry as our criterion for evaluating methods. This move gives us empirical grounds for evaluating methods, permits us to use the methods as our criteria for evaluating theses (presumptive truths), and yet avoids the equation of truth with non-cognitive success. The justificatory structure, then, is the following:

Figure 1.   *The instrumental justification of an inquiry method*

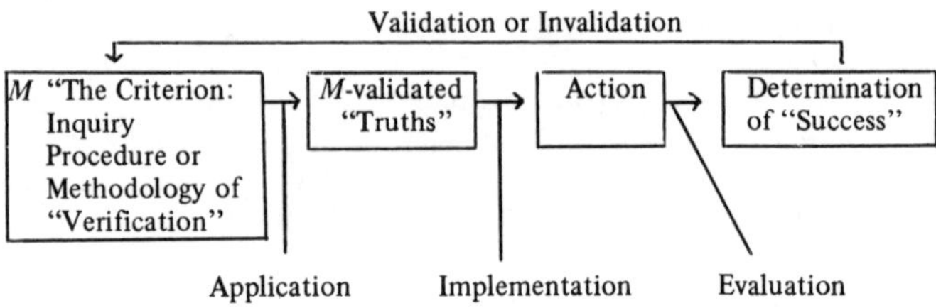

Note. From Rescher ([7], p. 25). Reproduced with permission from Basil Blackwell, Oxford.

As our criterion of truth we adopt a method of inquiry, M, which we then apply to the evaluation and validation of theses. Next, those theses that are validated by the method, the "truths", are implemented, that is, we act on them for non-cognitive purposes. We then evaluate the outcome of our action, determine the degree of our success, which validates or invalidates our method. In the absence of practical success our method is invalidated, and we start over again with a new method.

This justification, Rescher concedes, is still circular, and it might be thought that the circularity is "vitiatingly vicious" (sic). The determination of success is itself a factual inquiry; what we want for the purpose of such determination is factual truth, and if M is our criterion of truth, then we are bound to apply M for the purpose of its own validation. Rescher replies that there is no way of avoiding circularity in justificatory epistemology. Like Peirce, Dewey, Quine, et al., he insists that there is no Archimedean point from which to attack the problem of knowledge; we have to start *in medias res*, applying the whole apparatus of unjustified knowledge which we have already acquired. The circularity need not, however, be vicious. Our prior knowledge can be treated as a set of "plausible presumptions", which we may tentatively make use of until we have raised them to the status of "certified truths" — or else have replaced them by such truths.

Hence we need not claim the status of certified truth for our determination of success in action. This determination may be made tentatively as a plausible presumption which does not necessarily involve any use of the method M.

Rescher contrasts his own "methodological pragmatism" with the "thesis pragmatism" of the classical pragmatists. Peirce and James, in Rescher's view, went astray by directing their pragmatism towards theses, rather than towards methods. They thereby fell into the error of equating truth and utility. This error, for which Rescher holds James chiefly responsible, is dispelled by the following argument. Suppose a person hunts for an object x, valued at $12u$ (utiles), hidden in a grid composed of 9 squares; then a belief which will guarantee that he picks out x in one trial will have the utility $12u$, whereas a belief which guarantees that he will not pick out x will have the utility $0u$. Rescher stipulates two conditions which must be met for truth to be identical with utility: acceptance of a true belief must have a high utility ($8u$ or higher), and it must have a higher utility than acceptance of its (false) negation. Now consider the following set-up:

	x	x
x		x
x	x	x

Note. From Rescher ([7], p. 49). Reproduced with permission from Basil Blackwell, Oxford.

The false belief that there are no x's on the principal diagonal will here yield the highest possible utility, namely $12u$, whereas its true negation will yield only $4u$. Clearly neither of Rescher's two conditions is met, and truth cannot be equated with utility. There are other arguments, of which the principal one is that utility, unlike truth, does not obey the laws of logic.

Rescher ([7], p. 59) also takes issue with Peirce's definition of truth, which he interprets as "survival in point of acceptance." This definition of truth is taken by Rescher (p. 61) to be a variant of James' definition, open to the same fundamental objections:

"The main defect of Peirce's position is in fact one it shares with that of James's (sic), namely its *orientation toward theses*." Peirce's definition appears more plausible than James' because we do in fact determine the truth of a thesis by its ability to survive tests aimed at falsifying it; nonetheless, a false thesis may escape falsification indefinitely, for purely fortuitous reasons.

A large part of Rescher's book is devoted to the formulation of an evolutionary epistemology, labelled "methodological Darwinism" and contrasted with Karl Popper's "thesis Darwinism". Rescher is here conscious of following in the footsteps of Peirce — up to a point. What he takes exception to is Peirce's insistence that scientific hypothesis formation can lead us towards the truth only if guided by an instinct for guessing the truth:

> The only point at which our present position parts company with Peirce is in its explicit and deliberate substitution of the *methodology* of inquiry and substantiation in place of an otherwise mysterious capacity of *insight* or *instinct*. ([7], p. 164)

This objection, incidentally, is repeated almost word for word in Rescher's more recent book *Peirce's Philosophy of Science* ([8], p. 61). As someone with a personal stake in questions of what Peirce did or did not say, I cannot forbear to point out that Rescher's reading of Peirce is controversial. Rescher would, I gather, agree that Peirce also formulated a methodological pragmatism, and that he devoted considerable effort to the methodology of inquiry and substantiation. There is, however, textual evidence which strongly suggests that Peirce ([CP], V.408; VIII. 12) was not a thesis pragmatist at all. Peirce is a notoriously difficult philosopher, and there is legitimate room for alternative interpretations; since an extended polemic over interpretations would be out of place in this paper, I simply wish to put my disagreement on record.

Evidently, Rescher's pragmatism is relatively moderate; it is not clear to me whether it would even be recognized as a pragmatism from the more radical perspective of Richard Rorty — but, then, Rorty has disputed even Peirce's claim to belong to the pragmatist tradition. Rorty's radical pragmatism, developed in several articles throughout the seventies, has found its clearest expression in his *Philosophy and the Mirror of Nature* (1979) and in his 1979 presidential address to the Eastern Division of the American Philosophical Association (1980). The thesis of the former work is that the mainstream of the philosophical tradition of the last few centuries — the tradition which includes Descartes, Locke, Kant, Peirce, Husserl, and Russell — is based on a fundamentally wrongheaded picture of what knowledge is, and what the mind is. This tradition views knowledge as a series of more or less accurate *representations*. This picture alone motivates the two dominant disciplines within today's analytical philosophy: epistemology and the philosophy of mind. The former attempts to "ground" knowledge by demonstrating the accuracy of representations. The latter attempts to portray the mind as the representing medium, the "mirror of nature". In fact, in Rorty's view, there is nothing for either discipline to be about. Once we accept Sellars' and Quine's arguments to the effect that there are no privileged representations, and hence no standard by which to measure the accuracy of representations, the very notion of representation ceases to exert any compulsion on us. (1979, pp. 136, 209-210) With it go both the world and the mirroring mind. And, once we have learned from Dewey and Wittgenstein that particular knowledge claims are always justified by reference to the social practices of a particular culture, we realize that knowledge is an interesting — or even an intelligible — phenomenon only when understood simply as one of the social practices of our culture. (*Ibid.*, pp. 136, 170) Once the task of rationally grounding or justifying knowledge has been abandoned, what is left for philosophers to do is simply to help carry on the "conversation" of culture, taking as their models such philosophers as James, Dewey, Heidegger, and the later Wittgenstein.

PRAGMATISM IN SCHOLARLY LITERATURE

The emphasis placed in this chronicle on metaphysics, epistemology, and the philosophy of language should not be taken to imply that there has been no recent interest in the contributions of the pragmatists to other areas of philosophy, such as ethics, esthetics, and social and political philosophy. Such an interest is indeed in evidence; for the most part, however, it has taken the form of historical, critical, and interpretative work, rather than that of professedly original theorizing.

As mentioned earlier, the last decade has seen a prodigious growth of scholarly, expository, and critical literature about pragmatism. An exhaustive list of recent scholarly contributions is not my present purpose; in the following pages I wish only to take note of those contributions which appear to me most interesting and significant. For the purpose of this survey a convenient chronological point of departure is the year 1968. As it happens, this was the year in which Peirce's thought was brought to the attention of wide audiences in Europe through the very different, though in this one respect parallel, efforts of A.J. Ayer and Jürgen Habermas.[4] Since European thought falls outside the scope of the present discussion, it is for a different reason that 1968 may here be regarded as a landmark year. Although Peirce had gradually become philosophically respectable as an *individual* thinker, this was the year in which the pragmatic *movement* might be said to emerge as a respectable object of philosophico-historical scholarship. The literary landmarks in this respect are two publications which appeared in 1968, one by Murray G. Murphey [10], the other by H.S. Thayer [11].

Murphey established his reputation in 1961 with his impressive, albeit controversial, interpretation of Peirce — an interpretation which has later found its way into Habermas' *Knowledge and Human Interests* ([30], p. 107), as well as into *The Encyclopedia of Philosophy* [31]. In this 1968 article 'Kant's Children: The Cambridge Pragmatists' [10], Murphey turned his attention to the pragmatic movement in general, or, to be precise, to that strain within the movement which has been domiciled in Cambridge, Massachusetts. The article examines the thought of three of the classical pragmatists, Peirce, James, and Royce, and traces their philosophical concerns and preoccupations through the thought of C.I. Lewis down to Quine and Goodman. Murphey's article begins with the observation, later repeated by other scholars, that the logical empiricists who took refuge in the U.S. in the thirties and forties thoroughly misunderstood pragmatism by seeing in it a half-hearted and somewhat muddle-headed empiricism. Murphey then proceeds to the more extreme claim that pragmatism was never any kind of empiricism, but rather an American brand of Kantianism, chiefly preoccupied with limiting the domain of science to make room for religion, morality, or common sense.

H.S. Thayer, a prominent interpreter of John Dewey, does not take up the extreme position defended by Murphey. Thayer's monumental *Meaning and Action: A Critical History of American Pragmatism* [11] is devoted to showing the unity of the pragmatic movement, as well as its distinctive character vis-à-vis twentieth-century empiricism. Thayer, however, takes seriously the empiricist pretensions found in the writings of the pragmatists, and interprets their common project as an effort to render justice to the methods of the empirical sciences within a fundamentally moral perspective. Writing at the height of the Vietnam war, Thayer ([32], p. 233) sees a contemporary relevance for pragmatism in its recognition of, and attempt to overcome, a deep-rooted dualism in American culture once described by James as the dualism of "angelic impulses and predatory lusts." Another interesting theme in Thayer's book is his recognition of the similarities between Peirce's theory of meaning and the philosophy of language espoused by the later Wittgenstein and his intellectual heirs. More recently, this theme has been expanded on by Richard Bernstein in his *Praxis and Action* [12], which explores similarities as well as differences between Marxism, existentialism, pragmatism, and analytic philosophy.

Two interesting philosophical works on pragmatism which appeared in the seventies are Charles Morris' *The Pragmatic Movement in American Philosophy* [13] and Israel Scheffler's *Four Pragmatists: A Critical Introduction to Peirce, James, Mead, and Dewey* [14]. Morris is himself a pragmatist of long standing, and a pupil of George Herbert Mead. Over the last four decades he has contributed significantly to the development of pragmatic philosophy, especially in the field of semiotic, where he ranks as one of the pioneers. His book *The Pragmatic Movement* is less a history than an attempt to systematize the philosophical contributions of Peirce, James, Mead, and Dewey. Scheffler deals with the same four thinkers, but with a greater distance from his subject-matter, and, it seems fair to say, with a greater sensitivity to the individual differences between these four pragmatists. All the same, as noted earlier, Scheffler's interest in his subject is not purely historical. Himself an eminent philosopher of science and of education, he relates the ideas of the original pragmatists to present-day developments in the philosophy of science and attempts to draw out the implications of their thought for present-day philosophy of education.

Although I agree with Morton White that the distinction between philosophy and the history of philosophy is a somewhat arbitrary one, it seems appropriate to describe his *Science and Sentiment in America* [15] as a more historically oriented work than either of the two aforementioned. White's book is not confined to the history of pragmatism, but places this movement within a continuous tradition stretching from Jonathan Edwards to John Dewey. Common to puritanism, transcendentalism, and pragmatism, in White's view, is the endeavor to reconcile "science" with "sentiment" without opening the door to "enthusiasm". This endeavor is traced back to John Locke, who thus appears as the real progenitor of pragmatism. The Lockean pedigree of American philosophy has more recently been further explored by White in his latest book, *The Philosophy of the American Revolution* [16].

Like Morris, Sidney Hook is a pragmatist of long standing, whose most noteworthy contributions to philosophy fall outside the time-span here under consideration. A pupil of John Dewey, and a prominent Marx-scholar, Hook has recently published two collections of articles in defense of pragmatism and the liberal-democratic faith, as an alternative to revolutionary Marxism. Especially interesting for present purposes is the interpretation of pragmatism offered in his *Pragmatism and the Tragic Sense of Life* [17], a collection of articles published over a number of years. The title sounds like a juxtaposition of two antitheses: pragmatism has generally been thought of as a naively optimistic philosophy which totally lacks a sense of the tragic. Hook's interpretation is, on the contrary, that pragmatism essentially embodies a tragic sense of life, in that it fully acknowledges man's finitude and the impossibility of final or total solutions to social problems.

Whereas all the works mentioned so far in this section straddle philosophy and the history of philosophy, the last couple of years have witnessed the emergence of a puristic movement which advocates the strict separation of philosophy and history. Among the foremost spokesmen for this new "historicism" is Murphey ([33], p. 16) who, in 1979, published what may be seen as a partial recantation of his anachronistic treatment of the pragmatists 11 years later. As a model of how the history of American philosophy should be written, Murphey instances Bruce Kuklick's *The Rise of American Philosophy* [18]. This does not mean that Kuklick is to be held responsible for Murphey's recent views on historiography, Murphey is right, however, that *The Rise of American Philosophy* is a strictly historical work, without philosophical pretensions. Kuklick's chief contribution to our understanding of the classical pragmatists — specifically, the original Harvard pragmatists — lies in his examination of the social and economic conditions under which this movement arose, conditions which included the professionalization and secularization of philosophy through the emergence of graduate education in late nineteenth-century America.

A less pronounced purism is evinced by John E. Smith's *Purpose and Thought: The Meaning of Pragmatism* [19]. In one respect, Smith's outlook differs markedly from Murphey's: the former obviously sympathizes with the thinkers of whom he writes. Also, like Thayer, Morris, and Scheffler, Smith does think that the ideas of the classical pragmatists have a relevance for the present. Where he sides with Murphey is in denying that Peirce, James, or Dewey can be understood by relating their thought to present-day philosophical problems and concerns. In particular, Smith deplores the tendency — exemplified by Ayer — to interpret the pragmatists through *our* predominant concern with epistemology. To Peirce and James, he holds, metaphysics and the philosophy of religion were prior concerns, to which epistemology played a secondary role.

Although the treatment of pragmatism as a purely historical phenomenon is currently fashionable, it can hardly be said to have won the day. It is still possible for Rescher ([8], p. IX) to say, in his previously mentioned *Peirce's Philosophy of Science*, that he regards Peirce "not as a thinker of bygone days, but as a colleague and co-worker on issues of abiding interest." In a forth-coming book on Peirce, the present chronicler [25] has attempted to strike a middle course, more or less after the examples of Thayer and Scheffler. The disputed question of how one should write the history of pragmatism undoubtedly involves more general questions of the philosophy of history, transcending our present topic. A couple of closing comments are in order, however. Needless to say, those concerned with the present-day philosophical relevance of the classical pragmatists have every reason to welcome the growth of "pure" historical scholarship on pragmatism — as a complement to their own work and as a valuable aid in their work. I know of no one besides Ayer who ever thought he could interpret the philosophies of Peirce and James without taking account of their intellectual-historical context; Rescher, whose interest in Peirce is professedly ahistorical, nonetheless utilizes intellectual-historical material for the purpose of understanding Peirce. What is debatable is not the legitimacy of the purely historical approach to pragmatists of the past, but rather the neo-historicist thesis that this is the *only* legitimate approach to the subject. Against this thesis, it might be urged that the methodological decision to treat pragmatism as *only* a dead past, in itself involves a tacit philosophical decision against pragmatism. It involves the dismissal of an important corollary of Peirce's pragmatic maxim, to wit, the corollary that a statement is increasingly better understood as its logical consequences are gradually unravelled in the course of continued inquiry. And, by excluding the use of present-day problems and interests as tools for interpreting past thoughts, the historicist thesis may be held to involve a violation of Peirce's most fundamental maxim: Do not block the road of inquiry!

NOTES

1. In Skagestad [2], I attempted to uphold a more restrictive definition of 'pragmatism'; this, however, would be impracticable for the present purpose.
2. There are frequent references to Peirce in Quine's works; as far as I have been able to tell, most of these are either neutral or critical.
3. I do not have a reference for this thesis, which I have repeatedly heard Quine state in his lectures.
4. Gunnar Skirbekk has kindly reminded me that Habermas was in this respect anticipated by Karl-Otto Apel. On this subject, cf. Skirbekk's contribution to this volume.

BIBLIOGRAPHY

Ayer, A.J. *The Origins of Pragmatism*. London: Macmillan, 1968.
Bernstein, R.J. [12] *Praxis and Action*. Philadelphia: University of Pennsylvania Press, 1971.
Goodman, N. [4] *Ways of Worldmaking*. Indianapolis, Ind.: Hackett, 1979.
Habermas, J. [30] *Knowledge and Human Interest*. Boston: Beacon Press, 1971. Eng. transl. of 1968.
— *Erkenntnis und Interesse*. Frankfurt a.M.: Suhrkamp, 1968.
Hook, S. [17] *Pragmatism and the Tragic Sense of Life*. New York: Basic Books, 1974.
— *Revolution, Reform, and Social Justice*. New York: New York University Press, 1975.
James, W. [23] *Pragmatism: A New Name For Some Old Ways of Thinking*. New York: Longmans, Green, and Co., 1907.
Kuklick, B. [18] *The Rise of American Philosophy*. New Haven, Conn.: Yale University Press, 1978.
Morris, C. [13] *The Pragmatic Movement in American Philosophy*. New York: George Braziller, 1970.
— [31] Peirce, Charles Sanders. In *The Encyclopedia of Philosophy*, Vol. 6, pp. 70-78. New York: Macmillan, 1967.
Murphey, M.G. [10] Kant's Children: The Cambridge Pragmatists. In *Transactions of the Charles S. Peirce Society*, Vol. 4, pp. 3-33. 1968.
— [33] Toward an Historicist History of American Philosophy. In *Transactions of the Charles S. Peirce Society*, Vol. 15, pp. 3-18. 1979.
Peirce, C.S. [CP] *Collected Papers of Charles Sanders Peirce*, Vols. 1-6. Ed. by C. Hartshorne and P. Weiss; Vols. 7-8 ed. by A. Burks. Cambridge, Mass.: The Belknap Press of Harvard University Press, 1931, 1958.
Putnam, H. [5] Meaning and Reference (1973). Reprinted in Schwartz (Ed.), *Naming, Necessity, and Natural Kinds*, pp. 119-132. Ithaca, N.Y.: Cornell University Press, 1977.
— [6] *Meaning and the Moral Sciences*. London: Routledge and Kegan Paul, 1978.
— [24] Is Semantics Possible? (1970). Reprinted in Schwartz (Ed.), *Naming, Necessity, and Natural Kinds*, pp. 102-118. Ithaca, N.Y.: Cornell University Press, 1977.
Quine, W.V.O. [1] *Ontological Relativity*. New York: Columbia University Press, 1969.
— [2] *Word and Object*. Cambridge, Mass.: The M.I.T. Press, 1960.
— [3] *The Roots of Reference*. La Salle, Ill.: Open Court, 1973.
— [22] *From a Logical Point of View*. Cambridge, Mass.: The M.I.T. Press, 1960.
Rescher, N. [7] *Methodological Pragmatism*. Oxford: Basil Blackwell, 1977.
— [8] *Peirce's Philosophy of Science*. Notre Dame, Ind.: University of Notre Dame Press, 1978.

Rorty, R. (1979). *Philosophy and the Mirror of Nature*. Princeton, N.J.: Princeton University Press, 1979.
— (1980). Pragmatism, Relativism, and Irrationalism. In *Proceedings and Addresses of the American Philosophical Association*, Vol. 53, No. 6, pp. 719-738. 1980.
Scheffler, I. [14] *Four Pragmatists: A Critical Introduction to Peirce, James, Mead, and Dewey*. New York: Humanities Press, 1974.
— [26] *Science and Subjectivity*. Indianapolis, Ind.: Bobbs-Merrill, 1967.
— [27] In Praise of the Cognitive Emotions. *Teachers College Record*, Vol. 79, No. 2 (December 1977): 171-186.
Skagestad, P. [21] Peirce and Pearson: Pragmatism vs. Instrumentalism. Paper read at the Boston Colloquium for the Philosophy of Science, Boston, Mass., 6 February 1979.
— [25] *The Road of Inquiry: Charles Peirce's Pragmatic Realism*. New York: Columbia University Press, 1980.
Smith, J.E. [19] *Purpose and Thought: The Meaning of Pragmatism*. New Haven, Conn.: Yale University Press, 1978.
Thayer, H.S. [11] *Meaning and Action: A Critical History of Pragmatism*. Indianapolis, In.: The Bobbs-Merrill, 1968.
— [20] Pragmatism. In *The Encyclopedia of Philosophy*, Vol. 6, pp. 430-436. New York: Macmillan, 1967.
— [32] *Meaning and Action: A Study of American Pragmatism*. Indianapolis, Ind.: Bobbs-Merrill, 1973. Abridged version of 1968.
White, M.G. [15] *Science and Sentiment in America*. Oxford: Oxford University Press, 1972.
— [16] *The Philosophy of the American Revolution*. Oxford: Oxford University Press, 1978.

Pragmatism in Apel and Habermas

GUNNAR SKIRBEKK
University of Bergen

When we talk about pragmatism in Apel and Habermas, we do not have in mind the cruder sense of this term, which emphasizes "what works" and what is unreflectively taken to be "useful." Afterall, a critique of instrumentalistic fallacies and ethical short-sightedness belongs to the core of their thinking. The sense of pragmatism at stake here is primarily a conception of scientific investigation and validation, i.e. a pragmatic conception of truth in a broad sense. Its relatedness to pragmatism is realized by its affinity to basic ideas in Ch.S. Peirce (say, validity by consensus through an unlimited community of investigators).

Both Apel and Habermas have given extended interpretations of Peirce's pragmatism. In connection with the two-volume German translation (published 1967 and 1970) Apel wrote a long introduction which was later published separately as a book (Apel [1]). Here, as well as in various other publications in the early seventies (Apel [2, 3], later published in [4]), Apel elaborated Peircean pragmatism in the direction of transcendental semiotics. It especially focused on the community of researchers, conceived as an ideal community engaged in an ongoing interpretive and experimental validation process, for whom a future agreement on the ultimate truth is presupposed as a necessary regulative idea. (Cf. also Habermas' extended interpretation of Peirce in Habermas [5], 1968, pp. 116-178.)

These catchwords indicate how a transcendental-pragmatic interpretation of Peircean pragmatism is closely related to conceptions of truth and rationality. They also show how the question

Contemporary philosophy. A new survey. Vol. 4, pp. 387–416.
©*1983, Martinus Nijhoff Publishers, The Hague/Boston/London.*

of "pragmatism in Apel and Habermas" is basically a question of pragmatic conceptions of truth — or better, of validity and validation which depend upon concepts like rational consensus and argumentative validation, unlimited community of investigators and self-reflective ultimate justification.

We shall here delineate the main conceptions of the "transcendental-pragmatic" and "universal-pragmatic" conception of truth and validity worked out by Apel and Habermas during the last decade (approx. 1967-1977), through which the affinity to pragmatism in a Peircean sense will become evident.

Before entering the elaboration of pragmatic conceptions of validity in Apel and Habermas, it might be useful to call into mind why the validity question plays such an important role in the philosophical projects of both Apel and Habermas.

Apel, with his background in the hermeneutic tradition, came to the conclusion that intersubjective and argumentative aspects of validation and validity are insufficiently taken into account in this tradition (Apel [4], Vol. 1, pp. 22-52). This insufficiency shows itself in some self-referential uneasiness (a relativistic tendency) and in an inadequate grasp of the scientific endeavour; and it also implies a premature resignation to the impossibility of ultimate justification of basic norms. — The immediate need in our time for ultimate justification of basic norms, and the theoretical obstacles to recognizing its possibility, are both related by Apel to the scientification of the world (Apel [4], Vol. 2, pp. 359-378): On the one hand we live in a civilization based on technology and science, which has created a set of extremely consequential and global problems (e.g. in the field of ecological destruction, military potentials, economic and political inequalities and tensions), on the other hand we possess an overly restrictive conception of scientific rationality, which makes the idea of a rational justification of basic norms seem impossible (and as a result, what is then seen as a struggle between equally a-rational particular interests and preferences gets its pseudo-legitimation). In Apel's view, a rational and just treatment of these problems not only requires scientific insight in a technological or result-oriented sense, but also an open sphere of dialogue and rational formation of will and preferences; and, in the last instance, it requires a compelling justification of a rationally founded universal normative base, over and beyond all particular divisions in nations, races, blocks and generations. Philosophy cannot implement these norms, but philosophy can contribute positively by uncovering the (often overlooked) possibility of ultimate justification.

Apel's project might be described as an attempt at overcoming, in an Hegelian sense of that term, the prevailing, overly restrictive self-interpretation on the part of science, by showing a deeper sense of rationality, including communicative rationality and possible normative justification, more or less hidden within the presuppositions of the scientific enterprise itself. This is where a transformation of the Peircean pragmatic conception of scientific rationality fits in.

In the case of Habermas similar points can be made. (As an introduction to Habermas' development, cf. McCarthy [6].) Given his background in the Frankfurt School of critical theory, Habermas was in need of a rationally founded notion of normative validity, in order to legitimate the notion of critical philosophy. Without some rationally grounded standard the programme based on that notion would remain theoretically deficient. In Habermas' view at least a well-founded notion of procedural natural-rights is required. This goes hand in hand with a critique of a notion of rationality which is ultimately tied to control and domination. Habermas' attempt at elaborating the conception of rationality is well known from the discussion about the three cognitive interests, where communication and emancipation are included (cf. Habermas [5], also [7, 8]; the main contributions in this discussion are published in Dallmayr [9]). But in this theory of the three cognitive interests and forms of rationality validity problems are still not adequately taken care of; not only the validity problems of norms, but also theoretical and categorial validity problems are insufficiently treated in the Habermasian position of the mid-sixties (cf. Habermas [5] and his self-criticism on this point in the postscript of 1973). Against this background, an elaboration of the notion of validation — i.e. a pragmatic conception of truth — is a reasonable next task. (Cf. Habermas [10, 11], seel also Bernstein [12].)

Apel generally argues in a hermeneutic-dialectical way, interpreting other philosophers to the point where insufficiencies in their positions become clear. In Apel the overcoming of these insufficiencies points in the direction of an explicitly formulated transcendental-pragmatic conception (cf. his comments on Searle's shortcomings concerning normative justification and pragmatic unrejectability, Apel [13], pp. 56 ff.). A crucial argument in Apel's thinking is an attempt at showing the fallacy of a "semanticist" framework. If one thinks exclusively in terms of semantic categories, overlooking the internal relation between language and subject, important philosophical insights get lost (cf. Apel [2], or more recently [14, 15, 16]). One tends to regard this relation as an empirical one. Transcendentality becomes at most a question of "constitutive frames" in the sense of the paradigm case of chess where no self-reflective necessity (no strict "unrejectability", and therefore no transcendental-pragmatically grounded necessity) is involved. The prescriptive aspects of speech acts are overlooked as an issue for philosophical reflection, and conceived of as an empirical problem to be treated by sciences like psychology and linguistics. In such a semanticist view there is in this sense a reduction of validity (normativity) into factuality. The narrowness of this semanticist conception has to be overcome by a pragmatic conception, but it must be a philosophical, i.e. a reflective and transcendental one, and not merely an empirical pragmatics.

However, validity may be conceived of as being *institutionally dependent* in the sense in which a set of norms (say, for football) is valid within its social setting (the game). In this case the norms are not valid universally, i.e. for all people, but only *inside* the "language game." In juridical terms this position is one of positive rights, not of natural rights. For this position, in which validity is not reduced to factuality but conceived as contextually relative, the problem still remains of realizing the concern for self-referential consistency, the possibility of transcultural understanding, and an ultimate ethics in the sense of natural rights. This is the point where philosophical pragmatics becomes important: Do we, in our situated speech-acts, raise validity claims which in a pragmatic perspective can be shown by argument (undeniably, and by their inherent meaning) to transcend the bounds of any particular institution and to presuppose a universal validity?

Apel (like Habermas) argues that in our speech acts in various situations we already raise validity claims of such a non-relative nature (Apel, e.g. in Oelmüller [17], pp. 162, 165; cf. also Habermas [10, 11]). In social interaction we presuppose that what one says or does is understandable by other people; if not immediately, it can be made so by appropriate translation and explanation. In principle, it is understandable. We presuppose that people in principle are accountable by virtue of knowing what they say and do, and why. If this were not so, we could not interact. We assume that, as a rule, one means what one says and that one assumes that there are good enough reasons to support it and to justify why one is acting the way one does. Ultimately, this requires that the institution within which one acts be itself legitimate. When superficial doubts or dissents about these validity assumptions occur, they can be settled inside the given setting (institution, culture). But if the doubt becomes more profound, its resolution requires special measures in the way of research and argumentation. In an implicit sense this is already presupposed in our pragmatically raised validity claims, Apel argues (e.g. [4], Vol. 2, pp. 400-401). In elaborating these implicit, pragmatically given presuppositions the idea of an unlimited community of researchers emerges. An intersubjectively valid resolution, ultimately settled by discursive consensus, constitutes a pragmatically founded regulative idea (e.g. Apel [15]).

In this connection Apel finds support in Ch.W. Morris' semiotics (cf. e.g. [4], Vol. 1, pp. 138-166, Vol. 2, pp. 178-219). His semiotic division into semantics, syntax and pragmatics is used to stress the inter-subjective character of natural language. It is *inter*subjective because sign interpretation necessarily transcends the idea of methodological self-sufficiency of the individual ("methodical solipsism", cf. also the Wittgensteinian argument against the possibility of private rules, often referred to by Apel, e.g. [4], Vol. 2, p. 399), and it is inter*subjective* because it involves persons capable of reflection (not only of semanticist metalanguage/ objectlanguage thinking), of raising validity claims that presuppose intersubjective validation, and of communication with each other about something (the "double structure" of communication, cf. Habermas [18], pp. 224 ff.).

Armed with this transcendental interpretation of Morris' semiotics, Apel works out the Peircean conception of an unlimited community of researchers ([4], Vol. 2, pp. 188 ff.).

Apel appears to interpret Peirce in a Kantian way so that the resulting transcendental-semiotic conception of Peirce is proposed as a paradigmatic "transformation" of the consciousness-oriented paradigm of traditional transcendental philosophy (cf. Apel's thesis about "transformation of philosophy", [4]; and [19], p. 48 for a programmatic statement on Peirce in this perspective).

This elaborated version of Morris' semiotics is thus used by Apel to demonstrate the existence of transcendental-pragmatic presuppositions in everyday life/language. A speech act by virtue of presupposing implicitly mutual understanding is already an act of reciprocal recognition of the other subjects. It necessarily involves the counterfactual assumption of a possible redemption of implicitly and explicitly raised validity claims concerning the truth of what is claimed to be the case, the rightness of the norms involved, the general intelligibility of what is communicated, and the truthfulness of the speech actor (following the Habermasian terms, cf. the so-called four universal validity claims in Habermas [10, 11]). The revised Peircean conception of the unlimited community of investigators — of interpreters and experimenters — is seen as an adequate articulation of the implied presupposition of possible intersubjective redemption. Validity is thus intersubjective, not subjective and relative, and it is not merely founded on data and perception, but redeemed through intersubjective interpretation and argumentation, by the free consensus of all. (For a recent elaboration of the problem of factuality versus normativity in Peirce, leading up to Apel, see Bertilsson [20].)

Normative validity is found in the procedural norms themselves. They imply reciprocal recognition among the participants and universalization as a normative standard. This is, one may say, a procedural version of the categorical imperative with its mutual egalitarian recognition and validity through universalization. (But an adequate interpretation of needs is part of the evaluation process — cf. rational will-formation and need-interpretation, e.g. Apel [4], Vol. 2, p. 425 — creating some distance from the Kantian version.)

The Kantian *Ding-an-sich* is in Peirce transformed into a conception of the "recognizable, in the long run." Reality qua ultimate recognizability is contrasted to the notion of the fallibility of the actually recognized events. Apel agrees with his Peircean position: truth is rational consensus, and reality is what by a rational consensus is recognizable ([4], p. 14).

In his interpretation of Morris' semiotics and Peirce's pragmatism, Apel has passed beyond everyday communication to a consideration of fullfledged scientific activity. However, the central core of this pragmatic conception of scientific rationality is for Apel the unavoidability of argumentative rationality (e.g. Apel [13], pp. 122-123, "vom *methodischen Primat der Selbstbegründung des argumentativen Diskurses*"). This is the foundation to which Apel returns again and again (cf. his arguments against the deductivist dilemma of ultimate justification, the trilemma of regress, circle or decisionism, and cf. Albert [21] against Apel's transcendental argument): If we argue seriously, we have to take arguments seriously, and thereby accept the normative preconditions of argumentation, e.g. mutual equal recognition, as well as the force of the better argument at each moment. This is no proof in a deductive sense, but a rationally realized unrejectability, in the sense that all attempts at seriously arguing against it, already presuppose the preconditions for arguing. This is for Apel the rock bottom, where rationality shows its compelling nature. This binding force of rationality – as unrejectable and already accepted – not only holds for explicit arguing, and counter-arguing, but also for scientific activity in general, as well as for validity claims raised in everyday life, since these claims implicitly require argumentative redemption in the last instance, according to Apel.

Apel conceives his own way of arguing as a "meaning criticism" (*Sinn-Kritik*, e.g. [15], pp. 16 ff., [4], Vol. 2, p. 173; in Oelmüller [17], pp. 165, 176), i.e. as an indication of how the meaningfulness of implicit claims of truth and rightness is presupposed in a way which cannot be denied or neglected without self-defeating implications. When applied to arguing, this "meaning criticism" exhibits pragmatic/semiotic preconditions in the very act of arguing (and of thinking, Apel adds; see [15], p. 24). This implies a self-referential structure. However, when applied to everyday (non-argumentative) communication, the argument for the undeniability of the norms for argumentation, itself requires an extended argument. It must show that universal validity claims are really raised in all speech acts even when not consciously formulated by the actors themselves, and that the meaningfulness of these claims implies that they are redeemable, through intersubjective argumentation resulting in a consensus. When it comes to the elaboration of this transition Apel and Habermas apply different strategies. Apel relies more on self-refutability while Habermas elaborates a universal pragmatics of communicative competence and extends the application of his views to theories of socialization and historical evolution (Habermas [22, 23]).

We have validation of norms on two levels: the validation of the constitutive, procedural norms themselves and the validation of various normative questions brought into the argumentative checking process. The reflective resolution of the former is in principle definitive; we claim to know that they are valid, here and now. On the other hand, which of the thematized normative validity claims will turn out to be found valid in a discussion is an open question to be decided in the actual process of argumentation between the persons involved. One cannot predict these results, though one can predict that egoistic and ethnocentric conclusions, such as fascism, are ruled out, because of the egalitarian universalization inherent in the validation process. But beyond this, what will in each concrete case be found to be the right answer, e.g. about hierarchy and authority, is in principle an open-ended question. And there are normative questions, e.g. about taste and style, for which there might never be any rational consensus, so that in these cases the differing views are all legitimate. This is the field of rational tolerance and legitimate pluralism.

What has been said here about the unrejectability of argumentation and the universality of argumentatively-settled validity claims does not imply a denial of the historicity of argumentative activity, nor does it imply a guarantee against regression into irrationality. But inherent in our pragmatically raised validity claims and their presupposition of possible redemption there is a peculiar appeal for rational thinking and action, and for a practical concern for the improvement of argumentative rationality (cf. Apel [4], Vol. 2, p. 429).

Such argumentative validation implies a right to evaluate the legitimacy of different societies and cultures, even in cases where argumentative rationality has not developed or has been repressed. This right to evaluate others is however no *carte blanche* for autocratic and elitist decisions, since it is based on the possible assent of all persons involved. Furthermore, even when transcultural evaluation in this sense is legitimate, as in cases of ritual homicide, the question remains as to whether such an evaluation (recommendation, criticism) actually ought to be made, and if so, in what form this should be done. (For the discussion of these problems, and for the discussion of the possibility of motivating those who do not participate in genuine normative discourse to become participants, see Apel et al. in Oelmüller [17], e.g. pp. 160 ff.; for the relation between the use of argumentation in order to obtain an ultimate validation, and the use of argumentation in order to bring about will-formation and need-interpretation, see Habermas e.g. [23], pp. 280 f., 330-332, 344.)

We have delineated, in somewhat free formulations, the main arguments in Apel's pragmatic conception of validity. In order to bring out its philosophically puzzling aspects more clearly, we shall add a few critical remarks. (From the general objections, see e.g. Albert [21]; Berk [24], pp. 160-165; Dallmayr, McCarthy et al. in Oelmüller [17], e.g. pp. 29 ff. and p. 96; and Wellmer [25], pp. 49-51.)

If the criterion of validity (truth) is defined by argumentatively achieved consensus (Apel [15], p. 4), one may ask whether this conclusion applies to itself. In fact, to support his view Apel does not appeal to consensus, but primarily to what he sees as the unrejectability of self-referential arguments (Apel [13], p. 123). To elucidate the structure of this argument he refers to Aristotle's argument for the unrejectability of the principle of contradiction (e.g. in Oelmüller [17], p. 197). This is not a case of validation by consensus, or even by an intersubjective procedure. In this case one single person could in principle recognize the validity of the argument. One may certainly point out that all rational beings in this case will reach the same conclusion: there will be consensus. But to say that truth implies consensus among rational beings is not to say that consensus is what we understand by truth, or the way we decide what is true. This objection may be met by drawing a distinction between the self-referential validation *of* this conception of procedural validation *and* the argumentative validation of disputed issues *within* this validation process. The latter may then, without inconsistency, be described in fallibilistic and melioristic terms, whereas the former is claimed to be definitive. This is a strategy found in Apel (cf. [26], pp. 155 ff.). However, if one still wants to use the term "consensus theory of truth" to characterize this position, one should add that in this case there are quite important distinctions inherent in the term "consensus".

The transition from everyday (non-argumentative) interaction to full validating argumentation presents serious problems (e.g. McCarthy, in Oelmüller [17], p. 96), which also arise for the transition from actual to pure argumentation (e.g. McCarthy, ibid. p. 205, and Schnädelbach [27], p. 140-172). To say that in arguing seriously one has to take arguments seriously, is one thing; to say that we have to take arguments seriously once we take part in some actual but incomplete or even distorted discussion, is something else. There is, to be sure, something compelling in arguments, even in distorted contexts. (Try, for example, to defend clearly inconsistent views in a court!) This point supports the view that there is some "driving force" in actual discussions toward pure argumentation that is free from hindrances and distortions. In actual discussions there are, however, various specific institutional standards and rules for what is "sufficient" and "reasonable" in arguing, and these tell us when we have obtained enough clarification and well-foundedness to regard the problem as solved in the sense that we are entitled to claim that we understand and know. In everyday life special reasons are required to go on arguing, beyond this point. Even if one accepts that validity claims are raised in everyday life, presupposing some real redemption, one might doubt whether this entails the further presupposition that the only acceptable validation is one carried out intersubjectively under the conditions of an ideal discussion.

In order to uncover such basic presuppositions an *empirical* analysis of the validity claims raised in everyday speech-acts will *not* do. (For instance, the use of questionnaires — asking people whether they in their speech acts really presuppose validation by rational consensus, obtained through ideal speech situations — will not be successful, since most people do not have these concepts in any explicit sense.) This is the reason why an elaboration of transcendental semiotics or of universal pragmatics is required. This is also the point where a negative strategy is applied. Apel ([15], pp. 8 ff.) and Habermas ([11], pp. 230-238) both present criticisms of alternative conceptions of truth, as an introduction to their own notion of validity. In the case of Apel his transcendental-semiotic interpretation of Peirce is presented as a superior notion of truth, integrating other conceptions ([15], pp. 19-20). In this notion Apel sees a synthesis which both accounts for the connection to reality and the ongoing intersubjective interpretation, a notion by which "the problem of an adequate explanation of the truth conception that underlies modern empirical science" (Apel [15], p. 1) is reached. Since this represents a position superior to other conceptions of truth, the truth claims inherent in speech-acts *have to* be interpreted according to this conception.

Seen from some distance Apel's version of truth and validation is fairly close to Habermas' conception. Some main points of dispute between the two authors should however be pointed out.

The status of *reality* in these intersubjectivist notions of validity presents a source of uneasiness. Apel (see [15], pp. 18-19) regards Habermas as being ambiguous in this respect since on the one hand he presupposes that "the abstract *facts* which are the correlates of true propositions are asserted by us with respect to *objects* in the world"; and on the other hand makes "a rigorous distinction between the question of truth about *abstract facts* which for him [Habermas] is a question of *reflective validity-claims* to be settled on the level of *argumentative discourse* and the question of *evidence* about *objects of experience* which for him [Habermas] is a question of pre-discursive *information* within the frame of *pre-reflexive communicative* interaction between people." This uneasiness, we shall see, influences the core notions of validity and consensus.

For Apel the answer lies in the Peircean conception of reality as the recognizable in the long run, viz. in the ultimate consensus. (Apel [1], pp. 51 ff.) However, if reality as recognizability is taken to mean "what all investigators can agree upon," the problem remains as to whether they actually will *reach* such an agreement. Furthermore it is an open question of how we should know that some future consensus really is the *final* one. The expression "in the long run" serves to avoid a reduction (factualization) of the character of argumentation and agreement as validation, but it implies a lack of determinateness (as to what is the true consensus, by which true reality is recognized, whereby true consensus can be said to be a true consensus!). It is therefore doubtful whether this Peircean conception of the interrelation between truth, reality and recognizability is as good an answer as Apel apparently takes it to be.

Another main point of dispute turns around the question of *transcendentality* (cf. Apel [13], pp. 94 ff., Habermas [18], pp. 198-204, and in Oelmüller [17], e.g. pp. 190 ff., p. 207, pp. 225 ff.). This is partly a question of terminology. Habermas is reluctant to use the term "transcendental," with its Kantian associations, in connection with preconditions for communication and validation; he therefore prefers to talk about universal pragmatics, not about transcendental pragmatics. But it is also a question of methodological emphasis. Apel places emphasis primarily on self-reflective argumentation (and on more traditional philosophical reasoning, especially hermeneutical criticism), whereas Habermas places emphasis on justification through social scientific theory. This methodological difference implies philosophical differences. In Apel's opinion Habermas introduces empirical contingency beneath the transcendental rock bottom. In Habermas' opinion, Apel overstresses the strength and extension of transcendental (self-referential) argumentation.

We shall now discuss Habermas' conception of truth and some of the main comments and objections.

In Habermas (as in Apel) the concept of truth is not analysed in connection with semantic entities, but in connection with pragmatic entities where the preformative aspect implies truth claims (and thus the expression "is true" is rendered non-redundant, cf. [11], p. 213 ff.). The validity of these claims rests on their acceptance, i.e. acceptance for sufficient reasons, as Habermas also puts it ([11], p. 213). (Here two interpretations are possible: validity through mere intersubjective assent, and validity through good reasons; a consensus theory and a discourse theory, cf. [11], fn. 33.) Habermas takes "institutionally unbound," explicit speech-acts as paradigm cases ([18], p. 223). ("I hereby nominate..." is a case of an institutionally bound speech act in a sense which "I promise you..." is not, cf. [18], p. 221.) — For

Habermas there are four universal validity claims: intelligibility, truth, rightness, truthfulness ([11], p. 222). They are "universal" in the sense, first, that the validity claims are meant to be valid independently of any particular institution or situation, and second, that all speakers are able to raise them. The ability to do so belongs to our common communicative competence. These four validity claims are operative in all communicative speech acts, and in other types of speech acts they are involved in deficient modes. In everyday life there is a basic mutual trust in the implicit validity claims, a background consensus. (In asking for a cup of tea one presupposes that the cup is available and portable, that the other person understands the question and takes the questioner to be serious, and that both persons find it appropriate to make this request.) Through doubts and disagreements the implicit validity claims may become explicit; then resolution can be sought and possibly obtained by various reasons — the extreme case involving a radical switch into fully specialized investigation and argumentation.

Habermas relies on a distinction (developed in Ramsey and Strawson, cf. [11], pp. 215 ff.) between facts and objects of experience. Facts are what true statements state, and they are not in the world as things are. You can break a thing, e.g. a glass, but not a fact, e.g. the fact that the glass is fragile. Habermas elaborates this point into a distinction between the validity of fact-stating utterances and the objectivity of object experience ([11], pp. 215-218), and he brings this distinction to bear on his general criticism of correspondence conceptions of truth: correspondence theory mixes up validity and objectivity ([11], pp. 215 ff., pp. 231-234, [5], p. 382). — However, even if one agrees with Habermas' general criticism of correspondence conceptions (e.g. [11], pp. 230-238), his use of this dichotomy between objectivity and truth — which goes together with similar dichotomies between "action" and "discourse", "constitution" and "validation" — may seem puzzling, since the two factors apparently intertwine (as we shall point out later in this article; cf. p. 397 above, see also critical remarks from Beckerman [28], Höffe [29], and Ilting [30], and cf. Puntel [31] who comes close to regarding Habermas as a coherence theoretician).

For Habermas, truth and rightness are the two discursively (=

argumentatively) redeemable universal validity claims ([11], p. 222). Truthfulness is tested in subsequent interaction, and intelligibility (language related, cf. [11], p. 221, [18], pp. 257-259) is an indispensable condition for discourse (= argumentation).

The further steps in Habermas' presentation of his pragmatic conception of validity will be discussed with reference to his most extended exposition, *Wahrheitstheorien* from 1973 ([11]).

"Freilich liegt es sozusagen in der Natur von Geltungsansprüchen, dass sie eingelöst werden können; ..." ([11], p. 239). This is the notion of pragmatically rooted validity claims whose meaningfullness presupposes redemption.

"Die Herbeiführung eines Konsensus unter Bedingungen des Diskurses ist die 'Handlungswiese', durch die ein diskursiver Geltungsanspruch eingelöst wird..." ([11], p. 239). This is an interpretation of the pragmatically rooted validity claims from the standpoint of a consensus theory. We recall the fact that a draft of a criticism of alternative interpretations of validity and validation is already presented in the first part of Habermas [11] (pp. 230-238). However, irrespective of how this criticism of rival conceptions turns out, the concept of consensus is certainly ambiguous. We have a moderate version saying that if a validity claim is found to be valid, then all competent persons of good will should be able to agree upon it. Consensus is an implication of validity. In a strong version of the consensus theory, validity is defined by consensus. A view is valid because there is a consensus about it. Furthermore the term consensus may be defined in different ways, e.g. by various requirements for competence and number of participants.

A contingently achieved consensus cannot represent a criterion for the right answer, Habermas says. For that purpose we need a grounded, or rational, consensus ([11], p. 239). (This is the point from which Mans [32] develops his criticism: Habermas betrays an intersubjectivist conception by bringing in qualifications.)

To avoid a circle (by defining rational consensus by another rational consensus) rational consensus is defined by Habermas as "the formal properties of discourse", i.e. as an argumentation in which only arguments count and no irrelevant factors interfer (only "the unforced force of the better argument" determines the conclusion; [11], p. 240). The notion of discourse is thus tied up with a notion of a free speech situation where intersubjective obstacles are eliminated (the realm of action and experience is blacked out; [11], p. 214) and cooperative search for truth is the only motive. (Cf. the notion of an unlimited community of investigators in Apel's transformed version of Peirce, and cf. the notion of communication free from domination in Habermas. For a discussion of this notion, see e.g. Spaemann [33].)

Discourse is explicated in three stages, first with reference to Toulmin's scheme of non-deductive inference (in order to elaborate a pragmatic conception of reasoning; [11], pp. 240-244), second by emphasizing reflection upon, criticism and change of given linguistic frames as essential characteristics of discourse ([11], pp. 252-254), and finally by the notion of an ideal speech situation (including e.g. elimination of inequality of status between the participants, and elimination of time limits for the discussion, [11], pp. 254-259).

"Language system", historically generated and transmitted by socialization, is a basic notion here. Language system (should we say: horizons, traditions, categorial frameworks?) are not themselves true or false, Habermas emphasizes; they make true or false assertions possible. But their adequacy can be checked and changed, by reflective activity. Such reflection is an essential part of discourse.

This reflection, inherent in discourse, is defined by various steps, in a continuously more radical direction. First an earlier, implicitly accepted validity claim is thematized and questioned with regard to its validity. Then counter arguments (at least one) are put forward. By an ongoing process of questioning, the hitherto implied language system is reflectively put into question. The fourth and final step is a validating reflection upon this language system with the intention of criticizing it and finding a more adequate one ([11], p. 253).

To make this reflective-critical activity possible, an undistorted and free speech situation is required. Freedom and equality of chances among the participants are characteristics of this ideal speech situation. All participants should have the same chances to apply the various speech acts (ask, answer, assert, etc.), all participants should be truthful and transparent to their inner nature, and all should have the same chances to use sanctions ([11], pp. 255-256). Thus the ongoing argumentation should be free to treat any issue from any perspective. (Liberality and equality are in this sense conditions for rationality.) The consensus obtained under these conditions is a grounded (rational) consensus, which is said to be a "sufficient criterion" ([11], p. 255) for the redemption of validity claims.

The ideal speech situation is thus primarily determined "negatively", viz. by elimination of all discourse-conditioned and interpersonal hindrances to a free argumentative activity (elimination of harmful inequality among the participants and of deadlines), though with the additional "positive" characteristics of personal authenticity and of motivation for validation (and *only* for validation).

At this stage we survey the various steps in this exposition: pragmatically raised universal validity claims in communication, presupposing a redemption by consensus, viz. by rational consensus in the sense of discursively obtained consensus; discourse implies critical reflection on given frames and perspectives in order to improve them; free discourse requires an ideal speech situation; consensus obtained under these conditions is not merely factual, but a criterion of validity. In other words, the implicit validity claims imply the notions of ideal speech situation and discursively obtained consensus, *qua* unavoidable, regulative ideas, at the same time as the possibility of redemption is counterfactually presupposed in argumentation and communicative action and in this sense these notions are constitutive for argumentation and communication. There is, however, no external criterion for whether or not an ideal speech situation is realized (and mostly it is not; [11], p. 257). Finally, there is a distinction between discourse and therapy, i.e. between validation and efforts to establish the personal conditions for discourse ([11], p. 259).

From here on we shall discuss some of the main objections raised against this pragmatic conception of rationality and assertibility, and we shall focus on three aspects: the question of the external delimitation and internal shortcoming of a purely discursive theory of validity (e.g. Ilting, Höffe), the question of the unavoidable situatedness of discourse (e.g. Gadamer), and the question of the normativity of actual consensus (e.g. Höffe).

To the thesis that language systems are not true or false, one may object that even when the terms true and false are reserved for assertions, this terminology does not rule out a kind of *validation* of the so-called language systems (or, one may say, a validation of "constitution", since language systems have a constitutive function). This modifies the sharp dichotomy made between validity and constitution (cf. [5] postscript). Furthermore, this reflective validation of language systems has to be related somehow to *reality*. Conceptual adequacy, even when it is decided by an argumentative reflection (and not by a "looking in between concepts and phenomena"), must nevertheless come somehow to grips with *that* which concepts are about. This seems intuitively evident. This view can also be supported by pointing out that in an intersubjective free discussion — where only the better argument counts — that which distinguishes the better argument from the next best cannot itself be part of the intersubjective setting, since this setting (ideal speech situation, or something less but similar to it) is presupposed to be the *same* in both cases. It therefore has to be something *"in* the argument", which in a sense is its "content", as opposed to the "formal", or purely intersubjective, characterization of the ideal speech situation, that is decisive for the validation. Granting all difficulties in talking about "correspondence" or "reference", this much of an "objective" element has to be accounted for in a theory of validation. Habermas underlines that he rejects an interpretation of the discursive check of language systems in terms of correspondence theory, but without making it clear how the "adequacy" (*Angemessenheit*) of language systems is related to the realm of things and experience ([11], pp. 246-253).

However, if elements of "content" are necessary in conceptual checks, then the same holds true for both theoretical (empirical) and normative validations, since the question of the adequacy of the given language system is part of all discursive validations. And this is to say that a consensus theory, or a discourse theory, cannot be said to be "pure", if that is taken to mean that only consensus (intersubjective assent and no content) or only discursivity (merely structures in the discourse and no content) is sufficient to characterize the notions of validation and validity.

At the outset Habermas focuses on the argumentative aspect of validation, somehow leaving aside the more empirical aspect, and in dealing with the sources of failure he tends to concentrate exclusively on the sources of failure located on the intersubjective level. But there are sources of failure stemming from the empirical aspect, and there are linguistic (categorial) inadequacies. The latter type of failures is certainly meant to be taken care of by Habermas, partly through processes like therapy, rational socialization and criticism of ideology, partly through the free, discursive reflection upon language systems. The question is, however, whether Habermas' conception of reflective discourse is sufficient for an elimination of linguistic inadequacies, and whether empirical aspects can be left aside the way Habermas tends to do.

Habermas says ([11], p. 255) that a rational consensus obtained in an ideal speech situation is a "sufficient criterion" for the redemption of validity claims. In disregarding the difficulties of thinking and realizing an ideal speech situation and a rational consensus connected to it, one may raise the following question in terms of the logic of necessary and sufficient conditions: Is the ideal speech situation (the rational consensus) a sufficient condition for validity? Is the ideal speech situation (the rational consensus) a necessary condition for validity?

In our daily life we think we know various things. This we do without questioning it. In some cases we are mistaken, but not in all. Insofar as we often possess the truth, without an ideal speech situation and its rational consensus, they are not necessary conditions for validity. This is a trivial point, which nobody denies.

But if we question a validity claim and ask for a grounded answer, can we then reach such an answer without the ideal speech situation and the rational consensus connected to it? This question is rhetorical, since there evidently are various culturally dependent or institutionally conditioned ways for getting "sufficiently good" answers, without any ideal speech situation or rational consensus. In this sense, in these cases ideal speech acts are not a necessary condition of taking-something-to-be-true (and sometimes even of having-the-truth).

But what about the case when the answer has to be really certain? Even in this case an ideal speech situation, or even an actually realizable degree of free communication, is not always necessary. Imagine a colour-blind person (example borrowed from L. Böök, [36]) who wants to know with a high degree of certainty whether non-colour-blind persons do distinguish things according to objective properties and not only by conventions (as when speaking of "blue sky" and "green grass"). He compels some research persons with ordinary colour sight to sit in isolation from each other, and they are told (they are given the order, not asked in free communication) to separate a number of scraps, each with a colour and an individual number under it, according to their colours. Without going into greater detail with this example, we claim that this colour-blind person can in this way get quite a certain answer to his question. In this case neither an ideal speech situation nor any realizable degree of free communication is a necessary condition for obtaining this strongly grounded answer.

This example can of course be commented on in various ways. One can for instance point out that the implied compulsory action presupposes a communicative competence among the persons carrying out the experiment, and also among the research persons insofar as they understand the order. However, the question is here satisfactorily settled by looking, without discursive check or change of language. The foundation for validation can therefore most reasonably be said to be located at the level of the phenomena rather than on the intersubjective level – which is not to deny that these phenomena (coloured scraps) are already constituted by language and therefore mediated by the intersubjective level.

This example does not rule out the possibility of an ongoing discourse, but it denies its necessity, since in this case there is *no point* in going on with a reflective discussion. As a case of validation it has its relative autonomy over against the discursive demand to question any issue from all perspectives. It indicates a kind of truth redemption in its own right (not naturally "hintergehbar" by discursive redemption). It does not without resistance fit into Habermas' paradigm case of validation.

Some of Habermas' own examples illustrate the same point. In the section on Toulmin ([11], p. 242) he refers to the question whether Harry is a British citizen. To settle the question one pays attention to the fact that Harry was born on Bermuda. In addition one refers to British law which says that people born on Bermuda are in general British citizens. This law is a warrant which allows us to assert that Harry is in fact a British citizen, once it is proved that he was born on Bermuda — though one should add a backing to this warrant: "under normal circumstances". If Harry's British citizenship was ever a matter of doubt or dispute, the question would now be settled, i.e. beyond reasonable doubt and dispute, to the extent that the fact of his birth and the rules of British law are sufficiently well checked. What is explicitly referred to in order to settle the question, are facts and rules, both cast in a common language (containing concepts like person, time and place, and membership in a nation). There is no reflection on this language, and no attempt at critizing or improving it (it may even be pointed out that this question — Harry's British citizenship — is only meaningful inside this linguistic frame). No reference is made to consensus. In fact, no reference is made to the participants in the process of reasoning, or to any community of participants. The question is redeemed merely by appeal to facts and rules in the given frame of reference. These facts and rules can be checked by one individual alone, though if doubts occur one may need the help of qualified persons (knowing more about his birth or the given laws).

This is not an example of a piece of discourse in Habermas' terminology (including critical reflection on given frames and validation through a consensus by an ideal speech situation). This case, too, shows a rational redemption of a validity claim which does not naturally fit into Habermas' conception of truth and validation, with its paradigm in theoretical and universal-political questions: "Paradigmata der Erkenntnis, anhand deren der Sinn von Wahrheit expliziert werden kann, sind nicht die Wahrnehmungen oder singulären Aussagen, in denen Wahrnehmungen mitgeteilt werden, sondern generelle, negative und modale Aussagen" ([11], pp. 232 f.). This basic paradigm of validity has its great merits (for one thing by catching validation better than any static subject-object model); and the question whether *all* cases of validation (as e.g. the legal case of Harry's British citizenship) equally well fall into this paradigm, does not imply a denial of its overall importance, but it does situate this paradigm in relation to relatively autonomous cases of validation.

Whereas the question of categorial adequacy indicates an

internal element of "content" in this pragmatic conception of validation — thus restricting the possible meaning of the terms discourse theory and consensus theory of truth — these examples indicate the reasonableness of some external delimitation of this theory over against empirical truth problems — having a relatively self-sufficient form of validation, where it is pointless to go into a discursive questioning of the frames.

The next question is whether the ideal speech situation is a sufficient condition for validity.

If the rational consensus is said to be a "sufficient condition" in a weak (non-modal-logical) sense, it is clear that such consensus does not logically imply validity. We then talk about having good-enough reasons for asserting something — a "warranted assertibility" ([11], p. 240). In this case it would be more appropriate to talk about a theory of assertibility than of validity.

If however "sufficient condition" is used in a strict modal logical sense, can we then say that *if* we really have reached an ideal speech situation and a rational consensus, then the consensus guarantees the validity of the answer? One may deny this, by arguing for an inescapable, continuous possibility of consensus-modifying innovations both on the conceptual and the experiential level. Even if one had all discursive-structural hindrances simultaneously eliminated and we did reach a consensus which therefore would count as rational, it is still always thinkable that new concepts and new informations might turn up, and modify or correct our consensus. There is nothing in the premises, i.e. in the concept of an ideal speech situation, which can rule out this possibility. Only the elimination of intersubjective and discursive-structural hindrances is included in the premises. If we have a free, reflective validation in this sense, all issues and aspects should hopefully be brought into the discursive procedure as time goes on. But it does not follow that we can ever decide *when* the goal is reached (or whether it can be reached). At no definite moment can we really know that from now on nothing that might modify our consensus, can ever turn up. Even if the ideal speech situation were realized, and we knew it, we could still never know that we had reached the definite rational consensus which logically implies validity.

Since there is no logical implication between rational consensus (ideal speech situation) and validity, the concept of rational consensus and ideal speech situation do not suffice for a strict definition of validity, nor can they serve as a criterion in a strict sense (even if the ideal speech situation were realized). This consensus theory of discursive validation can therefore more appropriately be called a theory of validation than of validity.

However, despite this criticism of the term validity, our pragmatically grounded claims (in communication and argumentation) are thereby not denied. They do represent a peculiar obligation to rationality, even if they have to be given a more flexible and pluralistic interpretation. In this sense we may still talk about this conception as being about validity, i.e. first as pragmatically grounded validity claims, second about validity as a compelling, regulative idea in argumentative validation.

Rational consensus is tied up with the notion of discourse and ideal speech situation in order to avoid a regress in the determination of rational consensus ([11], p. 240). Disregarding the question about how an ideal speech situation can be conceived, or even actualized, one may ask how we possibly could *know, if* it were actually realized. It is tempting to answer: by a rational consensus. But to the extent that rational consensus is something we reach in an ideal speech situation, we have to actualize that ideal speech situation first, in order to reach a rational consensus about it. Thus we seem to end up in another regress! (This suggests the need for a distinction between the evidence for this theory itself and the validity of questions falling inside the process of discourse.)

The demand for a possible concrete realization of the ideal speech situation is rooted in the fact that it represents an ideal form of life, not merely a formal principle. But in which sense is this concept realizable, in reality and in thought? (Cf. Wellmer [25], pp. 44 ff.)

To the extent that one conceives of an ideal speech situation as a form of argumentation where all discursive-structural obstacles are eliminated, one can only think this as an open-ended concept: One starts by eliminating this and that concrete obstacle, e.g. the obstacle of the social status of the participants determining who is allowed to speak and whom one listens to. Then one may imagine a continuous process of elimination until all obstructions are overcome. But in order to conceive of this in concrete terms, we have to know all possible hindrances and we have to know that they can be eliminated simultaneously. This we have to know here and now. It is apparently not only difficult to decide whether or not we have got an ideal situation right here ([11], p. 257). The very concept is difficult (cf. e.g. Ilting [30], Schnädelbach [27]). – But still we may talk meaningfully about our efforts in making the situation better, and about our pragmatically grounded obligation for doing so.

If one asks for the conditions under which any discourse may be realized, it is not trivial to note that we always have to apply *one* organizational form, or one material structure, instead of another. One has either to write or to speak, and thus to use specific techniques and rules in each case. We can certainly change and improve the given institutional frames, and we can pass from the one to the other. But we can never leave the status of being in one definite setting or another. (This means, for one thing, that we do not only have "constitutive norms" on the universal level, but that we also always have particular "constitutive norms" connected to the particular organizational setting in each case. We can in this sense talk about constitutive norms on two levels, the universal and the various particular ones.) Even if discourse may be said to be a "counter institution" (Habermas, [34], p. 201) – in the sense that no preconditions are allowed to be sheltered from critical reflexion – every possible discourse has to be realized in one organizational form or another. This point is certainly not denied by Habermas, the question is whether he pays sufficient attention to it, and how this affects the relationship between universality and situatedness (cf. Gadamer's criticism of the ideal speech situation along these lines, e.g. [35], pp. 316-317, and also D. Böhler [37], pp. 369 ff.).

Each one of us not only has a limited amount of knowledge, thus creating the need to rely on others for supplementary information, but our categorial grasps are delimited by our special situatedness or special professional training. Therefore the presentation of other perspectives and views is indispensable to get us to see our own perspective *as* a perspective. It is indispensable to the creation of a reflective discussion in which one can try out the relative adequacies of other perspectives, possibly bringing them into some synthesis, possibly agreeing on the legitimacy of some rival perspectives (rational tolerance for legitimate pluralism), and hopefully in realizing a common basis (in communicative competence and pragmatically grounded validity claims). We may sharpen the point by saying that finitude is a precondition for discourse. (If God is omniscient, knowing everything from all possible points of view, in which sense can He take part in a discussion as a genuine participant?If all participants had the same preferences and abilities, should they then count as one or as many? What would be the point of letting more than one person speak?) Thought experiments indicate that discursive validation does not merely presuppose universal communicative and argumentative competence, but also a diversity of finite subjects, with different outlooks and different situated views and interests. In arguing, we do not only mutually recognize each other as rational, but also as finite, whereby everybody can learn from everybody, and in common effort mutually meliorate our insight. (Cf. Gadamer [35].)

One may, as Habermas does (in Oelmüller [17], p. 126), distinguish between legitimation of norms and justification of individual acts, thinking in terms of a distinction between justification inside a frame and justification of this frame itself. Legitimation of norms can be defined as the question whether the validity claims connected to norms of action can be rationally redeemed by arguments. Thus one apparently has the question of normative validation on the one hand (normative *Letztbegründung*) and a question of the appropriate understanding of the various situated actions on the other (situational justification of institutional acts, and judgment of their reasonableness in the concrete setting). This distinction may serve to avoid a totalization of merely situational, institution-bound justification, through which the critical potential of free argumentation and validation is overlooked. (Cf. Habermas' critical remarks on hermeneuticians of Gadamer's type, concerning the natural-rights issue, in [23], p. 296.)

But even if one holds on to this distinction and hence to the notion of ultimate and universal normative validation, there are still important conceptual interrelations between universal validation and situational concreteness: In order to discuss the validity of a universal norm (e.g. "all people are born equal"), one has to understand what it means (i.e. that "people" are "born equal", or "have the same rights"), and for this understanding a learning process through concrete situations in everyday life is required. The same holds true when it comes to the application of this general norm (then, too, one has to be able to judge the various situations where people can be said to have the same rights). One may object that problems of learning and of applying general norms are nevertheless conceptually external to the question of the validation of these norms. However, how could one meaningfully discuss the validity of a general norm (e.g. "all people are born equal"), without knowing "what it is about", what it means to follow or to violate the norm in concrete situations (i.e. what it means to be "equal" and "unequal" in various cases)? One does not have to have any complete knowledge (whatever that might mean, in this field), but some basic insight into the situational meaning (an insight which can then be further elaborated) has to be present already at the stage of normative validation and agreement. In this sense it is unavoidable for any meaningful validation and agreement (if it is to be more than empty words) to be conceptually related to an understanding of possible concrete cases.

It is worth emphasizing that the point we are now making is less intrusive in some clearcut juridical cases, like the trial in Nuremberg, where the situation is nevertheless fairly obvious: Nearly everything depends on whether or not some general norms can be rationally validated. And certainly, Apel and Habermas seem to a large extent to have these kinds of cases in mind.

This last point illustrates the importance of being aware of what examples a philosopher has in mind. It is tempting to suggest that by focusing on such implicit paradigm cases some further clarification might hopefully be expected, for instance in the discussion between Gadamer (stressing finitude and situatedness) and Habermas (stressing universal validity).

Some further remarks should be made of the concept of consensus.

In his criticism of Habermas Höffe says ([29], p. 272): "Die Aporie dieser Ansätze liegt darin, dass sie entweder die Wahrheit von historischen Zufälligkeit abhängig machen, das heisst dem verzerrenden Zugriff von Rhetorik, Suggestion, Manipulation, Täuschung und Selbsttäuschung aussetzen; dann aber geht der Invarianzanspruch von Wahrheit verloren. Oder sie führen normative Qualifikationen des Konsenses ein, Qualifikationen, die wie: unbegrenzte Forschergemeinschaft (Peirce), kritische Nachprüfung kompetenter Beurteiler (Kamlah, Lorenzen), potentielle oder begründete Zustimmung (Habermas) bei näherem Zusehen erstens kein operationales Legitimationskriterium darstellen und zweitens das Charakteristische von Konsens auflösen: das Resultat eines geschichtlichen Einigungsprozesses konkreter Personen (und nicht abstrakter Kommunikatoren) zu sein."

Even if one accepts that an actually given consensus can be "too weak", and that the notion of an ideal consensus implies something unreal and therefore cannot serve as a criterion in a more operational sense, one may still argue for the following points: Nevertheless the notion of an ideal consensus (rational consensus under the conditions of ideal speech situation) represents a particular binding orientation, a necessary regulative idea, which is not arbitrarily introduced, but which presents itself as the result of a reflection on preconditions inherent in argumentation. It makes furthermore sense to talk about a third concept of consensus characterized as the continuously improved consensus, over against the actual best-possible consensus, viz. as the best-possible improvement of the consensus which at each time is obtained. This is a notion of a realistic, realizable obligation to advance toward greater rationality.

If one accepts that "ought implies can", i.e. that we can only be said to be obliged to what is possible for us, we shall have to distinguish between the obligation to the ideal consensus and the obligation to the best-possible improvement of the consensus which at each time is actualized. The former is rooted in the recognition of preconditions for arguing, and it represents what we might call our "ultimate obligation". The latter obligation is, in addition, rooted in the recognition of our fallibility, in the sense that fallibility implies that every actual consensus may embrace something that demands correction, every consensus points toward its further improvement. We are obliged to accept as valid what under the best possible conditions until now we have recognized to be valid; and at the same time we know what we have accepted in this way as the best argument, may still (in various ways, according to the case) be overthrown by an even better argument. What we ultimately are obliged to accept as valid, is therefore that which can turn up as the still better argument. Thus, in principle, there is some "call" for constantly transcending the given actual consensus in favour of the even better.

This obligation "forward" — toward the better, in the last instance toward the ideal — is equally directed "backward", against meaninglessness and untruth, what is less well grounded and acceptable. The rejection of the *un*acceptable is the immediately compelling task in this version of human rationality. (Cf. the relation between criticizing a given scale of scientific professions as being *in*sufficient to grasp a problem adequately, e.g. a case of building a nuclear reactor where ecological expertise is lacking, and the question about what is *the* complete and adequate composition of scientific bodies of experts. Often the former, "negative" question is fairly easy to answer, whereas the latter, "positive" question remains unsettled; cf. e.g. the problem of possible future innovations, possibly making new professional perspectives and approaches a reality.)

The *dynamics* between the actual consensus and the constant formation of a better consensus is not adequately taken into account in Höffe's reflection on actual and ideal consensus.

In this background it makes sense to talk about a melioristic fallibilism (cf. Apel [26], pp. 151 ff.), even though such labels may create more confusion than clarification. Given the courage of using such labels, one should add that this melioristic fallibilism is based on transcendental pragmatics for argumentative reason.

We may say what we like, as long as it is clear what we mean. The discussion delineated above indicates that the title "theory of truth", applied to this pragmatic conception of argumentative rationality, is somewhat inappropriate. On the one hand this title seems to promise more than it redeems. We refer to the relative neglect of experiential truth problems and of the "content" element in question about conceptual adequacy, the former demanding some delimitation, the latter demanding an integration

of elements transcending the purely discursive and intersubjective
level. On the other hand it seems to provide more than it promises.
We refer to the procedural conception of natural rights.

This pragmatic conception of rationality pretends to be more
than a piece of theoretical insight. It pretends to imply a recognition of an obligation, not only to argumentative-scientific rationality, but to argumentative rationality in society in general.
This involves the formation of more adequate views and preferences, for better evaluations and decisions – a more human and
rational society. Finally, this obligation expresses the deeper concerns of Apel and Habermas underlying the elaboration of their
pragmatic conception of discourse and consensus.

BIBLIOGRAPHY

Albert, H. [21] *Transzendentale Träumereien*. Hamburg 1975.
Apel, K.-O. [1] Der Denkweg von Charles Sanders Peirce. Frankfurt a.M.
    1975. Also in K.-O. Apel, *Charles Sanders Peirce, Schriften I und II*.
    Frankfurt a.M. 1967 and 1970.
– [2] Szientismus oder transzendentale Hermeneutik? Zur Frage nach dem
    Subjekt der Zeicheninterpretation in der Semiotik des Pragmatismus.
    In R. Bubner et al. (Eds), *Hermeneutik und Dialektik*, Vol. 1.Tübingen
    1970. Also in Apel [4].
– [3] From Kant to Peirce: The Semiotical Transformation of Transcenden-
    tal Logic. In L.W. Beck (Ed.), *Proceedings of the Third International
    Kant-Congress*. Dordrecht 1972. Also in Apel [4].
– [4] *Transformation der Philosophie*, Vols. 1 and 2. Frankfurt a.M. 1973.
– [13] Sprechakttheorie und transzendentale Sprachpragmatik zur Frage
    ethisher Normen. In K.-O. Apel (Ed.), *Sprachpragmatik und Philoso-
    phie*. Frankfurt a.M. 1976.
– [14] Transcendental Semiotics and the Paradigms of First Philosophy.
    Philosophic Exchange 2/4 (1978).
– [15] *C.S. Peirce and the Question of the Truth – Conception of Modern
    Science (Toward a Transcendental-pragmatic Theory of Truth)*.
    Manuscript. Frankfurt a.M. 1979.
– [16] C.S. Peirce and the post-Tarskyan Problem of an Adequate Explica-
    tion of the Meaning of Truth. *The Monist* 63/3 (1980).
– [19] Der semiotische Pragmatismus von Ch.S. Peirce und die 'abstractive
    fallacy' in den Grundlagen der Kantschen Erkenntnistheorie und der
    Carnapschen Wissenschaftslogik. In A.J. Bucher et al. (Eds.), *Bewusst
    sein. Gerhard Funke zu eigen*. Bonn 1975.
– [26] The Problem of (Philosophical) Ultimate Justification in the Light
    of a Transcendental Pragmatic of Language. *Ajatus* 36 (1976).

Beckermann, A. [28] Die realistischen Voraussetzungen der Konsensustheorie von J. Habermas. *Zeitschrift für allgemeine Wissenschaftstheorie*, Vol. 3 (1972): 63-80.

Berk, U. [24] *Konstruktive Argumentationstheorie*. Stuttgart 1979.

Bernstein, R.J. [12] *The Restructuring of Social and Political Theory*. New York 1976.

Bertilsson, M. [20] *Toward a Social Reconstruction of Science Theory: Peirce's Theory of Inquiry, and Beyond*. Lund 1978.

Böhler, D. [37] *Über das Defizit an Dialektik bei Habermas und Marx. In* Dallmayr [9], pp. 369 ff.

Böök, L. [36] Argumentation och giltighet. In T. Nordenstam and G. Skirbekk (Eds.), *Kommunikasjon og moral*. Department of Philosophy, University of Bergen 1979.

Dallmayr, W. [9] *Materialien zu Habermas' 'Erkenntnis und Interesse'*. Frankfurt a.M. 1974.

Gadamer, H.G. et al. [35] *Hermeneutik und Ideologiekritik*. Frankfurt a.M. 1971.

Habermas, J. [5] *Erkenntnis und Interesse*. Frankfurt a.M. 1968. Second edition with a postscript 1973.

— [7] *Zur Logik der Sozialwissenschaften. Philosophische Rundschau* 1967.

— [8] *Technik und Wissenschaft als 'Ideologie'*. Frankfurt a.M. 1968.

— [10] Vorbereitende Bemerkungen zu einer Theorie der kommunikativen Kompetenz. In J. Habermas und N. Luhmann, *Theorie der Gesellschaft oder Sozialtechnologie — Was leistet die Systemforschung?* Frankfurt a.M. 1971.

— [11] Wahrheitstheorien. In H. Fahrenbach (Ed.), *Wirklichkeit und Reflexion. Walter Schulz zum 60. Geburtstag*. Pfullingen 1973.

— [18] Was heisst Universalpragmatik? In K.-O. Apel (Ed.), *Sprachpragmatik und Philosophie*. Frankfurt a.M. 1976.

— [22] *Legitimationsprobleme im Spatkapitalismus*. Frankfurt a.M. 1973.

— [23] *Zur Rekonstruktion des Historischen Materialismus*. Frankfurt a.M. 1976.

— [34] Theorie der Gesellschaft oder Sozialtechnologie? In J. Habermas und N. Luhmann, *Theorie der Gesellschaft oder Sozialtechnologie?* Frankfurt a.M. 1971.

Höffe, O. [29] Kritische Überlegungen zur Konsensustheorie der Wahrheit (Habermas). *Philosophisches Jahrbuch* 83 (1976). Also in O. Höffe, *Ethik und Politik*. Frankfurt a.M. 1979.

Ilting, K.-H. [30] Geltung als Konsens. *Neue Hefte für Philosophie* (1976): 20-50.

Mans, D. [32] *Intersubjektivitätstheorien der Wahrheit*. Diss. Frankfurt a.M. 1974.

McCarthy, T. [6] *The Critical Theory of Jürgen Habermas*. London 1978.

Oelmüller, W. (Ed.) [17] *Transzendentalphilosophie, Normenbegründung*. Paderborn 1978.

Puntel, L.B. [31] *Wahrheitstheorien in der neueren Philosophie*. Darmstadt 1978.

Schnädelbach, H. [27] *Reflexion und Diskurs*. Frankfurt a.M. 1977.
Spaemann, R. [33] Die Utopie der Herrschaftsfreiheit. *Merkur* 292 (August 1972).
Wellmer, A. [25] *Praktische Philosophie und Theorie der Gesellschaft. Zum Problem der normativen Grundlagen einer kritischen Sozialwissenschaft*. Konstanz 1979.

Wilfrid Sellars' philosophy of mind

JAY F. ROSENBERG
University of North Carolina

Nowhere within philosophy is it more difficult to draw lines of demarcation than in an attempt to isolate the philosophy of mind as a coherent subregion of the total philosophical terrain. The philosophy of mind grades off smoothly into questions of epistemology (the structure of sensory awareness and perceptual cognition), of ontology (the nature and multiplicity of substances), of the theory of action, of the philosophy of language and representation, of moral and social and political philosophy, and nowadays even into questions centered in the philosophy of science, in the theory of theories. In the case of Wilfrid Sellars, these difficulties are especially acute, for Sellars' philosophy of mind is intricately and inextricably woven into the fabric of a systematic philosophical vision of classical scope.

Such considerations collaborate to render near hopeless the task of a sympathetic expositor. Particularly in a survey as limited in scope as the present effort, something important must necessarily be sacrificed. The expositor is faced with an unpleasant choice. He can attempt to secure a limited range of his subject's key insights by tracing their interconnections with, anchorage in, and argumentative buttressing by collateral theses more properly belonging to other, although related, areas of philosophical thought; or he can attempt to communicate a sense of the overall sweep, structure, and design of his subject's philosophical tapestry, at the risk of leaving his audience with the feeling that this whole pattern of thought is arbitrary, dogmatic, and inadequately grounded by cogent argumentation.

Contemporary philosophy. A new survey. Vol. 4, pp. 417–439.
© *1983, Martinus Nijhoff Publishers, The Hague/Boston/London.*

Despite the magnitude of the risk, I have elected to pursue the latter course. I shall attempt, in other words, to sketch *what* stands Sellars takes within the philosophy of mind, while saying relatively little about *why* Sellars takes the stands he does. What will emerge, if I am successful, will be a coherent, intricate, and powerful systematic vision of "the mind and its place in nature". What will be lost will be a family of insightfully reasoned considerations which conduce to render that vision as compelling as it is powerful. From the perspective of what is philosophically ideal, this remains an unsatisfying compromise, but circumstances permit no better. To the task, then.

Sellars' philosophical orientation in general may usefully be characterized as a sophisticated Kantianism tempered by the insights of an indigenous, especially Peircean, American pragmatism. In the philosophy of mind, in particular, these broad tendencies manifest themselves, negatively, in Sellars' firm rejection of the Cartesian picture of mind as *res cogitans*, and, positively, in his continuing commitment to the project of integrating the distinctive mentality of persons into the framework of that concept of the world which is being increasingly sharply delineated by the advances of a maturing natural science. The negative moment here forms an essential prolegomena to the positive. It secures, indeed, the possibility of the integration which Sellars' positive programme aims, at least in principle, at actualizing.

Sellars follows Kant in bringing critical pressure to bear against both elements of the *res cogitans* formula — returning from the bare, substratal Cartesian *res* to a more Aristotelian view of persons as natured, unitary "first substances", and dismantling Descartes' overarching "*cogitatione*" (the "ideas" of the British Fmpiricists) by enforcing a sharp distinction between sensation ("raw feels") and cognition (thought).

On Sellars' view, the Cartesian picture of mind as *res* is part and parcel of the enterprise which seeks to erect upon the foundation of the *cogito* — correctly viewed as capturing "the basic and irreducible form of self-awareness with respect to distinctively human states of one's person" ([1], p. 236) — a *science* of Rational Psychology with ontological import. Like Kant, Sellars denies the *possibility* of such a science.

Traditional metaphysicians had argued that the subject of representations ... is a simple, non-composite substance which is "strictly" ... identical through time.... Kant argues, *per contra*, that for all we know the subject or representer might be:

> (a) an attribute of something more basic
> (b) a system (composite)
> (c) a series.

([1], p. 236)

Sellars endorses Kant's account of the classical arguments to the contrary as fallacious or "paralogistic". On Sellars' reconstruction, these arguments share a common form:

> *The representation of the I is not the representation of*
> (a) an aspect of something more basic,
> (b) a composite of parts,
> [(c) a series]:
> Therefore, *the I* is not
> (a) an aspect of something more basic,
> (b) a composite of parts,
> [(c) a series].

([2], pp. 69-71; cf. [1], pp. 236-239)

These arguments would not be fallacious "if we could add the premise that our concept of the 'I' is the concept of a determinate kind of object" ([1], pp. 236-237) and, indeed, "Descartes takes it for granted that '*res cogitans*' is a proper sortal concept...." ([2], p. 67).

> But the concept of the "I" is the concept of that which thinks..., and concepts pertaining to mental acts are "functional" in a way which leaves open the question as to the "qualitative" or ... contentual character of the items that function in such a way as to be the kinds of mental acts they are. ([1], p. 237; cf. [2], pp. 67-68)

It is, in fact, "in the literal sense a category mistake to construe 'substance'... as an object-language sortal word that differs from ordinary empirical predicates by being a *summum genus*." ([3], p. 53)

Instead, Sellars endorses the thesis of the mediaeval terminist logicians, itself extended and deepened by Kant, "that certain statements (thus 'Man is a species') which seem to be about queer entities in the world are actually statements that classify constituents of conceptual acts." ([3], p. 53) The categorial apparatus of classical metaphysics, in short, is to be understood as encoding a taxonomy of the "most generic logical powers" of conceptual representings. It is thus in itself devoid of any ontological import. (Vide [4-6]) This is the understanding which opens the way for Sellars' complete delegation of the *positive* ontological task to natural science in his much-remarked *"scientia mensura"*:

> ...that in the dimension of describing and explaining the world, science is the measure of all things, of what is that it is, and of what is not that it is not. ([7], p. 173)

From this metaphysical perspective, it follows straightforwardly that the fundamental concept of a person is not that of a Cartesian *res cogitans* but that of a *living organism* which both moves and thinks, feels and acts — an Aristotelian "first substance" which is the subject of both "physical" and "mental" predications. This ur-conception admits of an initial refinement, then, in terms of the picture of the world yielded by an emerging science, which produces a *trivial* version of what is typically called "the Identity Theory", to which Sellars, as a first step, unproblematically subscribes:

> ...There is a sense in which it is perfectly legitimate to suppose that [mental states] *are identical with* certain states of the empirical brain. This, for the simple reason that it makes sense to suppose that they *are* states of the empirical brain. Imagine a person who has been defleshed and deboned, but whose nervous system is alive, intact, and in functioning order. Imagine its sensory nerves hooked up with input devices and its motor nerves hooked up with an electronic system which enables it to communicate. Without expanding on this familiar science fiction, let me simply suggest

> that we think of what we ordinarily call a person as a nervous system clothed in flesh and bones. In view of what we know, it makes perfectly good sense to introduce the term "core person" for the empirical nervous system, and to introduce a way of talking according to which [mental states] are in the first instance states of "core persons" and only derivatively of the clothed person. ([8], p. 380)

While this version of the Identity Theory is "almost undoubtedly true", it is also, as Sellars remarks, "relatively non-controversial and unexciting. ...All of the important philosophical problems pertaining to the relation of mental states to physical states remain." ([8], p. 381)

On Sellars' view, a (perhaps, the) significant challenge for contemporary philosophy is the enterprise of uniting what he calls two "images" of man-in-the-world into a single "stereoscopic" synoptic understanding.

> [The] philosopher is confronted not by one complex many-dimensional picture, the unity of which, such as it is, he must come to appreciate, but by *two* pictures of essentially the same order of complexity, each of which purports to be a complete picture of man-in-the-world, and which ... he must fuse into one vision. ([9], p. 4)

These competing perspectives Sellars refers to as the *manifest* and the *scientific* images of man-in-the-world.

The manifest image is "the framework in terms of which, to use an existentialist turn of phrase, man first encountered himself...." ([9, p. 6) It is that image of man-in-the-world which is both endorsed and refined by the so-called "perennial philosophy", a tradition — spanning the centuries from Plato and Aristotle to G.E. Moore and P.F. Strawson — whose defining characteristic, indeed, is "an acceptance of the manifest image as the real". ([9], p. 19) At the same time, the manifest image is constitutive of that which it depicts, for "man is that being which conceives of itself in terms of the manifest image." ([9], p. 18)

The scientific image — even more of an idealization than the manifest image, since it is still in the process of coming to be —

is that conception of man-in-the-world which emerges from the fruits of postulational theory construction. Like the manifest image, the scientific image purports to offer (the schematism of) a *complete* picture of man-in-the-world, but one radically different from — and at first sight in many ways incommensurable with — the picture embodied in the manifest image. From the metaphysical perspective of Sellars' scientific realism, the picture embodied in the manifest image is viewed (*sub specie* the scientific image) as codifying a system of "*appearances*" to human persons of a reality which is *constituted* of, e.g., systems of imperceptible particles. It is the fact that the human organism (which, within the manifest image, *is* — *qua* Aristotelian "first substance" — the person) is, within the scientific image, represented as one such "system of imperceptible particles" among others, which sets the philosophical problematic of mind and body.

> For if the human body is a system of particles, the body cannot be the subject of thinking and feeling, *unless thinking and feeling are capable of interpretation as complex interactions of physical particles*; unless, that is to say, the manifest framework of man as *one* being, a *person* capable of doing radically different kinds of things, can be replaced without loss of descriptive and explanatory power by a postulational image in which he is a complex of physical particles, and all his activities a matter of the particles changing in state and relationship. ([9], p. 29)

Securing the possibility of such a replacement would constitute a defense of an "Identity Theory" in a non-trivial sense, and it is, indeed, to such a *significant* Identity Theory of mind and body that Sellars himself is philosophically committed.

The Cartesian concept of self (mind) as *res cogitans* unites under the rubric '*cogitatione*' a variety of classically separate capacities. Cognitions (thoughts), sensations ("raw feels"), and volitions ("acts of will") are all *cogitatione*. The guiding thread of Descartes' ontological unification here is essentially the *epistemological* fact of "privileged access". As Sellars reconstructs the epistemology of the mental, however, the first-person reporting role of the language of the mental constitutes a "dimension of the use of these concepts which is *built on* and *presupposes* [an] intersubjective status." ([7], p. 189) The ability to report, using the language of the mental, one's own mental states is an *acquired* ability — for the language of the mental, like all languages, must be learned.

In his seminal "Empiricism and the Philosophy of Mind" [7], Sellars sketches the learning process — in essence, that of operant conditioning — by which what *begins* as a language with a purely theoretical use can *gain* a (first-person, self-descriptive) reporting role. His account shows

> ...that the fact that language is essentially an *intersubjective* achievement, and is learned in inter-subjective contexts...is compatible with the 'privacy' of 'inner episodes'. It also makes clear that this privacy is not an 'absolute privacy'. For if it recognizes that these concepts have a reporting use in which one is not drawing inferences from behavioural evidence, it nevertheless insists that the fact that overt behavior *is* evidence for these episodes *is built into the very logic of these concepts*, just as the fact that the observable behaviour of gases is evidence for molecular episodes is built into the very logic of molecule talk. ([7], p. 189)

Seeing the epistemological fact of "privileged access" in this way not as constitutive of the concept of the mental but as a derivative status accruing to the concepts of certain "inner episodes" and thus as devoid of ontological consequences, Sellars is free to un-couple what Descartes brings together as *"cogitatione"*. Thoughts, sensations, and volitions, on Sellars' view, pose *different*, if related, challenges to the fusion of the manifest and scientific images, and Sellars proceeds to offer different, if related, discussions of these diverse dimensions of the mental.

Sellars distinguishes in [10] among the "logical (semantic)", "action", and "causal" sense of "the expression of thoughts". An utterance by some person can be said to express *the* thought that-p, a remark which *classifies* the utterance according to its place in the "logical space" of inference and argumentation; to express *his* thought that-p, a remark which classifies the occurrent speech episode as a speech *act* (an intentional action caught up in an economy of means and ends); or simply to be the expression of *a* thought, a remark which identifies the overt episode as the culmination of a causal process which beings with an "inner episode", an occurrent thinking. Only the last of these engages the *ontology* of thoughts. While thoughts *qua* occurrent thinkings are prior to meaningful utterances in the causal order, the *intentionality* of speech, on Sellars' view, is not derivative from the intentionality of thought. Rather, he sees the language of intentionality in general as functional and classificatory, employed for sorting episodes according to their roles in structuring the total behavioral economy of the speaking and thinking organism. (See, e.g., [11], [12].)

In [7], Sellars began what has become a continuing project of understanding the *epistemic* status of the concept of occurrent thought-episodes after the pattern of theoretical postulations. The *model* for his mythological "theory of thoughts" (mythological in Plato's sense — enlightening through its plausibilities) are the candid utterances ("thinkings-out-loud") of a hypothetical sophisticated "Rylean community" — "Rylean" in lacking the concept of covert "inner episodes", but sophisticated in having a command of the full repertoire of logical and semantic notions (validity, inference, meaning, truth) in their application to *sayings* and proximate *dispositions to say*. Sellars' myth introduces the concept of thoughts into this community in two stages. In the first stage, "Verbal Behaviorism", the (ur-) concept of a thought just *is* the concept of a proximate, although perhaps unactualized, disposition to think-out-loud (i.e., to *say*). In the second stage, thoughts are explicitly postulated (by one "Jones") as occurrent thinkings, covert ("inner") episodes (N.B.: not entities) which have, in effect, the *semantic place* of certain thinkings-out-loud — that is, which play an equivalent role in a system of responses to noncognitive stimuli ("language entries"), inferential passages from cognitive item to cognitive item ("intra-linguistic moves"), and the triggerings of overt behavior ("language exits"). (See [13], [14], Ch. IV)

The key to this account of thoughts lies in the recognition that, while the items of the *model* for Jones's theory have, *qua* acoustical disturbances, a determinate intrinsic character, the episodes (hypothetically) *postulated* by his theory as covert (mediating) states of persons — initially to explain the appropriateness and intelligence of conduct in contexts where no thinking-out-loud is occurring — are introduced by a purely *functional* analogy. The concept of a thought (occurrent thinking) is not the concept of something encountered *propria persona* but that of a causally mediating *logico-semantic role-player*, the ontological instantiation of which is, so far, left open. It is thus possible to discover, in the order of being, that these role-players intrinsically *are*, for example, determinate states of the central nervous system. (This would, parenthetically, supply part of an explanatory account of why it *is* possible to train people to have "privileged access" to some of their thoughts — i.e., to respond directly and non-inferentially to the occurrence of an "inner episode" with the (meta-) thought that one is thinking a determinate thought; to respond, that is, with *another* "inner episode".) The manifest image conception of persons as thinkers, then, can fuse smoothly with the concept of organisms of determinate neurological structure, which, from the standpoint of the scientific image, those persons *are*. On Sellars' account, the concept of a thought is at ground the concept of a *functional* kind, and so no ontological tensions are introduced by the scientific image's identification of items of that functional kind as *being*, structurally, states and episodes of the central nervous system.

In the case of sensations, however, the fusion of the two images cannot be achieved with an analogous unproblematic smoothness. Few aspects of Sellars' philosophy have provoked as much comment and resistance as his theory of sensations. (See, e.g., Cornman [15], Delaney [16], Hooker [17]) Here it becomes necessary to supply considerably more detail.

For a time, Sellars' account of sensations does run parallel to his account of thoughts. Sellars, however, sharply separates the "of-ness" of sensations from the "of-ness" of thoughts. The "of-ness" of thought is the "aboutness" of intentionality. To think of, for example, Socrates is to think *something* of Socrates, i.e., to think *that* ...Socrates...., where the open context is filled by the remaining elements of a complete sentence. Thinking-of is thus, on Sellars' view, an elliptical thinking-that, and the "propositional" idiom of 'that'-clauses, in turn, is once again a functional classificatory idiom which abstracts from specific material embodiments to sort logico-semantic role-players (overt or covert) *according to* their logico-semantic roles.

Like thoughts, sensations are merely "nominal objects". The hypothetical explanatory postulation of Jones's mythological "theory of sensations" within Sellars' account is a postulation of *states* of persons rather than of entities. And, as in the case of thoughts, talk of "of-ness" is again fundamentally classificatory. Here, however, the *sort* of classification is not logical or semantic.

> The "rawness" of "raw feels" is their non-conceptual character. The sense in which "raw feels" are "of something" is not to be assimilated to the intentionality of thoughts. ([8], p. 376)

Sellars illustrates his understanding of the place of sensations *within the manifest image* through a series of grammatical transforms from the customary "nominal" style of sensation-attributions, e.g.,

(a) S has a sensation of a red triangle,

to an ontologically-more-perspicuous, contrived "adverbial" style. 'Of a red triangle' is first represented as a classificatory modifier of 'sensation', thus:

(b) S has an of-a-red-triangle sensation.

The contrived adjective 'of-a-red-triangle' is, second, itself represented as a form of *analogical* predication, the fundamentum of which is the attribution of sensory qualities to manifest (physical) objects, thus:

(c) S has a red_s triangular_s sensation,

where the subscripts signal the invocation of the analogical transposition. Finally, viewing the "verbal noun" 'sensation' as a nominalization of the verb 'to sense', Sellars transforms the noun-adjective construction of (c) into a verb plus adverbs, roughly:

(d) S senses red$_s$ly and triangular$_s$ly

(paralleling the understanding of, e.g., "S wore a wry seductive smile" as "S smiled wryly and seductively".) The *person*, S, then emerges explicitly revealed as the only ultimate *ontological* subject of attributions of sensation. (See [7], [18], [19])

The *analogy* underlying the categorial transposition of redness and triangularity from qualities of manifest objects to modes of sensing is, as in the case of thoughts, mediated by viewing sensations, *qua* sensory states, as having the epistemic status of postulates of a mythological explanatory theory. Here, too, "privileged access" is treated as an added and derivative dimension of use of concepts essentially intersubjective in character. But where thoughts were (hypothetically) postulated as causally mediating logico-semantic role-players to explain the intelligence and appropriateness of conduct in certain contexts, sensory states are introduced as elements of an explanatory account of the appropriateness of certain *cognitions* ("propositional attitudes") themselves, whether covert (thinkings, believings) or overt (sayings, thinkings-out-loud). In particular, the state adverted to in (d) above is invoked to explain the occurrence of *thoughts* ("perceptual takings") of red triangles, both in instances in which a person's eyes are directed toward a red triangular object in good light and, more importantly, in cases of "non-veridical perceptual takings", where no red triangular objects are suitably positioned in the proximate environment of the perceiving subject at all.

In the *first* instance, then, the concept of a state of sensing red$_s$ly (dropping 'triangular$_s$ly' for compactness) is introduced by an *extrinsic causal* analogy: It is that sort of state which is brought about in normal perceivers in standard conditions by the action of red objects upon the eyes.

The temptation is to stop at this — that is, to hold that the concept of sensory states within the manifest image is the concept of causal role-players in the same way that the concept of occurrent thinkings within the manifest image amounts to the concept of certain causally mediating logico-semantic role-players. It is precisely here, however, that Sellars' treatment of sensations parts company from the account which he has offered of cognitions.

The key to this departure is a recognition of the different *explanatory* role which sensory states are being (hypothetically) pc ..ed to fill. Grasping the important of this difference, however, requires a metaphysical excursis.

The fundamental *concept* of color in the manifest image is the concept of a *content* (what Kant called "an intensive magnitude" and, more revealingly, "the real in space"). The conceptual space of colors as the qualities of natured substances (wood, ice, metal, pigment, etc.) rests upon a more basic conceptual framework in which colors are themselves the *stuffs* of which objects consist. The natures of natured substances are clusters of transformational, interactive, and causal powers, propensities, and dispositions. While such powers and propensities are implicitly adverted to in the perceptual *judgment* that, to take a favorite Sellarsian example, there is a pink ice cube before one, they are properly no part of the correlative perceptual *taking*. We do not *see* the natures of what we see, but *see* only what is conceived as thus natured. The concept of a pink ice cube, then, is in the first instance the concept of a *cube of pink* with determinate causal powers and transformational propensities – e.g., the power to cool tea and the propensity to melt in the process. Sellars insists, in other words, that we take seriously Berkeley's argument that there can be no primary qualities (form) in the absence of secondary qualities (contents) and thereby reverses Descartes' conclusions vis-à-vis "the real wax". Colors are not modes of appearing of bare *res extensa* but rather fundamentally to be conceived as *themselves* the extended (space-filling) continua in which empirical natures inhere. And the *basic* logical grammar of color space, in turn, is not at ground adjectival but rather is analogous to the familiar grammar of mass terms. It is *this* family of observations and considerations which Sellars summarily expresses by saying that the concepts of colors are concepts of *"ultimately homogeneous* (henceforth 'UH') qualities" [9], [20].

The fundamental explanatory job which must be done by the posited sensory states of persons is to account for the appropriateness of certain cognitions. We can now flesh out this bare constraint in greater detail. The crucial point is that the cognitions at issue *include* the concepts of color-contents – that is, the concepts of UH qualities – *as* UH. What the postulated sensory states must explanatorily do, in other words, is in part to supply an account which renders intelligible the occurrence of *concepts of UH qualities* as a response to irritations of the sensory surface of the human organism. But they can satisfy this specific explanatory demand, Sellars argues, only if these states themselves are posited as having a determinate *intrinsic* character. They must, in fact, be conceived of as themselves *instantiating* a logical space formally analogous to the logical space which color-contents are conceived as occupying — as preserving, within the logical space of states of a person *qua* perceiver, the resemblances, differences, orderings, exclusions, and the UH (in short, the "topology") of the logical space of color-contents which is the fundamentum of the *analogy* in terms of which these sensory states are (hypothetically) originally introduced. The concept of a state of sensing $red_s ly$, in other words, cannot be *simply* the concept of a state which is brought about in a certain fashion. Rather, it must be the richer concept of a state of a perceiver which resembles and differs from states of, e.g., sensing $blue_s ly$, $pink_s ly$, $green_s ly$, etc. in a manner formally analogous to the way in which red, blue, pink, green, etc. contents are conceived to resemble and differ from one another — and which *is* (*qua* state) itself UH.

The reason that characterizing such states as sensing $red_s ly$ only extrinsically, according to their paradigmatic causes, cannot do the relevant explanatory job here is that, already in the manifest image, *there are no color-contents*. Since the fundamental conceptual/experiential sense of 'red' is that *of* a red content, this seems puzzling, but the point is relatively straightforward: Considerations of the sorts mobilized in the classical (skeptical) Argument from Illusion already suffice to establish the conclusion that the basic *ontological* locus of color-contents must lie on the side of the subject, that is, must be somehow "within" the perceiving organism. It is crucial here to separate the order of understanding from the order of being. In the order of understanding, the basic *concept* of color is that of UH space-filling contents, and the concept of such states of perceivers as sensing $red_s ly$ is a concept formed by an analogical transposition into the category of *states* of those fundamental concepts belonging to the category of *stuffs*. This view, however, is compatible with the conclusion that, in the order of being, there are no such stuffs.

It is the states which alone *instantiate* the logical space which colors-qua-contents are conceived of as instantiating — and both our experiences of color-contents-in-space and our *having* concepts of such contents are properly to be (explanatorily) accounted for in terms of our being in such states. To postulate states to explain such experiences and the possession of such concepts *when there are no color-contents*, and then to characterize these states *only* "extrinsically", in a manner which makes essential *ontological use* (as posited *causes*) of the notion of such color-contents, is clearly self-defeating. We must consequently think of our mythological theory as postulating a family of states which themselves instantiate the topology of the logical space which colors are conceived of, *qua* contents, as occupying. Unlike the extrinsic (causal) characterization, this *intrinsic* characterization makes sense even if there are no color-contents, since such contents do not enter into this account ontologically, as the causes of sensory states, but only via their *concepts*, as paradigms for analogical concept formation. The upshot is that, within the manifest image, the concept of a sensory state, unlike the concept of an occurrent thinking, is not the functional concept of a role-player but the contentual concept of something with a determinate intrinsic character. It is sensory states *thus* conceived, then, which must be accommodated within the scientific image if the two images are to be fused, and this accommodation *cannot* be simply a matter of leaving it entirely to the scientific image to supply structural, ontological (intrinsic) specifications for items conceived within the manifest image purely functionally (extrinsically).

When we now turn to the emerging scientific image with which this purified manifest-image conception of sensations is to be fused, what we note first and foremost is that the *persons*, who within the manifest image are the single, basic logical subjects of sensory states, come themselves to be reconceived as *systems* of more basic logical subjects (cells, neurons, molecules, atoms, etc.). Such a system of logical subjects is the *counterpart* within the scientific image of the single logical subject which is a perceiver within the manifest image. Let us write "perceiver-ctpt".

Such an ontological reconceptualization of the subjects of

sensory states demands an analogous reconceptualization of the states themselves, since "sensing $red_s ly$", for example, is *analytically* the state of a single logical subject. Let us put "senses-$red_s ly$-ctpt" for the state of a system, within the scientific image, which "corresponds" to the state of sensing $red_s ly$ attributed within the manifest image to the unitary person which, as conceived within the manifest image, that system *is*. In Sellars' account, then, colors have so far gone through *two* ontological relocations and also through *two* categorial transpositions, from:

	(i) is (made of) red	a content "in the world"
to	(ii) senses $red_s ly$	a state of a person-*qua*-perceiver (= single logical subject)
to	(iii) senses-$red_s ly$-ctpt	a state of a perceiver-ctpt (= system of logical subjects)

In this process, analogical concept formation has been invoked twice as well: once *within* the manifest image to form a "trans-categorial" analogy between the concept of a family of contents (the *basic* color concept) and the concept of a family of states; and once *between* the manifest and the scientific images to form a "trans-framework" analogy between the concept of a family of states of a single logical subject and the concept of a family of counterpart states which are states of the system of logical subjects which is the theoretical counterpart of that pre-theoretically unitary single subject.

Just as the logical topology (formal properties) of colors conceived as contents is carried over from (i) to (ii) in order that the appeal to the states (ii) be able to explain our possession of the concepts of contents (i), so, too, the logical topology of colors conceived as contents should be carried over *again* from (ii) to (iii) in order that these states, now theoretically reconceived, of persons, also theoretically reconceived, can explain *both* the states (ii) of persons pre-theoretically conceived *and* the success of our appeals to those states (ii) in explaining what they were introduced to explain, namely, our possession of the concepts of the contents (i). *But*, Sellars argues, we *cannot* carry over the logical topology of color-contents from (ii) to (iii) in this way *on metaphysical grounds*. No state of a system or multiplicity of basic logical subjects *could* instantiate the logical topology of color-contents. In particular, no state of a system of basic logical subjects could *be* ultimately homogeneous. Position (iii) must therefore be rejected. It is metaphysically incoherent. Counterparts to those sensory states of persons which, within the manifest image, are the ultimate ontological locus of, e.g., colors must be introduced into the scientific image by a different route.

Sellars' ground for his rejection of position (iii) is what he calls a "principle of pure *a priori* metaphysics", the "Strong Principle of Reducibility" (SPR):

> If an object is *in a strict sense* a system of objects, then every property of the object must consist in the fact that its constituents have such and such qualities and stand in such and such relations. ([9], p. 27)

The argument then runs as follows: Since a perceiver-ctpt *is* "in the strict sense" a system of objects, the SPR implies, with repect to the supposed property (state) of sensing-red$_s$ly-ctpt

> (e) some or all of the constituents of the perceiver-ctpt (the neurons, atoms, etc.) *themselves* have the property (or are in the state) of sensing-red$_s$ly-ctpt,
>
> or (f) the perceiver-ctpt's being in that state (having that property) is "analyzable" ("without residue") into the atoms, etc. having *other* properties and standing in certain relations.

Since "sensing-red$_s$ly-ctpt" was to be the scientific image analogue of the state "sensing red$_s$ly" of manifest image *persons*, (e) is ruled out. But, since "sensing-red$_s$ly-ctpt" was to *instantiate* the logical topology of colors-conceived-as-contents, (f) is ruled out as well — for the *ultimate homogeneity* of a state or property of a system *logically* cannot be a matter of the objects composing that system having, separately, certain properties and standing in certain relations. Position (iii) is thus incompatible with the Strong Principle of Reducibility.

Nor can it be argued that the UH of colors-*qua*-contents is a mere *appearance*. For, to put it briefly, what our hypothetical postulations have been designed from the outset to *explain* is just *the appearance of UH*. The explanations here operate in a "transcendental mode". What was to be accounted for was the fact that we possess the *concepts* of "features" or "aspects" of experience or the world which are UH. Position (iii) proposes to supply such an explanation against the background of a set of ontological posits which imply that *literally nothing* actually *instantiates* the (formal, topological) property of UH. But, argues Sellars, if nothing actually *is*, in some sense, an UH continuum, then nothing can be *mistaken* for such a continuum either, for to mistake something for a continuum requires that we already possess the concept of such a continuum. While our possession of the very concept of a multiplicity of discrete entities *can* ultimately be explained by appeal to actualities which *are* continuua (locally qualitatively differentiated, for example), our possession of the very concept of an ultimately homogeneous continuum itself *cannot* in the last analysis analogously be explained by appeal to actualities which are *not* (or do not include) such homogeneous continuua.

The upshot, Sellars concludes, is that the fusion of the manifest and scientific images at the point of sensations will require the postulation of a further family of *basic entities* which themselves actually *do* individually ontologically instantiate the logical topology of colors-*qua*-contents, i.e., which themselves actually *are* UH. For reasons external to the philosophy of mind (deriving, instead, from the metaphysical problematic of constancy and change), Sellars foresees here another categorial transposition as well. Such "sensa", as he calls them, will need, on his view, to be postulated, not in the category of substances or states of substances but rather as "absolute processes", as, for example, "reddings". A perceiver-ctpt within the scientific image will thus ultimately emerge as conceived as a "harmony" or system of diverse such "absolute processes" ("reddings", "electronings", etc.), only *some* of which are "sensa". The final ontological locus of sensation (and color) within the scientific image will thus be not (iii) but

    (iv)   is a redding   a *constituent* (not: state) of a perceiver-ctpt (= system or "harmony" of diverse such "absolute processes")

The scientific image as we have it today, in other words, is arguably *incomplete*. Fusing the manifest image fact of sensory consciousness with the scientific image, on Sellars' view, will turn out to demand *more science* — that is, the postulation of further basic constitutive entities, parallel to the postulations of, e.g., electrons required to integrate the pre-theoretical appearances of what turned out to be electromagnetic phenomena into the mechanical world-picture of Newtonian physics. Sensa, thus understood, will be what Sellars calls physical$_1$ (belonging in the space-time network) but not physical$_2$ ("definable in terms of theoretical primitives adequate to describe completely the actual states ... of the universe before the appearance of life"). ([21], p. 252; cf. [7], [18], [9], [8]) They would need to be appealed to only in explanatory accounts of the behavioral competences (cognitive and non-cognitive) of those systems of basic entities which are sentient organisms. This, however, would be no more mysterious — and would no more support a *Cartesian* dualism — than the fact that electrical charge must be appealed to in explanatory accounts of lightning bolts but not of the motions of the planets.

There remains only the question of accommodating volitions, intentions, and the like — in short, of accommodating *practical* cognitions, "reason in its practical employment" — within the synoptic stereoscopic vision of the fused images. This is, in effect, the most crucial moment of Sellars' three-part story, for it amounts, in the end, to the question of whether it is possible to put *persons* into the scientific image, to

> the task of showing that categories pertaining to man as a *person* who finds himself confronted by standards (ethical, logical, etc.) which often conflict with his desires and impulses, and to which he may or may not conform, can be reconciled with the idea that man is what science says he is. ([9], p. 38)

The reason is that

> to think of a featherless biped as a person is to construe its behaviour in terms of actual or potential membership in an

embracing group each member of which thinks of itself as a member of the group. Let us call such a group a 'community'. ([9], p. 39)

Now, the fundamental principles of a community, which define what is 'correct' or 'incorrect', 'right' or 'wrong', 'done' or 'not done', are the most general common *intentions* of that community with respect to the behaviour of members of the group. It follows that to recognize a featherless biped or dolphin or Martian as a person requires that one think thoughts of the form, 'We (one) shall do (or abstain from doing) actions of kind A in circumstances of kind C'. To think thoughts of this kind is not to *classify* or *explain*, but to *rehearse an intention*.

Thus the conceptual framework of persons is the framework in which we think of one another as sharing the community intentions which provide the ambience of principles and standards ... within which we live our own individual lives. A person can almost be defined as a being that has intentions. ([9], pp. 39-40)

The challenge that this last accommodation poses to the fusion of the two images is radically different in kind from those already discussed. It is not, so to speak, an *ontological* challenge. Ontologically, indeed, intentions and volitions just *are* thoughts (occurrent thinkings) — although they are thoughts of a special (functional) kind. They are *practical* thinkings, which is to say that their unique functional role within the total cognitive-*cum*-behavioral economy of a person is to be understood in terms of their special relationship to *conduct*. (Analogous to the way in which the unique functional role of those cognitions which are perceptual takings or judgments is understood in terms of their special relationships to *sensations*, i.e., their status as non-inferential *responses*.) Sellars signals this unique conduct-structuring role by a contrived use of the auxiliary 'shall' as an operator on logico-semantically classified thinkings. (Categorical) intendings are time-determinate future-tensed shall-thinkings:

(g)   Shall (I will do X at t),

and volitions ("acts of will") are those special cases of intendings in which the time-determination is the immediate present:

(h)   Shall (I will *now* do X).

Such practical thinkings mediate between reasoning and conduct. They are related to the former by a single principle which unites practical and theoretical reasonings:

If ⌜p⌝ imples ⌜q⌝ then ⌜Shall(p)⌝ implies ⌜Shall(q)⌝.

And they are related to the latter by being caught up in a network of (acquired) causal propensities which guarantee, roughly, that intentions of the form (g) regularly give rise *at t* to volitions of the form (h), which, in turn, (barring paralysis and the like) regularly give rise then and there to those bodily movements which (further circumstances being suitable) *are* the initial stages of a doing of X. (For detailed accounts of these interfaces, see [22], [23], and [24], Ch. VII.)

The manifest image concept of an intention or a volition — of a practical thinking — is thus again the concept of a causally mediating logico-semantic role-player, and thus again not the concept of something with a determinate intrinsic character, given *propria persona*. The *ontological* accommodation of practical thinkings within the scientific image consequently proceeds as does the accommodation of thinkings in general — an emerging scientific understanding progressively supplying structural (e.g., neurophysiological) ontological cash to back the purely functional promissory-note conceptions of the manifest image.

But here, Sellars insists, such an accommodation cannot be the end of the story. Taking seriously the idea that the scientific image purports to be a *complete* image of man-in-the-world and presents itself as (potentially) an *alternative* to the manifest image requires that the categories pertaining to persons reappear within the scientific image *as such*. To be authentically a candidate to *replace* the manifest image — "the framework in terms of which...man first encounters himself" — the scientific image must itself become a framework within which man can continue to encounter himself *as man*. Thus, Sellars concludes,

> to complete the scientific image we need to enrich it *not* with more ways of saying what is the case, but with the language of community and individual intentions, so that by construing the actions we intend to do and the circumstances in which we intend to do them in scientific terms, we *directly* relate the world as conceived by scientific theory to our purposes, and make it *our* world and no longer an alien appendage to the world in which we do our living. ([9], p. 40)

Unlike the framework of thoughts and sensations, "the conceptual framework of persons [*as such*] is not something that needs to be *reconciled with* the scientific image, but rather something to be *joined* to it." ([9], p. 40). Such a "direct incorporation of the scientific image into our way of life" is something which, from our present perspective, we can only speculatively imagine. But, with the possibility of *ontologically* accommodating within the scientific image the thoughts and feelings of the organisms which *are* thinking and feeling persons now argumentatively secure, no irreducible dualism remains to stand as an in-principle obstacle to our imagining it. And *that* possibility, in the end, stands as the strength and culmination of the systematic synoptic vision which is Wilfrid Sellars' philosophy of mind.

BIBLIOGRAPHY

By WILFRID SELLARS

[1]   Metaphysics and the Concept of a Person. In K. Lambert (Ed.), *The Logical Way of Doing Things*, pp. 219-252. New Haven, Conn.: Yale University Press, 1969. Reprinted in [25]. Page citations to [25].

[2]   ...this I or we or it (the thing) which thinks.... *Proceedings of the American Philosophical Association* 44 (1970-1): 5-31. Reprinted in [25]. Page citations to [25].

[3]   Some Remarks on Kant's Theory of Experience. *The Journal of Philosophy* 64 (1967): 633-647. Reprinted in [25]. Page citations to [25].

[4]   Abstract Entities. *The Review of Metaphysics* 16 (1962-1963): 627-671. Reprinted in [26].

[5]   Towards a Theory of the Categories. In L. Foster and J.W. Swanson (Eds.), *Experience and Theory*, pp. 55-78. Amherst: University of Massachusetts Press, 1970. Reprinted in [25].

[6]   Empiricism and Abstract Entities. In P.A. Schilpp (Ed.), *The Philosophy of Rudolf Carnap*, pp. 431-68. LaSalle, Ill.: Open Court, 1963. Reprinted in [25].

[7]   Empiricism and the Philosophy of Mind. *Minnesota Studies in the Philosophy of Science, vide* [21], pp. 253-329.

[8]   The Identity Approach to the Mind-Body Problem. *The Review of Metaphysics* 18 (1964-1966): 430-451. Reprinted in [26]. Page citations to [26].

[9]   Philosophy and the Scientific Image of Man. In R. Colodny (Ed.), *Frontiers of Science and Philosophy*, pp. 35-78. Pittsburgh: University of Pittsburgh Press, 1962. Reprinted in [27]. Page citations to [27].

[10]   Language as Thought and Communication. *Philosophy and Phenomenological Research* 29 (1968-1969): 506-527. Reprinted in [25].

[11]   Notes on Intentionality. *The Journal of Philosophy* 61 (1964): 655-665. Reprinted in [26].

[12]   Meaning as Functional Classification. *Synthese* 27 (1974): 417-437.

[13]   Some Reflections on Language Games. *Philosophy of Science* 21 (1954): 204-228. Reprinted in revised form in [27].

[14]   *Naturalism and Ontology*. Reseda, Calif.: Ridgeview Publishing Company, 1979.

[18]   Phenomenalism. In H.N. Castañeda (Ed.), *Intentionality, Minds, and Perception*, pp. 215-274. Detroit: Wayne State University Press, 1967. Originally printed in [27].

[19]   The Adverbial Theory of the Objects of Sensation. *Metaphilosophy* 6 (1975): 144-160.

[20]   Seeing, Sense Impressions, and Sensa: A Reply to Cornman. *The Review of Metaphysics* 24 (1970-1): 391-447.

[21]   The Concept of Emergence (with Paul Meehl). In H. Feigl and M. Scriven (Eds.), *Minnesota Studies in the Philosophy of Science*, Vol. 1, pp. 239-253. Minneapolis: University of Minnesota Press, 1956.

[22]   Imperatives, Intentions, and the Logic of 'Ought'. *Methodos* 8 (1956): 228-268.

[23]   Actions and Events. *Nous* 7 (1973): 179-202. Reprinted in [25].

[24]   *Science and Metaphysics: Variations on Kantian Themes*. London: Routledge and Kegan Paul, 1967.

[25]   *Essays in Philosophy and its History*. Dordrecht: Reidel, 1975.

[26]   *Philosophical Perspectives*. Springfield, Ill.: Charles Thomas, 1967.

[27]   *Science, Perception, and Reality*. London: Routledge and Kegan Paul, 1963.

About WILFRID SELLARS

Essays cited

[15]   Cornman, J. W. Sellars, Scientific Realism, and Sensa. *The Review of Metaphysics* 23 (1969-70): 417-451.
[16]   Delaney, C. F. Sellars' Grain Argument. *The Australasian Journal of Philosophy* 50 (1972): 14-16.
[17]   Hooker, C.A. Sellars' Argument for the Inevitability of the Secondary Qualities. *Philosophical Studies* 32 (1977): 335-348.

Books

Castañeda, H.-N. (Ed.), *Action, Knowledge, and Reality: Studies in Honor of Wilfrid Sellars*. Indianapolis: Bobbs-Merrill, 1975.
Delaney, C.F., et al. *The Synoptic Vision*. Notre Dame, Ind.: University of Notre Dame Press, 1977. Contains an exhaustive primary and secondary bibliography through 1975.
Pitt, J.C. (Ed.), *The Philosophy of Wilfrid Sellars: Queries and Extensions*. Dordrecht: Reidel, 1978.

NOTE

Sellars extends and clarifies his account of (intentional) thinking in "Mental Events", *Philosophical Studies* 39 (1981): 325-345. His Carus Lectures ("Is Consciousness Physical?", "Naturalism and Process", and "The Lever of Archimedes" – published in *The Monist* 64 (1981): 3-90) offer a detailed elaboration and supplementary argumentative support of his complex theory of sensation. The same issue of *The Monist* contains preliminary responses, by, *inter alia*, Daniel Dennett and Roderick Firth, to the issues raised in these lectures. A subsequent issue – *The Monist* 65 (1982) – is devoted entirely to the philosophy of Wilfrid Sellars. For a further discussion of Sellars' views on sensation, see there especially this author's essay "The Place of Color in the Scheme of Things", pp. 315-335.

Abbreviations used by some contributors

SPR   =   strong principle of reducibility

t.t.s.   =   total temporary state

UH   =   ultimately homogeneous qualities

Index of names

Abraham, 176–178
Adler, M. 240
Albert, H. 393, 395, 414
Alexander, P. 195, 197
Allemann, B. 287, 317
Alston, W.P. 82, 95, 199
Anaximander, 310
Anscombe, G.E.M. 139, 209, 210, 239, 324
Antoni, C. 315
Apel, K.-O. 387–398, 401, 413, 414.
Applegarth, A. 192
Aquila, R.E. 238, 241, 252, 266
Archimedes, 376
Aristotle, 107, 110, 111, 115, 135, 136, 144, 159, 161, 225, 226, 240, 241, 288–290, 292, 297– 304, 306–309, 312, 373, 395, 418, 420–422
Armstrong, D. 4, 5, 49–52, 55, 56, 60, 69, 70
Arnaud, R.B. 238
Audi, R. 195, 196
Austin, J.L. 81
Ayer, A.J. 81, 380, 383, 384
Axelos, K. 317

Bain, A. 363

Baker, G. 322
Ballard, B. 315
Bartels, M. 317
Bartuschat, W. 125, 126, 130
Basch, M. 186–188, 216
Bausola, A. 225, 226
Beaufret, J. 315
Beckermann, A. 399
Beloff, J. 77
Bennett, J. 37, 217
Bergman, H. 227, 238, 239
Bergmann, G. 227, 228, 241, 242
Berk, U. 395
Berkeley, G. 87, 253, 254, 256, 428
Bernfeld, S. 217
Bernstein, R.J. 54, 178, 381, 389
Bertilsson, M. 392
Biemel, W. 287, 315
Birault, H. 287
Blackwell, B. 376, 377
Bloor, D. 186
Boden, M. 216
Boehm, R. 106, 249, 317
Boer, T. de, 240
Bogen, J. 322
Böhler, D. 409, 415
"Boltrafio", 206
Bolzano, B. 252, 268, 269

Böök, L. 405
"Botticelli", 206
Bradley, M. 51
Brandt, R. 194
Brenner, C. 196
Brentano, F. 2, 216, 217, 223–
    242, 249, 257, 274, 289–291
Brentano, J.C.M. 223
Breuer, J. 203, 204, 207
Broad, C.D. 112
"Brownson", 16–18, 20, 21, 31
Bucher, A. 316
Butler, J. 13, 14, 16, 26, 28, 39

Cäcelie, Frau, 204
Cairns, D. 249
Campbell, D.T. 379
Campbell, K. 45, 70–73, 75, 76
Canaletto, A. 369
Caputo, J. 317
Carnap, R. 282, 368
Carr, D. 238, 252
Carrella, M. 196
Carterette, E.C. 82
Castañeda, H.-N. 82, 226, 439
Cavell, S. 181, 322, 328
Cheney, J. 195, 200
Chiodi, P. 288
Chisholm, R.M. 26, 27, 28, 30, 34,
    35, 37, 41n., 82, 83, 88, 96,
    226, 227, 229–235, 237, 240,
    242
Chomsky, N. 216
Cioffi, F. 196, 198, 199, 201, 202,
    208
Clark, R. 82
Climacus, Johannes, 162
Coburn, R.C. 19
Cohen, L.J. 233
Collins, A. 195, 197
Condillac, E.B. de, 148, 149

Constable, J. 369
Cornman, J. 82, 425
Cousineau, R.H. 318
Courturier, F. 315
Curley, E.M. 109–112, 114
Currie, G. 45

Dallmayr, W. 389, 395
Darwin, C. 363, 378, 379
Davidson, D. 5, 60–64, 134, 186
Declève, H. 317
Dedekind, R. 213
Deely, J.N. 238
Delaney, C.F. 425, 439
Demske, J.M. 287
Dennett, D.C. 230, 231, 241
Derrida, J. 252, 273, 276–278,
    316
Descartes, R. 1–4, 7, 46, 81–85,
    89, 113, 134–137, 139, 141,
    142, 145, 148, 159, 194, 253,
    281, 293, 326, 368, 418, 419,
    422, 428, 434
Deutscher, M. 20, 204, 217
Devitt, M. 45, 48
Dewey, J. 363–366, 372, 376,
    381–383
Dietrichson, P. 178
Dijn, H. de, 123
Dilman, I. 196
Dilthey, W. 294
Doherty, J. 318
Donogan, A. 109
"Dora", 208, 209
Doz, A. 108
Dretske, F.I. 89
Dreyfus, H.L. 249, 251, 260, 261,
    262, 265, 267, 272, 273, 278,
    280
Dufrenne, M. 317
Dummett, M. 92, 101

Eccles, J.C. 77
Edelson, M. 216
Edwards, J. 382
Elliston, F. 252
Elrod, J.W. 158
Embree, L.E. 250, 279

Fawkes, Guy, 19
Fechner, T. 186, 187
Feick, H. 315
Feigl, H. 45–48, 52, 59, 65
Feldman, F. 68
Feuerbach, L.A. 175
Feyerabend, P.K. 52, 54
Fichte, J.G. 139
Field, H. 94, 230, 231
Findlay, J.N. 240, 269, 271, 277
Fingarette, H. 212
Fink, E. 249
Firth, R. 81, 82, 85, 88
Fischer, K. 240
Fløistad, G. 122, 315, 317
Fodor, J.A. 55–59, 63
Fogelin, R. 322, 333–335
Føllesdal, D. 238, 249–253, 255,
    257–263, 265, 266, 268, 269,
    272–280
Fox, M. 196
Franklin, B. 65
Franzen, W. 315
Frege, G. 23, 77, 160, 231, 238,
    250–252, 264–269, 272, 273,
    276, 283, 322, 325, 326
Freud, S. 2, 3, 127, 129, 130, 143,
    174, 185, 186, 186n., 187,
    187n., 188–203, 203n., 204–
    207, 207n., 208–210, 210n.,
    211–217
Frings, M. 315, 318

Gadamer, H.-G. 287, 315, 402,
    409–411
Galatzer-Levy, R. 186, 192, 193
Gale, R. 22
Geach, P. 20, 22–24
Gebhard, C. 121, 123
Gelven, M. 316
George, R. 226
Gethmann, C.F. 318
Gethmann-Siefert, A. 318
Gill, M. 186, 189, 215
Gilson, L. 227
Gogh, V. van, 369
Goldberg, B. 335, 336
Goldman, A.I. 89
Golomb, J. 240
Goodman, N. 4, 6, 91, 363, 369,
    370, 375, 380
Gould, S.J. 311
Grice, H.P. 13, 15–18, 20, 25, 27,
    30, 33
Grossmann, R. 82, 241, 269–273
Guerault, M. 106–108, 123
Guilead, A. 287
Gurwitsch, A. 249–253, 256–265,
    269–271, 273–282
Guzzoni, G. 316

Habermas, J. 4, 380, 387–392,
    394, 397–401, 403–406,
    409–412, 414
Hacker, P.M.S. 322, 327, 339
Hall, H. 6, 9, 251, 350
Haller, R. 241
Hallett, G. 322
Hamlyn, D.W. 212, 239
Hampshire, S. 120, 130, 179–181
Hannay, A. 3, 183n.
Harman, G. 83, 84, 88, 89, 94
Harries, K. 317

Harris, E.E. 5, 113–115, 126
"Harry", 405 f.
Hedwig, K. 238
Hegel, G.W.F. 2–4, 113–115,
    133, 133n., 136, 140–146,
    148, 150–154, 159–170,
    174–179, 389
Heidegger, M. 2, 3, 6–9, 154,
    252, 287–297, 299–314,
    343, 357
Heidelberger, H. 88
Heraclitus, 192, 308, 310
Herder, J.G. von, 149, 150
Herrmann, Fr.W. von, 287, 316,
    318
Hintikka, J. 82, 252, 282, 283
Höffe, O. 399, 402, 403, 411, 413
Hölderlin, F. 307
Holmes, O.W., Jr. 363
Holt, R. 192
Hook, S. 382
Hooker, C.A. 425
Hopkins, J. 340
Horowitz, M. 192
Hume, D. 1, 13, 61, 83, 119, 120,
    127, 253, 254, 256, 281
Husserl, E. 2, 203, 238, 240,
    249–254, 256–283, 288,
    290–297, 304, 349, 352

Ihde, D. 316
IJsseling, S. 288, 318
Ilting, K.-H. 399, 402, 409
Isaac, 176

Jackson, F. 73, 82
Jaeger, P. 316
James, W. 363–365, 368, 370,
    373, 377–381, 383, 384
Joachim, H.H. 113

Joyce, J. 369

Kamlah, W. 412
Kant, I. 12, 109, 136, 138–140,
    143, 144, 187, 203, 208, 217,
    241, 321, 322, 327, 380, 381,
    392, 398, 418, 419, 420, 428
Kastil, A. 223–225
Kenny, A. 320, 322, 326, 330,
    332–334
Kierkegaard, S.A. 2, 3, 157–181,
    344
Kim, C.T. 239, 241
Kim, J. 194, 241
King, M. 287
Kisiel, T. 318
Klein, G. 186, 192
Kleist, H. von, 147
Klostermann, V. 315
Kneale, W. 238
Kockelmans, J. 287, 316
Körner, S. 241
Kotarbinski, T. 241
Kraus, T. 224, 225, 235, 238
Krell, D. 317
Kripke, S. 65–70
Kucklick, B. 383
Kuhn, T. 373
Küng, G. 240, 251

Lacan, J. 203
Lad, J.F. 251
Laffoucrière, O. 316
Landgrebe, L. 240
Langan, T. 287, 317
Laplace, P.S. 120, 121
Lehrer, K. 83, 86, 89
Leibniz, G.W. von, 30, 48, 52, 53,
    117, 136, 203
Leichti, T. 25

Levin, D.M. 67–69, 252
Levinas, E. 252, 287, 317
Lewis, C.I. 81, 100, 363, 364, 380
Lewis, D.K. 5, 25, 49, 50, 51, 52, 55, 56, 60, 69
Lisska, A. 238
Locke, J. 12–14, 16–20, 27, 30, 33, 37, 39, 41, 89, 149, 372, 382
Lorenzen, P. 412
Lotz, J.B. 317
Löwenstein, K. 216
Löwith, K. 287
Luce, D. 233
Lycan, W.G. 68, 69, 233, 331

MacAlister, L. 226, 235, 237, 238
McCarthy, T. 389, 395, 396
McCormick, P. 252, 316
Macdowell, J.A. 316
MacIntyre, A. 195
McIntyre, R. 251, 252, 264, 265, 277, 281–283
Mackey, L. 157, 158
Mackie, J.L. 89
Macomber, W.B. 318
McTaggart, J.E. 15
Magnus, B. 316
Malantschuk, G. 158
Malcolm, N. 319, 320, 339, 340
Mans, D. 400
Marbach, E. 252
Marks, C.E. 41
Marras, A. 226, 235, 237
Martin, C.B. 20, 204, 217
Marx, K. 170, 382
Marx, W. 287
Matte Blanco, I. 212–215
Mayer-Hillebrand, F. 223, 224, 227, 235, 241

Mead, G.H. 381
Mehta, J.L. 315
Meiner, F. 225
Meinong, A. 231, 241, 252, 268, 269, 270, 271, 272, 274
Mendel, G. 56
Merleau-Ponty, M. 2, 3, 5, 6, 8, 9, 280, 343–346, 348–361
Mijuskovic, B.L. 241
Mill, J.S. 269
Miller, I. 251, 280
Mischel, T. 200, 211, 212
Mohanty, J.N. 251, 266, 267, 269
Moore, G.E. 83, 109, 270, 421
Morris, C.W. 381–383, 391–393
Morrison, J.C. 239
Morscher, E. 227
Mullane, H. 195–197, 199
Murphey, M.G. 380, 381, 383

Naess, A. 121, 122
Nagel, T. 41, 73–76, 186, 186n.
Natanson, M. 252
Nestor, 13
Neu, J. 127–130
Newton, I. 434
Nicholson, G. 318
Nietzsche, F.W. 309
Nijhoff, M. 281
Noller, G. 318
Nordentoft, K. 174

O'Connor, D.J. 233
Odegard, D. 116–119
Oelmüller, W. 391, 393, 395, 396, 398, 410
Olafson, F. 252
Oppenheim, P. 4, 58

Palmer, R. 316
Palmier, J.-M. 318
Parfit, D. 31, 36–39
Parkinson, G.H.R. 117, 121,
    123–125
Parmenides, 310
Pastin, M. 2, 81, 82, 84, 86, 94, 95,
    97–99
Pears, D. 322, 329, 331, 334
Peirce, C.S. 4, 26, 89, 363–366,
    368, 372, 373, 376–381, 383,
    387, 389, 391–393, 397, 398,
    401, 412, 418
Penelhum, T. 36
Penso, G. 317
Perrotti, J. 318
Pitt, J.C. 439
Pivčević, E. 227, 252, 269, 277
Place, U.T. 45–50, 52, 57, 65
Plato, 77, 162, 231, 276, 309–312,
    352, 421, 424
Pöggeler, O. 287, 315, 316, 318
Pollock, J.L. 83, 88, 92, 94
Popper, K.R. 77, 124, 378, 379
Price, H.H. 83, 88
Prior, A.N. 37, 238
Prior, E. 45
Puccetti, R. 41
Pugliese, O. 287
Puntel, L.B. 399
Putnam, H. 4, 55–58, 60, 63, 92,
    101, 369, 371–373, 375

Quine, W.V.O. 6, 23, 64, 101, 363,
    365–371, 375, 376, 380
Quinton, A. 18, 240

Radden, J. 195–197, 202
Ramsey, F.P. 399
Rancurello, G. 226

Regina, U. 316
Reid, T. 14, 16, 83, 224, 238
Rescher, N. 84, 375–378, 383, 384
Rice, L.C. 119, 120
Richardson, W.J. 287, 318
Ricoeur, P. 202, 203, 203n.,
    204–207, 207n., 208n., 252,
    318
Roberts, R.C. 182
Robinson, L. 107
Rorty, A.O. 39, 41n.
Rorty, R. 52–55, 75, 84, 101, 187,
    187n.
Rosales, A. 318
Rosenberg, J.F. 3
Rosenblatt, A. 187, 192, 193, 217
Royce, J. 12, 364, 380
Rubinstein, B. 192, 206
Russell, B. 15, 60, 109, 231, 322
Ryle, G. 46, 49, 50, 179, 208,
    319, 424

Sallis, J. 315, 316
Sanford, D. 233
Sartre, J.P. 208, 344, 346, 349,
    358, 359, 361
Sass, H.-M. 315
Saussure, F. de, 207
Saw, R.L. 118, 119
Schafer, R. 186, 190, 191, 193,
    208–210, 212
Scheffler, I. 373–376, 381–384
Schelling, F.W.J. 139
Schimek, J. 207
Schmitt, R. 316
Schnädelbach, H. 396, 409
Schopenhauer, A. 139, 144, 154,
    322
Schrag, C. 318
Schröder, R. 267
Schrödinger, E. 7

Schulz, W. 287
Schur, M. 192
Schurmann, R. 317
Schutz, A. 249
Schwan, A. 318
Scott, C. 315
Scruton, R. 238
Searle, J. 390
Seidel, I. 288
Sellars, W. 3, 82, 85, 86, 89, 94,
    231, 417–429, 431–437
Severino, E. 316
Shaffer, J. 210
Sheehan, T.J. 3, 317
Sheridan, G. 55
Sherover, C. 317
Shimony, A. 379
Shoemaker, S. 12, 14–18, 20, 22,
    24, 26–31, 33–36, 38
Shope, R.K. 3, 187n., 189,
    192–194, 200, 202–206,
    206n., 207–210, 217
"Signorelli", 195–197, 206
Silverstein, A. 216
Sini, C. 316
Skagestad, P. 4, 373
Skinner, B. 210
Skirbekk, G. 4
Sklar, L. 94
Sleigh, R. 233
Slote, M. 217
Smart, J.J.C. 4, 45, 46, 48–52, 56,
    65, 69
Smith, B. 252
Smith, D.W. 2, 251, 252, 264,
    265, 277, 281–283
Smith, J.E. 383
Smythe, T. 194, 195
Socrates, 162, 163, 179, 287, 310,
    425
Sokolowski, R. 252, 281
Solomon, R.C. 188, 192–194,

239, 266–268
Spaemann, R. 401
Sperry, R.W. 73, 75
Spiegelberg, H. 227, 235, 237, 238,
    288
Spinoza, B. 1–3, 5, 7, 105–130
Spriggle, T.L.S. 111–113, 117
Srzednicki, J. 226, 241
Stampe, D. 208
Stanescu, H. 216
Starr, D. 317
Stassen, M. 316
Stine, G. 89
Stoa, 268
Strawson, P.F. 160, 319, 399, 421
Stroud, B. 4
Suppes, P. 216
Swanson, D. 189, 192, 193

Taminiaux, J. 317
Taylor, C. 3, 135, 139, 142, 153
Taylor, M.C. 158, 160, 179
Terrell, B. 2, 239, 241
Thalberg, I. 189
Thayer, H.S. 363, 364, 380, 381,
    383, 384
Theristes, 13
Thickstun, J. 187, 192, 193, 217
Thomas, St. 226, 238, 312
Thompson, J. 183n.
Toulin, H. 405
Toulmin, S. 401
Tragesser, R.S. 252
Tugendhat, E. 252, 273–277, 318
Twardowski, K. 252, 268–271,
    274

Unger, P. 83
Urmson, J.O. 233

Vail, L. 318
Vattimo, G. 288, 315
Verdi, G. 215
Verra, V. 317
Vesey, G. 41n.
Vico, G. 138
Vitiello, V. 318
Vitiis, P. 316
Volkmann-Schluck, K.H. 287, 316
Volpi, F. 317
Vycinas, V. 288

Wagner, R. 215
Wahl, J. 160, 287
Wallerstein, J. 193
Warren, H. 216
Wellmer, A. 395, 408

White, M.G. 382
Wiggins, D. 20–22, 24, 26, 28, 30, 31, 37
Williams, B. 18–20, 22, 24, 28, 31–36, 136
Williams, M. 84, 89, 94, 101
Wilson, N.L. 64
Wiplinger, F. 287, 316
Wisdom, J. 208
Wittgenstein, L. 2, 3, 12, 14, 15, 17, 35, 46, 81, 94, 109, 139, 150, 179–181, 238, 319–340, 373, 391
Wolf, K. 241
Wolfson, H.A. 107, 111
Wollheim, R. 201, 202, 233
Wright, G.H. von, 5

Zimmermann, M. 318

Index of subjects

Abortion, 11
Abschattungen, 275
Absolute, 177 f.
Abstraction
    theory of, 224
Acceptance
    perceptual, 83
Access
    and excess, 305 ff.
    privileged, 423, 425, 427
Accident, 242
Actions
    causal theory of, 136
    vide Causation
    conditional, 208 f.
    directed, 137, 141
    effective, 152 f.
    expressive, 149, 152 f.
    fantasizing of, 209
    logical, 423
    obsessive, 200
    philosophy of, 133 ff.
    qualitative theory of, 136 ff.,
        140 f., 146 ff., 153 ff.
    scene of, 186 f.
    semantic, 423
    trans-individual, 153
    vs non-action, 134 f.
Activity, 133, 139 ff.

bodily, 149
conceptual, 143
expressive, 149
intentional, 211
knowledge as cognitive, 3
of formulating, 144
of self-formulation, 145
of the self, 139
transformation of, 141
unconscious, 141
unreflecting, 147
Acts, 239
    vide Actions
    de re vs de dicto mental, 282
    direct intentional *vs* reflective
        intentional, 295
    mental, 253, 282
    of consciousness, 253, 276
    of will, 436
    speech, 424
Actuality, 140
Adumbrations, 275
Affectus, 126 ff.
    vide Emotions
Affirmation, 239
Agency, 137, 140, 152, 168
Akrasia, 172
    vide self-deception
Aletheia, 290, 292, 302, 308,
    310 f.

vide Appearance; Appropriation;
    Disclosure; Truth
Alreadiness, 306, 309
Analogies, 427
    extrinsic causal, 427
    transframework, 431
    transcategorial, 431
Analysis
    causal, 49 ff., 71
    linguistic, 239, 241
    micro-, 57
Annihilation
    self-, 163
Antedetermination, 121
Anthropocentrism, 311
Anthropology
    existential, 314
Anxiety, 171, 179, 199 f.
    signal, 211 f.
Appearance, 250, 256, 308, 311
    vide Aletheia
Apperception, 224
    immanent, 290
Appetite, 125
Appropriation, 290, 295, 304 ff.,
    308 f.
    vide Aletheia
    and metaphysics, 309 ff.
Argument
    Nonduplication –, 31
    private-language –, 326 ff.
    Reduplication –, 19 ff., 24 ff.
As
    apophantic, 303
    – for, 303
    hermeneutical, 303 f.
Ascent
    semantic, 230
Associations
    free, 205
Assurance
    self-, 161, 166, 168

Atomism, 151 f.
    logical, 109, 112
Attention, 198 f., 210
Attitudes
    vide Cognitions
    emotional, 239
    propositional, 231, 320, 427
Attributes, 106 ff.
    theory of, 106 ff.
    of extension, 107, 110, 112, 119
Awareness, 150, 165
    preconscious, 211
    reflective, 153
    self-, 143, 148, 418
Axioms, 109

Bats, 76
Bedeutung, 258, 265, 273, 276
    vide Reference; Meaning;
        Noema; Sense and Reference;
        Sinn
Befindlichkeit, 296
Behaviour
    neurotic, 202
Behaviourism, 46 f., 319, 330, 339
    verbal, 424
Being, 228
    vide Ontology
    as appropriation, 305
    forgetting, 311 ff.
    – in-the-world, 295
    meaning of, 289 ff., 304 f.
    of intentionality, 292
    situated, 6
    symmetrical, 213 ff.
    towards death, 306
Beliefs, 50, 55, 62 f., 230, 252,
    282, 352
    unconscious, 195, 197, 200 f.,
    211
Bewandtnisganzheit, 8

Body
   and mind, 1 f., 4 ff., 12, 20,
      106, 111 f., 115 f., 127,
      229, 241, 348, 315 ff.,
      422
   identity of, 35
   livèd, 5 f., 9, 344 ff.
   mobility of, 345, 348
   soul and, 144, 165 f., 170 f.
   spatiality of, 345
   — transfer, 32 ff.
Brain
   mind and, 45 ff., 113
   split, 41, 74
Bundle theory, 1, 13 f., 76, 256

Camshafts, 57, 59, 60
Care, 305 f.
   bivalent structure of, 305 f.
   temporal structure of, 306
Castration, 199 f.
Categories, 160
Causality, 61 ff.
   Principle of the nomological
      character of, 61 ff.
Causation, 21, 40
   final, 125
   of human actions, 120
Causes
   efficient, 125
   final, 125
   mental, 151, 209 f.
   psychological, 134
Certainty, 82, 168
Character
   noematic, 255
   thetic, 258
Charity
   Principle of, 64
Choice, 173 ff., 357 ff.
Classification

of mental phenomena, 226, 229,
   239
Cogitans, res
   vide Res cogitans
Cogitatione, 418 422 f.
   vide Cognitions; Consciousness;
      Mind; *Res cogitans*; Thought
Cognitions, 418, 422, 427 f.
   vide Consciousness; Mind;
      Res cogitans; Thought
   perceptual, 85
Coherence, 82
Coherentism, 84, 86
   second-order, 94
Colour, 48, 51 f., 428 ff.
   concept of, 428 ff.
   — content, 428 ff.
   logical topology of, 429 ff.
Communication
   double structure of, 391
Community
   Rylean, 424
Competence
   communicative, 394, 399 ff.
Completeness
   epistemic, 96 ff.
Comportment
   everydayness *vs* theoretical,
      293 f.
Computer, 58
   simulation, 216
Conatus, 120, 122 ff.
Concept
   — formation, 4
   of colour, 428 ff.
Conception
   abstract, 240
Conditionals
   fallacy of irrelevant, 208
Conflict, 211
Conscience
   call of, 295, 306

454   *Index of subjects*

individual, 175
Consciousness
  vide Cognitions; Intentionality;
    Mind; Noema; Thought
  act of, 253, 276
  co-, 74
  continuity of, 12
  directedness of, 249, 253,
    257 ff.
  intentional, 249
  noetic, 224
  objects of, 254
  of identity, 253, 256, 281
  perceptual, 353
  pure, 293 ff., 346
  reflective, 146
  secondary, 240
  self-, 147 f.
  sensory, 224
  transcendental, 293
  unhappy, 160
  unity of, 229, 241
Consensus, 388 ff.
  discursive, 391, 402 ff.
  rational, 388, 392 ff.
  the concept of, 396, 400, 411 ff.
  true, 398
Content, 428 ff.
  act-, 274
  colour, 428 ff.
  ideal, 273, 294
  intentional, 274
  mental, 224, 235
  predicate, 264
  real, 274
Context
  grammatical, 238
Contingency, 68
  illusion of, 67 f.
Continuity
  psychological, 36, 39 f.
  spatio-temporal –, 20 f.

Corpus callosum, 73
Correctness
  truth as, 275
Criterion
  logical – of intentionality, 232
  of intentionality, 233
  of the mental, 229
Criterionism, 330
Criticism
  meaning –, 393
Cupiditas, 126 f.

Daring
  act of, 168
Darwinism
  methodological, 378 f.
  thesis –, 378 f.
Dasein, 3, 6, 287 f.
Das Man, 295
Data
  hyletic, 278 ff.
  sense, 250, 278 ff.
Death
  being towards, 306
Deception
  self-, 172, 196, 210, 212, 346,
    358, 412
Decision, 11, 168
Definition
  genetic, 123
Denkbestimmungen, 160
Dependence
  causal, 110
  logical, 110
Descriptions
  absolute, 136
  Australian, 69
Designators
  non-rigid, 65 ff.
  rigid, 65 ff.
Desires, 63, 127, 134, 137, 141 ff.,

147, 151, 206, 208 f., 211, 230,
320
vide Wishes
first-order, 202
higher-order, 202
strength of, 208
unconscious, 197, 207
Despair, 168 ff., 179
Destruction
self-, 130, 168
Desymbolization, 206
Determinism, 53 f., 120 ff., 190,
358
hard, 54
Development
historical, 153
Diairesis, 302 ff., 306
Dialogue, 4
vide Discourse
Directedness
vide Intentionality
co-, 265, 281
of actions, 137, 141
of consciousness, 249, 253,
257 ff.
of mental phenomena, 238
upon objects, 235, 291 f.
Disappearance, 53 ff., 75
Disclosure, 155, 289, 291 f., 298 ff.
vide Aletheia; Appearance;
Appropriation, Truth
kinetic structure of, 307 ff.
levels of, 302
linguistic, 300 ff.
phenomenology of, 300
self-, 298, 306 f.
world-, 303 f., 307
Discourse, 401 ff.
situatedness of, 402 f.
Discovery
contingent associated, 67 ff.
Discrimination, 89 ff.

Dispositions, 49
Dividing
vide Diairesis
Dolor, 128
Doubt
method of, 83
Dream
Physicalist, 48, 59
Dreams
as rebus, 206n.
healthy, 204
interpretation of, 188, 194, 198
latent, 186 f., 212
manifest, 186 f.
meaning of, 198
Dualism, 5, 56, 70 ff., 135, 137 f.,
141, 159, 186, 278 f., 330, 351,
357, 381, 434, 437
anti-, 135
interactionist, 76 ff.
Dynamis, 307 f.

Ego
empirical, 294
pure, 2, 13, 34
transcendental, 296
Eidos, 298, 301, 311 f.
Embodiment, 145, 149, 166 f.
principle of, 142, 145
Emotions, 126 f.
active, 129
cognitive, 374 f.
passive, 129
Empiricism, 1, 12, 13, 109, 134 ff.,
141, 147, 253, 365, 381
logical, 365, 368
Encroachment, 353 f., 356
Energy
conservation laws of psychic,
192
of the unconscious, 194

456 *Index of subjects*

psychic, 109 ff., 199
Entia irrealia, 226
Entschlossenheit, 313
Epiphenomenalism, 70 ff., 76
Episodes
    inner, 423 ff.
Episteme, 298 f.
Epistemology, 228
Ereignis, 290, 304, 308, 313
    vide Appropriation
Eros, 190
Erschlossenheit, 8
Essence, 109, 111, 123 f., 160 f.,
    169, 266, 296
    act-, 266
    of an instinct, 191
Ethics, 226, 228
    objective, 152
    teleological suspension of, 176,
        178
Events
    mental, 134 f., 147 f., 228, 230
Everydayness, 294 f., 297
Evidence, 224, 226, 239
    theory of, 224
Evidenz, 240
    vide Evidence
Excess
    and access, 305 ff.
Existence, 2, 109, 111, 162 f.,
    166 f., 169, 296
    historical, 294
    intentional, 239
    self-contained, 165
Existentialism, 343 f., 381
Existentiality, 305
Experiences
    co-personal, 13
    direct, 215
    mental, 290 f.
    momentary, 13
    perceptual, 348 ff., 358 ff.

sensory, 81 ff.
situated, 350
Explanations
    best, 89
    psychological, 134
    teleological, 125
Extension
    and thought, 110
    attributes of, 107, 110, 112, 119
Externalization, 166

Facticity, 294 ff., 300, 305 f.
    vs pure consciousness, 294 ff.
Fact, 228
Factor
    motor-, 191
Facts
    accidentally general, 110
    nomological, 110, 114
    singular, 110
Faith, 179
    vide Beliefs
    vide Self-deception
    bad, 346
    knight of, 176 ff.
    unintelligibility, 178
Fallacy
    ceteris paribus, 208
    conditional, 208
    of irrelevant conditionals, 208
    phenomenological 47 f.
Fallenness, 295, 306, 312 f.
    vs apodictic self-givenness, 295
Fantasy, 206, 217
    space of, 206
Fear, 199
    quasi-, 36
Feeling, 127
    intellect and, 144
    nontactual, 117
    perspective, 374

Feels
   vide Feeling; Sensation
   raw, 47 f., 418, 422
   rawness of raw, 426
Finitude, 106 f., 164, 166, 169,
   306, 411
Firth-Bosanquet, 94
Fluid
   coloric, 52 f.
Forgetting, 195
Form
   vide Ideas; Mind
   and matter, 135, 144
Formation
   concept-, 4
Formulating
   activity of, 144
Formulation, 145
   activity of self-, 145
   self-, 145
Foundationalism, 82 f., 96, 277
   first-order, 94
Foundations
   psychological, 229
Fragments
   synsemantical, 234, 236 f.
Freedom, 11, 121, 122, 139,
   164 f., 169, 171 f., 350, 351,
   357 ff., 401 f.
Functionalism, 55 f., 60 f., 64, 71,
   75
Future
   existential, 306, 309
   self and, 31 ff.

Game, 310
   language, 390
Gegebenheitsweise, 260, 265, 274
Gegenstand, 263, 267, 269 f., 273
   vide Object
Geist, 133

vide Spirit
Gelassenheit, 313
Generalizations
   accidental, 109
   existential, 232
   nomological, 109
   principle of, 213
Gerede, 302
   vide Speech; Talk
Gestalt
   – psychology, 250, 349
   – theory, 250
Gewesenheit, 306
   vide Alreadiness
Givenness
   apodictic self-, 295
   horizonal, 348
   self-, 276 f.
   ways of, 260, 265, 274
God, 139
   psychological proof of the
      existence of, 229
Good, 228
Guilt, 11

Habits
   mental, 352, 359 f.
Hate, 228, 239
Hemisphere, 73 ff.
Hermeneia, 294, 300 f.
   vide Understanding, 294
Hermeneutics, 203, 287
   second-order, 297
Hexeis, 299
Hilaritas, 128
Historicism
   new –, 383
Holism, 63 f., 99
Homophony, 207
Horizon, 280 ff.
   predelineation of, 281

Hylé, 278 ff.
  vide Sensation
Hypnosis, 197 f.
Hypothesis
  constancy, 279

Id, the, 185, 189 ff., 207n., 213f f.
Idea, 263
  absolute, 140
Idealism, 12, 102, 112 ff., 242,
    256, 265, 277
  absolute, 113, 179
  phenomenological, 275
  speculative, 161, 175
  structural, 228, 242
  transcendental, 256, 275
Ideas, 252 f., 263, 268, 418
  complex, 3, 270
  intention of, 270
  object of, 270
  objective, 268
  subjective, 268
Identifications
  theoretical, 50 f.
  token-token, 57
  type-type, 57
Identity
  bodily, 35
  collective, 4
  consciousness of, 253, 256, 281
  criteria of, 120
  individualistic conception of
      personal, 2, 4
  mind-brain, 113
  of body, 12, 17, 35
  of man, 3, 12
  of spiritual substance, 12
  personal, 2 ff., 11 ff., 118 ff.
  relative, 23 f.
  self-, 12, 15 ff., 118
  subject-object, 139 f.
  – theory, 108, 111, 241, 420 ff.

transitivity of, 30
  type-type, 61
Idioms
  intentional, 230 f., 233
  nonintentional, 233
Image
  after-, 47 ff.
  scientific, 421 f.
  stereoscopic, 421, 434
Imagination, 206, 215
  productive, 203
  theoretical, 374
Immanence
  worldliness *vs* –, 294
Immediacy, 138
Immortality, 139
  of the soul, 229
Import
  ontological, 96
Incongruity, 169
Incorrigibility, 54 f., 138 f.
Indeterminacy
  of the intentional object, 233
  of translation, 64, 101, 367
Indifference
  existential, 232 f., 237
Individualism
  moral, 176
Individuals, 115
Individuation, 38, 119
  relativity of, 23
Induction
  hermeneutical – *vs* phenome-
      nological reduction, 296 f.
Inexistence
  intentional, 224, 231, 233, 235,
    237
Inference
  principles of, 89
Infinite
  passion of the, 168
Information

– theory, 216
Inscrutability
　of reference, 367
Instinct, 186n., 190 f.
　biological, 207
　energy and, 190
　essence of an, 191
　reason and, 144
Institutions, 144
　signs by, 148
Instrumentalism, 201
Intellect
　vide Cognitions; Mind; *Res
　　cogitans;* Thought
　and feeling, 144
Intentio, 235
Intentionality, 2, 8, 179, 207,
　211 f., 224, 226, 228 ff.,
　249 ff., 288 ff.
　vide Directedness
　aboutness of, 425
　and individuation, 280 ff.
　grammatical concept of, 238
　logical criteria of, 232 f.
　modes of, 292
　of speech, 424
　ontology of, 292
　the being of, 292
Intentions, 5, 134, 137, 141, 147,
　151, 209, 211, 270, 320, 345,
　435 ff.
　empty, 292
　signifying, 203
Interaction
　causal, 62 f.
　mind-brain, 77 f.
　mind-body, 127
　of mind and world, 7
Interiority
　achieved, 145
Interiorization, 142
Interpretations

of dreams, 188, 194
Intersubjectivity, 391 ff., 423
Intimation
　self-, 198
Introspection, 189, 193, 210, 240,
　291
Intuition, 5, 252, 275 ff., 298
　categorial, 291, 293 f.
　fulfilled, 292
　intellectual, 139
　noetic, 299, 302
　sensuous, 291, 299
Intuitionism, 277
Inwardness, 178 f.
Irony, 162, 179
Irreducibility, 233

Jemeinigkeit, 296
Judgment, 228, 239 f.

Kinesis, 289 ff., 307 f., 312
　vide Movement
Knight
　of faith, 176 ff.
Knowledge, 228
　active, 3
　analytic theory of, 3
　as cognitive activity, 3
　dynamic, 3
　empirical, 138
　experimental, 3 f.
　immediate, 138 ff.
　inferential, 138
　intuitive, 129
　non-observational, 139
　self-, 7, 12, 15 ff., 129, 139,
　　207n.

Laetitia, 127

Language, 177, 230, 300 f., 323 ff.,
  371 ff.
  vide Speech; Talk
  as forms of life, 4
  as intersubjective achievement,
    423
  – game, 390
  indirect, 203
  intentional, 233
  logical private, 328
  meta-, 366 f., 391
  necessary unteachable, 329 ff.
  picture theory of, 373
  private, 326 ff.
  system, 401 ff.
Law
  Leibniz's, 30, 48, 52 f.
Laws
  causal, 61
  of nature, 109
  physical, 64
  psychological, 58
  psycho-physical, 62 f.
  strict, 61 f.
Libertarianism, 54
Libido, 130
  permanent reservoir of, 192
Life
  everyday, 6
  – views, 179
Lifters
  valve, 57, 59 f.
Linguistics
  Chomskian, 216
Locality
  psychical, 187
Locanism, 206
Logic, 228
Logos, 298 ff., 303, 310
Love, 228, 239

Magnitude
  intensive, 428
Man
  identity of, 3, 12
  in-the-world, 421 f., 436
  kinetic structure of, 305 ff.
  practical, 6
  primitive, 207
Marxism, 381
Materialism, 4, 46, 55, 58, 66 ff.,
  70 ff., 186, 230
  anti-, 54, 56, 72
  complete, 71
  type-type, 63, 66
Maxims, 212
Meaning
  vide Bedeutung; Noema;
  Reference; Sense and Reference;
    Sinn
  and metaphysics, 92 ff.
  and understanding, 372 f.
  concept of, 206
  – criticism, 293
  linguistic, 254, 262 f., 265,
    276 f.
  objective, 326
  of dreams, 188, 194, 198
  of mnemic symbols, 204 f.
  perceptual, 349 f.
  theory of, 143, 148 ff., 154
Medium
  notion of, 149 f.
Melancholia, 128
Memory, 12 ff., 188 f., 195 f., 198,
  204 f., 207, 217, 255, 322 f.,
  336
  causal theory of, 20 f., 40
  links of, 17 f., 35
  quasi-, 29 f., 36
  – theory, 13 f., 18 ff., 25, 27,
    40
  trace, 189

traumatic, 204 f.
unreliability of, 332 f.
Mental
criterion of the, 229
Mentalism, 141, 210
Metaphysics, 161, 223
and appropriation, 309 ff.
as the forgetting of being,
311 ff.
meaning and, 92 ff.
of presence, 277
pragmatism in, 365 ff.
scientific, 321
Method
of doubt, 83
Mind, 288
vide Cognitions; Consciousness;
Res cogitans; Thought
and body, 1 f., 4 ff., 12, 20,
106, 111 f., 115 f., 127,
144, 159, 229, 241, 319 f.,
348, 351 ff., 422
and brain, 45 ff., 113
and its object, 159
and matter, 7, 105, 115
and world, 1 f., 4, 6 f.
contextual character of, 8 f.
cosmic, 112
multiplying —s, 18 ff.
unity of human, 115 f., 118
Mineness
vs pure consciousness, 296
Mobility
of the body, 345, 348
Mode
of reference, 239
ontological, 228
psychological, 228
Models
linguistic, 240
Modification
hysterical, 204

Modo
obliquo, 236 f., 239
recto, 236 f., 239
Monad, 203
Monism, 166, 193
anomalous, 60 ff.
Monologue
interior, 277
Moralität, 175
vide Morality; *Sittlichkeit*
Morality
vide Sittlichkeit
individual, 175
social, 174 f.
Motivation, 208
Motives, 205
vide Intentionality
unconscious, 194 f.
Motor factor, 191
Movement, 292, 303 ff., 307 f.,
310
vide Kinesis
phenomenological, 227
Myth
of reincarnation, 352

Nature
laws of, 109
Necessity, 160, 164, 166
Neurosis, 199, 203 f.
types of, 204
Neutrality
topic-, 48, 52
Noema, 238, 249 ff.
and noesis, 253, 256, 263,
268
of higher order, 256
Noemalism, 256
Noesis, 253, 256, 263
Noumena, 140, 213 ff.
Nous poetikos, 225

462   *Index of subjects*

Nucleus
   noematic, 255
Nulldimensionality, 241

Object
   act-, 274
   autosemantic, 236
   complete, 271 f.
   external, 253
   incomplete, 271 f.
   indeterminacy of the
      intentional, 233
   intended, 249 f., 255 ff.
   intentional, 224, 230 ff., 250,
      257, 263, 271, 274 f.
   intentionally inexistent, 216,
      230, 234
   in the manner of determination,
      274
   nominal, 426
   of an idea, 270
   of consciousness, 254
   of thought, 233 ff.
   primary, 237
   simpliciter, 274
   transcendent, 256
   vorgestelltes, 235
Objectivity
   immanent, 235
Observation
   inner, 229
Objectivism, 51
Objectivity, 136
Obligation
   ultimate, 412
Observation
   inner perception *vs* inner —, 229
Observe *vs* reverse, 349 f.
Occurrence
   nonextensional, 232
Of-ness

of sensations, 425 f.
of thought, 425 f.
Ontology, 6 f., 228, 289 f., 209 f.,
   312, 366 f.
   of intentionality, 292
   of thoughts, 424
Opacity
   referential, 232 f.
Ousia, 310 ff.
Ousiology, 312

Paganism, 162 f.
Pain, 127 f.
Panpsychism, 72, 112
Paradox, 162, 177
   the brave officer —, 14
Parapraxes, 198 f., 202, 208 ff.
Parapsychology, 77
Parsimony
   ontological, 241
Passion
   of the infinite, 168
   rational, 374
Perception, 2, 6 ff., 203, 252, 255,
   278 ff.
   inner, 224, 229, 236 f., 239 f.
   inner — *vs* inner observation,
      229
   little, 117
   modes of, 224
   noematic character of, 255
   outer, 224
   phenomenology of, 250
   philosophy of, 81 ff.
   primacy of, 346 ff.
   principles of, 85
   psychology of, 82
   self-, 143
   sense-, 240
Person, 159, 163
   the concept of a, 11 ff.

Perspective, 90
  mental, 352
Phenomena
  based on presentations, 239
  classification of mental, 226,
    229, 239
  mental, 224, 226 ff., 237 ff.
  physical, 228 f.
  private mental, 239
Phenomenalism, 59, 102, 250,
  256
  epi-, 70 ff., 76
  linguistic, 81 f., 86
  ontological, 59
  translation, 59
Phenomenology, 6, 231, 249 ff.,
  290, 292 ff.
  of disclosure, 300
  of perception, 250
  of religion, 313
Philosophy
  analytical, 4, 6, 12, 109, 139,
    251, 381
  common sense, 83
  of action, 133 ff.
  of perception, 81 ff.
  perennial, 421
  speculative, 175
  Thomistic, 226
  transformation, 392
Phobia, 200, 212
  Hans', 199 ff.
  —, proper, 199
  zoö, 199
Phronesis, 298 f.
Physicalism, 46 f., 51 f., 54, 58, 62,
  340, 368
  anti-, 65
  ontological, 62, 64
  token-token, 61
Physis, 310 f.
  vide Aletheia; Appropriation

Pleasure, 127 f.
Polis
  the Greek, 151
Position
  self-, 295
Positivism, 365
  logical, 321
Power, 122 f., 128
Pragmatism, 4, 6, 363 ff., 387 ff.
  American, 363 ff., 418
  Harvard, 370 ff.
  in metaphysics and
    epistemology, 365 ff.
  methodological, 376 f.
  universal *vs* transcendental, 398
Preconsciousness, 195, 205n., 208,
  211 f.
Predelineation
  of horizon, 281
Predicates
  psychological, 239
Prefix
  intentional, 232
  modal, 232
Pre-grasp, 293
  vide Vorgriff
Pre-having, 302
  vide Vorhabe
Presence
  metaphysics of, 277
  self-, 277
Presentations, 238 ff.
  modes of, 224, 239 f.
  thing, 206
  vs judgments, 240
  word, 206
Presentness, 309 f. 312 f.
Presumptions
  plausible, 376
Principles
  categorematic inductive, 88
  deductive, 88

general warrant, 2, 92 f.
of causal interaction, 63
of charity, 64
of embodiment, 142
of generalization, 213
of inference, 89
of perception, 85 ff.
of projectability, 93
of symmetry, 213
of the nomological character of
    causality, 61 ff.
specific warrant, 2, 92 f.
sui generis epistemic, 92
Privacy
absolute, 423
logical, 328
of inner episodes, 423
Problem
Brentano's, 230
ontological, 229
Processes
absolute, 433
Programme
Oppenheim-Putnam, 4
Projectability, 91, 93
Properties, 60 ff., 71 f.
experimental, 230
functional, 60
mental, 228
phenomenal, 72
second-order, 60
Propositions, 230 f.
amplifying, 87
basic, 2, 85 ff.
foundational, 82
ground, 87
nomological, 109, 111, 114
non-basic, 2, 85 ff.
singular, 109, 111
true, 111
Psychoanalysis, 3, 129, 185, 193,
194, 197, 209, 211, 214, 216

Psychologism, 224, 251, 266 ff.
anti-, 266 f., 325
Psychology
a priori, 293
definition of, 227
descriptive, 229, 236, 239 f.,
    290
epistemological status of, 229
explanatory, 240
genetic, 240
Gestalt, 250, 349
history of, 226
introspective, 240
meta-, 186, 189 f., 192, 208
moral, 172 f.
of perception, 82
phenomenological, 239
transcendental phenomeno-
    logical, 240
without a soul, 227
Purposes, 50, 55, 62, 135, 137,
141, 145 f., 152, 206

Qualities
colour, 51, 428 ff.
experienced, 71, 76
phenomenal, 71 ff.
primary, 428
secondary, 48 f., 51 f., 71, 428
sensible, 238
ultimately homogeneous, 428 f.,
    432 f.
Quantifiers, 232
Questions
meta-epistemic, 95 f.

Rationalism
epistemological, 155
Rationality, 4, 64, 387, 413 f.
Rat-man, 201 f., 207, 209

Realism, 265, 373
  causal, 102
  direct, 102
  metaphysical, 373
  representative, 102
  scientific, 46, 49, 422
Reality
  inner, 138
  outer, 138
  status of, 397 f.
Realization
  effective, 145
  expressive, 145
Realms
  emotive *vs* cognitive, 373 f.
Reason
  and instinct, 144
Rebus
  dream as, 206n.
Recognition, 145 f.
  reciprocal, 146
  self-, 147
Reconciliationism, 53
  anti-, 54
Rede, 299
  vide Speech; Talk
Reducibility
  Strong Principle of, 432
Reduction
  eidetic, 296
  phenomenological, 261, 279, 296 f.
Reductionism, 4 f., 86 f., 100, 365
Reduplication Argument, 19 ff., 24 ff.
Reference, 300 f.
  vide Bedeutung; Meaning; Sense and Reference; *Sinn*
  intentional, 224, 231, 233 ff., 239
  inscrutability of, 367
  linguistic, 263
  mental, 237
  mode of, 239
  secondary, 236
Reflection
  phenomenological, 280
  transcendental, 278
Registration, 207, 216 f.
Reismus, 223 f., 226, 233, 236 f., 241 f.
Rejection, 239
Relations
  abductive inferential, 88
  Brentanist, 238
  categorematic inductive, 87 ff.
  equivalence, 24 f.
  master-slave, 144 ff.
  mind-body, 2, 106, 111, 115, 241, 351 ff.
  mind-matter, 105
  substance-attribute, 106 ff., 111
  thought-extension, 110
  transcategorematic inductive, 87 ff.
  unity −, 23 ff., 39
Relationship
  intentional, 238
Relativism, 369
Relativity
  of individuation, 23
  ontological, 6, 366
Reliability, 89 ff.
Religion
  phenomenology of, 313
  philosophy of, 229
Remembering, 206
  quasi-, 29 f.
Rendering
  rightness of, 370
Repräsentanz, 207
Representation, 150, 207 f., 216 f., 323

and will, 139
mental, 301
Representatives, 190
Repression, 196, 204 ff., 211, 212,
215
Res cogitans vs res extensa, 159,
418 ff.
vide Cognitions; Consciousness;
Mind; Thought
Responsibility, 11, 31, 173, 177,
212, 357 f.
quasi-, 31, 36
Revelation, 292
vide Aletheia
self-, 148
Revolutions
scientific, 373
Richtigkeit
truth as, 275
Right, 228
Rightness, 369 f.
of rendering, 370
Rights, 11
Roles
causal, 5, 50 f., 57, 60, 71
Romanticism, 143, 147

Scepticism, 82 ff., 327
Scholasticism, 230, 235, 238, 240
Science, 420
Hegelian, 174
of spirit, 174 f.
psychological, 228
unity of, 58
Scientism, 321
Sedimentation, 352
Selbstsein, 125 f.
Selbsttätigkeit, 139
Self, 159, 163 f., 169, 171 f., 252
activity of, 139
activity of – formulation, 145

and future, 31 ff.
– annihilation, 163
– assurance, 161, 166, 168
– awareness, 143, 148, 418
– consciousness, 147 f.
– deception, 172, 196, 210,
212, 346, 358, 412
– destruction, 130, 168
– disclosure, 298, 306 f.
dividing, 18 ff.
– formulation, 145
– givenness, 276 f.
– harm, 202
– identity, 12, 15 ff., 118
– intimation thesis, 198
– knowledge, 7, 12, 15 ff., 129,
139, 207n.
nature of, 105
– perception, 143
– position, 295
– presence, 277
– recognition, 147
– revelation, 148
– subsistence, 122
– transparency, 142 f., 145
– understanding, 135 f., 143 f.,
147 ff.
unity of, 105
Semiotics, 206 f.
Sensa, 433 f.
Sensation, 5, 50 ff., 328, 337 f.,
418, 422 ff.
vide Feels, raw
data of, 278
felt, 127
hyletic phase of, 278
of-ness of, 425 f.
private, 328 f.
Sense and Reference, 263 ff., 268,
276, 331 ff., 371 f.
vide Bedeutung; Meaning;
Noema; Reference; *Sinn*

Sense-data, 250, 278 f.
Senses
    predicate, 264
Sensibility
    extensionalistic, 231
    naturalistic, 231
    nominalistic, 231
Signifying, 202 f., 207
    pre, 207 n.
Signs, 148 f., 206
    accidental, 148
    by institution, 148
    conventional, 148
    natural, 148
Silence
    phenomenological, 277
Simulation
    computer, 216
Sinn, 249 ff., 263 ff.
    vide Meaning; Noema;
        Reference; Sense and
        Reference
    noematic, 257 f., 262 f., 264 ff.
    noematischer, 258
    -*Kritik*, 393
Sittlichkeit, 152 f., 175, 178
Situatedness, 350, 359, 402 f.,
    409 ff.
Solipsism
    methodological, 391
Sophia, 298 f.
Soul, 164 f., 170 f., 225, 240
    and body, 144, 164 f., 170 f.
    immortality of, 229
    intellectual, 241
    psychology without, 227
    sensitive, 241
Space, 185 ff., 214, 216
    semantic, 239
Spacelessness, 214
Spatiality
    of the body, 345

Speech, 390 ff.
    act, 424
    intentionality of, 424
Spirit, 140, 144 f., 147, 152, 161,
    165 ff., 169 ff., 174 f., 181
    objective, 174
    science of, 174 f.
    subjective, 174
Sprachkritik, 241
State
    conative mental, 199
    content of mental, 217
    mental, 49 ff., 60, 64, 151,
        216, 228, 420 f.
    physical, 52, 54, 320
    preconscious mental, 195 ff.
    psychological, 320
    sensory, 430
    total temporary, 13 f.
Subject
    body-, *vide* Body, lived
    -object-distinction, 7, 139 f.
    transcendental, 349
Subjectivism, 51, 76, 153
Subjectivity, 178, 288, 311, 349
    inter-, 319 ff.
    philosophy of, 297
Substance, 241 f.
    first —, 418, 420, 422
    mental, 227 ff., 240, 420
    modifications of, 107
    physical, 229, 420
    spiritual, 227
    theory of, 106 ff.
    truth of, 107
Substrata, 281
Supervenience, 86 f.
Suspension
    teleological — of the ethical,
        176, 178
Symbolization, 203 f.
Symbols, 143 ff., 203, 203n.,

468   *Index of subjects*

204 f., 208n., 215
  mnemic, 204 f., 210n.
Symmetry
  principle of, 213
Symptoms, 198 f., 202, 204 f.,
    208
  hysterical, 204
Synsemantic fragments, 234, 236 f.
Synthesis, 302 ff.
  and *diairesis*, 302 ff., 306
Systems
  deductive, 109
  language, 401 ff.
  mnemic, 188

Takings
  vide Thought
  non veridical perceptual, 427
  perceptual, 427 f.
Talk, 301 f.
  vide Language; Speech
  apophantic, 301 f.
  assertoric, 302
  categorial, 302
  mere, 301 f.
  vs mere utterance, 301
Tätigkeit, 133
Techne, 298 f.
Teleology, 140
Temporality, 306, 310
Thanatos, 190
Theology, 229, 289, 312
Theory
  bundle, 1, 13 f., 76
  causal, 64, 75, 136, 141, 358
  genetic, 56
  Gestalt, 250
  identity –, 108, 111, 241,
    420 ff.
  information, 216
  memory, 13 f., 18 ff., 25, 27, 40

neuro-physiological, 134
  of abstraction, 224
  of evidence, 224
  of meaning, 143, 148 ff., 154
  physical, 134
  possible – worlds semantic, 252
  psychoanalytic, 194
  qualitative, 136, 138, 140 f.,
    146 ff., 153 ff.
  three world, 77
Thesis
  ontological, 231, 233 f., 237 f.
  psychological, 231 ff.
  self-intimation, 198
Thinker
  existential, 162
Thinking-out-loud, 424 f.
Thought, 418, 422, 427
  vide Cognitions; Consciousness;
    Mind; *Res cogitans*
  and expression, 144
  and extension, 110
  attribute of, 112
  existential, 162
  object of, 233 ff.
  of-ness of, 425 f.
  ontology of, 424
  unity of, 288
Throwness
  vs self-position, 295
Time, 185, 214
Timelessness, 214, 216
Titillatio, 128
Topology
  logic – of colour, 429 ff.
Trance
  hypnotic, 198
Transcendence, 3, 288 ff., 303 ff.,
    310 f., 313
Transcendentality, 398
Transfer
  body –, 32 ff.

Transformation
  kinetic, 289 f.
  of activity, 141
  of philosophy, 392
  phenomenological, 281
Transgression, 353 f., 356
Transitivity
  of identity, 30
Translation
  indeterminacy of, 64, 101, 367
Transparency
  self-, 142 f., 145
Tristitia, 127
Truth, 226, 228, 297 ff.
  vide Aletheia; Disclosure
  a posteriori, 66
  a priori, 66
  as correctness, 275
  as correspondence, 275
  as rational consensus, 392 ff.
  certified, 376 f.
  correspondence theory of, 399
  empirical, 66
  factual, 375 f.
  necessary, 66, 109
  places of, 298
  presumptive, 375 f.
  synthetic *a priori*, 138 f.
  transcendental-pragmatic, 388
  universal, 399
  universal-pragmatic, 388

Uhrmensch, 207
Unconsciousness, 185 f., 191,
  194 ff., 207n., 208 f., 211,
  214 ff.
  dynamic, 199
  energy of, 194
  levels of, 215
Understanding, 294
  meaning and, 372 f.

objective, 136
  of the world, 6 ff.
  reflective, 147 f.
  self-, 135 f., 143 f., 147 ff.
  self-conscious, 150
Undetermination
  epistemic, 101
Unity, 239
  noematic, 261
  of consciousness, 229, 241
  of human mind, 115 f., 118
  of mind and body, 7 ff.
  of noemata, 256, 275, 278
  of science, 58
  of subject and object, 7 ff.
  of the self, 105
  of thought, 288
  − relations, 23 ff., 39
Universality
  strict, 109
Unrejectability, 390, 393 f.
Urmensch, 207
Utilitarianism, 38
Utility, 377

Validation, 388 ff.
Validity, 388 ff.
  vide Truth
  vs constitution, 403
View
  double-aspect, 186
Vitalism, 192
Volitions, 436
Vorgriff, 293
Vorhabe, 302
Vorstellungen, 150, 263, 267 ff.
  vide Ideas

Wants
  unconscious, 195

Warrant, 87 f.
Weakness
    of will, 172
Wesen, 266
    vide Essence
Will, 170, 172, 175
    and representation, 139
    free, 53 f., 83, 105
    weakness of, 172
Wirklichkeit, 140
Wishes, 217
    fulfilment of, 203
    repressed, 212
    unconscious, 195, 216
Words
    use of, 323
World, 369 f.
    actual —s, 369
    and mind, 1 f., 4, 6 f.
    — disclosure, 303 f., 307
    — making, 369 f.
    possible —s, 280 ff., 370
    possible —s semantic theory, 252
    three — theory, 77
    understanding of the, 6 ff.
Worldliness,
    vs immanence, 294 f.

X-noema component, 264, 281

Zukunft, 306
    vide Future